RACE,

REDISTRICTING,

AND REPRESENTATION

American Politics and Political Economy
A series edited by Benjamin I. Page

RACE, REDISTRICTING, AND REPRESENTATION

The Unintended

Consequences of

Black Majority Districts

David T. Canon

THE UNIVERSITY OF CHICAGO PRESS

CHICAGO AND LONDON

David T. Canon is professor of political science at the University of Wisconsin, Madison. He is author of *Actors, Athletes, and Astronauts* (1990), also published by the University of Chicago Press, and *The Dysfunctional Congress?* (with Kenneth R. Mayer, 1999).

The University of Chicago Press, Chicago 60637
The University of Chicago Press, Ltd., London
© 1999 by The University of Chicago
All rights reserved. Published 1999
Printed in the United States of America
08 07 06 05 04 03 02 01 00 99   1 2 3 4 5
ISBN: 0-226-09270-4 (cloth)
ISBN: 0-226-09271-2 (paper)

Library of Congress Cataloging-in-Publication Data

Canon, David T.
   Race, redistricting, and representation : the unintended consequences of
Black majority districts / David T. Canon.
      p.   cm.—(American politics and political economy)
   Includes bibliographical references and index.
      ISBN 0-226-09270-4 (cloth : alk. paper).—ISBN 0-226-09271-2 (paper : alk.
paper)
      1. Gerrymandering—United States.   2. United States. Congress. House—
Election districts.   3. Election districts—United States.   4. Apportionment
(Election law)—United States.   5. Representative government and representa-
tion—United States.   6. Afro-American legislators.   I. Title.   II. Series.
JK1341.C36   1999
328.73′07347′08996073—dc21   99-24134
                                                                          CIP

To Sarah

CONTENTS

TABLES AND FIGURES

Tables

Figures

PREFACE

Reading the U.S. Supreme Court decisions on racial redistricting, the popular literature on the topic, and the testimony presented at the various Judiciary subcommittee hearings and roundtables on voting rights is a sobering experience. The racial divide in our nation leaps from the pages. Supreme Court justices, members of Congress, political pundits, and the nation's leading voting rights experts look at the same set of facts and reach diametrically opposed positions. One side looks at the evidence and sees apartheid, balkanization, polarization, and disenfranchisement; the other sees integration, diversity, harmony, and empowerment.

Differences in perceptions of racial issues should come as no surprise to even the most casual observer of American politics. Well-publicized public opinion surveys provided ample evidence of the racial divide in the 1990s. For example, racially divergent assessments of the fairness and legitimacy of law enforcement and the judicial system helped produce startling polls showing that 60 percent of African Americans believed that O. J. Simpson did not murder his wife and Ronald Goldman, while 68 percent of white Americans believed he was guilty (Gallup poll, cited in Raspberry 1994, A23). This racial divide is perpetuated by racial stereotyping by blacks and whites. Many blacks' assessments of the Simpson case were rooted in perceptions that blacks receive unequal treatment in the criminal justice system. Whites engage in similar rushes to judgment when they avoid black youths on the street or when a white cab driver refuses to pick up a well-dressed black business person. Political scientists have demonstrated that such racial stereotyping has a significant impact on perceptions of government assistance programs (Sniderman and Piazza 1993) and violence and crime (Hurwitz and Peffley 1997).

The distinctive quality of the racially divergent perceptions of black majority congressional districts is that *both* sides of the debate are using the same stereotype—that black politicians represent only black constituents—while reaching different normative conclusions about the value of that type of representation. I argue that both sides of the debate are wrong: a careful assessment of the nature of representation in these districts shows that most black members of the U.S. House of Representatives represent their entire district, not just the African-American voters. Because this issue will be litigated well into the next century, it would be useful to ground the legal debates in concrete evidence about the impact of these districts rather than in unfounded stereotypes.

Providing objective, scientific evidence is difficult in such a highly charged area. I cannot claim that I am completely objective and neutral on this subject. Obviously I care deeply about issues of race and representation. Thus, I took many precautions to insulate the data collection process and statistical analysis from my normative commitments. While such attempts cannot be completely successful, potential biases may be minimized. Another aspect of my approach to this research influenced my interpretation and evaluation of the evidence: I was willing to change normative judgments based on the evidence. At the beginning of the project I had a grudging acceptance of the districts. I was uncomfortable with the odd-looking districts, but on balance I thought they were required by the Justice Department's interpretation of the Voting Rights Act and believed that they were a useful tool to enhance black representation in Congress. I also shared the stereotypical view of black representation held by supporters and critics of the districts.

But after examining the political campaigns in the new black majority districts in 1992, it became clear to me that many of the newly elected African-American representatives were committed to a biracial politics rather than "political apartheid." I developed, with Patrick Sellers and Matthew Schousen, a "supply-side theory" of congressional elections to explain the type of representative that emerged from the various black districts and then applied this theory to the behavior of these representatives in the U.S. House. It was only by discarding the previous stereotypes and recognizing the various groups within the black community and the power of biracial appeals that I was able to explain more fully the patterns of black representation in the U.S. House. Thus, by the time I completed the project, I remained supportive of the districts, but for entirely different reasons. Rather than seeing these districts as a vehicle for "authentic black representation," to use

Lani Guinier's term,[1] I saw them as the basis for creating a broader biracial politics that would help move us closer to the pluralist, tolerant society that Martin Luther King, Jr., dreamt about. These reasons may not be acceptable to partisans on either side of the debate: opponents of the districts will still view them as creating "political apartheid," while supporters will lament the dilution of "authentic representation." However, I hope that the evidence I present here will change some readers' minds about the consequences of the black majority districts that were created in 1992.

*   *   *

As with all projects that span the better part of a decade, I have accumulated many personal debts along the way. The massive data collection and coding effort was undertaken by Jesse Gray, Aaron Olver, Andrew Shaw, Robert Turner, Steven Yonish, and especially Elizabeth Wiebe and Gregory Streich. Greg spent more than two years on the project, and Liz dedicated nine months. This book would not have been possible without their diligent work, and the quality of the final product was greatly improved by their comments and suggestions. The evolving work also benefitted greatly from the comments of anonymous reviewers of articles that appeared in the *Journal of Politics* and *American Politics Quarterly;* from reviewers of my National Science Foundation proposal; from the chairs and discussants of various panels at the Midwest and American Political Science Associations' meetings; from Thomas Weko and his colleagues at the University of Puget Sound and Jim Rhodes at Marquette University, who hosted talks on this topic; from my colleagues at the University of Wisconsin who helped sharpen my arguments in two "brown bag" seminars; and from Thomas Kazee and Bernard Grofman, who edited books in which early versions of this work appeared. Charles Franklin, Mark Hansen, Kevin Price, Ben Marquez, Richard Merelman, Marion Smiley, David Rohde, and Crawford Young provided invaluable critiques and advice. I am very grateful to the Graduate School and Alumni Research Foundation of the University of Wisconsin and the National Science Foundation (Grant no. SBR-9411028) for their generous support and to my friends Jean and Mark Raabe, who opened their home to me while I was doing interviews in Washington, D.C.

Patrick Sellers and Matthew Schousen deserve special recognition. They became involved in the very early stages of this project while I was teaching at Duke University. They conducted much of the interviewing for the case study of the 1st Congressional District in North Carolina and coauthored three chapters in edited books and the *Journal of Politics* article on work related to this research. These papers serve as the basis for chapter 3 of this book (they are listed as coauthors on that chapter). It was very rewarding working with Pat and Matt; the overall quality of this book was enhanced through their involvement. The standard claim of responsibility for all remaining errors applies.

My family deserves tremendous thanks for their love and support. My parents and my sisters and their families provided frequent breaks with visits from or roadtrips to Minnesota. My wife Sarah juggled her career and our children while providing me with a judicious mix of encouragement and nudging on the book. When a friend suggested that maybe all of those hours at the computer had turned me into Jack Nicholson's character in the horror movie *The Shining* (was I just cranking out hundreds of pages with nothing on them except the words "all work and no play makes David a very dull boy . . ."?), Sarah started to worry that this project would *never* get done. Two of our three children were born while the project was under way. While the sleepless nights and general chaos around the house certainly slowed the progress on the book, I cannot imagine what life would be like without Neal, Katherine, and Sophia.

INTRODUCTION

Race, Redistricting, and Representation in the U.S. House of Representatives

A central problem for representative democracy is to provide a voice for minority interests in a system that is dominated by the votes of the majority. The legitimacy and stability of any democracy depend, in part, on its ability to accomplish that difficult goal. The Founders' institutional solution of the separation of powers within and across levels of government provided multiple points of access for various interests and some assurance that no single interest would dominate government for extended periods. Hailed by generations of pluralists within political science, this competitive political process was thought to produce optimal results.[1] Majority tyranny was prevented by a pluralist politics in which "minorities rule," to use Robert Dahl's famous phrase (Dahl 1956, 124–151). However, for at least forty years, scholars and politicians have recognized that the system did not provide adequate representation for certain groups in society, especially racial minorities (see McClain and Garcia 1993 for a review of research on this topic).

Early legislation to provide equal representation for minorities fell within the pluralist tradition: Congress passed process-oriented laws, such as the Voting Rights Act (1965) and the Civil Rights Act (1964), aimed at providing equal access and opportunity. In the 1970s the courts moved toward results-oriented standards in affirmative action cases that corrected for discriminatory employment practices, but representation cases in electoral politics maintained a process orientation ("one person, one vote" and equal access to the polls) until Congress amended the Voting Rights Act in 1982. Instead of mandating a fair *process,* this law and subsequent interpretation by the U.S. Supreme Court in the 1980s mandated that minorities be able to "elect representatives of their choice" when their numbers and configuration permitted (see Schockley 1991, 1041). This shift meant that the legislative redistricting process now had to avoid discriminatory *results* rather than being concerned only with discriminatory *intent.* Consequently, in 1992, fifteen new U.S. House districts were specifically drawn to help elect African Americans to Congress and ten districts were drawn to provide opportunities to elect new Latino members (Lublin 1997, 23).

The goal of most proponents of racial redistricting was to "empower" minority voters by giving them more adequate representation in the national policy-making process.[2] This goal is extremely controversial. Critics on the left argue that the new districts provide only descriptive rather than substantive representation (Guinier 1991a, 1134–1153). The right ridicules them as affirmative action for black politicians or, worse, a form of "political apartheid" that racially segregates voters (Henry Hyde, House 1993, 3–5; *Shaw v. Reno* 1993). Most recently, political observers have debated whether the new districts were pivotal in the Republican takeover of Congress in 1994 by weakening southern white Democrats (Petrocik and Desposato 1998; Guinier 1995; Lublin 1995; Bullock 1995; Engstrom 1995). The Supreme Court's *Miller v. Johnson* decision on June 29, 1995, weighed in against the minority-majority districts, arguing that race could not be the "predominant factor" in the drawing of district lines, but the Texas case of *Bush v. Vera* (1996) made it clear that each case would be decided on its own merits and that minority districting could be constitutionally permissible.

While scholars may disagree about many aspects of black majority districts, they generally concur that these districts were created to increase the representation of black interests by black representatives. This "blacks must represent blacks" or "politics of difference" school of thought lies at the heart of racial redistricting. In the majority opinion in *Shaw v. Reno,* Justice Sandra Day O'Connor states that "[w]hen a district obviously is created solely to effectuate the perceived common interests of one racial group, elected officials are more likely to believe that their primary obligation is to represent only the members of that group, rather than their constituency as a whole" (1993, 2827). This line of reasoning leads to the inescapable conclusion that white voters will not be adequately represented in black majority districts.[3]

I regard Justice O'Connor's position as a testable proposition rather than an uncontroversial assumption. This book will test this proposition by examining the nature of racial representation in the U.S. House of Representatives. My thesis is that the process of candidate emergence and political campaigns exerts a powerful influence on representation in black majority districts. I challenge the prevailing notion that there are monolithic black interests that could produce *a* "representative of their choice" in most districts. Instead, factions within the African-American community produce candidates with different ideological backgrounds and different visions of the representation of racial interests. One significant effect of this ideological diversity among black candidates is to give a centrist coalition of moderate white and black voters the power to elect the black candidate of *their* choice in many districts (Canon, Schousen, and Sellers 1996).

This "supply side of redistricting"[4] provides a new understanding of the electoral sources of representation in the new black districts. The traditional demand-side perspective on redistricting focuses on voters and elections, addressing such topics as incumbency safety, partisan bias, racial bloc voting, political geography and demographics, vote dilution, and runoff primaries. In contrast, the supply-side perspective examines the supply of candidates—how individual politicians respond to the changing electoral context imposed by new district lines and how, in turn, their decisions shape the electoral choices and outcomes in a given district. Rather than simply assuming that goals for minority representation translate into a specific configuration of district lines and predictable consequences, the supply-side perspective cautions that all outcomes depend on the calculations of potential candidates. A similar point is often made in the broader literature on representation in Congress: the type of representation a district will get depends, at least in part, on the type of politician who is elected (Kingdon 1968; Fenno 1978; Bianco 1994). However, it has not been applied to the racial representation literature on Congress.

These supply-side effects—outcomes that are rooted in the decisions of individual candidates acting in their own self-interest—have important implications for the normative debate raging in the minority politics and women's studies literature concerning the "politics of difference" versus the "politics of commonality" (Gilligan 1982; MacKinnon 1987; Young 1990; Eisenstein 1988; Gitlin 1993; Taylor 1992; Phillips 1995; Streich 1997). This debate centers around the question, Should politics be organized around certain purportedly universal principles such as "life, liberty, and the pursuit of happiness," or should one recognize that the political process is not neutral in applying these principles to people of diverse ethnic, cultural, racial, and gender identities? How society answers this question influences policy outcomes. A politics of commonality strives to provide equal protection of the laws without special treatment for any single group, while a politics of difference calls for proper remedies for previous discrimina-

tion and exclusion. In the context of racial representation the politics
of commonality would be rooted in a biracial politics and would argue
that blacks can represent whites and whites can represent blacks. A
politics of difference would maintain that only a member of a given
race can truly represent the interests of that racial group. Most political observers, including proponents and opponents of the strategy,
see the creation of minority-majority districts as an embodiment of
the politics of difference (Walters 1992; *Shaw v. Reno* 1993; Thernstrom 1987).

This study will contradict that common wisdom. The supply-side
effects of racial redistricting show that many of the African-American
politicians who were elected in the new districts embody the politics
of commonality rather than the politics of difference. Furthermore,
even those who *campaign* by appealing only to black voters do, in fact,
spend a substantial proportion of their time in Congress representing
the interests of white and black voters alike. This is a story of unintended consequences: the Madisonian-style institutional engineering
that attempted to implement a politics of difference was trumped by
individuals operating as sovereign actors (the candidates and potential
candidates) within the broader Madisonian system that is based on the
politics of commonality. The "commonality" roots of our republic are
evident in the Federalists' desire to overcome sectionalism and get citizens to start thinking like "Americans" rather than "Virginians" or
"New Yorkers." While making concessions to the Anti-Federalists, the
institutional engineering implemented by the Federalists to encourage
a politics of commonality was nothing short of revolutionary (of
course, with the important caveat that "commonness" applied only to
white, primarily landholding men). In contrast, the attempt to elect
black leaders through the creation of black majority districts is typically viewed as promoting a politics of difference. I will argue that
because of these unintended consequences, minority districting should
be embraced in a political system that continues to be riven by racial
fear, animosity, and discrimination.

Unfortunately the Supreme Court seems to be moving in the opposite direction, with its recent challenges to racial redistricting. If the
Court persists in its current line of logic, additional damage could be
done to race relations in our country, as many African Americans
could interpret this as another bit of evidence that the system works
against their interests. My work suggests that new minority districts
may give African Americans a greater voice in the political process

while simultaneously helping to promote a politics of commonality rather than creating the "political apartheid" feared by Justice O'Connor (1993, 2827).

The Critics of Racial Redistricting

Despite the potential benefits of minority districting, the practice has been attacked from all sides. As I noted above, critics from the right, such as Henry Hyde (R–IL), argue that black majority districts undermine color-blind representation and promote racial segregation (House 1993, 3–5). Critics on the left argue that the "electoral success" strategy is limited because it provides descriptive rather than substantive representation (Guinier 1991a, 1134–1153). Moderates, such as State Representative Milton F. "Toby" Fitch, a key architect of North Carolina's redistricting plan, worry about losing influence in districts that give up black voters to create the new black majority districts. Fitch criticized the creation of "political reservations" that would marginalize black interests (Denton 1991). John Lewis, the civil rights leader and representative from Georgia, echoed this concern, noting that black majority districts will "ensnare blacks in separate enclaves, the exact opposite of what the civil rights movement intended" (Wilentz 1996, 22). A related and more partisan concern is that Democrats will lose seats in districts that are adjacent to the black majority districts. Thus, Republicans tend to oppose the districts on principle, but quietly support them for political reasons, while many white Democrats support the districts in principle, but privately hope that they will be abolished. In some of the state legislative battles over redistricting the alliance between Republicans and black Democrats was very evident. I will discuss these concerns and briefly outline how my evidence addresses them.

The argument from the right has two components: (1) white voters are disenfranchised or harmed by black majority districts, and (2) any racial classification undermines the goal of a color-blind society. The former is demonstrably false. As I will discuss in more detail in chapter 2, the courts have not required the proof of harm as a condition for standing; therefore, this is not a crucial legal question. However, harm is alleged by most plaintiffs in challenges to black majority districts and is of central importance to the theoretical and policy questions in this book. For example, in *Moon v. Meadows,* the 1997 U.S. district court decision that struck down Robert Scott's (D–VA) district, the plaintiffs alleged, "Plaintiffs are all adversely affected by the racial gerrymandering which is the subject of this complaint" (Plaintiffs' Complaint, section 6, November 29, 1995). Plaintiffs Donald Moon and Robert Smith claimed that they had been "stigmatized" by the district, and Moon argued that his job as the Republican chairman of the 3rd Congressional District had been made "exceedingly difficult" by the "tortured construction" of the district lines. Organizing political events and building networks were more difficult in the far-flung district than in a more compact district (Plaintiffs' Interrogatories in *Moon v. Meadows,* section 2, April 1, 1996). However, such organizational difficulties are also present in many districts that were not affected by racial redistricting. Furthermore, on the more substantive point of whether white voters in the district were being represented by Robert Scott, I provided testimony for the State of Virginia showing that Representative Scott balanced the racial interests of all the voters in his district (this balancing approach to racial representation will be explored more fully in chapter 1).

The second point, that any racial classification undermines the goal of a color-blind society, is a stronger argument. To some extent this is a normative position that is not subject to empirical refutation. However, there are two relevant counterarguments. First, if the ultimate goal is a color-blind society, one must consider the *long-term* impact of the racial classification, not the simple act of making distinctions between people based on race. The implications of the biracial representation provided in the new black majority districts summarized above are examined in more detail in chapters 4 and 5. If blacks *do* represent whites and gain their support, providing the opportunity for black representation in areas where whites previously had not supported black politicians may help break down racial barriers.

Second, treating all racial classifications as morally equivalent ignores historical context. For example, there are important differences between the racial gerrymander in Tuskegee, Alabama, struck down by the Supreme Court in *Gomillion v. Lightfoot* (1960), and the racial redistricting in North Carolina in *Shaw v. Hunt* (1996, often referred to as *Shaw II*). In both instances the Court held that classifications based on race were constitutionally suspect. However, the 1960 case was an explicit attempt to disenfranchise black voters, while no white voters were prevented from voting in an election due to the 1992 redistricting.[5] Furthermore, the Tuskegee gerrymander was "created in a climate of bitter white supremacist feeling" and "conceived in secret by whites and executed without any black consent," while the North Carolina redistricting reflected, in part, the desire of a white-controlled state legislature (with a black speaker) to provide "black empowerment and a just American democracy" (testimony of Robert J. Norrell, House 1993).[6] Ira Glasser of the American Civil Liberties Union (ACLU) argues that this difference in context should permit racial classification when it is a response to past patterns of discrimination:

> While it may be true in some perfect world that if we were starting on a blank slate, all racial classification should be subject to strict scrutiny and be presumptively invalid. Some of us have worked a long time to reach that day and are rather despondent that we have not yet done so. But it's important to remember that you can't have a situation where the original discrimination and the original district lines in this setting were not subject to strict scrutiny and were done for the purpose of grouping based on race and then come in and apply the strict scrutiny at the level of remedy. (House 1994a, 26–27)

From the other side of the political spectrum critics on the left argue that black majority districts will not help black constituents because (1) many blacks elected from these districts are not "authentic black" representatives and (2) even the authentic blacks will have little impact in Congress. Their first concern maintains that black representation has come full circle in the past forty years: from the early black politicians who were products of white urban political machines (or of the Reconstruction Era in the South), to authentic black leaders of the civil rights era, to the new-style "accommodationist" or "deracialized" African-American politician (Walters 1992; Smith 1990). Ronald Walters argues that black leaders of white majority districts should not be considered authentic black leadership as it "emerged from the civil rights/black politics movement" (1992, 204). Black politics, and the representation of black interests, can be produced only by African-American politicians. Guinier takes the next step and argues:

> Establishment-endorsed blacks are unlikely to be authentic because they are not elected as the representatives of choice in the black community. In addition, these officials are often marginal community members whose only real connection with the black community is skin color. Electoral support by a majority of black voters is thus a convenient proxy for political authenticity. (1991a, 1104)

Though Guinier does not explicitly address the topic of primary elections, it seems clear from her argument that if an authentic black who has majority black support is defeated in the primary by another African American who wins with a biracial coalition, the winner does not become authentic by defeating token Republican opposition in the fall.

John Lewis, a black leader with impeccable civil rights movement credentials (and the scars to prove it), has been rebuked by black critics who claim that he is "not black enough" and "too much of a party man, too chummy with whites, [and] that he had lost touch with the alienated hopeless inner-city mood" (Wilentz 1996, 22). The criticism came to a head in the fall of 1995, when Lewis refused to participate in Louis Farrakhan's Million Man March, but one can trace the suspicion that Lewis is "Tommin' it" (as Lewis himself characterized his critics) to his victory over Julian Bond in the 1986 Democratic primary. Bond had the support of most black leaders in Atlanta and nearly won a majority of the vote in a five-way primary. Lewis was able to prevail in the runoff primary with 80 percent of the white vote and 40 percent of the black vote (Thernstrom 1987, 226–227), which raises the rather incredible possibility that Lewis would be classified as an "inauthentic" black, using Guinier's criteria (of "white establishment" support and lack of a majority of the black vote).

Furthermore, these critics maintain, black majority districts have symbolic value at best because black representatives, authentic or not, cannot have a substantive impact in a majoritarian, white-dominated institution (Guinier 1991b, 1476–1492). The only solution is institutional change, such as cumulative voting schemes or minority veto power over a subset of policies (Guinier 1991a, 1134–1154). It is true that members who promote a racial agenda in Congress do not have much maneuvering room to build majority coalitions. Most blacks would gain nothing from siding with the Republicans, as became clear during the intense budget negotiations in the summer of 1993, and threatening to form a third party as a means of inducing more Democratic support would not be seen as credible by most members of Congress.[7] Short of the institutional reforms suggested by Guinier, the only viable alternatives, according to these critics, are a politics of protest and one of accommodation. The former has a long been an essential role for the Congressional Black Caucus (CBC), as it provides a conscience for the nation and a voice for poor people (Clay 1993). Adam Clayton Powell, Shirley Chisholm, Mickey Leland, William Clay, John Conyers, and Maxine Waters are among the most visible advocates of this critical role in our political system in the last fifty years.

However, the politics of confrontation has been complemented by a centrist strategy that has moved many members of the CBC into leadership roles and enhanced the clout of the CBC (Canon 1995): William Gray, John Lewis, Mike Espy, Augustus Hawkins, and Alan Wheat were the pioneers of this approach. Many members of the 1992 class, such as Sanford Bishop, James Clyburn, Albert Wynn, and Robert Scott, have moved comfortably into this role. Critics may view these members as accommodationists and somehow tainted by gaining biracial support. However, this normative perspective is not supported by the empirical evidence. The notion of "authentic" representation paints differences in representational styles too starkly and does not capture the reality of legislative politics in the U.S. House. As I will discuss in the next chapter, all black representatives in Congress operate on a continuum of racial representation. The most avid supporters of black interests, such as John Conyers and William Clay, also spend a substantial proportion of their legislative work on issues that are important for all Americans. Likewise, the members of the CBC who are most sensitive to the interests of their white constituents spend substantial amounts of time on black interests. Chapter 4 provides evidence to support these claims.

Finally, the concern of moderate critics, summarized by Toby Fitch's comment about "political reservations," is that black majority districts dilute overall black representation. There are two versions of this argument: (1) The "wasted vote" perspective is concerned that "supersaturated" districts with more than 60 percent black population reduce the total number of potential districts blacks can win. These moderate critics would like to maximize the number of blacks in Congress, but they do not see black majority districts as the most efficient means to that end. The more optimistic in this group argue that African Americans can win from constituencies that are less than 50 percent black; therefore, black majority districts are not necessary and may place an artificial ceiling on potential black gains (Swain 1993). (2) The "color-blind" approach argues that the race of the member does not matter and that creating black majority districts diminishes the overall representation of black interests by reducing the number of sympathetic white Democrats. This perspective is distinguished from the conservatives' "color-blind" perspective outlined above, as these critics actually want to maximize the representation of black interests. I will briefly examine both arguments.

While there is some merit in the "wasted vote" argument, in areas where racial bloc voting is especially severe, a 60–65 percent black population may be required to ensure the election of a black representative (if, indeed, that is the goal) given the differential turnout rates of blacks and whites. However, there is little support for the optimistic view that blacks will win many House seats in white majority districts. The numbers are stark: of the 26,670 U.S. House elections since the adoption of the 15th Amendment in 1870, only 415 (1.6 percent) produced black winners (ninety-two individuals).

A more meaningful statistic for the purposes of this discussion is the proportion of blacks who have been elected in black majority and white majority districts since the passage of the Voting Rights Act in 1965 (before the Voting Rights Act the distinction between white majority and black majority districts was fairly meaningless because a large proportion of blacks was disenfranchised). In the 6,667 House elections in white majority districts between 1966 and 1996 (including special elections), only 35 (0.52 percent) were won by blacks. This number is even more striking when one considers the unusual circumstances surrounding nearly all of those elections. First, eleven of the thirty-five victories are accounted for by Ron Dellums (D–CA). He represented what the *Almanac of American Politics* describes as "the most self-consciously radical district in the nation" (Barone, Ujifusa, and Matthews 1975, 66; the eleven elections were from 1970 to 1990; the district has not been majority white since 1992). The combination of the urban ghetto of Oakland and the radical white voters from Berkeley makes this district an extreme outlier. Six elections are accounted for by Alan Wheat, who was elected in 1982 by winning the Democratic nomination with only 31 percent of the vote. As the only black candidate in the field of eight, he was able to rely on his base of black votes (he had been a state legislator in a black majority district before running for the House). After winning the primary over a field that split the white vote, he was able to win the general election in the heavily Democratic district. Subsequently, Representative Wheat was able to appeal to white voters after gaining the power of incumbency and was easily reelected to the seat in a district that was only 25 percent black, until he lost a bid for the U.S. Senate in 1994.

Katie Hall (D–IN) also won election under fortuitous circumstances, but she was not able to maintain her seat in a district that was only 22 percent black. When Adam Benjamin (D–IN) died of a heart attack in September 1982, the congressional district party chair was mandated by state law to name the party's nominee (the primary had already passed). Richard Hatcher, the black mayor of Gary, was the district chair and named Hall for the slot. Party leaders were outraged that Benjamin's widow was not named, but Hall narrowly won the general election against a Republican whom the *Almanac* described as "pathetically weak" (Barone and Ujifusa 1985, 452; the Republican nominee spent only $10,526 in losing the election). In the next election Hall managed only 33 percent of the vote in the Democratic primary, a strikingly low figure for an incumbent, and one that closely matches the 30 percent minority population of the district. Andrew Young (D–GA) and Harold Ford (D–TN) account for seven elections and will be discussed below. Gary Franks (R–CT) and J. C. Watts (R–OK), who account for five of the cases, won as Republicans and are not considered by black leaders as sympathetic to black interests. In fact, Franks waged a vicious battle simply to be included in the CBC.

The 1996 elections raised hopes that blacks would start winning more often in white majority districts. Five black incumbents, all in the South, lost significant numbers of black voters when their black majority districts were ruled unconstitutional, but were still able to win. Three of those, Cynthia McKinney (D–GA), Sanford Bishop (D–GA), and Corrine Brown (D–FL), won in white majority districts. Even more significant, Julia Carson (D–IN) won an open seat race in a district that is 69 percent white and had been held by Andrew Jacobs (D–IN) for twenty years. These results led to headlines such as "Is the South Becoming Color Blind?" (Fletcher 1996, 13; Sack 1996, A1). However, McKinney and other supporters of majority black districts argued that black incumbents were able to win through the power of incumbency (McKinney 1996, 62). Therefore, only one of the thirty-five elections (Carson's) provides much hope for a significant number of black victories in white majority districts.[8] On the other hand, 200 of the 249 elections (80.3 percent) between 1966 and 1996 in black majority House districts have produced black representatives, including all but one of the elections in 1996. (Districts that are neither black majority nor white majority are not included in this analysis.)

Given the concentration of black voters in the South and the legacy of legal discrimination, it is important to separate the South in this analysis. Before the 1990 reapportionment, the South held a majority of the nation's districts with between 10 and 30 percent black voters and a large majority of the "black influence" districts (30–50 percent). However, no districts in the South were majority black in the 1970s, and only three were majority black in the 1980s. Given the patterns of racial bloc voting, no blacks were elected from majority white districts in the South in the 1980s or the 1990s. Two, Andrew Young (D–GA) in 1972 and Harold Ford (D–TN) in 1974, were elected in districts that were 44 percent black and 48 percent black, respectively, but both districts became majority black after the 1980 redistricting. Thus, the creation of fourteen new black majority districts in the South in 1992 gave blacks a realistic opportunity to elect black politicians for the first time since Reconstruction.[9]

The success of black politicians noted above in white majority House districts and the elections of Douglas Wilder as governor of Virginia, Carol Moseley Braun (D–IL) to the Senate, and Norm Rice as mayor of Seattle indicate that blacks *can* win in white majority districts. However, as David Lublin points out, "their victories attract attention precisely because of their exceptional nature. Empirical evidence indicates that racial composition of the electorate overwhelms all other factors in determining the race of a district's representative" (Lublin 1995, 112–113). The numbers bear repeating: only 35 of 6,667 elections in white majority U.S. House districts have provided black winners since 1966, and most of those were in unusually liberal districts or occurred in some other idiosyncratic context that prevents generalizing to other districts. While the Voting Rights Act and its amendments, in my opinion, only provide an opportunity for black voters to elect candidates of choice rather than guaranteeing that outcome, 35 of 6,667 elections are not much of an opportunity.

The color-blind perspective is based on two assumptions: (1) that sympathetic white Democrats were hurt by the creation of black majority districts and (2) that whites are just as able to represent black interests as blacks. There is some support for the first point, but very little support for the second claim. Benenson estimates that only three white Democratic incumbents who were weakened by racial redistricting lost in 1992 (1992, 3580–3581). Instead, Democratic legislators were able to employ creative cartography to protect white Democrats while creating new black districts (North Carolina is probably the best example; all the Democratic incumbents won, one African American replaced a retiring white Democrat, and another won a newly created district). I will examine this argument in more detail in chapter 2, but there is evidence that Democrats lost about ten seats in 1994 due to racial redistricting.

The representational consequences of racial redistricting are more subtle than simple wins and losses. The cost of black majority districts for black representation is not only that Republicans will win more seats, but also that Democrats who survive will have fewer black voters and therefore not be as sensitive to their needs. One study concluded that the representation of black interests would be maximized by creating as many 42 percent black districts as possible (Cameron, Epstein, and O'Halloran 1996). Such a strategy could produce 60 sympathetic white Democrats, but no black incumbents. This is preferable, they argue, to the distribution of black voters in the 1992 districts, in which only six districts were between 40 and 50 percent black and thirty-three were majority black.

While it is certainly true that some white incumbents, such as Lindy Boggs (D–LA) and Peter Rodino (D–NJ), have been very attentive to black constituents (Swain 1993, chap. 8), the color-blind approach ignores the importance of descriptive representation and the real differences in the substantive representation provided by white and black politicians. Perhaps the most surprising finding of my research is the extent to which white representatives from districts with substantial black populations do not emphasize racial issues. I will support this argument in chapters 4 and 5 with a comprehensive array of data.

A central conclusion of chapter 4 can be stated quite simply: race matters. To rephrase Guinier's argument, white representatives from districts that are 30–40 percent black *can* largely ignore their black constituents, and many do. Black representatives from districts that are 30–40 percent white cannot ignore their white constituents *because they are operating in an institution that is about 86 percent white and a nation that is 82.5 percent white.*[10] Therefore, as I noted above, even the most race-conscious members of the CBC spend a majority of their legislative efforts on nonracial issues. However, race matters in complex and subtle ways. The supply-side theory presented in chapter 3 explains some of that complexity.

Chapter Outline

This discussion has provided a brief overview of the central concerns of this book. At this point I will provide a brief description of what is to follow. Chapter 1 will discuss the various concepts that provide the basis for my analysis of race and representation in the U.S. House: black interests (subjective and objective), the politics of difference and the politics of commonality, and representation (substantive and descriptive). Chapter 2 examines the legal debates surrounding the creation of minority-majority districts. This continues to be a very confusing area of law with few absolutes and massive areas of shifting terrain. In these first two chapters I attempt to present the linkages between my research and the normative and legal literature on race and representation. While I cannot hope to provide a comprehensive overview of the relevant literature, my aim is to facilitate communication across the subdisciplinary "separate tables" described by Gabriel Almond (1988).

In chapter 3 I present my supply-side theory of racial redistricting, which provides an explanation for the nature of racial representation that emerged in the new black majority districts. This theory is illustrated with a case study from the two North Carolina districts that were created in 1992 and is tested with a systematic analysis of all candidates who ran for the U.S. House in 1972, 1982, and 1992 in districts that were at least 30 percent black. The theory explains why some districts produced a winner who campaigned on the basis of a politics of difference and others on the basis of a politics of commonality.

The next chapter examines the links between campaigning and governing. That is, do the styles of racial representation that emerge in the campaign carry over to the legislative arena? The nature of racial representation in the U.S. House is examined with a comprehensive data set that includes most dimensions of legislative behavior of all members of the CBC in the 103rd Congress. This chapter also examines the behavior of white House members in the 103rd Congress who represented districts with at least 25 percent black voters and a more limited data set from the 104th Congress for this same group of members. I also conduct more traditional (and limited) analyses of legislative behavior for all members of Congress in the 103rd and 104th Congresses, examining leadership positions, committee assignments, and roll call behavior.

Chapter 5 completes the analysis of representation by examining the various dimensions of member-constituency linkages. While chapter 4 analyzes what members do, this chapter tries to figure out how much of that activity is evident to the constituents. Four linkages are examined: the racial composition of members' staffs, the location of members' offices, the content of constituency newsletters, and the newspaper coverage of the members. The concluding chapter summarizes the argument and explores its broader significance.

A Note on the Scope and Methods of This Project

One limitation of previous studies of racial representation in Congress was their narrow scope. Just as a more complete understanding of racial representation in Congress must cut across the subfields of political science, no single research method can uncover all the relevant relationships. For example, the research that has concluded that white representatives are equally as capable of representing black interests as black representatives are is almost exclusively based on roll call vote analyses (Cameron, Epstein, and O'Halloran 1996; Lublin 1997) or detailed case studies (Swain 1993; though Swain also includes some roll call analyses in her study). More confidence can be placed in research that triangulates methods and data (Tarrow 1995, 473–474; King, Keohane, and Verba 1994; 1995, 479–480). My research utilizes elite interviews, participant observation, legal analysis, content analysis, and statistical analysis of eleven new data sets that I created for this project and existing voter surveys. The detailed case study of North Carolina presented in chapter 3 relies heavily on interviews with thirty-seven political elites, including state legislators, all of the candidates in the 1992 1st District race, newspaper reporters, members of Congress, and party leaders. The analysis of congressional behavior in chapter 4 examines thousands of roll call votes, and thousands of speeches and bills were content analyzed for their racial perspectives. I also conducted interviews with thirty-two congressional staffers and eight members of Congress for this part of the research. Chapter 5 presents a content analysis of more than 11,000 newspaper stories on the activities of House members in the 103rd Congress from districts that are at least 25 percent black. Thus, the research methods I employ run the full range from "soaking and poking" (as Richard Fenno, the leading proponent of participant observation in congressional politics, described the method) to large-scale quantitative analysis. A more detailed outline of the data is provided in Appendix A.

Understanding and Explaining

In her recent book on race, class, and the "American Dream," Jennifer Hochschild notes the obstacles that white scholars face when studying race and politics in the United States. Hochschild notes, "I have been told that I either cannot or should not write this book." She then outlines the various reasons for this position: "[W]hite scholars studying black problems are parasitic or engaging in intellectual imperialism, white scholars' voices will drown out black scholars' voices in what remains a racially biased intellectual world, and whites cannot ever really understand and convey what it means to be black in America" (1995, 9).

I, too, experienced some of the resistance noted by Hochschild, but this view was not typical. Many colleagues in the Race, Ethnicity, and Politics Section of the American Political Science Association enthusiastically welcomed me; their position is "The more attention that can be focused on racial issues, the greater the potential for theoretical development, understanding, societal awareness, and policy change." The success of the Race, Ethnicity, and Politics Section; the impact of Afro-American and Hispanic studies programs at universities all around the country; and the proliferation of journal articles and books by African-American scholars suggest that the first two points noted by Hochschild—intellectual imperialism and the establishment and dominance of a hegemonic discourse by whites—are less of a concern now than even ten years ago. While resistance to white scholarship on racial politics was understandable, and indeed even warranted, a generation ago as the subfield developed, supporting this view today only undermines the potential for the broadest possible debate.

Hochschild's final concern—obstacles to understanding—is formidable. She addresses the point by noting that a woman can have empathy for the black middle-class experience. Women often experience rejection, discrimination, and harassment. Hochschild also points out that studying African Americans in politics almost always involves simultaneously studying the white experience (1995, 10).[11] I obviously cannot claim the former, but the latter is central to my supply-side theory of redistricting and its implications for legislative behavior.

An additional obstacle posed by being a white male was the problem of potential bias in interviews. Early in the project I had reservations about my ability to receive straight answers about racial issues from African-American members of Congress, their staff, and other political elites interviewed for this study. Carol Swain reports that several representatives would not have talked to her if she were white and one "would not even speak openly in front of his white staffers. In their absence, he 'talked black talk'" (Swain 1993, 229). My coauthors of chapter 3 experienced this in interviews in the 1st District in North Carolina. Several African-American politicians and party leaders thought they were spies for the Republican Party or the leading white candidate in the Democratic primary and were reluctant to be interviewed. Furthermore, I feared a pattern of bias in cooperation that would undermine the systematic use of interview data: before conducting the interviews I feared that black members who see themselves as representatives of all voters would be more likely to cooperate than those whose primary goal is to represent the black community. However, these concerns were largely unfounded. All the staffers, representatives, and elites I talked to, with just one exception, were cooperative and helpful, and there was no systematic pattern in willingness to be interviewed based on the representational style of the member (politics of difference versus politics of commonality).[12]

However, the problem of interpretation and understanding remains. Peter Winch argues that all meaningful behavior is rule-governed (1958, chap. 2). Therefore, outsiders may have a difficult time understanding behavior in a specific context because they will not be privy to the rules. Clifford Geertz's "thick description" of the Balinese cockfight is probably the most famous example of how an outsider would entirely miss the deeper meaning of behavior (1973, chap. 15). Winch also argues for the importance of empathy. He says, "[A] historian or sociologist of religion must himself have some religious feeling if he is to make sense of the religious movement he is studying and understand the considerations which govern the lives of its participants" (1958, 88). These two insights provide the basis for the argument that white scholars can never understand the black experience in America.

Taken to an extreme, this position poses insurmountable obstacles to social science. Comparative politics would be impossible, as scholars from one culture could never truly understand another (see MacIntyre 1971; Said 1978). In the context of American politics, in addition to the limitations placed on racial understanding, it would mean, for example, that Jews and Muslims, or even Catholics, Episcopalians, and Lutherans, could not study the impact of the evangelical Christian Right. I disagree. "Outsiders" may bring fresh insights or a different perspective that "insiders" may not see because they are too close to the subject of study. Furthermore, given the scope of this project, I cannot hope to *understand* the individual motivations and thoughts of the millions of constituents represented by the actions of the House members in this study. I have greater confidence in my ability to understand the motivations of the politicians I examine. However, the ultimate goal of this work is to *explain* the patterns of racial representation in the U.S. House, while providing some level of understanding.[13] The case study in chapter 3, the interviews used through the book, and the national surveys employed in chapter 1 help provide the micro-level foundations for understanding racial representation from the perspective of the actors. The supply-side theory provides the theoretical basis for presenting broader empirical patterns and causal relationships that support an explanation of racial representation in the U.S. House.

So why write this book given the obstacles? In short, because I believe that race continues to be the central problem of American politics, and I hope that I can help explain an important aspect of racial politics. Living in North Carolina for five years changed my thinking about racial politics. Racial issues at Duke University, where I started my teaching career, were not that different than they are at the University of Wisconsin. However, local and state politics in North Carolina are permeated by race. Race constantly simmers below the surface, as in the debate in the late 1980s over merging the Durham county and city school systems, and occasionally boils over, as in the 1990 Senate contest between Jesse Helms and Harvey Gantt.

However, race did not have a predictable impact on politics. The 1986 nonpartisan race for mayor of Durham pitted Wib Gulley, a popular white incumbent, against Howard Clement, a conservative black. The Durham Committee, a group of black political leaders, turned out huge majorities for Gulley, while Clement drew most of his support from white voters. The complexities of racial politics in North Carolina became more evident when I began studying the redistricting process as part of a project on candidate emergence organized by Thomas Kazee. We were interested in finding out what motivates some candidates to run and others to stay on the sidelines; the district we examined as part of this broader study was one of the newly created black majority districts (the 1st). Some of the racially motivated strategic behavior was simply stunning (see Canon, Schousen, and Sellers 1994, 1998, and chapter 3 of this book). From this case study it appeared that the supply-side effects that I outline in chapter 3 can have a profound effect on the nature of representation provided in a congressional district.

However, it was not until the *Shaw v. Reno* decision in June 1993 that I decided to write a book on this topic. That decision and the outpouring of commentary on the "political apartheid" districts simply did not square with what I had observed in North Carolina and the broader study of the supply-side effects in the 1992 elections that I was working on with Matt Schousen and Pat Sellers. It appeared to me that an important part of the story was missing: many black candidates were reaching out to white voters and winning on that basis. These new districts seemed to promote a politics of commonality rather than a politics of difference; furthermore, nobody had noticed that it was the decisions of individual candidates that determined whether or not that outcome would be produced rather than a carefully legislated institutional remedy to patterns of discrimination. This book provides a systematic test of these supply-side influences on racial representation in the U.S. House.

CHAPTER ONE

Black Interests, Difference, Commonality, and Representation

I recently attended a lecture by a prominent political theorist on the topic "the politics of difference." The speaker's analysis of identity politics and the government's role in promoting or hindering group politics was fascinating and thought-provoking. In the question-and-answer period, several people asked the speaker to support empirically some assumptions and asked about the practical implications of the argument. Do members of one racial or ethnic group have distinct interests from one another? How could governments operate if they were required to provide groups with veto rights on specific policies? How would the protected groups be defined? The speaker offered a few anecdotes and suggestions, but finally took refuge in the disciplinary division of labor. "I will leave these practical details to the policy folks and the empirically oriented scholars" was the candid, but somewhat unsatisfying, reply.

Political scientists who sit at the empirically oriented "separate table" (Almond 1988) are equally guilty of ignoring the other side of the disciplinary divide. The leading journals of the field are filled with articles on representation or racial politics that make an obligatory reference to Hanna Pitkin, Charles Taylor, Anne Phillips, Will Kymlicka, or Iris Young and move on to data analysis without engaging the debates that occupy an entire subfield of our discipline. For example, Stephan Thernstrom and Abigail Thernstrom's book (1997) does not cite the prominent theorists noted above in 545 pages of text; nor are these theorists mentioned in 160 encyclopedic pages of endnotes. While specialization and a division of labor are necessary in a maturing discipline, both types of work would be improved by a dialogue that seriously considers scholarship on the "other side."

This chapter attempts to promote such a dialogue by discussing the central theoretical concepts used in this book—black interests, the politics of difference and commonality, and representation—in the context of the normative and empirical work on these topics. Are black interests distinct from white interests? If so, how should these be defined? Is the "politics of commonality" inherently in conflict with a notion of distinctive black interests? If not, how can this conceptual tension be resolved? What theory of representation is most useful for examining racial politics in the U.S. House of Representatives?[1]

Black Interests

African Americans have occupied a distinctive, and difficult, place in our nation's history. Thus, it is not surprising that blacks should have different interests and ideas about politics and the role of government than whites. Exploring the contours of the racial divide has been a focus of social science research for at least a half-century. The first generation of research examined the various dimensions and causes of black interests, but did not challenge the notion that blacks and whites wanted different things from the political system. The next generation of work explored more carefully the explanations for the differences in the objective conditions of blacks and whites that gave rise to distinctive black interests. Are blacks responsible for their own social and economic problems, or could these problems be explained by broader societal forces, such as racism, white flight, the absence of jobs in the inner city (Wilson 1996), or failed social policies (Murray 1984)? More recent work has also started to question the notion of "black interests." Thernstrom and Thernstrom urge blacks to move beyond the "figment of the pigment," which only serves to undermine black progress, and focus on the positive role models of Asian and European immigrants (1997, 535; Thernstrom and Thernstrom cite Donald Horowitz [1985, 46] as the source of this colorful phrase).

Race relations and the objective condition of blacks in our nation have dramatically improved in the past sixty years. Thernstrom and Thernstrom's chapter on the Jim Crow laws and norms of the pre–Civil Rights era is a useful reminder of how far we have come. In 1940, 87 percent of black families lived in poverty; there were *no* black police officers in the five deep southern states, in which nearly 40 percent of the nation's black population lived; about half of black Southerners twenty-five years and older had less than five years of schooling; and most were not allowed to vote. Blacks in the South could not go to the same schools, restaurants, hotels, or hospitals as whites. Even graveyards were segregated by race. Blacks were not allowed to shake hands with whites or enter the front door of a white person's house; these simple acts would have been seen as tacit indicators of equality (Thernstrom and Thernstrom 1997, chap. 1).

Conditions have dramatically improved since 1940, but there are still clearly identifiable black interests, in both objective terms (their income, unemployment, death rates, crime, education, and health relative to whites) and subjective terms (the gap between blacks' and whites' opinions on policy and politics). Alternatively objective and subjective interests may be thought of as "needs" and "wants": What needs would have to be met for African Americans to raise their social and economic position to parity with whites? How do African Americans see their position within society, and what policies would they want to have implemented to improve their position relative to whites?

I will not contribute to the debate over the *causes* of the racial divide and the dismal conditions faced by many blacks in this nation. Rather, I am interested in the *consequences* of black interests in the political process. Given that distinctive black interests exist, how are they represented in Congress? This is the topic of chapters 4 and 5. My immediate purpose is to provide a brief overview of the massive literature on the nature of black interests. I will argue that despite substantial improvement in the objective position of blacks and a narrowing gap on some measures of public opinion between blacks and whites, the racial divide figures prominently in American society and politics. This conclusion is supported by a variety of methods from the macro-sociology of Andrew Hacker (1992) to David Shipler's micro-sociology (1997) in the tradition of Erving Goffman and survey-based work in political science (Dawson 1994; Tate 1993; Kinder and Sanders 1996).

Objective Interests (Needs)

African Americans have faced adverse economic and social conditions since they were first brought to this country against their will. The scourge of slavery tarnished our Constitution, helped produce the most serious and violent rift in our history (the Civil War), and left an ugly legacy that has yet to be fully reconciled. In 1944 Gunnar Myrdal chided America for not addressing its distinctive "dilemma."[2] A quarter-century later, after many of our nation's largest cities smoldered with racial unrest and violence, the Kerner Commission painted a stark portrait of the objective conditions faced by blacks. The commission feared that we were heading toward two Americas, one black and one white, that were becoming increasingly separate and unequal.

There has been undeniable progress on many fronts since the 1960s: 37.5 percent of blacks twenty-five years or older had attended college in 1995, compared to only 7.2 percent in 1960; the median income for black men was only 41 percent of the median income for white men in 1940 and increased to 67 percent in 1995; the comparable gains for black women were even more encouraging, increasing from 36 percent of white female income in 1940 to 87 percent of white female income in 1995. Perhaps the most dramatic figure that demonstrates the explosion in the size of the black middle class is the increase in the proportion of black families with incomes that are at least double the poverty line from 1 percent in 1940 to 44.9 percent in 1996 (the comparable increase for whites was from 12 percent to 75 percent) (the 1940 figure is from Thernstrom and Thernstrom 1997, 190–197; the 1996 figure is from Lamison-White 1997, 4). More blacks own homes, more blacks have white-collar jobs, the proportion of blacks living in suburbs doubled between 1950 and 1995, more blacks live in integrated neighborhoods (Thernstrom and Thernstrom 1997, 211, 218–219), and de jure discrimination is a thing of the past.

But is the glass half full or half empty? Even as the gap between blacks and whites has shrunk in some areas, the objective conditions faced by the typical black and white citizens in the United States are far from equal. The 1988 Commission on Cities reached many of the same conclusions as the Kerner Commission (McCartney 1992, 4), and more recent observations by scholars such as Andrew Hacker (1992), David Shipler (1997), and Michael Dawson (1994) are more depressing than encouraging. Dawson's analysis of economic data and public opinion surveys in the 1980s led him to conclude that "the Kerner Commission's judgement that the United States was moving toward two societies—one black, one white—is clearly reflected in the American landscape" (1994, 33).

Huge gaps remain between whites and blacks, and in some cases the racial divide is growing. Nearly three times as many black families are below the poverty line as white families (26 percent compared to 9 percent in 1996), which is substantially higher than the black-to-white poverty ratio in 1940 (87 percent compared to 48 percent, or 1.8 times) (1996 data from Lamison-White 1997, vii; 1940 data from Thernstrom and Thernstrom 1997, 233; the respective rates of poverty for black and white individuals were 28.4 percent and 8.6 percent in 1996). Thern-strom and Thernstrom try to put a positive spin on these numbers by pointing to the absolute decline in black poverty rather than blacks' position relative to whites.[3] However, they do not completely sugarcoat the poverty statistics, citing the persistence of black poverty at around 30 percent for the past twenty-five years as the "single most depressing fact about the state of black America today" (1997, 234). Furthermore, while black median family income now stands at about 60 percent of white median family income (which is still a huge gap), the gap in wealth is much more dramatic: the average white household has ten times the assets of the typical black family (in 1993 the median house-hold net worth was $45,740 for whites and $4,418 for blacks).[4]

Other indicators show similar patterns. The unemployment rate of black adult males has been about twice as high as that for white adult males for the past forty-five years (which is substantially higher than the nearly equal ratio of 1.26 in 1940); in 1997 the black unemployment rate averaged 10.1 percent, compared to 4.2 percent for whites; in Jan-uary 1998 the gap had narrowed slightly to 9.3 percent and 4 percent.[5] The other most depressing statistic on the objective position of blacks is that only one-third of black children lived in two-parent households in 1995 (compared to 76 percent of white children). In 1940 two-thirds of black children and 91 percent of white children lived with two par-ents. Blacks are more likely than whites to be victimized by crime; for some crimes, such as murder of young black men, the figures are stun-ning. A black male between the ages of eighteen and twenty-four is 10.5 times as likely to be murdered as a white male in that same age range (Thernstrom and Thernstrom 1997, 265).

One of the largest remaining gaps between blacks and whites is their respective quality of health. On every imaginable measure—life ex-pectancy, infectious diseases, infant mortality, cancer, heart disease, and strokes—the gaps are large and in many cases growing. In 1995 the life expectancy for blacks was about 10 percent shorter than that for whites (seventy years for blacks, compared to seventy-seven for whites), the infant mortality rate was double for blacks (15.1 deaths per 100,000 births for blacks, compared to 7.6), and maternal mortal-ity was more than triple (22.1 deaths per 100,000 live births for blacks, compared to 7.1). The death rate for women with breast cancer fell by 10 percent for all women between 1990 and 1995, but did not change for blacks (and now stands at 27.5 deaths per 100,000 for blacks, com-pared to 21 for all women). Maternal mortality for blacks increased by 47 percent from 1987 to 1995, compared to a 7.6 percent increase for all women (which means that white women had virtually no increase in their rate of maternal mortality). Between 1980 and 1995 the number of new cases of diabetes increased by a third among blacks, which was three times the increase among whites. The cancer rate among black men has risen by 67 percent since the early 1960s, but only by about 11 percent among white men. Deaths caused by stroke and heart disease are also substantially more frequent among blacks, though the gap between blacks and whites did not increase between 1990 and 1995 (all the data cited here are from the Department of Health and Human Services, as reported in Kilborn 1998, A16).

Differences in income and education account for some of the gap, but even after these factors are controlled, racial differences persist in the quality of health for Americans. Some practitioners argue that the gap is explained by the inferior health care received by blacks: "'When you take black and white Americans and exactly the same situation like being hospitalized for a heart attack and having the same insurance, the chance that the black patient will get the advanced care is much less than it is for the white patient. The medical system appears to treat them differently'" (quoted in Kilborn 1998, A16).

The half-empty, half-full debate has been resolved by some scholars by pointing out that both may be right: there are two black Americas—a middle class that has become better off and a lower class that has been left behind (Wilson 1987; Marable 1980). The African-American middle class fled the inner city, following the path of ethnic whites who left a generation before them. Conservative critics point to the institution of marriage as a key explanation for the intraracial divide. Among married couples 9.1 percent of black families and 5.1 percent of white families were below the poverty line, compared with 43.7 percent of black female-headed households and 27.3 percent of white female-headed households (Lamison-White 1997, vii). Liberals also recognize the split within the black community, but argue that race and class interact in complex ways. Dawson notes that an intraracial divide is evident on some issues, such as economic redistribution. As income increases, blacks are increasingly less interested in redistribution, an effect that swamps Dawson's measurement of racially "linked fates" (1994, chap. 8).[6]

The election of the new members of the Congressional Black Caucus (CBC) from the South in 1992 drew attention to a third group within black America: the rural poor. The "truly disadvantaged" have typically been portrayed as residing in inner-city ghettos. However, the poor southern districts now represented by members of the CBC have different interests than the urban districts of the older CBC representatives. State Representative Toby Fitch, the cochair of the House Redistricting Committee in North Carolina in 1992, testified in federal district court in the *Shaw v. Hunt* case that his goal was to create one urban black district and one rural black district because "'I don't think [blacks] all act alike, or look alike or have the same interests.'" To illustrate the differences between urban and rural blacks, he noted, "'A good friend of mine, Rep. Mickey Michaux, came down to Eastern North Carolina from Durham when there was water laying in the tobacco fields wearing patent leather shoes and a silk shirt driving a black El Dorado Cadillac. Yes sir, there is a difference'" (quoted in Patterson 1994, 3A).

Differing circumstances produce varying needs, which, in turn, are linked to subjective interests, or wants. Christopher Eisgruber notes, "Interests . . . will sometimes track racial lines for reasons that ought not to seem especially surprising or disturbing. For example, interests will track racial lines to the extent that racial minorities have a special interest in fighting racial discrimination—just as farmers will have a special interest in certain issues of agricultural policies . . ." (1996, 523–524). In the following section I will show that the divide between the races is vast on racial issues, but does not exist on issues that are not related to race. In other words, wants are very strongly rooted in needs.

Subjective Interests (Wants)

Just before President Bill Clinton initiated his "national conversation on race," two national polls reflected the racial divide. The headline of an article reporting on a Gallup poll summarizes the divide in these terms: "Whites positive on race relations . . . but blacks believe whites are much more prejudiced and less than half feel they are treated the same as white people" (Eversley 1997, 2A). Indeed, whites see themselves as quite tolerant. Only 1 percent of whites say they would move out if a black moved in next door, and 91 percent would vote for a black person for president. Seventy-six percent of whites think that blacks are treated as well as whites, but only 49 percent of blacks feel the same way. A CBS News poll taken a few days after the Gallup poll had more negative numbers. Sixty-six percent of blacks and 53 percent of whites thought that race relations in the United States are "generally bad," and most (58 percent of the survey's respondents) thought that doing anything to resolve racial problems was beyond the president's control (the latter view was up 12 percent from the previous year). The racial gap was also evident in whether the respondent thought that improving race relations is among the most important things that America needs for its future: 71 percent of blacks, but only 32 percent of whites, thought it was.

Public opinion researchers have dissected these basic impressions of race relations and identified a "principle-implementation gap" (Tuch and Hughes 1996b, 724) whereby the gap between whites and blacks has declined dramatically on general *principles* of racial equality, but huge differences remain on *policies* aimed at producing equality between the races. There is also a lively debate over the causes of this gap: symbolic racism (Kinder and Sears 1981; Sears 1988; Sniderman and Piazza 1993), differences between policy areas (Tuch and Hughes 1996a, 1996b; Stoker 1996; Sears and Jessor 1996), or a complex interplay among material interests, group interests and resentment, principle, and the framing of issues (Kinder and Sanders 1996). The intraracial division noted above in basic demographic data is also evident in survey research. Dawson (1994) concludes that race trumps class in most instances, but Jennifer Hochschild argues class differences are central: middle-class blacks have become discontent, but the lower class still believes in the American dream (1995). Michael Alvarez and John Brehm add the cautionary note that there is a great deal of uncertainty about racial issues, in part because racial attitudes revealed in surveys are highly sensitive to question wording (1997, 369).

For my purposes the causes of the gap are not crucial; that it exists is evident. However, the picture is far more complex than often portrayed. I will present survey evidence on three types of issues—racial, implicit racial, and nonracial—that demonstrates varying levels of differences between white and black respondents. Figure 1.1 shows the familiar racial divide that has been chronicled so thoroughly by others (Tate 1993; Kinder and Sanders 1996; Lublin 1997). In fact, the methods used here are the same as those used by Donald Kinder and Lynn Sanders to produce their figure 2.2 (1996, 27). My results on racial issues are nearly identical to theirs, but the gap has grown slightly wider between 1986 and 1994.[7] The figure shows the distribution of opinions of black and white respondents to twenty questions on a range of racial issues, including affirmative action and quotas, the posi-

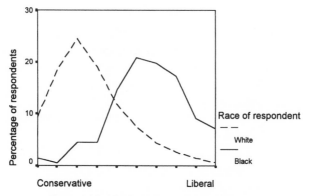

Figure 1.1 Public Opinion on Racial Issues
Source: 1992 and 1994 National Election Study

tion of blacks in our society (including items like "Have blacks gotten less than they deserve?" and "If blacks tried harder, they could be as well off as whites."), the pace of civil rights progress, and the government's role in promoting integration. That blacks would be more supportive of the pro–civil rights position is not surprising, but the size of the gap is stunning given the often heard view that the significance of race is waning. Nearly three-fourths of whites (71.6 percent), but only 11.2 percent of blacks are in the four most conservative deciles. More than half of blacks (53.3 percent) are in the most liberal four deciles, while only 9.2 percent of whites are equivalently supportive of racial issues. The mean for blacks was nearly twice as large as that for whites (.61 compared to .32 on the 0–1 scale, *t*-test for difference of means = 20.2, sig. at .0001).

However, the divide in public opinion on racial issues tells only part of the story. A second set of issues implicitly involves race, such as welfare programs, food stamps, the death penalty, and policies dealing with urban unrest (others, such as foreign policy toward South Africa and Haiti, would also be in this category, but there were no National Election Studies [NES] questions in the 1994 survey on these issues, so they are not included here). An index derived from fifteen questions on these topics[8] reveals a large racial divide on part-racial issues between whites and blacks, but one that is somewhat smaller than the gap on purely racial issues. The mean for blacks on this index was .49, compared to .28 for whites (*t* = 12.5, sig. at .0001). One interesting difference between the distributions in figures 1.2 and 1.1 is that a far greater proportion of whites is bunched in the most conservative dec-

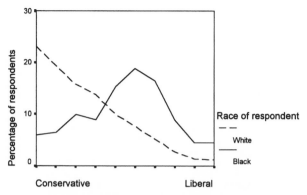

Figure 1.2 Public Opinion on Part-Racial Issues
Source: 1992 and 1994 National Election Study

iles of the implicit racial index than on the explicit racial index (42.6 percent in the bottom two deciles, compared to 24.6 percent on the racial issues). Blacks are normally distributed in figure 1.2, while they were heavily skewed in the liberal direction on the racial issues displayed in figure 1.1. In fact, there are more blacks in the most conservative three deciles (22.3 percent) than in the most liberal three deciles (17.6 percent) on the implicitly racial issues. Blacks are clearly more supportive of welfare and food stamp spending and policies to support urban areas, and less supportive of the death penalty, than whites, but they are actually quite moderate on these issues, while whites are extremely conservative.[9]

The third set of issues does not involve race and covers the broadest range of issues of the three indices. I attempted to make the index comparable to the Americans for Democratic Action (ADA) ratings for the 103rd Congress, which were based on thirty-nine roll calls on twenty-three issues. I was able to find NES questions on twelve of those topics (a total of twenty-eight questions), including health care, supplemental appropriations, taxes/deficit, abortion, gay rights, defense, the North American Free Trade Agreement (NAFTA), immigration, the environment, education, the death penalty, and the CBC budget (the final two were dropped because they are implicitly related to race). I calculated a weighted and an unweighted index, and the results were the same: there were few to no differences between white and black respondents.[10] As figure 1.3 shows, the distributions are nearly identical, and the means, amazingly enough, *are* identical (.4654 and .4653 for whites and blacks, respectively, for the weighted index). The unweighted index of all twenty-eight questions, including the implicit

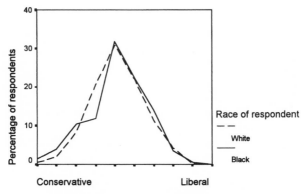

Figure 1.3 Public Opinion on Nonracial Issues
Source: 1992 and 1994 National Election Study

racial issues, revealed a mean for blacks that was .03 more liberal than
the mean for whites (.453 compared to .423, $t = 3.5$, sig. at .001). On
this broad range of issues blacks have the same preferences as whites.
On some issues they are slightly more conservative (abortion and the
environment), and on some they are slightly more liberal (spending for
education and the government's role in health care).

I was surprised by these results. Previous research led me to expect
that blacks would be more liberal than whites. I should reemphasize
that these were issues chosen by the ADA to best distinguish liberals
from conservatives in the House; thus, if there is any general pattern
of blacks being more liberal than whites, the differences should have
been evident on this range of issues.[11] These were not issues such as
spending on highway programs or education, which tend to be more
consensual. Furthermore, the data do not make a distinction between
Democrats and Republicans. *Blacks have the same preferences as whites
on nonracial issues, irrespective of political party.*

These results challenge the validity of standard measures of racial
representation. Nearly all research on race and representation measures congressional behavior with general ideological ratings such as
the scores from the ADA, LCCR (Leadership Conference on Civil
Rights), COPE (the AFL–CIO's Committee on Political Education),
or NOMINATE (Keith Poole and Howard Rosenthal's measure of the
dimensionality of member roll call voting [1996]). All of these general
measures correlated very highly with each other (Lublin 1997, 79) and
are used interchangeably in the literature (Swain 1993; Cameron, Epstein, and O'Halloran 1996; Whitby 1998; Lublin 1997), but they have

very little to do with race. Of the thirty-nine roll calls used by the ADA in the 103rd Congress, one was directly related to race (the Racial Justice Act) and four implicitly involved race (District of Columbia statehood, the CBC budget vote, the death penalty, and U.S. policy toward Haiti). Thus, general ideological indices are flawed measures of racial representation from the member side of the equation, but figure 1.3 conclusively demonstrates that they are worthless as an indicator of behavior that addresses constituents' racial wants. The standard practice of regressing ADA, LCCR, COPE, or NOMINATE scores on district characteristics, such as percentage black, percentage urban, and income, can no longer be justified as a reasonable approach for measuring racial representation.

Critiques

There are two central critiques to my focus on black interests (and the implicit comparison to whites): multiracialism and deracialization. The first of these is known as the Tiger Woods phenomenon, in reference to the golf star who calls himself a "cablinasian" (Caucasian, black, Indian, and Asian). Proponents of this view argue that it does not make sense to talk about biracial (i.e., black-white) politics in a multiracial world (MacManus 1995). This argument also received extensive attention early in 1997 when Representative Tom Petri (R–WI) introduced a bill to create multiethnic categories on the U.S. Census. Currently the Census categories include white, black, American Indian or Alaskan Native, Hispanic, Asian or Pacific Islander, and "other." The number of people classifying themselves as "other" has risen from 5,000 in 1940 to 9,850,000 in 1990 (U.S. Census). This trend will continue in the next few decades as interracial marriages, which were banned in nineteen states until the U.S. Supreme Court's 1967 decision *Loving v. Virginia,* have increased more than fourfold in the last generation, from 676,000 to more than 3 million marriages from 1970 to 1994 (Galloway 1997, 1A).

A few congressional staffers I interviewed noted the decreasing relevance of the black-white focus of racial politics. One pointed out: "Even the black and Hispanic populations are very mixed: African Americans, Jamaicans, Haitians and Cubans, Puerto Ricans, Dominicans, and Mexicans. It's all just a jumbled mix" (S31; S16 made a nearly identical argument).[12] President Clinton seemed to be moving toward the multiracial perspective with his nomination, and subsequent intersession appointment, of Bill Lann Lee, an Asian-American lawyer, to be assistant attorney general for civil rights. A *New York Times* reporter argued that the president recognizes that "the country's changing demographics have moved the issue of race relations beyond interactions between whites and blacks and now encompass relations among an array of races and ethnic groups" (Holmes 1997, A18). This is the first time the position has been held by someone other than a black or a white.[13]

Many black leaders oppose the multiracial category on the Census, arguing that it would further undermine blacks' political power. Joseph Lowery, the president of the Southern Christian Leadership Conference, points out that new categories would "affect race-sensitive government actions ranging from the enforcement of fair-housing laws to the reapportionment of minority voting districts," fail to change the way people think about race, and risk "weakening the nation's already tenuous commitment to affirmative action as a means of remedying inequities and including the excluded" (Lowery 1997, 21).

Despite the ascendance of a multiracial society, there are many reasons why the black-white divide maintains special *political* prominence, if perhaps a decreasing social position. Even the distinctive social and cultural position of the black-white divide has not disappeared. The most recent Census data reveal that for married people between the ages of twenty-five and thirty-four, 70 percent of Asian women and 39 percent of Hispanic women have white husbands. Only 2 percent of black women in the same age group were married to white men in 1990. Transracial adoptions of black babies are very rare; despite a tremendous need to find homes for black children, many white parents travel to Latin America or Southeast Asia to adopt children (Fogg-Davis 1998). On both a social and a political level, the biracial divide has a distinctive historical legacy rooted in slavery, segregation, and the civil rights movement. For more than two hundred years race relations in this nation were clearly defined by tensions between blacks and whites. Other ethnic groups suffered economic and social discrimination, but nothing that paralleled the experience of African Americans.

The political distinctiveness of biracial politics is even more significant for this study: while black interests, and the political expression of those interests, are by no means monolithic, they are far more cohesive than those of any other racial or ethnic minority in the United States. African Americans vote more cohesively and demonstrate more consistent political opinions (on racial and part-racial issues) than Hispanics, Asian Americans, Jews, or other racial or ethnic groups. Kinder and Sanders's landmark study of racial attitudes concludes that the black-white gap is a "divide without peer" and that "[d]ifferences as drastic as these simply have no counterpart in studies of public opinion" (1996, 27). Finally, the decision to focus only on black and white constituents and members of Congress was partly dictated by pragmatic considerations: the scope of the project was already vast; testing the supply-side theory with data on other minority groups will have to be left for future research.

The deracialization perspective brings a two-pronged attack against the notion of distinctive black interests.[14] First, there is the empirical claim that race is declining in significance in American politics and society more generally. Second, the policy implication of deracialization is obvious: abandon all racial preferences and affirmative action policies to promote a "color-blind" society. This view has been associated with scholars to the left of center, such as William Julius Wilson, and those to the right, such as Thernstrom and Thernstrom. Jeffrey Elliot argues, "'Despite what many whites may believe, the agenda of black America is not that different from that of white America. African-American values are not different. They too want to share in the American dream and have a part in the basic things all families and all Americans want: a good life'" (quoted in Donohoe 1993, E1). Abigail Thernstrom delivers the punch line that flows from this perspective: "It's time to forget the message of the Kerner Commission, and start treating Americans simply as individuals" (1997, A19).

The color-blind dream picked up momentum in the mid-1990s from the conservative wing of the Supreme Court, Proposition 209 in California, and a general reaction among whites against affirmative action. However, the evidence presented above indicates that blacks' objective interests are very distinct from those of whites over a range of areas and that their subjective interests are sharply divided on issues that are explicitly and implicitly related to race. I concur with Mel Watt's (D–NC) assessment of circumstances in the late 1990s:

> [W]e all do strive for a time that we don't have to take race into account. I don't think there is any black or white person that could honestly say as an American that we don't aspire to that high goal. My response, though, is that in the interim, until we get to that point, minority people, Hispanics, blacks, deserve to have representation in every process. And if at some point we can reach the goal where it is not necessary to draw

minority districts or take race into account to assure that people have
representation in the process, then I think I will be the first to join [the
color blind theory]. (House 1993, 85)

The Politics of Difference and the Politics of Commonality

Given the distinctive nature of black interests, at least over a range of
relevant issues, how should these interests be represented in Congress?
Can white politicians adequately represent African-American interests? Should African Americans have congressional districts explicitly
drawn to maximize their political power, even if it requires tortuous
district lines? Once the districts are created, should black representatives focus their attention on black constituents or attempt to represent
the entire district? What does the creation of black majority districts
mean for the quality of democracy? What impact do these districts
have on the nature of representation, accountability, legitimacy, and
equality?

One basis for answering these questions is found in the debate in
the minority politics and women's studies literatures concerning the
"politics of difference" versus the "politics of commonality" that I discussed briefly in the Introduction (Gilligan 1982; MacKinnon 1987;
Eisenstein 1988; Gitlin 1993; Young 1990; Connoly 1991) and in the
broader literature on community, identity, and democracy (Phillips
1995; Kymlicka 1995; Taylor 1992; Gates 1992; Beitz 1989; Streich
1997; Gutmann and Thompson 1996). I cannot do justice to the complexity and scope of the normative literature on these topics,[15] but I
will briefly outline its contours, starting with the more general literature. I will then discuss two relevant dimensions of the more specific
"commonality-difference" debate for the topic at hand—how it in-
forms notions of racial representation, especially among members of
the CBC, and how it directly relates to racial redistricting. In the following section I will review the empirical literature on representation
that examines the actual relationships between the elected and the voters rather than the ideal arrangement. As I note in the Introduction,
the normative and empirical literatures often ignore each other, much
to their mutual impoverishment. I hope that my work will help bridge
that divide.

The broader literature on identity, community, and democracy helps
sort out the general principles that should govern the relationships
among groups and between politicians and constituents. Stated in general terms, the racial politics questions posed above look like this:

Should government treat everyone as individuals or recognize group differences? If group differences are recognized, what are the proper mechanisms for ensuring fair representation? Should group differences be confined to the private sphere and only tolerated in the public sphere within a broader Madisonian system of majority rule (Rawls 1971), or should identity politics be embraced, recognizing that permanent majorities may be tyrannical (Guinier 1994)?

These questions reveal the central fault lines in current democratic theory. Does the ideal democracy place more emphasis on individualism or identity, community or liberty, rights or responsibility (for citizens), accountability or autonomy (for politicians), authenticity or assimilation, equality of opportunity or outcomes? There are no obvious groupings across all these dimensions that can be captured in a single belief system or theory, nor could consistent choices across pairs be made by those who seek racial justice and equality.

Greg Streich's excellent dissertation, "After the Celebration: Theories of Community and Practices of Interracial Dialogue," outlines five general theories of politics that have implications for racial commonality and difference and the dualisms outlined above: American national identity, liberalism, communitarianism, deliberative democracy, and difference theory. These five are arrayed, roughly, in order of increasing acceptance of important differences between whites and blacks. Advocates of American national identity, such as Arthur Schlesinger, Jr. (1992), and Allan Bloom (1987), have an overriding belief in commonality. America is strongest when it focuses on common beliefs and values, the "American Creed," and the "American Dream." Differences should be subsumed within the "melting pot," and all Americans should focus on what they share as Americans rather than on the racial, ethnic, or religious differences that may separate them. Streich summarizes this view in these terms: "[D]ifference is a problem and a source of conflict in community that threatens to undermine our communities, and commonality is the cure" (1997, 16).

Political liberalism favors individualism, liberty, rights, assimilation, and equality of opportunity across the pairs outlined above; however, there is a great deal of variation among political liberals. In general, political liberalism attempts to downplay, or even avoid, difference while emphasizing shared values, consensus, and toleration (Rawls 1971). However, unlike American national identity, there is room for cultural and racial differences within a Rawlsian liberalism (Kymlicka 1995; Dworkin 1989, 499–504). Kymlicka attempts to resolve the tension between liberalism and group rights by arguing for a "societal culture" that allows individuals to express their political and cultural identities (1995).

Communitarians focus on shared meanings and values, the common good, and consensus that bonds communities together. Difference is not easily incorporated into a theory that focuses on unity and common experiences, but Michael Sandel (1982) and other communitarians argue that "outsiders" can fit in by expanding shared meanings to encompass new experiences. Taylor makes additional room for difference in his "politics of recognition" by balancing procedural liberalism with the distinctive interests of racial or ethnic groups (French Canadians are of special interest to Taylor) (Taylor 1992). Communitarians share a link with advocates of American national identity with their interest in shared values, but they tend to focus on smaller political units than the nation. Some communitarians also overlap with deliberative democrats in arguing that shared meanings and values are open to a variety of perspectives and may be shaped through discussion and debate (Downing and Thigpen 1986). In general, the balance that communitarians strike between commonality and difference is likely to be unsatisfactory to both sides. Advocates of commonality would see too much emphasis on recognition and incorporation of difference, while difference theorists (and liberals for that matter) are concerned about the exclusive practices implied by dominant shared values.

Deliberative democrats do not fare much better in resolving these tensions, but they provide a strong normative argument in favor of minority representation in Congress. Advocates of deliberative democracy argue that deliberation itself is an important component of representation. How members vote on roll calls may be important, but the words they speak are equally important. Speeches can changes debates, agendas, and even preferences. After outlining the versions of deliberative democracy as discursive (Drysek 1990), communicative (Young 1994), civic republicanism (Sunstein 1993), and strong democracy (Barber 1984), Phillips argues that the common element in this work is that "political engagement can change initial statements of preference and interest. All combine in criticism of that interest-based democracy which sees political activities as primarily in terms of instrumental rationality; which reduces the act of representation of pregiven unchanging preference; and conceives of government as engaged in aggregation" (Phillips 1995, 149). While I part company with deliberative democrats in their critique of interest-based democracy, I see great value in their focus on deliberation, participation, and agendas and on how minority voices can contribute to the richness of this debate.

Kathryn Abrams was one of the first to make the connection between deliberative democracy and minority districting. She recommends creating the maximum number of districts that have a relatively even split between majority and minority voters, arguing that different races will be more likely to understand each other if the opportunities for cooperation across difference are promoted by racially conscious districting (Abrams 1988, 477). Phillips is less convinced, arguing that there is a logical inconsistency between group representation and deliberative democracy, at least in its more extreme "difference" or essentialist manifestations, in that true deliberation requires movement from initial positions; if a politician is held on a short group-identity leash, there is no room for cooperation and compromise (1995, 154–156). "One of the worries about the strategy of 'safe seats' of minority representatives," Phillips says, "is that the politicians may not even bother to cloak themselves in any garb of political ideas. The presumption of authentic, or what Adolf Reed calls 'organic,' representation can then reduce the vitality of political debate" (1995, 102). However, Phillips goes on to argue that if politicians are provided some autonomy and are not simply "messengers, sent there to pass on pre-agreed programmes and ideas" (1995, 159), then the "politics of presence" (that is, descriptive representation) becomes increasingly important for democracy. Phillips concludes, "All this [deliberative democracy] depends in turn on some guarantee of political presence, for if certain groups have been permanently excluded, the process of deliberation cannot even begin" (1995, 151).

Amy Gutmann and Dennis Thompson provide a compelling account of how the politics of presence shook up the status quo in the U.S. Senate as Senator Carol Moseley Braun (D–IL) successfully challenged the Daughters of the Confederacy's renewal of their patent on the Confederate flag insignia. The measure was about to sail through as a noncontroversial, nongermane amendment that had been attached by Jesse Helms (R–NC) and Strom Thurmond (R–SC). Braun, as the only African American in the Senate, was outraged. Her passion carried the day as twenty-seven senators switched their votes on the amendment, which was defeated by a 75-to-25 vote (Gutmann and Thompson 1996, 135). It is quite likely that the Helms amendment would have not been questioned had Braun not been in the Senate.[16]

Students of Congress are increasingly enamored of deliberative democracy. Prominent scholars, such as Lawrence Dodd, Steven Smith, Tom Mann, Norman Ornstein, and Joseph Bessette, have all called for a greater role for deliberation within the institution as a way to improve the policy-making process and enhance the public's understanding of the institution. The quality of that debate would certainly be improved by enlarging its scope.[17]

Difference theorists are concerned that all the talk advocated by deliberative democrats will simply serve to obscure the real issues of power differentials, permanent exclusion, and coercion. "It also can become a rhetorical substitute for the concrete action needed to reach racial equality and social justice" (Streich 1997, 24, citing Carby 1992 and Gates 1992). While some difference theorists, such as Iris Young (1990), advocate dialogue across differences, "essentialist" or radical difference theorists question whether meaningful communication across the racial divide is possible. Richard Merelman points out that cultural conflict between whites and blacks, as manifested in the symbolic debate over "multiculturalism," demonstrates that "preservation of cultural differences is a legitimate way of advancing economic and political equality between the races. We can see, therefore, that multiculturalism challenges the received conceptions of American social structure and identity to which most whites adhere" (1994, 17). While multiculturalism has not yet developed a "fully articulated vision of the American nation as a whole" (Merelman 1994, 17), it may provide an alternative to liberalism that can bridge the gap between theories of difference and commonality.

To sum up, political liberals would prefer to ignore racial differences, but also tolerate them and in some cases accept them as part of a multicultural society (Kymlicka 1995). Advocates of American national identity are even less tolerant of difference, while difference theorists are critical of the homogenizing assumptions made by communitarian and liberal theorists who emphasize common ground. However, there are liberals, communitarians, and difference theorists who all share some of the hopes of deliberative democrats that we can talk out our differences, or at least get to the point where shared understandings promote tolerance and recognition.

Political Applications of Difference and Commonality

Given the difficulty in mapping these general theories of politics onto notions of commonality and difference, it would be useful to examine how politicians define these concepts. Though politicians do not "talk the talk" of political theorists, they "walk the walk." That is, all politicians who represent multiracial districts have implicitly answered, or at least confronted, the questions introduced in this section. Most politicians from racially diverse constituencies have fairly explicit understandings of racial representation, identity, and difference-commonality.

An extreme vision of a politically grounded racial representation that embodies the politics of difference is the separatist philosophy of the Nation of Islam and Louis Farrakhan. Not only do Black Muslims reject the possibility that whites can represent black interests, but also they call for the economic, social, and political separation of the races. Black Muslims' views of difference overlap with white supremacists at the other end of the political spectrum: both agree that separation is the only way to reduce racial friction. The black nationalist sentiment also is evident in the less extreme, but very urgent and vigorous debates in the nation's urban public schools over Afrocentric curricula, ebonics, and the utility of integration as a goal and busing as a means to achieve that goal.

Other core principles of Black Muslims—self-reliance, responsibility, and economic power—have roots in the proposal of Radical Republican Thaddeus Stevens after the Civil War to give "40 acres and a mule" to every freed slave. Huey P. Newton, Black Panther cofounder and leader, echoed these sentiments a century later, arguing that blacks needed an economic base from which to compete. Newton maintained that it was meaningless for blacks to try to participate in the system. "'When black people send a representative [to government], he is somewhat absurd, because he represents no political power'" (quoted in McCartney 1992, 8). For Newton, Marxist revolution was the only answer. Obviously, the difference perspective does not require embracing Farrakhan or Newton. Those who view politics through the lens of race and require representation of distinctive black interests by black representatives are practicing the politics of difference. Descriptive representation becomes critical if inherent differences are recognized in terms of identities and shared experiences rather than ideas and opinions (Phillips 1995, 6). From this perspective white politicians cannot represent blacks because they cannot understand what it means to be black, despite their best intentions and efforts.

Shifting to the opposite end of the spectrum, the extreme version of the politics of commonality is the deracialized, color-blind perspective outlined above. This perspective holds that the race of a member of

Congress does not matter because racial issues are no longer central (or at least *should* not be central) to American politics. Alternative views, which will be discussed in more detail below, hold that while there still may be some issues that divide Americans along racial lines, politicians should attempt to find common ground and represent the interests of all their constituents. Furthermore, the race of the member is irrelevant in providing substantive representation because policy positions and ideas matter more than the color of one's skin.

African Americans in Congress shy away from both extremes. In February 1994 an impassioned debate over the censure of an anti-Semitic and racist speech by Khalid Abdul Muhammad, a former minister in the Nation of Islam, provided insight into the views of many members of the CBC on this topic. Major Owens (D–NY) eloquently expressed the sentiment of many members of the CBC:

> Responsible African American leadership should cease the pursuit of total unity within the Black community. We must leave the ten percent who advocate hatred and violence and let them march off to their own destruction. These are copycats mouthing imitations of ancient European biases against Jews. We must also leave the five percent of Blacks who are educated, manipulative, self-serving opportunists openly toadying to racist benefactors on the right. Eighty-five percent of African Americans is enough to maintain the core of the Coalition of the Caring Majority. . . . No more time should be wasted on negotiations with hate-mongers and rank opportunists. Reject Muhammad and Farrakhan at one extreme. Reject Clarence Thomas, Roy Innis and their more subtle followers who strangle human and economic rights at the other extreme. (*Congressional Record,* February 3, 1994, E93–E94)

While its members reject the political extremes of racial politics,[18] until recently the CBC was firmly placed on the "politics of difference" side of the debate. The formative political experiences for the founding members of the CBC were in the civil rights movement of the 1960s. The battle against racism and discrimination that began in the streets continued in the halls of Congress as the CBC took on the self-proclaimed role as the "conscience of the institution." Many members saw themselves as spokespersons for all African Americans, not only those in their congressional districts. Their representation of black interests was without political bounds. "'We fought publicly with Jimmy Carter almost every day of his administration,'" William Clay (D–MO) recently said. "'It's no different, Democrat or Republican. We will challenge anybody who seeks to undermine the basic interests of our people'" (quoted in Cooper 1993a, 24).

The distinguishing features, then, of the politics of difference as practiced by current members of the House are to perceive politics in racial terms, to view differences between the races as central for understanding power relations and exclusion, and to see one's primary constituency as black voters (either nationally or in one's district). This style of representation is typical among the House members from the older, northern inner-city districts. The staffer for one representative from this type of district made it clear that her boss did not place a priority on the largely Republican, white suburbs. "He works to represent the people who are the most in need in the inner cities" (S6).

Some members of the 1992 class are more subtle than their senior colleagues in holding this perspective. Corrine Brown (D–FL) talked about the improvement in representation she would bring to the black voters in her district, saying, "'They have been represented by people who haven't paid attention to their districts. I don't say that white candidates can't represent the district. They can. They just haven't'" (quoted in Cooper 1994, 34). Cynthia McKinney (D–GA) echoes this view: "Black-majority districts create opportunities for African-Americans, particularly in the South, to choose someone who will represent *their* interests, as opposed to the person who will do them the least harm" (McKinney 1996, 64). Brown and McKinney shied away from explicitly saying that "blacks must represent blacks," but Bennie Thompson, who was elected to replace Mike Espy in Mississippi in 1993, was quite blunt. Thompson criticized his predecessor, who was noted for his moderation on racial issues and his appeals to white voters, saying that blacks voters "don't like how the district has gone back to the plantation owners." Thompson vowed to return more power to blacks and consistently rejected biracial politics during the campaign, saying, "'You've got to be one or the other. Ain't no fence. The fence is torn down now'" (quoted in Cunningham 1993b, 537). Later, in the runoff election, he scoffed at the idea that any black would vote for his white Republican opponent with the memorable quip, "'A vote for [Hayes] Dent is like a chicken voting for Colonel Sanders. There's no way you'll vote for your own execution'" (quoted in Cooper 1993b, A12; see Glaser 1996, chapter 5, for an excellent discussion of this election).

The politics of commonality, on the other hand, views politics in biracial or nonracial terms. "'I see myself as participating in an effort to enhance the quality of life for all Americans,'" says Representative John Lewis (D–GA). "'The point of the movement was to create in

America a truly interracial democracy, so what affects one segment of the population affects all of us. So it's not a civil rights concern, it's a people issue'" (quoted in Donohoe 1993, E1). The politics of commonality produces a different policy focus and a more pragmatic approach to the legislative process than is true of the confrontational and symbolic approach adopted by many practitioners of a politics of difference.

The Politics of Commonality and Difference in the New Districts

Many editorialists, pundits, and politicians have claimed that the new black majority districts undermined the politics of commonality and promoted difference. They thought the "tearing down of the fence" cited by Bennie Thompson was precipitated by the creation of black majority districts. With nearly one voice they regarded these new districts as a manifestation of the politics of difference. Racial polarization and a "blacks must represent blacks" vision of representation were inevitable if voters were racially categorized and strategically split, even within precincts. Thernstrom and Thernstrom argue that "congressional districts that were deliberately drawn to be overwhelmingly black invited the sort of ideological militancy that became the model for the black legislative candidate. In contrast to the more heavily white cities in which blacks have been elected mayors, these districts beckoned candidates with racially strident voices" (1997, 483; also see Sleeper 1997; Gutmann and Thompson 1996, 153).

However, members from the new districts tend to endorse commonality rather than difference. Kenneth Cooper, a *Washington Post* reporter writing for *Emerge* magazine, noted, "Caucus newcomers like [Cleo] Fields [D–LA] and [Mel] Reynolds [D–IL] tended to see themselves more as political agents for their constituents than as guardians of moral principles." Cooper then quotes freshman Albert Wynn (D–MD): "'I didn't come here to be anybody's conscience. I came here to negotiate'" (quoted in Cooper 1993a, 24). While Bennie Thompson would probably argue that he is an agent for his constituents by guarding moral principles, Cooper's assumption is that politicians in Congress who bargain and compromise will be more effective in delivering tangible benefits to their constituents than members who stake out more ideologically pure positions.

My interviews with members of the CBC and their staff confirmed this more moderate, biracial perspective among many of the new members. One staffer vigorously defended the districts using the language of commonality:

> [Rep. Henry] Hyde [(R–IL), a critic of the black majority districts,] doesn't have his facts straight. This district is more integrated than any other district. Not only by race, but also by interests. Minority districts are not a threatening issue to whites in this district. Minority members of Congress can represent white interests as well as black interests. Furthermore, many interests are the same—there is no such thing as white banking interests and black banking interests. We have more in common than not in common. We are responsive to all the interests in our district. White voters will see that as more and more blacks have an opportunity to serve; even people like Representative Hyde will see that blacks can be inclusive representatives. Fear will dissipate: fear of the unknown, fear that all we will do is help black folks. But we are the same where it counts. You only see these districts as polarizing if you hold racist conspiracy beliefs. (S12)

One staffer noted that his boss has always taken a biracial approach. Citing an early poll that showed the representative with an astonishingly low 6 percent unfavorable rating, the staffer suggested that the strategy appeared to be working: "Our district is made up of four overlapping demographic groups: urban and rural, veterans/military and civilian. Representative C tries to represent a balance and find the common ground. He fought for funding for a new POW museum and against any more base closures. He is against the Racial Justice Act and in favor of the death penalty. We have an understanding with the CBC—they know we can't support them on a lot of things" (S3). These comments are revealing. Notice that the staffer, who was black, did not mention race in his four demographic groups. However, the policy examples he raised were primarily aimed at showing that Representative C was independent from the CBC and reaching out to the white voters in his district. Another staffer bluntly claimed, "Representative D doesn't think in terms of black and white issues. She only tries to do what she thinks is right" (S5).

There is also a strategic element to the politics of commonality for some members. Clarence Page writes, "'I think there's a consensus in the black community: if we push our issues as special, we separate ourselves from other Americans. That encourages other Americans to ignore us completely'" (quoted in Donohoe 1993, E1). This pragmatism was clearly evident in many of the campaigns in the new districts. One staffer, after noting that his boss was the most moderate candidate in the four-person primary, said, "He almost had to be moderate. Unlike the northern urban districts that are 70 percent black, our district is 55 percent black. You can't neglect 45 percent of the electorate. We had to pick up the white voters if we wanted to win, and we did a better job of appealing to the white voters than any of the other three candidates. Also, the whites vote in higher percentages; therefore, the whites in our district even have more clout [than the black voters]" (S2).

Several hearings on voting rights held by the House Judiciary Subcommittee on Civil Rights provide excellent insight into how members and many voting rights experts view the nature of representation in the new districts. Representative Henry Hyde (R–IL) opened a hearing by supporting the polarization hypothesis:

> All prior principles of redistricting—geographic compactness, commonality of interests, unity of political entities—were overlooked as maps were drawn at all costs to create the maximum number of black and Hispanic majority districts. Instead of learning to engage in multiracial coalitions, Americans are being urged to act like tribal clans. Instead of moving toward the goal of a color-blind society, we are further entrenching a very race-conscious one. I am deeply troubled by these developments. . . . (House 1994a, 4)

Stuart Taylor, one of the nation's most respected legal journalists, echoed Hyde's remarks:

> I think the problem that racial gerrymandering as a remedial device poses when it is carried to extremes is twofold. One, it perpetuates racial polarization by encouraging politicians of all races to appeal only or primarily to members of their own race. If you put people in a district where they only need to appeal to members of their own race, that is what they are likely to do, whites and blacks alike, and when we stretch too hard to draw minority districts, an inevitable side effect is to create whiter districts in the surrounding area. That too, it seems to me, leads to racial polarization.
>
> I think this particular remedy also has a tendency to entrench racial bloc voting, to perpetuate it perhaps infinitum, by putting the law's imprimatur on the notion that it is natural and expected. I am reminded of a phrase Justice Scalia used many years ago in another context, "the disease as cure," and for those reasons, I am troubled as the Supreme Court was in *Shaw v. Reno* by extremes of racial gerrymandering. (House 1994a, 35–36)

Benjamin Griffith, an attorney who is active in voting rights litigation, has even deeper reservations:

> Racial gerrymandering sends us back light years because what it does,
> it allows the electorate not to be mobilized on the basis of enthusiasm for
> a candidate, enthusiasm over the issues, enthusiasm over the particular
> contest, but only on the basis of race. It completely destroys what we
> consider to be traditional criteria for candidates as well as for creation
> of districts. (House 1994a, 95–96)

Griffith's unsubstantiated claims about the nature of the elections in
the black majority districts in 1992 may sound hyperbolic. However,
the tone of his commentary is not unusual.

These assessments did not go unchallenged in the subcommittee
hearing. Barney Frank (D–MA) pointed out, though he did not use
the term, that most members of Congress practice a politics of commonality rather than a politics of difference:

> Mr. Taylor said one of the problems is that people only appeal to one
> race or another. I must say that is contrary to all the experience I have
> ever had as a representative or in watching other representatives. There
> are a few people in my district whom I make a conscious effort not to
> represent, but I could give you their names, and it is personal in every
> case. I think the overwhelming majority of us, frankly, spend a lot of
> time trying to conciliate people on the other side, and in particular with
> regard to our African American colleagues from the South who are rep-
> resenting these mixed districts, every one of them, in my experience,
> works very hard in trying to reach out to the white voters. So I think
> there you just have an empirical error. (House 1994a, 57)

The intense debate occasionally took a lighter turn. Following his
comments above, Representative Frank pointed out that many white
districts are also "bizarre" in shape. He summed up his argument by
saying, "So I will be listening with particular interest when we get
to bizarreness, because I think I am more bizarre than Mel [Watt—
the North Carolina Democrat who represents the infamous "I-85"
district]" (House 1994, 58). At that very moment Representative Watt
walked in, and Chairman Edwards asked him if he would like to make
a statement. Representative Watt quipped, "No. I just wanted to concur that Barney is more bizarre than me" (House 1994a, 59). Later
in the day Representative Watt contradicted the polarization hypothesis set forth in *Shaw v. Reno* (1993) and echoed by the critics noted
above:

> [W]hat happened in Espy's case is a prime example. He was able to get
> in. Once people got familiar with him, then he became an acceptable
> alternative to whites who might otherwise have been elected, and I think

the same thing I see happening in all of these States. Once we get in and people find out that we are not terrible people, it will help to undercut and shorten the period of racial polarization, and I hope that happens. I mean I can't prove it to you with any great degree of reliability, but I can tell you that I am willing to take my chances on that happening rather than just the regular course of events to happen while I am outside the system and waiting on nature to take its course. (House 1994a, 107–108)[19]

While these assertions (which are central to the argument of my book), if proven true, should assuage some of the concerns noted by Representative Hyde, Stuart Taylor, and other conservative critics, they will only stoke the fires of the critics on the left. A recent editorial in *Emerge* pointed out that some of the new members were more conservative and took positions that diverged from the older members of the CBC on issues like school choice and crime. The article noted the disadvantages of ideological divergence, quoting Ronald Walters, "'It isn't diversity but unity that has moved the civil rights agenda along,'" thereby implying that an exclusive focus on black interests may be more beneficial to the African-American community than diversity (Cooper 1996, 16). Writing in a different historical context, Hanes Walton, Jr., and Leslie Burl McLemore are more strident in their criticism of centrist blacks who reach out to white voters, labeling them "accommodationists." They argue:

> One can say that the accommodationists are, by and large, Blacks in skin color only—in other words oreos (black on the outside and white on the inside) in the *political process.* The political life of the accommodationists depends upon whites and so their being Black is only coincidental to their political involvement. In sum, the Black community should not expect any benefits from the accommodationists, for they are more concerned about the white community than the Black community. (1970, 12)

Even Martin Luther King, Jr., "'condemned political opportunism by black politicians deaf to the demands of their community'" (quoted in Guinier 1991a, 1090).

This critique of the politics of commonality assumes that any sensitivity to the needs of white constituents by black politicians proves that the latter are traitors to their race and unresponsive to black interests. Indeed, the very concept of "black interests" would be viewed by these critics as inherently contradictory with a politics of commonality. Recognizing the distinctive nature of black interests requires a politics of difference to ensure that those interests are represented, according to this view.

My "Balancing" Approach

The difference critique of commonality is flawed for three reasons: (1) it presents the styles of representation too starkly, (2) it characterizes the positions of different racial constituencies as nonoverlapping, and (3) it focuses on the mean positions of the member and the constituency rather than the variances in both. I will discuss each in turn. First, neither the accommodationist that is condemned by Walton and McLemore nor the radical black separatist exists in the U.S. Congress. The politics of commonality and the politics of difference should not be seen as neatly dividing black members of Congress into two categories, but rather the conceptual construct should be viewed as a continuum that ranges from Farrakhan's politics of difference at one extreme (the separatist position) to politics in a nonracist society, where a person's race is simply irrelevant at the other extreme (the deracialization perspective). Most black members of Congress would fall somewhere in the middle half of the spectrum. While they reject separatism, all members of the CBC, with the possible exceptions of former Representatives Gary Franks (R–CT) and J. C. Watts (R–OK), also reject the notion that racism and discrimination are no longer problems in our society.

Second, the accommodationist critique assumes that black and white constituencies within a district have nonoverlapping interests. This is not supported by the data presented in the first section of this chapter; even on issues that substantially divide the races, such as affirmative action and government assistance to blacks, there is some overlap. There are many positions that representatives can take that appeal to white and black constituents.

Finally, the accommodationist critique is flawed because it focuses only on the *mean* position of the representative on the continuum described above rather than on the distribution along the continuum (or, in statistical terms, the *variance* of the member's position). For example, two members who focus most of their time on issues with no racial content or on issues with implicit racial content could have the same mean on the hypothetical racial policy continuum, but very different representational styles. One member may have the accommodationist style critiqued by Walton and McLemore (1970) and spend almost no time on racial issues (a distribution that is tightly bunched around the mean), while the second member may split his or her effort between the black and white constituents (thus having a broader distribution on the racial policy continuum).

These hypothetical examples point to alternative conceptions of the politics of commonality. The *deracialization perspective* argues that there are no meaningful differences between constituents or policies on the basis of race. This could be thought of as the "we're all in the same boat" argument. The second is the *balancing perspective,* which notes the importance of racial difference, but makes an explicit effort to address both sets of concerns. Many members of Congress, and even some members of the CBC, *say* they believe in the first approach. White members of Congress are more likely to *act* on those beliefs, whereas black members of Congress are more likely to engage in the balancing version.

When I use the term "politics of commonality" in this book, I am referring to the balancing version rather than the deracialization version (unless I explicitly state otherwise). I emphatically reject the argument that race does not matter. One cannot spend more than a few minutes interviewing members of Congress and their staff without recognizing the centrality of race. However, I do not argue that race matters on all policies that Congress considers. Indeed, as I noted in the Introduction, a vast majority of issues in Congress have nothing to do with race.

The balancing perspective has both normative and empirical appeal. Normatively this approach has the advantage of recognizing differences between racial groups, without endorsing the divisive language of separatism. The approach is consistent with Phillips, who says, "It is in the relationship between ideas and presence that we can best hope to find a fairer system of representation, not in a false opposition between one or the other" (1995, 25). Streich agrees, arguing that we must discard the dichotomy between commonality and difference and recognize that they "can be balanced within the various communities in which we live" (1997, 5). His theory "allows for commonalities to vary so that even if people retain different identities they can still work together on the basis of some other commonality such as a shared concern about various local social problems" (1997, 33). One commonality member I interviewed expressed the balancing perspective perfectly:

> I had a white constituent come to me in February complaining that he wasn't getting any help from my staff [concerning a banking regulation]. He gave me the feeling that he thought that under no circumstances could a black man represent him. I looked into his issue and by July he was thanking me for my help. He saw that I would do what is the district's interests, not just the black community. Some people in my district see adversity between the banking and black communities. I don't see it that way. I try to balance them. I try to walk that line with more integrity than some of my predecessors who ignored the inner-city community entirely. You have to listen and understand the various interests in the district. Both blacks and whites in my district say that they have a member of Congress who will listen to their views. (M7)

Notice that he did not say that blacks and whites share all the same interests. Rather, the representational relationship must recognize differences and balance them, while also seeking common ground when possible.

Returning to the broader theories of democracy and community that started this section, my balancing position on commonality is a combination of liberalism and deliberative democracy with a heavy dose of good old-fashioned pluralism. I share the liberal assumptions of rationality, tolerance, and overlapping interests. While I agree with liberals that society is better off when it attempts to focus on common ideals and goals, I do not share the views of advocates of a common national identity. Even when blacks and whites share common values, such as equality and liberty, they have different perspectives on how those values should be attained. Deliberative democracy recognizes the importance of multiple perspectives and identities within the political process. Representatives of varying races bring perspectives to the legislature that can change agendas and alter preferences.

The balancing approach also shares many of the characteristics of pluralism. Groups that lose on one issue may win on the next round, and those with the most intense preferences are more likely to have their voices heard (Dahl 1956). However, the balancing approach differs from pluralism in two respects. First, pluralism focuses on organized group interests, while the balancing approach recognizes an important entrepreneurial role for the politician. Rather than taking the current balance of group interests as a given, the politician often activates latent group interests through advertising his or her services and promoting certain policy agendas. The politician has an active interest in making sure that diverse racial interests are balanced in the district. Second, the balancing approach recognizes that racial issues are of special importance. Many racial issues, such as affirmative action, require position-taking that will alienate some segment of the district. The balancing politician works to offset these controversial positions with work on other issues that have no racial content. For example, Mike Espy worked hard to support the racial interests of his black constituents, but also delivered Pentagon contracts to the largely white catfish farmers in his district.

Empirically the balancing perspective on commonality is sound because it captures the actual behavior of members of Congress. This is typically how *they* view the process of representing diverse constituencies. The balancing perspective is summarized nicely by Kenneth Spaulding, an African-American state legislator from North Carolina. Spaulding even hints at my supply-side theory when he articulates the electoral strategy for the "smart black candidate" when only blacks are running:

> [T]he Voting Rights Act is helping whites to have that opportunity of being able to see that once blacks are elected and are office holders that they can support them, that they do see that we, in fact, represent their interests as well as are sensitive toward minority interests. And I think that you are well aware, in the legislature when we served together, my legislation dealt with issues that were sensitive to the black community, and you know how I addressed it on the redistricting. But at the same time, I recognized responsibility to each and every voter of my district, and I worked just as hard to represent white constituents. . . . If you are a black candidate and nothing but black candidates are running, a smart black candidate is going to run and try to get as much of a black vote that he can get and then use the same amount of time to try to get the white vote, that 40 percent of that vote that is there; and he is going to try to get that to get elected.
>
> I think that is what Mel Watt did in his district. And I think the numbers would show that. Let's don't feel, oh, we have this black district, which is really an integrated district, and we have got a black representative. Oh, what is going to happen to the white constituents? Because what is going to happen is the same thing that is going to happen in any democratic society. The person that is holding that office is going to want to stay in that office, and he is going to represent a majority of that [district]. (House 1993, 77–78)

Some aspects of the balancing perspective are more amenable to empirical testing than others. The critical test of the analysis is to demonstrate the importance of the politics of presence. That is, *does* it make a difference having black representatives in Congress? A more diverse policy agenda in the legislature is one testable implication. The example of Carol Moseley Braun noted above is a dramatic example of how the politics of presence may change the nature of debate and introduce new ideas. But does it change preferences? Edward Carmines and James Stimson (1989) demonstrate that *revealed* preferences shifted rather dramatically on racial issues in Congress in the 1960s, but it is difficult to say how much of this can be attributed to the politics of presence or ideas.

Theorists and politicians alike were quoted above as arguing that having a black representative can change the preferences of white voters who recognize that their interests can be represented by a black politician. Anecdotal evidence to support this point is plentiful. Mike Espy clearly won over thousands of white voters with his biracial appeals. It is quite likely that such dramatic changes could not have happened as long as a white person represented that Delta district. However, more definitive tests await better data.[20] The 1992–1994 NES panel survey did not have enough respondents from the districts represented by black members of the 1992 class to allow statistical analysis of changes in voter preferences. While I will not be able to examine changes in the preferences of members of the House or of voters, chapters 4 and 5 will offer a broad range of testable implications of the impact of black representation in Congress.

To summarize the argument thus far, black members of Congress differ in their approaches to racial politics. The three perspectives range from those who deemphasize the racial aspect of issues (deracialization), to those who balance the interests of black and white constituents (commonality/balancing), to those who see themselves primarily as representatives of black voters (difference). Most political observers, including proponents and opponents of the strategy, see the creation of minority-majority districts as an embodiment of the politics of difference because districts are created to elect more African-American politicians to represent black voters (Walters 1992; *Shaw v. Reno* 1993; Thernstrom and Thernstrom 1997; Sleeper 1997). I argue that the balancing perspective is more common in the new districts than is the politics of difference, which has important implications for the nature of representation provided in those districts. The supply-side theory presented in chapter 3 provides an explanation for whether commonality or difference is more likely to emerge in a given district.

Representation

Having examined the nature of black interests and various normative perspectives on racial representation, I now turn to broader questions of representation. I obviously will not be able to provide even the most cursory review of the vast literature on the two-way representational linkages between politicians and constituents. However, I will attempt to outline the broad contours of the topic, while focusing on the nature of racial representation.

Descriptive Representation

A first set of concerns is rooted in the politician's side of the relationship. Does the member of Congress "look like" the constituent? Is the member black or white, male or female, Catholic or Protestant? There are three positions on the value of descriptive representation. The first argues that there is a distinct value in having role models and notes the benefits that come from the simple act of being represented by someone who shares something as fundamental as skin color. For example, Chandler Davidson and Bernard Grofman note:

> Tom McCain was one of the first blacks elected to office since Reconstruction in Edgefield County, South Carolina—home of the racist firebrand Benjamin "Pitchfork Ben" Tillman and of long-time opponent of desegregation J. Strom Thurmond. Speaking in 1981, McCain said, "There's an inherent value in office holding that goes far beyond picking up the garbage. A race of people who are excluded from public office will always be second class citizens." (1994, 16; Thernstrom [1987, 239] uses the same quote from McCain)

The intangibles of descriptive representation and the role models that help create greater trust in the system are important. Thernstrom, a critic of black majority districts, sees the advantages of having racially diverse political bodies. She writes:

> Whether on a city council, on a county commission, or in the state legislature, blacks inhibit the expression of prejudice, act as spokesmen for black interests, dispense patronage, and often facilitate the discussion of topics (such as black crime) that whites are reluctant to raise. That is, governing bodies function differently when they are racially mixed, particularly where blacks are new to politics and where racially insensitive language and discrimination in the provision of services are long-established political habits. (1987, 239)

Even if one could be assured that substantive representation was not affected by race or gender, it would not be fair if the nation were represented by 535 white men in Congress. Barney Frank (D–MA) argues that descriptively diverse representation is better representation:

> What we are saying is a representative assembly in which no one has lived the life of an African American in the South, in which no one has lived the life of a Hispanic in the United States, in which, let me add, there has been no gay person, or there haven't been any Jews, or there have been very, very few women, will not do as good a job of representing the country. That doesn't mean you automatically reproduce it, but that's the value that you are losing. (House 1994b, 74–75)

This same logic has produced a strong commitment to racial diversity in corporate America, in higher education, and in the public sector.

Jane Mansbridge argues that descriptive representation is valuable when "'communication between constituents and representatives is impaired by distrust,'" when "'important substantive interests of a descriptive group are relatively uncrystallized,'" or when a group is "'disadvantaged and dispersed'" (1996, 1 [quoted in Bianco 1997, 1]). William Bianco models these scenarios and concludes that if the constituents have relatively homogeneous interests, "constituents are more likely to trust a representative who shares their demographics compared to one who does not, and such trust will increase the chances that the representative's behavior is consistent with constituent interests" (1997, 6). However, trust and responsiveness will not prevail if constituent interests are heterogeneous (1997, 9).

The other two groups argue that descriptive representation by itself is not useful unless it is linked to substantive representation; the left-of-center perspective argues that having "black faces in high places" may come at too high a price. Robert C. Smith says, "Like the transformation of black music, it will be a hollow victory if in order to achieve equitable descriptive-symbolic representation blacks are required to sacrifice their substantive policy agendas. The new black politician would then be a shell of himself, more like a Prince or Michael Jackson than a B. B. King or Bobby Bland" (Smith [1990, 161], Pinderhughes [1987, xix], and Jones [1985] make similar arguments). The right-of-center perspective recognizes the value of descriptive representation in some limited contexts, but points out that whites can adequately represent black interests and that descriptive representation comes at a price (as noted above).

Phillips (1995) makes the case that empirical research has focused almost exclusively on representation of "ideas" (substantive) rather than "presence" (descriptive). While substantive representation receives a disproportionate share of attention, there are many studies that focus on descriptive representation. These works either describe how the presence of blacks in Congress has grown in the past century (Lublin 1997, chap. 2; Clay 1993, apps. A and B; Swain 1993, 20–34) or provide explanations for how blacks get elected (Lublin 1997, chap. 3; Grofman and Handley 1989; Handley and Grofman 1994; Grofman, Griffin, and Glazer 1992; Cameron, Epstein, and O'Halloran 1996, 803–805). All of this work concludes that there are significant differences in racial representation between the South and non-South (a greater percentage of black voters is needed to elect a black member in the South than in the non-South) and between Democrats and Republicans (above 40 percent black population it is extremely unlikely that a Republican would be elected). Grofman and Lisa Handley (1989b; Handley and Grofman 1994) make the strongest statement that black majority districts are nearly a necessary condition to elect blacks to office.

Descriptive representation is also important because the political world has recently shown a much greater sensitivity to having leaders who "look like America." The Clarence Thomas hearings created the perception that the "old white guys" on the Senate Judiciary Committee "just didn't get it." President Clinton's well-publicized efforts to appoint a diverse cabinet brought more attention to the importance of descriptive representation. Congress watchers, such as *Congressional Quarterly* and *National Journal,* also mention the racial, gender, and even occupational composition of every new Congress, and every Congress textbook dutifully mentions the similar sets of demographic figures.

My argument does not hinge on the importance of descriptive representation (in the absence, of course, of a link between descriptive and substantive representation). Judgments about the value of descriptive representation are inherently normative: either one thinks that the skin color, gender, and ethnic background of a representative are important, or one does not. I happen to think they are important, but it is difficult to imagine that any empirical evidence could change the mind of a person who thinks descriptive representation does not matter. However, the lines between descriptive and substantive representative are often quite fuzzy, as the previous discussion of "presence" and deliberative democracy made clear. My interviews revealed many examples of actions by black representatives that appear to be largely symbolic, even as they reflect substantive differences.

A staffer in a commonality member's office said, "There are many simple but important differences that come with having a black member of Congress in [our state]. There are many more African-American interns than this office has ever seen, we get to appoint some African Americans to the military academies, and we show more interest in the historically black institutions of learning in our state" (S1).

Others pointed out that many black members felt a duty to represent all African Americans, not just those who resided in their districts. One staffer noted the additional pressures this places on a member's schedule. "Representative X was the first and only black elected to Congress in our state in 100 years. So he is very sought after as a speaker, especially in the black churches on Sundays. He feels some pressure to go, so once a month or so he will travel outside the district" (S2). This type of pressure would not be felt by a first-term white member of Congress.

Substantive Representation

While descriptive representation supplies an important dimension to a complete theory of representation, it only goes so far. As A. Phillips Griffiths pointed out, we do not expect lunatics to be represented by crazy people. "'While we might wish to complain that there are not enough representative members of the working class among Parliamentary representatives,'" he says, "'we would not want to complain that the large class of stupid or maleficent people have too few representatives in Parliament; quite the contrary'" (quoted in Phillips 1995, 39).[21]

Substantive representation moves beyond appearances to specify *how* the member serves the interest of the constituents. Two models go back at least until the time of Edmund Burke: (1) the trustee who represents the interests of constituents from a distance, weighing a variety of national, collective, local, and moral concerns, and (2) the delegate who has a simple mandate to carry out the direct desires of the voters. Hanna Pitkin advanced the discussion by noting that both of these perspectives are right and that true representation must combine both approaches. Her definition, offered more than thirty years ago, serves as the basis for much empirical research on representation today:

> "Representation here means acting in the interest of the represented, in a manner responsive to them. The representative must act independently; his action must involve discretion and judgement; he must be the one who acts. . . . And, despite the resulting potential for conflict between

> representative and represented about what is to be done, that conflict
> must not normally take place. The representative must act in such a way
> that there is not conflict, or if it occurs an explanation is called for."
> (Pitkin 1967, 209–210 [quoted in Jewell 1983, 304])

This characterization of the representative-represented relationship
raises a host of empirical questions. How much do voters monitor their
representatives' behavior? Can representational linkages work if voters
are not paying attention? The most demanding theory of representation, known as "policy responsiveness," requires that voters express
basic policy preferences, the representative respond to those desires,
and then voters monitor and assess the politician's behavior (Miller
and Stokes 1963). Other scholars paint a more subtle picture. John
Kingdon (1989), among others, demonstrates that members of Congress behave *as if* voters are paying attention, even when constituents
may be inattentive. Richard Fenno (1978) points out that some segments of the constituency are more attentive and more important for
the member's reelection than others. These constituents will have a
different representational relationship than those who occupy one of
the more distant "concentric circles" in Fenno's characterization. Others argue that the representational linkages will vary depending on the
electoral context and the issue attentiveness of constituents: Aage
Clausen (1973) shows that representation varies by issue. Douglas Arnold (1990, 68–71) notes the importance of the "potential preferences
of inattentive publics" that could be aroused by a well-funded challenger, so members may be held accountable by *anticipating* what the
constituents would want *if they were fully informed.* Bianco (1994)
points out that the basis for one important dimension of representation depends on the trust that members of Congress develop under
varying circumstances. Therefore, constituents do not have to engage
in constant monitoring if they are convinced that the member will "do
the right thing."

Applying these basic components of representation to race adds a
layer of complexity. At the constituency level the racial composition of
the district intersects with Fenno's concentric circles (1978). Within the
district, reelection, and primary constituencies (and to some extent the
personal constituency, depending on the politician), race overlays a
complex set of relationships that vary from district to district. As noted
above, black constituents have distinct needs and interests that differ from those of white constituents. Blacks are disproportionately
affected by problems such as crime, drugs, poverty, discrimination,

and poor health. Politicians representing districts with a substantial African-American population differ in their responsiveness to the needs and interests of these constituents. Some members of Congress focus on one race within their reelection constituency, and others give attention to both races within one party, while some may focus on a single race at the district level. These patterns of representation obviously vary across issues. Most issues considered in Congress do not have any direct racial content, others are centrally concerned with race, and another substantial portion may or may not concern race depending on the member's framing of the issue.

Yet another layer of complexity that must be factored in is the homogeneity or heterogeneity of a district. As Morris Fiorina argued twenty-five years ago, heterogeneous districts are more difficult to represent (Fiorina 1974). This is especially true in some districts such as John Conyers's district in Detroit, which encompasses very poor urban areas and relatively wealthy suburbs. One white member who represents an urban/suburban district complained, "We have the poorest district in the state and the second richest.[22] This makes it pretty tough. No matter what we do on some issues, there will be somebody who is mad at us" (M5). Another district variable that is important for the inner-city northern districts is the relative electoral safety of those seats. As Carol Swain notes, these members have much more leeway than the members from more marginal districts (1993, chap. 3). This observation is consistent with several of the interviews I had with staffers from these districts. "He is free to take stands on whatever he wants because he is so popular. His issues are more nationally oriented that district-oriented. You can do and say what you want when you are from a safe district" (S21).

While factors such as district heterogeneity and electoral safety should apply equally to whites and blacks, there are two ways in which the substantive content of racial representation will play out in all districts with a substantial minority population (and interact with the race of the member): (1) how black and white representatives allocate their time to the racially diverse constituencies, in terms of both issue emphasis and who they spend time with, and (2) whether the member views racial representation through the lens of the politics of commonality or the politics of difference (the latter obviously has an impact on the former).

Several staffers I interviewed pointed out that many of the black areas in their districts had not been served by their white representatives. They reported traveling to counties that had *never* been visited by a member of Congress (S7, S8). Consequently, in some of the poor, rural areas of the South, the new members elected in 1992 often had to drum up their own business through extensive outreach efforts. One staffer said, "We have a very passive constituency. They very seldom write to us with their problems; they are not even aware of the basic resources offered by the federal government in many cases. So we have town meetings and radio call-in shows every week to try to get out the word" (S1).

White and black representatives are likely to differ not only in their efforts to reach black constituents, but also in the racial frames of reference they use to help them set legislative priorities and determine their behavior in the House. White representatives, I hypothesize, are more likely to adopt the "deracialization" perspective outlined above, claiming "we are all in this boat together." "Representative R focuses on the district as a whole; he sees interests as cutting across racial lines," said one staffer for a white member (S20). These members typically mentioned issues such as deficit reduction, the environment, or a specific industry or military base, rather than issues such as affirmative action, historically black colleges and universities (HBCUs), the Racial Justice Act, Haiti, and welfare (S20, S15, S25). One staffer for a white member was particularly adamant that "there are *no* racial differences on issues at all. Issues are not black and white but GREEN—education, jobs, and the economy" (S25). (I assume that the staffer noted examples to make sure that I would not mistake his boss for an environmentalist.) However, there were some white representatives who spent a significant amount of time on issues like "redlining" or "rent to own" scams that exploited inner-city blacks (S18). Some black representatives will also emphasize common interests, as the John Lewis quote above illustrates, but for the most part they act differently than white members on racial issues. Rather than striving to find common interests on all issues, black representatives who represent the commonality perspective will find common ground when possible, but always fight for *equal representation of different interests.*

These complexities of race and representation are usually ignored in the popular and academic literature on the topic, especially as it is applied to the new black majority districts that were created in 1992. As I will discuss more fully below, the latter focuses almost exclusively on roll call analysis, while the popular literature (and the Supreme Court) simply makes assumptions about the nature of racial representation provided in the new black districts.[23] Critics and supporters of the new districts agree that the fundamental nature of representation provided in these districts is the representation of black interests by black representatives. Furthermore, traditional theories of representation can *describe,* but not *explain* variations in racial representation. My supply-side theory, which will be presented in chapter 3, explains this variation in terms of the racial coalitions that elect members of Congress and the racial composition of the primary pool of candidates.

The issues raised in this chapter are important for theoretical and policy reasons. I hope that this work will contribute to discussions of the politics of commonality, difference, and identity. My "balancing perspective" commonality provides a pragmatic middle ground that probably will fail to satisfy theorists at both extremes. Difference theorists will point to ingrained power inequalities and the futility of attempting to balance various interests; national identity and deracialization theorists will resist the notion of distinctive black interests that require special attention. The balancing perspective should also contribute to the policy debate over racial redistricting. I will show that black majority districts produce better representation of black interests, while also representing white voters (to varying degrees depending on the supply-side factors that will be explored in chapter 3). The next chapter will show how white plaintiffs who challenged the black majority districts have been able to carve out a new understanding of the Fourteenth Amendment that completely ignores the balancing argument discussed in this chapter.

CHAPTER TWO

A Legal Primer on Race and Redistricting

The U.S. Supreme Court's adherence to a color-blind jurisprudence has thrown the constitutionality of black majority districts into doubt (*Shaw v. Reno* 1993; *Miller v. Johnson* 1995; *Bush v. Vera* 1996; *Shaw v. Hunt* 1996). However, there are at least five votes on the Court to uphold the Voting Rights Act of 1965 (VRA), and Justice Sandra Day O'Connor made it clear in *Bush v. Vera* that black majority districts are legal as long as they are "done right." Despite this basic affirmation of the VRA itself, the Court has not given state legislators much guidance on how race can be considered when drawing district lines. This continued uncertainty makes it clear that racial redistricting will remain a contested and heavily litigated area of the law well into the twenty-first century.

The purpose of this chapter is twofold. First, the chapter will provide a brief summary of the legal background on race and redistricting for readers who are not familiar with the topic. The jargon associated with redistricting court cases can be mystifying to the uninitiated and frustratingly vague to the participants in the legal battles: Section 5 preclearance, Section 2 vote dilution claims, compactness and contiguity, communities of interest, strict scrutiny, compelling state interest, totality of circumstances, candidates of choice, and the three *Gingles* preconditions all have subjective meanings and no consistent bases for operationalization. (Those familiar with these terms and the legal literature on this topic can skip the first two-thirds of the chapter). Second, the chapter addresses legal specialists by showing the links between my work and the current legal debates. Integrating the representational consequences of black majority districts that I present in chapters 4 and 5 could further muddy the unclear waters by raising a set of factors that thus far have not come into play in the *Shaw*-type cases. However, if these consequences are linked to the debate over whether or not white plaintiffs have standing to sue, it is possible that many challenges to the districts could be summarily dismissed because my research shows that white plaintiffs do not suffer any particularized harm (how- ever, as I discuss in the conclusion of this chapter, this outcome is unlikely given the current composition of the Court). While I could present my supply-side theory and evidence on racial representation without mucking around in the legal quagmire, developing these linkages is important to establish the broader significance of this work.

Both audiences, dabblers and specialists alike, should be warned that I will not provide a comprehensive review of the case law and legal concepts, but rather a primer that focuses on the central legislation, the court cases, and the relevance of this legal corpus for my work. There is a comprehensive literature on the VRA, its amendments, and the subsequent legal controversies that may be consulted for more in-depth treatments (Strong 1968; Ball 1986; Thernstrom 1987; Karlan and McCrary 1988; Parker 1990; Grofman, Handley, and Niemi 1992; Davidson and Grofman 1994; Grofman 1995).[1]

The First Century of the Struggle for Voting Rights

The goal of empowering African Americans through the creation of black majority districts is rooted in a century-long struggle to give blacks the right to vote. The Fifteenth Amendment to the Constitution, adopted on March 30, 1870, guaranteed that "the right of citizens of the United States to vote shall not be denied or abridged by the United States or any State on account of race, color, or previous condition of servitude." In the Reconstruction Era blacks in the South gained considerable political power through institutions such as the Freedmen's Bureau and the Union League, with substantial help (some would argue manipulation and exploitation) from the Radical Republicans. Between 1869 and 1901 twenty different blacks served a total of forty-one terms in the U.S. House of Representatives and two blacks served a total of eight years in the Senate—all of them from the South. However, after 1879, there was only token representation of blacks in Congress, with no more than three being elected in any given Congress (Congressional Research Service 1989).

When federal troops withdrew and the Republican Party abandoned the South (Valelly 1995), blacks were almost completely disenfranchised through the imposition of residency requirements, poll taxes, literacy tests, the "grandfather clause" (see note 2 for a definition), physical intimidation, other forms of disqualification, and later the white primary (Davidson 1993; Key 1949, 531–675; Parker 1990). While these provisions purported to be race-neutral on their face, their impact fell disproportionately on black voters. The most transparent of these was the grandfather clause, which, V. O. Key explains, "provided an exception to the literacy test that could be taken advantage of only by illiterate whites" (1949, 538).[2] Many states also had "understanding" or "good character" exceptions to the literacy tests, which gave election officials substantial discretion over who would be allowed to vote. The collective impact of these obstacles to voting was to virtually eliminate black voting; for example, only 6 percent of blacks were registered to vote in Mississippi in 1890, and only 2 percent were registered in Alabama in 1906 (Davidson 1992, 11).

After the last post-Reconstruction black left the House in 1901, it was seventy-two years until another black represented a southern district in Washington (Barbara Jordan from Texas). Blacks were not concentrated in large enough numbers outside the South to elect a black to Congress (and most whites were not willing to support blacks in the first part of the twentieth century); thus, no blacks served in Congress between 1901 and 1929. Between 1929 and 1945 one black served in the House (from Chicago), and one more black member was added in 1945 from New York City. Through 1969 no more than six blacks served in Congress at the same time (Congressional Research Service, 1989).

The VRA changed this legacy of political exclusion by eliminating direct obstacles to minority voting in the South, such as discriminatory literacy tests and other voter registration tests. The VRA is often cited as one of the most significant pieces of civil rights legislation passed in our nation's history (Days 1992, 52; Parker 1990, 1). In an address to Congress on March 15, 1965, President Lyndon Johnson compared the critical events at Selma, Alabama, which helped provide the impetus for passage of the VRA, to the American Revolution and the Civil War. He cited all three as moments when "history and fate meet at a single time in a single place to shape a turning point in man's unending search for freedom" (cited in *Congressional Record,* October 22, 1965, 28354). After its passage, President Johnson hailed the VRA as a "triumph for freedom as huge as any ever won on any battlefield" (quoted in Senate 1982b, 4). Even critics of the 1982 amendments to the VRA recognize the significance of the initial legislation; one such critic claims that the "passage of the act was an event that transformed

American political life" (O'Rourke 1992, 86; see also Thernstrom 1987, 1).

The statistics on the explosion in black participation in the South after the passage of the VRA are familiar, but bear repeating. The most dramatic gains came in Mississippi, where black registration increased from 6.7 percent before the VRA to 59.8 percent in 1967. As Chandler Davidson notes, "The act simply overwhelmed the major bulwarks of the disenfranchising system. In the seven states originally covered, black registration increased from 29.3 percent in March 1965, to 56.6 percent in 1971–1972; the gap between black and white registration rates narrowed from 44.1 percentage points to 11.2" (1993, 21).

The central parts of the VRA are Section 2 and Section 5. The former prohibits any state or political subdivision from imposing a voting practice that will "deny or abridge the right of any citizen of the United States to vote on account of race or color." The latter was imposed only on "covered" jurisdictions with a history of past discrimination, which must submit changes in any electoral process or mechanism to the federal government for approval.[3] Changes may be either "pre-cleared" by the Department of Justice (DOJ) or approved by the U.S. District Court for the District of Columbia. Most states use the pre-clearance option because the judicial route is more time-consuming and costly.

Patrick Leahy (D–VT) summarized the importance of these two sections of the VRA in a 1982 Senate Judiciary Subcommittee hearing: "If Section 5 is the engine that drives the Act and renders it enforceable as a practical matter, Section 2 is still the basic protection against discriminatory practices. . . . Preclearance is designed to stop voting discrimination before it can start in covered jurisdictions, and Section 2 is calculated to end it whenever and wherever it is found" (Senate 1982a, 45).

In the first decade after the passage of the VRA the central issues in voting rights cases involved the equal apportionment of population among legislative districts, or "one person–one vote" (this litigation built on the landmark cases *Baker v. Carr* (1962), *Wesberry v. Sanders* (1964), and *Reynolds v. Sims* (1964) under the Fourteenth Amendment rather than the VRA), and vote dilution claims. The latter became much more potent under Section 5 after the Supreme Court held in *Allen v. State Board of Elections* (1969) that "the preclearance provisions were applicable, not only to changes in laws directly affecting registration and voting, but all changes 'which alter the election law of a covered State in even a minor way'" (Senate 1982a, 1073). As *Allen* was applied, covered practices included not only literacy tests and other practices that directly restricted access to voting, but also actions such as switching from single-member to at-large elections, switching from elective to appointive office, establishing qualifications for independent voters and write-in votes, redistricting, annexing suburban areas to dilute black urban voting power, or engaging in other voting practices that could *abridge* the right to vote based on race or color (Senate 1982b, 6–9). Redistricting cases were primarily of the former type, while vote dilution cases typically involved the types of practices outlined in *Allen.*

Abigail Thernstrom argues that the more expansive interpretation of Section 5 undermined the original intention of the VRA, which was simply to ensure that blacks had "the right to enter a voting booth and pull the lever" (1987, 5). She says that after *Allen* there were "'meaningful' and 'meaningless' votes—votes that 'counted' and those that did not. . . . It was a subtle but important change: the shift from black ballots safe from deliberate efforts to dilute their impact, on the one hand, to a right to vote that fully counted on the other" (1987, 4). From *Allen* it was a relatively short step to the "black electoral success strategy" (Guinier 1991a, 1081–1134), whereby the VRA was seen as a tool not only to get more blacks to vote, but also to enhance political representation of their interests (Thernstrom 1987, 4–10). The Subcommittee on the Constitution's report on the 1982 VRA Amendments also maintained that *Allen* "improperly strayed from the original intent of Congress" (Senate 1982b, 7). However, this position was rejected by the full Senate Judiciary Committee and the Senate. The Judiciary Committee report says, "The legislative history of Section 5, as well as the careful and persuasive analysis of the history which the Supreme Court has made, fully refutes that suggestion" (Senate 1982b, 7; also see Grofman, Handley, and Niemi 1992, 129–130; Karlan and McCrary 1988, 755–762; Kousser 1992; and Handley 1991).

Furthermore, a series of Supreme Court decisions prior to the VRA concerning the "white primaries" cases of the 1930s and 1940s (e.g., *Smith v. Allright* 1944; see Key 1949, chap. 29) and the "one person–one vote" decisions of the 1960s (*Wesberry v. Sanders* 1964; *Reynolds v. Sims* 1964) made it clear that meaningful participation in the political process requires more than simple access to the voting booth. Whether the *Allen* decision signaled a shift in meaning of the 1965 VRA or not

(I side with Bernard Grofman, Pamela Karlan, et al., rather than Senator Orrin Hatch's (R–UT) subcommittee in this debate), it is clear the vote dilution litigation and Section 5 preclearance activity greatly expanded in the 1970s and 1980s.[4] The impact of the VRA would have been seriously undermined if the narrower interpretation advocated by Hatch had been adopted by the courts rather than the standards articulated in *Allen*.

Despite the dramatic gains in black participation, institutionalized resistance was still prevalent through the 1980s and into the 1990s (Davidson 1992; Senate 1982a, 9–15). The 1982 Senate Judiciary Committee report cites several examples, such as the elimination of twelve of thirteen polling places in Burleson County, Texas, leaving the closest polling place for the largest concentration of black voters 19 miles away and 30 miles from the concentration of Mexican-American voters. DeKalb County, Georgia, discontinued a practice of allowing community groups to hold voter registration drives, despite the fact that only 24 percent of black voters were registered, compared to 81 percent of whites (Senate 1982b, 11). Davidson chronicles many other tools of resistance, including withholding information about registration and voting procedures from blacks, moving polling places, and "causing or taking advantage of election day irregularities" (1992, 22). The heated 1990 Senate race between Jesse Helms (R–NC) and Harvey Gantt, the black former mayor of Charlotte, provided many examples of such "irregularities." The state Republican Party and the Helms campaign mailed 150,000 threatening postcards to black voters with misleading information in a "ballot security program" just days before the election (Edsall 1990, A13). The DOJ filed suit in 1992, and the Helms campaign and the state Republican Party signed a consent decree that prohibited them from engaging in such activity in the future (Duncan 1993, 1116). The Durham precinct my wife and I voted in was predominantly black, and lines were about two hours long because half of the voting machines were not working (strategically placed wads of chewing gum were reported as the cause of some of the malfunctions in our precinct). Apparently this happened at other locations around the state. In Greensboro there was only one sign-in book at many polling places, rather than the customary multiple copies, which also created long lines. A court order kept the polls open until 10 P.M. in Durham and 8:30 in Greensboro to give people a chance to vote. However, many people became discouraged by the long lines and went home. The *Washington Post* reported that "voting problems chiefly affected precincts with large numbers of black voters" (Cooper 1990, A27).

 It is difficult to prove sabotage, but forms of institutionalized vote dilution are also elusive targets. For example, many municipalities were sued under Section 2 of the VRA because plaintiffs claimed that at-large elections prevented substantial blocs of black voters from electing representatives of their choice to local office (e.g., *Whitcomb v. Chavis* 1971). If a city is 40 percent black and has ten city council members, blacks would have a good chance of electing four members if their votes were concentrated in single-member districts. However, with at-large elections it is conceivable that they would not win any seats (especially if "single-shot" voting[5] was not allowed, which was another tactic used to dilute minority voting). Other vote dilution techniques included annexing white suburbs to lower the percentage of black voters in a city and imposing majority runoff provisions, which could allow white voters to unite behind a single white candidate if there was a split field in the primary (Davidson 1992, 23).

Despite the difficulties of litigating vote dilution cases, fairly clear standards were laid down by the Court in *White v. Regester* (1973) and *Zimmer v. McKeithen* (1976) in a "totality of circumstances" approach to proving vote dilution.[6] This relatively settled approach to vote dilution cases was turned on its head in 1980 when the Court upheld a multimember district plan that appeared to favor white politicians, arguing that minority voters' Fourteenth Amendment protections were not violated unless it could be shown that district lines were *intentionally* drawn to dilute the votes of minorities (*City of Mobile v. Bolden* 1980). This was a major departure from precedent and placed a much greater burden on plaintiffs trying to prove a voting discrimination claim.

The 1982 VRA Amendments

With sections of the VRA set to expire and pressure from the civil rights community building against the *Bolden* decision, in 1981 Congress started to tackle the first major revision of the act since 1975. A division of labor developed between the House and the Senate, with the House focused on extending Section 5 preclearance and amending the bailout provisions and the Senate working on Section 2 modification. The division was somewhat accidental because the significance of the Section 2 changes was not recognized or debated in the House, as "potential opponents were asleep at the switch" (Thernstrom 1987, 83). However, by the time the bill moved to the Senate, the Section 2 changes became the focus of Orrin Hatch's Subcommittee on the Constitution. Opponents of extending the VRA and expanding its coverage thought they were in a strong political position with Republican control of the Senate (53–47) and a Republican president. However, Henry Hyde's (R–IL) attempts to water down the Section 5 changes and Hatch's efforts in the Senate did not prevail. The final version of the bill sailed through Congress with a twenty-five-year extension of Section 5 preclearance, tough "bailout" provisions, and language in Section 2 that restored the results standard to prove a vote dilution claim.[7]

The part of this debate that is most central to my work concerned the amended portion of Section 2. The changed version reads:

> (a) No voting qualification or prerequisite to voting standard, practice, or procedure shall be imposed or applied by any State or political subdivision in a manner which results in a denial or abridgement of the right of any citizen of the United States to vote on account of race or color. . . .
>
> (b) A violation of subsection (a) is established if, based on the totality of circumstances, it is shown that the political processes leading to nomination or election in the State or political subdivision are not equally open to participation by members of a class of citizens protected in subsection (a) in that its members have less opportunity than other members of the electorate to participate in the political process and to elect representatives of their choice. The extent to which members of a protected class have been elected to office in the State or political subdivision is one circumstance which may be considered: *Provided,* That nothing in this section establishes a right to have members of a protected class elected in numbers equal to their population. (U.S. Code, title 42, sec. 1973b)

There are two controversial aspects of the amended Section 2 that I will briefly discuss: the equality of opportunity to participate in the political process and proportional representation.

Equal Opportunity to Participate

The seemingly subtle change of Section 2 from "deny or abridge the right of any citizen of the United States to vote on account of race or color" to "which results in a denial or abridgement of the right of any citizen" effectively wiped out the *Bolden* decision. The Senate Judiciary Committee report explained the reasons for this change: requiring plaintiffs to prove the intent to discriminate undermined the origi-

nal legislative intent of Section 2, *Bolden* "marked a radical departure
from both Supreme Court and lower federal courts' precedent in voting discrimination cases,"[8] and the intent test of *Bolden* placed an un-
due burden on plaintiffs and "asks the wrong question" (Senate 1982b,
16–27, 36–39, quotes from p. 16). The report also defended the
amended Section 2, saying that proportional representation would not
be required, at-large representation would not be automatically suspect, and the results test (outlined below) is a "well-defined standard"
that will "provide ample guidance to federal courts" (Senate 1982b, 16,
27–35, quotes from p. 16).

Senator Robert Dole (R–KS) was pivotal in fashioning the compromise between the conservative forces in the Senate and the House version of the bill. Dole was concerned that the House version left open
the possibility that the revised Section 2 could require proportional
representation, but he also was worried that the intent standard of
Bolden placed too much of a burden on plaintiffs. He explained his
compromise on the floor of the Senate:

> What I have sought to accomplish with the compromise to Section 2 is
> to address both concerns. I believe that the results test is a provision that
> is well equipped to identify both overt and subtle methods of discrimina-
> tion while avoiding possible problems which might arise from the lack of
> specificity in the language contained in the House bill. The critical aspect
> of this compromise is that it clarifies that the focus is upon whether or
> not minorities have an "equal opportunity to participate" in the electoral
> process. In other words, the question to be decided is whether or not
> minorities have "equal access" to the political process. "Equal access"
> does not imply any right among minority groups to be elected in particu-
> lar proportions: it does not imply a right to proportional representation.
> (*Congressional Record,* June 18, 1982, 14316)

The opportunity to participate in the political process was to be ascertained by the set of factors outlined in *White* and *Zimmer.* No single
factor was determinative, but any combination of the following factors
could be used to prove an inequality of access:

> 1. the extent of any history of official discrimination in the state or
> political subdivision that touched the right of the member of the minor-
> ity group to register, to vote, or otherwise participate in the democratic
> process;
> 2. the extent to which voting in the elections of the state or political
> subdivisions is racially polarized;
> 3. the extent to which the state or political subdivision has used un-
> usually large election districts, majority vote requirements, anti–single

shot provisions, or other voting practices or procedures that may enhance the opportunity for discrimination against the minority group;

4. if there is a candidate slating process, whether the members of the
minority group have been denied access to that process;

5. the extent to which members of the minority group in the state or
political subdivision bear the effects of discrimination in such areas as
education, employment and health, which hinder their ability to participate effectively in the political process;

6. whether political campaigns have been characterized by overt or
subtle racial appeals;

7. the extent to which members of the minority group have been
elected to public office in the jurisdiction.

Additional factors that in some cases have probative value as part of
plaintiffs' evidence to establish a violation are:

whether there is a significant lack of responsiveness on the part of
elected officials to the particularized needs of the members of the minority group.

whether the policy underlying the state or political subdivision's use of
such voting qualification, prerequisite to voting, or standard, practice, or
procedure is tenuous. (Senate 1982b, 28–29)

The Senate report went on to note that "this is not an easy test"
(1982b, 31), but federal judges had substantial experience in applying
the test; thus, while defining "equal access" to the political process was
a somewhat subjective enterprise, it was a manageable task.

Proportional Representation

Critics of the amended Section 2 feared that "equal opportunity to
participate" would require proportional representation of minorities,
despite the explicit disclaimer in the legislation. In the closing debate
over the bill, Senator Hatch made one last plea: "The change may
appear to some of us as somewhat subtle today, but I assure you that
its impact will become clearer and clearer as the years pass. Rather
than moving in the direction of a single society, we have begun to give
legal and constitutional sanction to a restoration of separate but equal.
I hope that my colleagues think long and hard about what we are doing
today" (Senate 1982a, 74). Later he argued that the results test was not
based on any core principle and, therefore, would ultimately turn into
proportional representation (Senate 1982b, 95–101). Supporters of the
bill argued that the disclaimer means what it says: "[N]othing in this
section establishes a right to have members of a protected class elected
in numbers equal to their proportion in the population." The Senate
Judiciary Committee report argues: "Contrary to the assertion made

during the full Committee mark-up of the legislation, this provision is both clear and straightforward. . . . It puts to rest any concerns that have been voiced about racial quotas" (Senate 1982b, 30–31).

Thornburg v. Gingles

The first Supreme Court decision to apply the amended VRA clarified some issues, but left a great deal of confusion. The unanimous verdict obscures a fractured decision with four separate opinions; there was no agreement among more than four justices on any specific part of the decision (see table 2.1). The heart of the 1986 decision, authored by Justice William Brennan, established the "three *Gingles* prongs" by winnowing the nine factors that could be used to demonstrate a discriminatory result. The decision struck down parts of the 1984 North Carolina state legislative redistricting, holding that a minority group can claim discrimination under Section 2 if, "[f]irst, the minority group [is] able to demonstrate that it is sufficiently large and geographically compact to constitute a majority in a single-member district. . . . Second, the minority groups [is] able to show that it is politically cohesive. . . . Third, the white majority votes sufficiently as a bloc to enable it . . . usually to defeat the minority's preferred candidate" (*Thornburg v. Gingles* 1986, 50–51).[9]

The decision greatly pleased voting rights advocates because it upheld the results standard over the more difficult burden of proving intent. However, Justice Sandra Day O'Connor argued that the Court went too far in elevating the election of preferred candidates and vote polarization as the critical tests, saying that the Court created "the right to a form of proportional representation" (*Thornburg v. Gingles* 1986, 90). While the *Gingles* prongs do not require proportional representation, officials in the DOJ responsible for enforcing the VRA under its preclearance provisions and the state legislatures that drew the new district lines interpreted these actions as a mandate to create minority-majority districts. As I will discuss below, in some cases (Georgia and North Carolina especially) the DOJ seemed to be imposing proportional representation on the states.

The *Gingles* decision did not resolve the relationship between its three prongs and the more comprehensive approach laid out in the Senate report. Do the three prongs establish necessary conditions for a vote dilution claim, which then set the stage for a more complete "totality of circumstances" analysis, or are they sufficient by them-

Table 2.1 Summary of Major Court Cases on Minority Districting

Case	Vote	Majority Opinion	Concurring	Dissenting
Thornburg v. Gingles 6/30/86	9–0	Brennan, Marshall, Blackman, Stevens, and White	White O'Connor and Burger Powell and Rehnquist	Stevens, Marshall, and Blackman (on only one of the five districts; the Court was unanimous on four and split 6–3 on the fifth)
Growe v. Emison 2/23/93	9–0	Scalia	—	—
Voinovich v. Quilter 3/2/93	9–0	O'Connor	—	—
Shaw v. Reno 6/28/93	5–4	O'Connor, Rehnquist, Scalia, Kennedy, and Thomas	—	White; Blackman and Stevens joined Blackman, Stevens, and Souter
Miller v. Johnson 4/19/95	5–4	Kennedy; Rehnquist, O'Connor, Scalia, and Thomas joined	O'Connor	Stevens Ginsburg; Stevens and Breyer joined, Souter joined except as to Part III-B
Hays II v. United States 6/29/95	9–0	O'Connor; Rehnquist, Scalia, Kennedy, Souter, Thomas, Breyer joined	Breyer plus Souter Stevens Ginsburg	—
Bush v. Vera 6/13/96	5–4	O'Connor; Rehnquist and Kennedy joined	O'Connor Kennedy Thomas; Scalia joined	Stevens; Ginsburg and Breyer joined Souter; Ginsburg and Breyer joined
Shaw v. Hunt 6/13/96	5–4	Rehnquist, O'Connor, Scalia, Kennedy, and Thomas	—	Stevens; Ginsburg and Breyer joined as to Parts II, III, IV, and V Souter; Ginsburg and Breyer joined
Abrams v. Johnson 6/19/97	5–4	Kennedy; Rehnquist, O'Connor, Scalia, Thomas joined	—	Breyer; Stevens, Souter, and Ginsburg joined

selves? Furthermore, what is a cohesive minority, and how is geographic compactness defined? How do plaintiffs demonstrate that their preferred candidates are being defeated by white bloc voting?[10]

A more basic question that has special significance for my supply-side argument concerns the definition of "preferred candidates," or, in the language of Section 2, "candidates of choice." Even as the legislation was being written, the term was controversial. Hatch ridiculed it as "little more than a euphemistic reference to the idea of a right in such groups to the establishment of safe and secure political ghettoes so that they can be assured of some measure of proportional representation" (Senate 1982b, 100). Central to this critique is the assumption that candidates of choice for African-American voters must be black. While there is nothing in the language of Section 2 that requires this interpretation, five members of the Court in *Gingles* argued that the race of the candidate was important in determining "candidates of choice." Justice Byron White, in a concurring opinion, argued that if the race of the candidate was not considered, party and interest group politics could produce electoral results that are indistinguishable from those produced by racial bloc voting.

There are certainly instances when the race of the candidate is not crucial in determining the candidate of choice. Thernstrom notes that a black endorsing group, the Concerned Citizens of Norfolk, Virginia, occasionally supported white candidates over black candidates, who, in turn, received a majority of the black vote (1987, 225). Thus, if the definition of "candidate of choice" is simply the candidate who receives the majority or plurality of minority votes, these white candidates would meet that criterion.[11] However, many lower courts have rejected this argument, noting that actual voting patterns, including those in the *Gingles* decision itself, tend to be polarized when a black candidate runs against a white candidate (Soni 1990, 1658–1662). Also, there are many instances in which only white candidates are running and there is no candidate of choice (using the reasoning of the *Gingles* majority) for the black community.

An additional wrinkle is presented by cases in which at least two black candidates run in the Democratic primary with no white candidates and white voters become pivotal in deciding who will win the nomination (and in all likelihood the general election). Earlier I cited the election in which John Lewis defeated Julian Bond by receiving 40 percent of the black vote and 80 percent of the white vote (Thernstrom 1987, 226). One black politician who was defeated in a primary by another black who appealed to white voters made his feelings clear: "'He got all the white votes. . . . Doc is not classified as black to me. You black when black folks elect you. White folks don't vote for black folks'" (quoted in Thernstrom 1987, 241). However, because Lewis received an overwhelming percentage of the black vote in the general election, he would still be considered a "candidate of choice" for purposes of Section 2 litigation.

Knowing the candidates of choice is also critical for conducting an analysis of vote polarization. As Bernard Grofman, Lisa Handley, and Richard Niemi note: "To prove that minority candidates are usually defeated, it is necessary to know who the minority preferred candidates are" (1992, 75). To conduct polarization analysis, one must decide whether to include white versus white contests or only elections in which a black candidate runs against a white candidate. This obviously goes back to the definition of "candidate of choice." The relative confusion in *Gingles* over this issue opened the door for a variety of interpretations in the lower courts. Some lower courts have limited polarization calculations to races in which a black candidate ran (*Citizens for a Better Gretna v. City of Gretna* 1986), while others have included races in which no black candidate ran (*Collins v. City of Norfolk* 1989; *Sanchez v. Bond* 1989) (Soni 1990, 1658–1662). A reasonable compromise position is that all contests can be included, but evidence of polarization in black versus white contests has "higher probative value" (*Buchanan v. City of Jackson* 1988, 1531; *Meadows v. Moon* 1997, appeal to Supreme Court, 20; see Grofman, Handley, and Niemi 1992, 74–81, for a review of the various positions taken by the lower courts).

The Partisan Connection

While there was little consensus among the lower courts on the details of applying *Gingles,* there was strong agreement within state legislatures that the decision required the creation of black majority districts whenever possible. State legislators feared that a failure to create black majority districts when the three *Gingles* prongs were present could result in vote dilution lawsuits. The partisan implications of this new position became immediately obvious as the 1990s redistricting commenced. Partisan calculations mixed with racial motivations in two important ways, one from the Democrats' perspective and the other from the Republicans' vantage point; both are rooted in the tremendous loyalty that black voters show for Democratic candidates. Neither has been recognized as a central legal principle in the post-*Shaw* court cases, but both were critical in the pre-*Shaw* redistricting process.

The first involved the Democratic Party's effort to balance the need to create new black majority districts and the desire to protect white Democratic incumbents. Creating black majority districts may hurt white Democratic incumbents because surrounding districts lose substantial numbers of black voters, who tend to vote Democratic (see Brace, Grofman, and Handley 1987 for a balanced argument based on the pre-1990s redistricting data; see Lublin 1997, 111–114, for an summary of recent research showing that racial redistricting hurts white Democratic incumbents). Consequently Democratic-controlled state legislatures often attempted to mitigate the damage through very creative cartography. As I will discuss in the next chapter, North Carolina produced one of the most successful efforts in 1992, adding two new black districts, while protecting all seven white Democratic incumbents (one of the new black members replaced a retiring white incumbent). Thus, the massive defeat of wounded white Democratic incumbents did not materialize in 1992, as only a few were defeated due to racial redistricting (Bob Benenson [1992, 3580–3581] puts the number at three, Kevin Hill [1995] says four, Carol Swain [1995, 78–83] says five, and David Lublin [1997, 112] says "five or six"). In 1992 the main effect of the racial redistricting on the surrounding districts was not to hurt white Democratic incumbents, but to make Republican incumbents' districts more secure. This had little impact on the representation of black interests because Republicans are not as sympathetic to black interests as Democratic representatives (Swain 1993, 13–19; Overby and Cosgrove 1996).

Some have argued that the impact of black majority districts on white Democrats was far greater in 1994, but it is difficult to sort out the confounding influence of the general Republican landslide and the effect of having new constituents (Engstrom 1995; John Petrocik and Scott Desposato [1998] conclude that these effects had a greater impact on Democratic losses in 1994 than minority districting). The range of estimates of Democratic losses caused by racial redistricting in 1994 varies; one seat (NAACP 1994), between seven and eleven seats (Lublin 1997, 114), or twelve (Swain 1995, 78–83; see Lublin 1997, 111–114, for an summary of this conflicting research). In any event it seems clear that white incumbents have not been as harmed as Democratic partisans feared, nor as much as Republican partisans hoped. Furthermore, the anticipated Democratic payoff from dismantling some of the black districts did not materialize in 1996. In Georgia, where the shift of black voters to white majority districts was most dramatic, all Republican incumbents survived. Neither did black incumbents suffer; both Sanford Bishop and Cynthia McKinney, the black incumbents in redrawn districts, were comfortably reelected.

Most state legislators were not too concerned about having their plans overturned on partisan grounds because historically the Court has been reluctant to enter the "political thicket of partisan gerrymanders," recognizing that redistricting is an inherently partisan process. However, in *Davis v. Bandemer* (1986, 125) the Court recognized the justiciability of partisan gerrymander claims. In 1992 the North Carolina Republican Party used *Bandemer* as the basis for its challenge of the state's redistricting plan. State party chair Jack Hawke argued that the General Assembly created a "government of the Democratic incumbent, by the Democratic incumbent, for the Democratic incumbent." The suit specifically charged that the new plan violated the voters' rights to "freedom of association and to fair and effective representation" (Ruffin 1992, 1A). However, the Supreme Court refused to hear the initial challenge on March 11, 1992, and rejected a subsequent suit by the Republican Party (*Pope v. Blue* 1992). In the post-*Shaw* era the Court continued to minimize the significance of partisan motivations when compared to racial redistricting.

Republicans saw racial redistricting as an opportunity, rather than as an issue that had to be balanced against alternative goals. However, Republicans did not control the redistricting process in any of the states where black majority districts were to be added. Therefore, they needed help from two possible sources: the Bush DOJ, which wielded the substantial powers of Section 5 preclearance, and the Republican National Committee. There is disagreement over whether the Justice Department interpreted the VRA for partisan gain. Some critics argue that the DOJ went beyond the intention of the 1982 amendments (*News and Observer* [Raleigh, N.C.], January 19, 1992, 10A). Daniel T. Blue, the first black speaker of the North Carolina House, said, "I think that what the Republicans are trying to do is corrupt the Voting Rights Act to the extent they can go beyond what its goal and mission is and use it for their political advantage" (*News and Observer* [Raleigh, N.C.], January 5, 1992, 5A). In elevating the third *Gingles* condition (polarized voting and electing preferred candidates) over the first condition (geographic compactness), the DOJ put the state legislature on a collision course with the Supreme Court, which would state in *Shaw v. Reno* (1993) that "appearances matter." While the second black majority district the DOJ thought was going to be created (the Republican plan across the southern tier of counties) was more compact than the snakelike district that connected Durham and Charlotte along Interstate 85, the former was relatively elongated as well.

In a slightly different context involving trade-offs among black Democrats, white Democrats, and Cuban Republicans, Ronald Weber describes the motivations of the DOJ in Dade County, Florida (Weber was an expert witness in the case): "I am convinced that nothing other than partisan concerns motivated the decision of the U.S. Department of Justice to intervene. . . . The Cuban Republicans in Dade County were just too crucial to President Bush's reelection effort to leave them out to dry . . ." (1995a, 227).

Grofman argues that the DOJ did not blindly pursue partisan ends in all cases. He says, "[T]he claim that a Republican-controlled DOJ has been enforcing the Voting Rights Act in a selective and partisan manner is simply not supported by the evidence from 1990s redistricting" (1993, 1254). Grofman cites the case of *Garza v. County of Los Angeles* (1990) to show that sometimes the DOJ's actions actually hurt Republicans. The DOJ also precleared a Virginia state legislative plan that had seven pairs of Republican incumbents, but no pairs of Democratic incumbents. Grofman also argues that the DOJ often *tried* to use the VRA for partisan purposes, but it did not always work; this observation is consistent with the North Carolina experience (1993, 1256).[12] However, since Grofman's article was published, *Miller v. Johnson* (1995) favorably cited the district court's finding that "it was obvious . . . that [the Justice Department] would accept nothing less than abject surrender to its maximization agenda" (1995, 925). The *Miller* decision makes eleven references to the "maximization policy" or the "maximization agenda" of the Justice Department. However, whether this agenda was purely for partisan ends is still open to debate (see Blissman 1996, 542–547, for a discussion of these issues).

While the motives of the DOJ are not entirely clear, the same cannot be said of the Republican National Committee (RNC). According to Benjamin Ginsberg, the chief counsel for the RNC in the late 1980s, the RNC promoted an unusual alliance between blacks and Republicans. Ginsberg attributes the strategy to Lee Atwater. "'I began working at the RNC in 1989, and Lee Atwater's first words to me were, "Do something about redistricting"'" (quoted in Kelly 1995, 46). Michael Kelly reports, "Under Ginsberg's direction, the Republican National

Committee undertook a campaign of guerrilla warfare, working with black Democrats against white Democrats in legislatures throughout the South." According to Ginsberg, the impact was devastating. "The fact that black Democrats plotted with Republicans made the white Democrats greatly mistrust them, while the black Democrats looked at the white Democrats and said 'If you aren't willing to let us have a better level of representation, you must be a racist.' Ginsberg is convinced that the emotional impact of the black-G.O.P. alliance 'absolutely' shattered the old black-white Democratic alliance" (Kelly 1995, 52).

The Post-*Shaw* Era

The relatively orderly process of elaborating and refining the host of questions raised by *Gingles* came to an abrupt end with the landmark decision *Shaw v. Reno* (1993), which held that bizarrely shaped black majority districts violated the rights of white voters if they were created solely on the basis of race and ignored traditional districting practices. Justice O'Connor, in the most widely quoted passage of the decision, argued that the challenged reapportionment plan

> bears an uncomfortable resemblance to political apartheid. It reinforces the perception that members of the same racial group—regardless of their age, education, economic status, or the community in which they live—think alike, share the same political interests, and will prefer the same candidates at the polls. We have rejected such perceptions elsewhere as impermissible racial stereotypes. (1992, 2827)

The decision departed from recent precedent by creating a new basis for making a voting rights claim under the "equal protection" clause of the Fourteenth Amendment (also note that table 2.1 shows that the key decisions went from consensual 9–0 verdicts to conflictual 5–4 decisions). While *Shaw* did not reverse *Gingles* or *Beer v. United States* (1976) (no retrogression standard), it departed from precedent in several important respects. First, in *Voinovich v. Quilter* (1993) the Court upheld a state legislative districting plan that created several black majority districts. In that case the black plaintiffs claimed that their overall influence was reduced by packing black voters into a few districts. Justice O'Connor said black majority districts were permissible, arguing that "Section 2 contains no per se prohibitions against particular types of districts: It says nothing about majority-minority districts. . . . Instead, § 2 focuses exclusively on the consequences of apportionment.

Only if the apportionment scheme has the effect of denying a protected class the equal opportunity to elect its candidate of choice does it violate § 2; where such an effect has not been demonstrated, § 2 simply does not speak to the matter" (1993, 155). This focus on "candidates of choice" is quite different from the general stigmatic harms claimed by the white plaintiffs in *Shaw.*

Second, *Voinovich* reaffirmed the Court's adherence to judicial restraint on this political topic, while giving state legislatures substantial leeway to engage in racial redistricting. Justice O'Connor wrote, "Of course, the federal courts may not order the creation of majority-minority districts unless necessary to remedy a violation of federal law. . . . [T]hat does not mean that the State's powers are similarly limited. Quite the opposite is true: Federal courts are barred from intervening in state apportionment in the absence of a violation of federal law precisely because it is the domain of the States, and not the federal courts, to conduct apportionment in the first place. Time and again we have emphasized that 'reapportionment is primarily the duty and responsibility of the State through its legislature or other body, rather than of a federal court'" (1993, 156).

Shaw also did not adhere to a ruling in *United Jewish Organizations of Williamsburgh, Inc. v. Carey* (1977) (*UJO*) that strict scrutiny does not apply and that the districts are valid even though the state "deliberately used race in a purposeful manner" to create minority-majority districts (*UJO* 1977, 165).[13] A majority of the Court also held that the intentional creation of majority-minority districts does not produce an equal protection claim unless the districting diluted the majority's voting strength. Justice O'Connor argued in *Shaw* that *UJO* did not apply because the North Carolina case did not involve a vote dilution claim. However, Justice Ruth Bader Ginsburg challenged that view in her *Miller* dissent:

> Nor is *UJO* best understood as a vote dilution case. Petitioners' claim in *UJO* was that the State had "violated the Fourteenth and Fifteenth Amendments by *deliberately revising its reapportionment plan along racial lines.*" Petitioners themselves stated: "Our argument is . . . that the history of the area demonstrates that there could be—and in fact was—*no reason other than race* to divide the community at this time" (*Miller v. Johnson* 1995, 946 n. 11 [Ginsburg, J., dissenting], internal citations omitted, emphasis in original)

Justice O'Connor clearly erred in arguing that the plaintiffs in the *Shaw* case brought "an analytically distinct claim [from the plaintiffs in *UJO*] that a reapportionment plan rationally cannot be understood as anything other than an effort to segregate citizens into separate voting districts on the basis of race without sufficient justification" (1993, 2830). In fact, as Justice Ginsburg pointed out, that is precisely what the *UJO* plaintiffs claimed, at least in part.

While the extent to which *Shaw* deviated from precedent is somewhat disputed, there is no disagreement that the decision created a new basis for challenging the constitutionality of a voting district. Justice O'Connor's decision notes that *Shaw* "warrants different analysis" than previous voting rights cases. Prior to *Shaw* there were only two bases on which to challenge a district: "one person–one vote" and vote dilution. The U.S. District Court for the Eastern District of North Carolina noted in *Shaw v. Hunt* (the remand from *Shaw v. Reno*) that, "[u]ntil *Shaw*, no majority opinion of the Supreme Court had held that a state redistricting plan that did not cause concrete, material harm to the voting strength of an identifiable group of citizens in one of these two ways could nonetheless be challenged under the Equal Protection Clause on the grounds that it impermissibly took race into account in drawing district lines" (1994, 422). This new analysis emphasized "traditional districting practices" for the first time, citing the importance of compactness, contiguity, and respect for political subdivisions (respect for "communities defined by actual shared interests" was added in *Miller*). Or in Justice O'Connor's words, "we believe that reapportionment is one area in which appearances do matter" (*Shaw v. Reno* 1993, 2827). Richard Engstrom suggests that these criteria, which have no basis in the Constitution or federal statute, create a confusing "conceptual thicket" to compound the difficulties posed by the "political thicket" of redistricting that for decades the Court was loath to enter (1995b, 323–324).

Even those who see the landmark decision as a reasonable compromise recognized the problematic nature of the decision itself. Grofman argues that *Shaw* steers a course between "premature optimism that will lead to the elimination of safeguards vital to the continuing integration of minorities into American electoral politics, and an unrealistic pessimism that insists we will never get beyond judging people by the color of their skin," yet notes the decision is "somewhat muddled" (1995, 34, 29). Paul Peterson calls the decision "logically incoherent," but sees it as "politically correct" because it does not try to impose racial classifications on the political process (1995, 16). The critics of *Shaw* are far less charitable. Morgan Kousser says, "It is true that the abstract, deeply ambiguous, and often unreflective opinion suggested only vague and unworkable standards that have led to much-heightened judicial intrusions in the political process, and that it encouraged a cruelly ironic interpretation of the 14th and 15th Amendments, an interpretation surely unintended by their framers, that aims to undermine the sharpest minority gains in politics since the First Reconstruction" (1995, 1).[14]

Subsequent decisions expanded the scope of judicial scrutiny. *Miller v. Johnson* (1995) established that congressional districts were unconstitutional if race was the "predominant factor" in their creation, while moving away from the importance of the appearance of the district. Bizarrely shaped districts were no longer a threshold requirement for an equal protection claim. As Justice Ginsburg pointed out in her *Miller* dissent, this was a dramatic shift from the relatively proscribed language of *Shaw:* "[In *Shaw*] the Court wrote cautiously, emphasizing that judicial intervention is exceptional: '[S]trict [judicial] scrutiny' is in order, the Court declared, if a district is 'so extremely irregular on its face that it rationally can be viewed only as an effort to segregate the races for purposes of voting'" (*Miller v. Johnson* 1995, 939 [Ginsburg, J., dissenting]). *Miller* also held that compliance with Section 5 preclearance was not an adequate reason for creating a black majority district, even when the Justice Department insisted that additional black majority districts be added. *Abrams v. Johnson* (1997) upheld the dismantling of two of Georgia's black majority districts that followed the *Miller* decision, even though the state legislature had shown a clear preference for keeping one of those two districts during the redistricting process. This decision signals that the courts are becoming increasingly activist in this area of litigation rather than allowing the elected officials to settle the issue.[15]

Bush v. Vera (1996) established that protecting incumbents was not a strong enough reason to dislodge race as the predominant factor when both motivations were present. The Court recognized incumbency protection as a legitimate end of redistricting and thus categorized *Vera* as a "mixed motive" case; however, race was seen as predominant, and thus the district was subjected to strict scrutiny. This logic is problematic.[16] While race may have been predominant in determining that one or more black majority districts would have to be created in Georgia, Texas, and North Carolina, in the latter two states incumbency protection dictated the actual shape of the district. For example, the infamous I–85 district in North Carolina was largely a product of incumbency protection. As noted above, the Republican plan called for a more compact district that could have been drawn across the southern tier of counties. Texas also produced some of its irregularly shaped districts to protect incumbents, but the Court rejected this alternative "compelling state interest" because the state legislature improperly used black voters as proxies for Democratic voters (*Bush v. Vera* 1996). In other words, even if the districts were oddly shaped to protect incumbents, race predominated because the state legislature assumed that blacks would vote Democratic.

The only bright spot for advocates of the districts was *United States v. Hays* (1995, 739), when the Court narrowed the scope of standing, noting that a plaintiff must reside in the challenged district in order to file a Fourteenth Amendment claim.

Justice O'Connor realized that this string of decisions left state legislatures potentially "'trapped between the competing hazards of liability'" (quoting *Wygant v. Jackson Board of Education* 1986). After affirming the constitutionality of the VRA and its amendments, she stated, "I believe that States and lower courts are entitled to more definite guidance as they toil with the twin demands of the Fourteenth Amendment and the Voting Rights Act" (*Bush v. Vera* 1996, 990). Thus, in an unusual separate concurring opinion (she also wrote the plurality opinion) Justice O'Connor laid out the following steps to determine whether a given district would survive judicial scrutiny. First, the plaintiffs have to prove that race was the predominant factor in creating the black majority district by showing that traditional districting principles were subordinated to race. Violation of compactness, contiguity, communities of interest, or traditional political boundaries does not satisfy the burden of proof faced by the plaintiffs unless they can show that this neglect is predominantly due to race (*Bush v. Vera* 1996, 993).

For example, in the district court case of *Moon v. Meadows* the state of Virginia attempted to show that some irregularities of district lines (compactness) and splitting of precincts (respect for political boundaries) were caused by nonracial considerations, such as protecting incumbents and splitting two ship-building yards between two districts. One of the more amusing moments in this case came when the State showed that one of the split precincts was created to satisfy Governor Douglas Wilder's request to include a "close personal friend," Jacqueline Epps, in the new 3rd District (she wanted to run for the new open seat). General tittering in the courtroom indicated that most of the observers understood what was going on, but one of the three judges was in the dark and had to be filled in by a colleague. This incident could give new meaning to the term "compelling state interest." Despite these arguments, the district court ruled that race was the predominant factor in the creation of the 3rd District.

The second step of the process requires that if the predominance of race is established, the district come under strict scrutiny and the burden of proof shift to the state to demonstrate that the district was "narrowly tailored" to achieve a compelling state interest other than race. One important aspect of Justice O'Connor's concurring opinion in *Vera* is that compliance with Section 2 can be a compelling state interest if the *Gingles* preconditions are met and if the state does not violate traditional districting principles in the creation of the district for predominantly racial reasons.

While this may sound like a relatively straightforward procedure, there are practical difficulties and important political implications posed by the *Shaw* decisions. For example, Justice Stephen Breyer in his *Abrams v. Johnson* (1997) dissent points out:

> Legislators, for example, may ask just what the words "predominant racial motive" mean. The question has no obvious answer because racial motives (here efforts to include some additional African-American voters in a particular district) *never* explain a predominant portion of a district's entire boundary (most of which inevitably reflects county lines, other geographical features, and sometimes even a discriminatory history); yet those motives *always* predominate in respect to those voters (whether few or many) whom the legislature, with consciousness of race, places for that reason in one district rather than another. More importantly, here, unlike other cases that use somewhat similar words, the Court has not turned to other considerations, such as discriminatory intent, or vote dilution, or even a district's bizarre geographical shape, to help explain, or to limit the scope of, the words themselves. Thus, given today's suit, a legislator might reasonably wonder whether he can ever knowingly place racial minorities in a district because, for example, he considers them part of a "community" already there; because he thinks doing so will favor the Democrats (or the Republicans); because he wants to help an African-American incumbent; because he believes doing so will encourage participation in the political process by racial minorities in whom historical discrimination has induced apathy; because he believes that doing so will help those same voters secure representatives that better reflect their needs and desires; or simply because he wants to see more racial minorities elected to office in a Nation that has become increasingly diverse. (1997, 148 [Breyer, J., dissenting], internal citations omitted)

Tellingly the Court has made no effort to define its core principle—
race as the predominant factor—in a fashion that would help answer
Justice Breyer's questions.

Supporters of racial redistricting predicted dire political implications of *Shaw* and the subsequent decisions. Frank Parker said, "So
now we are seeing the first reduction in minority representation in
Congress and in state legislatures since the post-reconstruction period.
That act is going to have a very chilling effect on race relations in this
country, and a very damaging effect on democratic principles in this
country" (1996, 528). Representative McKinney was even more bitter.
Just before her district was dismantled by a federal court, she said
Shaw and its progeny will "turn Black voters back into spare parts for
the political machines of Dixiecrats. What Georgia does in redistricting
will set the tone for the rest of the nation as majority-minority districts
across America are sacrificed to feed the appetite of recently embold-
ened neo-Confederates . . . the leadership of my state seems eager to
make up for 'time lost' since the Voting Rights Act sought to give
Blacks a meaningful vote" (McKinney 1996, 66).

However, other observers of the Court see these concerns as overstated. Cass Sunstein argues that despite appearances, the Court has
taken a relatively tentative stand on redistricting and tends not to offer
definitive answers on a broad range of questions it addresses. "In fact,
following Justice Sandra Day O'Connor's cautious lead, the heart of
the current court avoids clear rules and final resolutions. It allows
room for Congress's and the states' continued democratic deliberation,
and to accommodate new judgments about facts and values. It is a
court that leaves fundamental issues undecided. . . . [T]he court has
avoided simple rules in its series of cases involving bizarrely shaped
voting districts redrawn to produce a different racial makeup; it has
insisted instead that constitutional challenges would have to be decided on the basis of the details" (1997, 22). Sunstein concludes that
in a dynamic political context the nation may be better served with
court decisions that are "ambivalent or catalytic rather than final or
decisive. If these points are right [about change], O'Connor's distinctive concurring opinions represent not a failure of judicial nerve, but
a healthy reminder that judges are mere participants in America's process of democratic deliberation" (1997, 23). While the Court has been
more restrained than it could have been (for example, it could have
struck down portions of the 1982 VRA Amendments), I think that

giving more latitude to the state legislatures in redistricting would be
preferable to the muddled process created by the courts.

Links to My Research

The *Shaw*-type cases raise important questions concerning representation, but ironically the Court's majority opinions have almost completely ignored these issues (vigorous dissents from Justices Ginsburg,
Stevens, Souter, Blackmun, White, or Breyer in nearly every decision
have developed the importance of representation through the topic of
standing). My central argument, which is shared by most of the dissenters, is that white voters did not suffer any "cognizable harm like
dilution or the abridgement of the right to participate in the electoral
process" (*Shaw v. Reno* 1993, 684 [Souter, J., dissenting]). Therefore,
white plaintiffs should not have standing to sue unless they can demonstrate a particularized harm. There is no harm because white voters
are adequately represented by blacks. As chapter 3 will show, whites
were the pivotal voters in many districts and were able to elect the
representatives of their choice. Chapters 4 and 5 show that black representatives pay attention to white voters and spend most of their time
on issues that are important to all constituents in their district.

Justice O'Connor's assertion in *Shaw* that "[w]hen a district obviously is created solely to effectuate the perceived common interests of
one racial group, elected officials are more likely to believe that their
primary obligation is to represent only the members of that group,
rather than their constituency as a whole" (1993, 648) is simply wrong.
Furthermore, the current approach taken by the Court ignores differences in the types of African-American candidates who are elected
and the type of representation they provide to the white and black
communities. Clearly a moderate like Mike Espy was very acceptable
to the white voters of the Mississippi Delta, while they probably would
not be as supportive of a radical former Black Panther. By ignoring
differences within the African-American community, a majority of the
members of the Supreme Court are guilty of racial stereotyping that
they claim is represented by the districts they reject.

My research is specifically linked to this body of law in two areas:
responsiveness of elected officials and standing. Responsiveness was
not included in the Senate report's first seven factors that could be used
to show that blacks did not have an equal opportunity to participate.
However, it was one of the two additional factors in the Senate report,

and Senator Dole mentioned it as an important consideration when asked by Senator Hatch how he would define "equal opportunity to participate." Dole responded, "Typical circumstances include a history of official discrimination, racist campaign tactics, racial polarity in voting, *unresponsiveness of elected officials,* and the use of voting practices or procedures which enhance the opportunity for discrimination" (Senate 1982a, 81, emphasis added).

In *Rogers v. Lodge* (1982, 625) the Court cited elected officials who were "unresponsive and insensitive to the needs of the black community" as one reason for striking down the at-large system of representation in Burke County, Georgia. More recently the plaintiffs in *Moon v. Meadows* (1997) tried to show that white politicians were just as responsive to blacks as black politicians and that blacks would lose representation with a black majority district (the same point developed by Lublin [1997] and by Charles Cameron, David Epstein, and Sharon O'Halloran [1996]). This was an unusual argument because lower courts (the 5th and 11th Circuits) have held that while evidence that white politicians are unresponsive to black voters may be useful in proving a Section 2 claim, demonstrating responsiveness is not probative because vote dilution may exist for other reasons (Grofman, Handley, and Niemi 1992, 43–44). Furthermore, white plaintiffs in the *Shaw*-type cases are making equal protection rather than vote dilution claims, and they have not been required to offer evidence of responsiveness. However, my research could aid defendants in *Shaw*-type cases whose districts come under strict scrutiny. My evidence that white representatives are not as responsive to black constituents as black representatives could help establish a Section 2 justification for the creation of a black majority district under a "totality of circumstances" analysis that demonstrates blacks did not have an equal opportunity to participate.

While responsiveness has no probative value in determining a vote dilution claim, it is relevant for the debate concerning standing. If black members of Congress are responsive to white voters, this undermines the claim of any particularized harm suffered by white plaintiffs. The Court has argued that white plaintiffs have standing because they suffer two types of concrete harms: "stigmatization," which occurs from the general classification by race in the racially gerrymandered districts, and "representational harms," which occur when black politicians focus their attention on black constituents (*Shaw v. Reno* 1993; *Hays v. Louisiana* 1993). As noted in the introduction, in *Moon v. Mead-*

ows (1997), one of the plaintiffs asserted, "I have been stigmatized by the fact that the Virginia General Assembly classified voters according to race and segregated us, to the extent it was practicable. . . . Additionally, the tortured construction of the Third District has made my job as the Republican Chairman of the Third Congressional District exceedingly difficult" (Plaintiffs' Answers to the First Interrogatories, April 1, 1996, 2–3). However, the plaintiffs did not provide evidence to support either claim, and white plaintiffs in voting rights cases have not been required to do so by the Court, which assumes that the harm flows from the simple act of classification and that the other harms *may* occur.

Critics of *Shaw* assailed this new basis for standing.[17] Representative McKinney quotes a *New York Times* editorial noting that the white plaintiffs in her district had their "feelings hurt" (McKinney 1996, 63). Arthur Baer testified before a House Subcommittee Roundtable on Voting Rights:

> In *Shaw* . . . there was no allegation of vote dilution on white voters. That is, there was no harm to them. So it is an extraordinary case, because essentially it is unique in terms of creating standing for a group without injury. We had never had ideological standing before. This is essentially ideological standing. (House 1994a, 76)

Morgan Kousser is blunt in his attribution of the motivation behind this expansion of standing: "In *Shaw v. Reno* the Court majority blatantly ignored their own broadly stated standards on standing in order to get to an issue that they wanted to decide" (1995, 12). David Kairys proposed a provocative "dual system thesis" in which one set of standards applies to black plaintiffs in discrimination and equal protection cases and another applies to white plaintiffs (1996; see p. 746 for a summary table). While Kairys takes the argument further than I would, there are clearly different criteria for standing and burdens of proof in the pre- and post-*Shaw* cases.

Other "standing" cases outside the area of voting rights also have great relevance. In *Lujan v. Defenders of Wildlife* (1992) the Court established clear guidelines for standing: plaintiffs must have suffered an "'injury in fact'" that is "'concrete and particularized'" and "'"actual or imminent," not "conjectural" or "hypothetical"'" (1992, 559–567, 571–578). In *Allen v. Wright* (1984) Justice O'Connor wrote for a six-person majority in denying standing to plaintiffs who were claiming an "abstract stigmatic injury" (1984, 755). However, in *Shaw* the stigmatic injury was sufficient for standing, as the simple classification of people based on race was held to be unconstitutional.

Pamela Karlan and Daryl Levinson point out that this is a "radical proposition." They continue: "If racial classification is itself the injury, then a wide range of government activities—from juror selection questionnaires to police descriptions of fleeing suspects to much of the census—may also be presumptively unconstitutional" (1996, 1214). Justice John Paul Stevens makes the same point concerning the Census in his dissent in *Shaw v. Hunt* (1996) and goes on to criticize the constitutional grounds for standing used in the *Shaw*-type cases:

> Given the absence of any showing, or, indeed, any allegation, that any person has been harmed more than any other *on account of race,* the Court's decision to entertain the claim of these plaintiffs would seem to emanate less from the Equal Protection Clause's bar against racial discrimination than from the Court's unarticulated recognition of a new substantive due process right to "color-blind" districting itself. Revealed for what it is, the constitutional claim before us ultimately depends for its success on little more than speculative judicial suppositions about the societal message that is to be gleaned from race-based districting. I know of no workable constitutional principle, however, that can discern whether the message conveyed is a distressing endorsement of racial separatism, or an inspiring call to integrate the political process. As a result, I know of no basis for recognizing the right to color-blind districting that has been asserted here. (1996, 924–925 [Stevens, J., dissenting])

The dubiousness of the stigmatic claim is further supported by noting its unique application in racial redistricting cases. In the early segregation cases cited in *Miller v. Johnson* (1995, 911)—*New Orleans City Park Improvement Association v. Detiege* (1958), *Gayle v. Browder* (1956), *Holmes v. Atlanta* (1955), *Mayor and City Council of Baltimore v. Dawson* (1955), and *Brown v. Board of Education* (1954)—classification by race was not allowed, but the context was entirely different than current redistricting cases. These cases were challenges to the Jim Crow laws that segregated the races in public parks, buses, golf courses, beaches, and schools, respectively. Blacks were clearly stigmatized by being *excluded* from participation because of their race. It is not clear why whites are stigmatized by being *included* in a district with large numbers of blacks (Karlan and Levinson 1996, 1214). Unlike blacks in the 1950s, whites are able to fully participate in the political process. Justice Stevens develops this argument in his *Shaw v. Hunt* dissent:

> Even if race-based districting could be said to impose more personal harms than the so-called "stigmatic" harms that *Hays* itself identified, I do not understand why any voter's reputation or dignity should be *presumed* to have been harmed simply because he resides in a highly inte-

grated, majority-minority voting district that the legislature has deliberately created. Certainly the background social facts are not such that we should presume that the "stigmatic harm" described in *Hays* and *Shaw I* amounts to that found cognizable under the Equal Protection Clause in *Brown v. Board of Education,* where state-sponsored school segregation caused some students, but not others, to be stamped with a badge of inferiority on account of their race. (*Shaw v. Hunt* 1996, 928 [Stevens, J., dissenting], citations omitted)

The basis for standing moves to even shakier ground when considering the more tangible "special representational harms" referred to in *Shaw* and *Miller.* Grofman, writing before the *Shaw* decision, explains why the precedents cited by the Court, such as *Adarand Construction v. Pena* (1995) and *City of Richmond v. J.A. Croson Co.* (1989), in which white contractors were denied business because of minority set-aside programs, are inappropriate in the context of voting rights:

[T]he nature of the remedy for minority vote dilution *does not require injury to innocent parties* as is the case, for example, in those situations where the future job prospects of whites may be threatened as a result of having been fired by a firm which is found to have been discriminating against blacks. The only possible losers when minority districts are created are the white *incumbents* whose districts will be severely reconfigured . . . and these white incumbent legislators have no "right" to their seats. As the majority cannot be said to have a right to elect *all* the candidates, white *voters* are being denied no entitlement when minority vote dilution is remedied, and white voters' rights to elect candidates of choice remain unimpaired. (1993, 1246, emphasis in original)

Even Thernstrom, who supports the general reasoning of the Court in the *Shaw* cases, agrees with Grofman's argument about white politicians: "Whites denied medical school admission as a consequence of minority preference have been arguably denied a right; those disadvantaged by a change in electoral rules cannot make that claim. There are no 'objective' criteria for elected office—no equivalent of the Medical College Aptitude Test. A white denied a seat on a city council cannot claim entitlement on the ground of 'merit'" (1987, 242). Indeed, the Court has never used the Fourteenth Amendment to "strike down a racial classification which has had no tangible consequences," other than in the *Shaw* cases (Karlan and Levinson 1996, 1214). The link to standing is developed by Justice Stevens:

To prove the representational harms that *Hays* holds are needed to establish standing to assert a *Shaw* claim, one would think that plaintiffs should be required to put forth evidence that demonstrates that their

political representatives are actually unlikely to provide effective representation to those voters whose interests are not aligned with those of
the majority race in their district. Here, as the record reveals, no plaintiff
has made such a showing. Given our general reluctance to hear claims
founded on speculative assertions of injury, I do not understand why the
majority concludes that the speculative possibility that race-based districting "may" cause these plaintiffs to receive less than complete representation suffices to create a cognizable case or controversy. (*Shaw v.
Hunt* 1996, 927 [Stevens, J., dissenting], citations omitted)[18]

Perhaps plaintiffs have not presented evidence of representational
harm for one simple reason: it does not exist. As the data in chapters 4
and 5 will demonstrate, whites are adequately represented by African-
American members of Congress.

Conclusion

A major shift in how the Supreme Court applies the Fourteenth
Amendment to congressional redistricting has left the status of black
majority districts in serious doubt. State legislatures have been told
that it is possible to consider race as a factor when drawing district
lines, but not as the predominant factor. The lack of an operational
definition of "predominant" may have a chilling effect on the creation
of black majority districts in the next round of redistricting (Parker
1996, 528). To reach this position, the Court loosened well-defined
conditions for standing, while moving toward a color-blind theory that
ignores history and the distinctiveness of voting rights law when compared to other areas of civil rights law, such as affirmative action and
discrimination. Unlike the white plaintiffs in *Regents of the University
of California v. Bakke* (1978) (medical school admissions), *Adarand*
and *Croson* (minority contracting set-aside programs), or *Wygant*
(considering race or seniority in laying off teachers), white voters were
not harmed by being placed in black majority districts. Justice O'Connor noted the hypothetical representational harms that come from the
district, but no such harms have been demonstrated, even though they
are claimed in some of the *Shaw*-type cases.

Thus, the motivation for the challenges to the black majority districts boils down to an extremely thin conception of "stigmatic harm."
One must look only as far as the dictionary to see what a distortion of
language and the law this is. The archaic definition of stigma is "a
mark burned into the skin of a criminal or slave; a brand." The current
definition is "a mark or token of infamy, disgrace, or reproach." To

stigmatize is "to characterize or brand as disgraceful or ignominious" (*American Heritage Dictionary,* 3rd ed. 1993). The use of the term by white plaintiffs in this context is certainly ironic (Justice O'Connor also used the language of slavery and racism in *Shaw* by noting the parallels to "political apartheid"). Slaves in this country were literally stigmatized. Their offspring were effectively "branded" by the Jim Crow laws in the century that followed the Civil War. It is difficult to see how white voters, who participate fully in the political process and dominate the political system at the national level ("virtual" representation), are branded as "disgraceful or ignominious" or suffer a mark of "infamy, disgrace, or reproach" by being placed in black majority districts.[19]

Furthermore, the notion of an individual right to color-blind districting[20] does not mesh with the group-based focus of the politics of drawing district lines and the history of the Voting Rights Act. State legislators make precise calculations, based on census data that is aggregated by demographic groups, about the political consequences of separating groups of voters in various ways. Districting decisions cannot avoid group-level analysis.[21] Similarly vote dilution claims under the VRA are based on patterns of group-level behavior (racial bloc voting and the ability to participate in the political process as the member of a group). As Karlan and Levinson note, "[O]nly a group of voters can suffer dilution from districting. A lone voter cannot" (1996, 1204 n. 16).

A meaningful basis for evaluating the constitutionality of black majority districts must be rooted in an assessment of their consequences. Do they dilute a group's voting power? Do they restrict a group's ability to elect candidates of choice and participate fully in the political process? Do voters suffer representational harms such as those endured by black constituents in the pre-VRA era (or, in the language of the 1982 Senate report, are elected leaders responsive to all groups of constituents)? The answer to all of these questions for the white plaintiffs in the *Shaw*-type cases is an unequivocal *no.* First, no claims of vote dilution have even been made by white plaintiffs. Second, as Thernstrom notes with the examples of Julian Bond and John Lewis, and as I will demonstrate more systematically in the next chapter, white voters often elect their preferred candidate. Critics of the black districts, such as Thernstrom, have argued that black support of white candidates should be considered in determining candidates of choice (1987, 225). By the same logic the courts should consider white support for black candidates and recognize that white voters were pivotal in choosing many of the black representatives who were elected in 1992 and thus are electing *their* candidates of choice. Unless the parallel logic is applied in both contexts, there is an implicit argument that whites can represent blacks, but blacks cannot represent whites. Third, as Justices Stevens and Souter note, the white plaintiffs have never provided any evidence of representational harms; indeed, these harms do not exist. Given this reality, it is difficult to see how Fourteenth Amendment complaints can be sustained.[22] When black plaintiffs bring a lawsuit under the Section 2 of the VRA, these patterns of concrete harms must be demonstrated. It seems only fair that white voters should bear the same legal burdens.

I have no illusions that the federal courts will suddenly alter the standards used to evaluate the constitutionality of a given district. I am convinced that the predominance of race in creating the districts and strict scrutiny will prevail given the current composition of the Court. I am sympathetic to the reasons why the Court would not want to open this can of worms—it is difficult to determine whose interests are being represented and whose are being ignored. However, the current array of concepts is as difficult to define and measure as "responsiveness" and standing: Was race the predominant factor in drawing the district lines? If so, is there a Section 2 liability (that is, was there racial polarization, voting cohesiveness, district compactness, and denial of candidates of choice)? Why should the courts privilege one type of question over another, especially when in other areas of Fourteenth Amendment law plaintiffs *have* been required to show specific discrimination rather than generalized patterns of discrimination (*Croson* 1989) and specific harm rather than vague, generalized stigmatic harm (*Adarand* 1995; *Bakke* 1978).

The important questions of representation and democracy have not been addressed by the Court's majority in the racial redistricting cases. *Candidates of choice, opportunity to participate, and vote dilution matter because representation matters.* If white politicians and black politicians were completely interchangeable in terms of representation, the fairness of the process would be much less important. However, my research shows that black and white politicians are not interchangeable. Most white representatives from black influence districts do not spend much time representing their black constituents, while most black members of Congress spend a substantial proportion of their time representing white constituents.

The legal questions surrounding racial redistricting are inextricably intertwined with policy and partisan politics. Ultimately the solution to the legal quagmire may be judicial restraint. As Justice Souter points out in his *Vera* dissent, the Court has confused the issue without resolving anything, and the political process had been making some progress with one of the nation's most persistent problems. Souter's plea to abandon *Shaw* as a "failed experiment" is worth quoting at length:

> While I take the commands of *stare decisis* very seriously, the problems with *Shaw* and its progeny are themselves very serious. The Court has been unable to provide workable standards, the chronic uncertainty has begotten no discernible reliance, and the costs of persisting doubt about the limits of state discretion and state responsibility are high. There is, indeed, an added reason to admit *Shaw*'s failure in providing a manageable constitutional standard and to allow for some faith in the political process. That process not only evolved the very traditional districting principles that the Court has pledged to preserve, but has applied them in the past to deal with ethnicity in a way that should influence our thinking about the prospects for race. (*Bush v. Vera* 1996, 1074 [Souter, J., dissenting])

Justice Souter goes on to note that redistricting built around ethnic neighborhoods played an important role in assimilating European immigrants into our political culture. "The result has been not a state regime of ethnic apartheid, but ethnic participation and even a moderation of ethnicity's divisive effect in political practice" (*Bush v. Vera* 1996, 1074 [Souter, J., dissenting]). The evidence I present in chapters 4 and 5 shows that the black majority districts put in place in 1992 could have that same integrative impact through the politics of commonality if the Court would abandon its "failed experiment" of judicial activism in this area.

CHAPTER THREE

The Supply-Side Theory
of Racial Redistricting

WITH MATTHEW M. SCHOUSEN AND PATRICK J. SELLERS

> What we have here is a situation in which blacks have been
> excluded because whites have written the laws to exclude
> black participation. They have dammed up the flow to both
> candidates and voters. Well, the floodgates are open. There
> are many people who have been waiting for this opportunity.
> State Representative Thomas Hardaway
> (personal interview, March 8, 1992)

This chapter provides a new understanding of the electoral sources of representation in the new black districts based on the supply-side theory of redistricting. The traditional demand-side perspective on redistricting examines voters and elections and includes hundreds of studies on such topics as swing ratios and incumbency safety (Tufte 1975; Gelman and King 1994) and partisan bias (Cranor, Crawley, and Sheele 1989; Cain 1985; Butler and Cain 1992; Niemi and Abramowitz 1994; Niemi, Hill, and Grofman 1985; Rush 1993). Demand-side research that examines minority redistricting includes studies of vote dilution (Davidson 1984; Schockley 1991), racial bloc voting (Grofman 1991; Loewen 1990; McCrary 1990; Schockley 1991), runoff elections (Bullock and Smith 1990; Ballard 1991), political geography and demographics (Grofman and Handley 1991; Niemi et al. 1990; Niemi, Brace, and Chapin 1992), racial transitions and incumbency advantage (Vanderleeuw 1991), and the partisan implications of black majority districts (Brace, Grofman, and Handley 1987; Lublin 1997).

In contrast, our supply-side perspective examines the process of candidate emergence: how individual politicians respond to the changing electoral context imposed by new district lines and how, in turn, their decisions shape electoral choices and outcomes in a given district. The crucial supply-side variables are the number of black candidates who run and their representational styles, and whether a white candidate decides to run. Thus the types of candidates who run define the voters' choices in primary elections and set the context for behavior during the "governing season" (Fenno 1989, 1996). In a strong party system the type of candidate who runs would not be as important because parties rather than individual candidates decide policy positions. However, in candidate-centered elections it becomes critical to understand the motivations and positions of each candidate.

We argue that individual politicians acting in their own self-interest may tip the balance of power in black-majority districts to a cohesive minority comprised of black and white moderates who will elect black racial moderates or even white candidates. We find that the former outcome prevails in a majority of the new districts where biracial coalitions elect candidates who embody a politics of commonality rather than a politics of difference. (*Note:* For ease of presentation we will often refer to "commonality" politicians as "new-style" and "difference" politicians as "traditional.") In a nutshell the supply-side theory argues that the type of racial representation provided in a district depends on the racial composition of the candidate pool in the Democratic primary. In most instances (necessary conditions will be discussed below), if only black candidates run, a new-style black candidate will win. If a white candidate and at least one traditional black candidate run, a traditional black candidate will win. Before testing these assertions, we will explain how the supply-side perspective forces a reexamination of the typical interpretation of the new black districts.

Empowering Blacks through Redistricting: The Supply-Side Challenge to the Common Wisdom

As noted in chapter 1, both supporters and opponents of the black majority districts see them as a manifestation of the politics of difference and a reflection of the assumption that black interests are monolithic. This chapter challenges both those assumptions. Even disregarding the black political right (Walter Williams, Thomas Sowell, Clarence Thomas, Shelby Steele, The Lincoln Institute, etc.), which is relatively small though growing, *black interests are not monolithic* (see Faryna, Stetson and Conti 1997).

This diversity of black positions opens up a dynamic in the supply-side effects within the new districts that potentially promotes a politics of commonality rather than a politics of difference. If black interests were monolithic, a single type of candidate would run for office in the new black districts. These traditional black candidates, with backgrounds in the civil rights movement and black churches, typically come from the liberal wing of the Democratic Party and embody the politics of difference. These candidates tend to think of themselves and the black community as political outsiders who must form political organizations separate from whites in order to battle for a greater share of the political pie. Many of these black politicians have little or no prior experience in party and elective politics and, more important, value their outsider status (Dymally 1971; Holden, 1973). Representative Adam Clayton Powell (D–NY) explicitly described this view: "'Black organizations must be black-led. The extent to which black organizations are led by whites, to that precise extent are they diluted of their black potential for ultimate control and direction. . . . Black people must support and push black candidates for political office first'" (quoted in Dymally 1971, 65–66). The campaigns of Bennie Thompson (D–MS), Alcee Hastings (D–FL), and Eva Clayton (D–NC) are examples of this style of representation in the 1992 elections, and Maxine Waters's (D–CA) leadership of the Congressional Black Caucus (CBC) in the 105th Congress clearly falls into this category.

These traditional blacks are not the only type of candidate in the new districts. The pool also includes more moderate new-style candidates who advocate compromise and accommodation with white voters rather than confrontation and separation (Perry 1990; Strickland and Whicker 1992). In pursuing this politics of commonality, the new-style black politicians tend to follow more mainstream lines of career development and are more closely tied to the party organization. Sanford Bishop, for example, served in the Georgia state legislature for sixteen years before defeating white incumbent Charles Hatcher (D–GA) in a 1992 primary. The black challenger campaigned on his political experience, arguing that he "represents a new generation of leadership" (Montgomery 1992, E1). In Louisiana's 4th District, State Senator Cleo Fields campaigned hard for the support of white voters. According to *Congressional Quarterly,* "Fields has always played down racial issues and done as much as possible to raise the comfort level of his white constituents. At one point in the campaign, he distanced himself from Jones (his runoff opponent, a black state senator), who attacked a white newspaper editor as 'some racist cracker'" (*Congressional Quarterly* 1993, 90).

With the creation of new black influence and black majority districts in 1992, for the first time in history dozens of ambitious black politicians—both traditional and new style—had a realistic chance of being elected.[1] The pent-up supply of black politicians, the absence of political institutions capable of channeling ambition, and racial bloc voting created the possibility of a white candidate defeating a split black field. For example, if one white candidate and four black candidates ran in a district that was 51 percent black, the white candidate probably would have won. While this has happened in many state and local races in the South, it is relatively rare in the U.S. House of Representatives. Although it was unlikely that whites would win in the new black majority districts, the diversity of black candidates running in 1992 placed white voters in a potentially pivotal position in terms of deciding the *type* of candidate who won. A relatively cohesive minority can usually help elect their preferred candidate when the majority is divided.[2] Thus, a Sanford Bishop or a Cleo Fields is far more likely to attract the support of white voters than a Bennie Thompson.

To summarize, we expect that supply-side effects (the number and race of candidates who run) will affect descriptive and/or substantive representation in the new black districts, or in any competitive district with a newly elected black member.[3] It is less likely that descriptive representation will be altered (because a black candidate is very likely to win). But it is quite likely that substantive representation will be greatly affected by supply-side considerations. Whether a district elects a candidate who practices a politics of commonality or a politics of difference depends on the candidates who run. The diversity of black candidates creates a context in which biracial coalitions may elect racial moderates. Specifically we are positing two causal effects (King, Keohane, and Verba 1994, 76–85):[4] (1) the presence of a new black majority district will stimulate more black candidates to run than in the older districts (a corollary effect is that large fields of candidates will have diverse representational styles), and (2) the presence or absence of a white candidate will determine which type of black candidate wins.

We test these causal effects with case studies of two black majority districts in North Carolina and a unique data set that includes the race of every candidate in House districts that were at least 30 percent black (total population) in 1972, 1982, and 1992. The case studies are especially useful for identifying causal mechanisms (Little 1991). King,

Keohane, and Verba provide a succinct summary of the utility of adding this type of analysis to the more typical quantitative causal models: "In our view, identifying the mechanism by which a cause has its effect often builds support for a theory and is a very useful operational procedure. Identifying causal mechanisms can sometimes give more leverage over a theory by making observations at a different level of analysis into implications of the theory. The concept can also create new causal hypotheses to investigate" (1994, 86–87).[5]

In our research the case studies provide two distinct advantages. First, the case studies provide an understanding of the personal ambition of and the strategic calculations made by the actual and potential candidates in the district. To what extent did the new districts, with the attendant racial implications, drive the decisions of the candidates to enter the House race? Second, how did the racial composition of the pool affect candidate behavior (in terms of the racial constituencies that each candidate targeted)? Without the case studies we would not know whether the politicians actually view racial politics in the manner laid out in the theory. Understanding the campaigns from the perspectives of the actors, the basic interpretivist starting point, provides the basis for understanding the causal mechanisms. District-level quantitative analysis can posit this strategic behavior, derive theoretical implications, and identify causal effects that *look right* and are consistent with the data. But to actually have a candidate reveal, "The only reason I ran was to split the white vote," drives home the centrality of race in a way that a regression coefficient never could. On the other hand, the case studies have the obvious drawback of limited external validity and generalizability. Therefore, the prudent research strategy is triangulation of research methods (Tarrow 1995, 471–472). The quantitative analysis provides a more comprehensive test of the causal effects (the causal effects are observed in the two districts, but after all it is only two districts), while the qualitative case studies provide an understanding of the causal mechanisms (personal ambition and race as an omnipresent filter).

Redistricting and Race in North Carolina

Congressional redistricting in North Carolina was thrown into the center of the national debate over minority redistricting in the summer of 1993, when the U.S. Supreme Court severely criticized the state's plan as a racial gerrymander (*Shaw v. Reno* 1993). The confluence of forces that produced this controversial plan makes it one of the most interesting and instructive case studies of the politics of empowering minority voters through racial redistricting. Ambitious African-American officeholders, self-interested Republican Party officials and Democratic House incumbents, Section 5 preclearance procedures, computer technology, and legal challenges to the new black districts all played important roles in the unfolding drama.

Though it is impossible at this juncture to assess the long-term effects of redistricting in North Carolina, the most obvious short-run consequence was to redistribute power toward black voters, black community leaders, and black politicians. In a state that had not elected a black to Congress since 1898, two new black majority districts attracted a very strong field of African-American politicians who gave a new voice to black voters. Some of the black candidates campaigned with the explicit message that "it's our turn." Even the black candidates who attempted to create biracial coalitions, such as Mel Watt in the 12th District and Willie Riddick in the 1st, gave more attention to the concerns of black voters than had been true in previous elections.

The other short-run effects of the redistricting process were confusion and uncertainty. The state legislature debated ten redistricting plans, including one that was passed (plan #6) only to be rejected by the U.S. Department of Justice. A second plan (plan #10) was written into law only weeks before the beginning of the filing period for congressional primaries. A lawsuit filed by the North Carolina Republican Party challenging the districts extended the filing period by one week, but a federal judge dismissed the suit, ruling that the new plan met federal requirements. The uncertainty affected potential candidates who were deciding whether to run, incumbents who were trying to map out reelection campaigns, and constituents who did not know which district they would vote in.

Ultimately two African Americans were elected in 1992 and reelected in 1994, 1996, and 1998 from two newly created black majority districts. Voters chose Mel Watt in the new 12th District and Eva Clayton from the redesigned 1st District. Both candidates won hotly contested primaries in 1992 (Clayton was forced into a runoff with a white candidate, Walter Jones, Jr., the son of the late incumbent, who had represented the district for twenty-six years), but easily defeated the token Republican opposition in the fall. Both representatives have been prominent in congressional politics, especially Clayton, who was elected president of the huge freshman class in the 103rd Congress.

This case study examines the supply-side forces that shaped congressional redistricting in North Carolina. We begin by examining the strategic and legal context of redistricting. We then turn to the interplay among the competing groups, individuals, and courts as the various redistricting plans unfolded. The section concludes by pointing out the significance of the redistricting process in North Carolina's congressional elections and the implications of this case for the supply-side theory.

Setting the Stage

THE PLAYERS. The conflicting preferences of individuals and groups involved in redistricting created a protracted process that was confusing and controversial. Civil rights advocates viewed the addition of one House seat in North Carolina (an increase from eleven to twelve) as an opportunity to create one or more minority-controlled districts. Progressively ambitious African-American state lawmakers looked forward to carving out districts that would provide outlets for their aspirations. United States House incumbents and other state legislators with more static ambition hoped to protect their existing turf, or even make it more secure.[6]

The two major political parties also had a stake in the redistricting process, hoping to strengthen their respective positions in the state. The Democrats held a seven-to-four advantage in House seats in 1990. The party hoped to keep that edge, strengthen its incumbents' seats, or even increase its advantage. Republicans, on the other hand, wanted to use the creation of minority districts to concentrate Democratic voters in a few districts, thereby weakening Democratic incumbents in neighboring districts and increasing Republicans' chances to pick up a few seats.

Other groups, such as the National Association for the Advancement of Colored People (NAACP) and the American Civil Liberties Union (ACLU), urged the creation of a second black district. But as we will discuss below, there was a split within the black community over the wisdom of this strategy. A prominent North Carolina group, the Black Leadership Caucus (BLC), did not get involved in the redistricting process. But the group played an active role in the recruitment process by trying to ensure that blacks would be elected in the new black majority districts. Technical support for redistricting came largely from the state legislature, but some Democratic House incumbents also got involved with the help of a New York–based political action committee. The National Committee for Effective Congress (NCEC), known for supporting Democrats, provided a computer and database that enabled House members to draw up potential district maps. When asked about the Democrats' reliance on the NCEC, Representative Tim Valentine (D–NC) responded that North Carolina House members were not paying for the services; the national Democratic Party had engaged the NCEC to help "handle redistricting issues." Representative David Price (D–NC) added that "it helped to have our own resource, so if we wanted to suggest something we weren't totally out to lunch" (*News and Observer* [Raleigh, N.C.], August 25, 1991, 6C).

THE CANDIDATES.   Seven Democrats (four blacks and three whites) and one Republican (a white) entered their parties' primaries to fill the seat vacated by the retirement of Walter Jones, Sr. Table 3.1 shows the name, background, party, race, percentage of the primary vote, and campaign finance figures for each of the candidates. We interviewed party leaders, journalists, politicians, and candidates to identify potential candidates in the district.[7] This process uncovered nine potential candidates, four of whom ran in the 1st District (one other leading candidate, Mickey Michaux, ran in the 12th District).

As shown in table 3.1, Walter Jones, Jr., won the initial primary with 37.4 percent of the vote, falling just short of the 40 percent required for an outright win. Eva Clayton, who came in second with 30.7 percent in the first round, won the runoff election with a unified African-American community behind her and 54.8 percent of the vote. The 1992 general election was not seriously contested by the Republican nominee, who spent only $7,055 in the district and received 32 percent of the vote.

Mel Watt had a surprisingly easy time in the 12th District. The race was expected to produce a runoff between Watt and Michaux, but Watt easily won with 47 percent of the vote (well above the 40 percent cutoff for the runoff). There were nine candidates in the race, four Democrats and five Republicans; seven of the candidates were black, including all of the Democrats and three Republicans. Watt received a stunning 86 percent of the vote in Mecklenburg County, the most populous county in the district (which includes Charlotte).

Table 3.1   Potential and Announced Candidates in the 1st District

Name	Background	Party	Race	Constituent Overlap*	Identified by Sources?	Primary Vote	Expected Money	Needed Money	Total Receipts
Frank Ballance	State senator, Warrenton	D	B	33.8%	Yes	—	—	$350,000	—
Thomas Brandon	Mayor, Williamston	D	W	3.0%	No	6.0	$15,000–30,000	$15,000–30,000	$29,883
Eva Clayton	County commissioner, Warren County	D	B	3.8%	Yes	30.7	$300,000–500,000	$300,000–500,000	$521,382
Toby Fitch	State representative, Wilson	D	B	13.2%	Yes	—	—	$200,000	—
Thomas Hardaway	State representative, Enfield	D	B	12.4%	Yes	7.2	"hard to say"	"hard to say"	$43,171
Howard Hunter	State representative, Murfreesboro	D	B	15.5%	Yes	—	—	"not too much"	—
Paul Jones	Attorney, Kinston	D	B	4.1%	Yes	—	—	$400,000–500,000	—
Walter Jones, Jr.	State representative, Farmville	D	W	13.0%	Yes	37.4	$250,000–300,000	$250,000–300,000	$226,611
Stacatto Powell	Reverend, Wilson	D	B	4.9%	No	6.8	$150,000–200,000	$150,000–200,000	$11,091
Willie Riddick	Legislative aide, Windsor	D	B	53.7%	Yes	10.4	$250,000	$250,000	$39,539
Don Smith	Househusband, Stokes	D	W	—	No	1.5	$1,250	$250,000	$1,250
Ted Tyler	Mayor, Rich Square	R	W	4.9%	No	Unopposed	$80,000	$300,000	$7,055

Sources: North Carolina General Assembly, Legislative Services Office; *Broadcasting Yearbook, 1990;* and personal interviews.

Notes: This table does not include Mickey Michaux, who was one of the front-runners for the first version of the district. Michaux ended up running in the new 12th District when Durham was removed from the 1st. Eva Clayton defeated Walter Jones, Jr., in the runoff 54.8 percent to 45.2 percent and defeated Ted Tyler in the general election 68 percent to 32 percent.

"Constituent Overlap" refers to the percentage of overlap between the candidate's previous political constituency (if an officeholder) or his or her hometown and the 1st Congressional District.

LEGAL REQUIREMENTS FOR REDISTRICTING.   The North Carolina General Assembly was keenly aware of the political and legal pressures to create at least one black majority district. Twenty-two percent of the state's 6.6 million people are black. Consequently Republicans and some black leaders argued that the state should have two and perhaps even three black majority districts (.22 times 12 equals 2.64 districts). This view was based on the 1982 Voting Rights Act Amendments, and their subsequent interpretations by the Supreme Court and the Justice Department. As noted in chapter 2, the 1986 Supreme Court decision in *Thornburg v. Gingles* (1986) made it possible for a minority group to claim discrimination if "(i) it is sufficiently large and geographically compact to constitute a majority in a single-member district, (ii) it is politically cohesive, and (iii) its preferred candidates are usually defeated as a result of bloc voting by a white majority" (Research Division, North Carolina General Assembly 1991, 10).

The first condition established in *Gingles,* size and compactness, created some problems for the redistricting committee in the General Assembly. Unlike some northern states, such as Illinois or Michigan, or even some southern states, such as Georgia, North Carolina does not have an African-American population that is concentrated in large urban areas. Instead, the minority population is scattered in smaller urban areas, such as Charlotte, Durham, Raleigh, Wilmington, Winston-Salem, and Greensboro and in the rural northeastern part of the state. Only three counties are at least 50 percent black, and when added together, they are not nearly large enough to comprise a single congressional district (fig. 3.1). Therefore, North Carolina lacked the luxury enjoyed by many states of debating the minimum percentage of black voters needed to guarantee the election of an African American. Instead, the North Carolina legislature had to use creative cartography to scrape together enough black voters to make a single black majority district.

The Research Division of the state legislature advised the redistricting committees that they could ignore the compactness standard: "Neither the State nor federal constitution requires districts to be compact. Critics often refer to the lack of compactness of a particular district or group of districts as gerrymandering, but no court has ever struck down a plan merely on the basis that it did not appear to be compact" (Research Division, North Carolina General Assembly 1991, 12). The legislature certainly followed this advice with impunity.[8]

While North Carolina's 1992 districts are not geographically com-

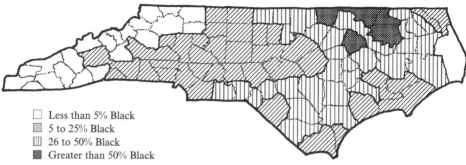

☐ Less than 5% Black
▨ 5 to 25% Black
▥ 26 to 50% Black
■ Greater than 50% Black

Figure 3.1 Black Population as a Percentage of Each County's Total Population in
North Carolina
Source: North Carolina General Assembly, Legislative Services Office.

pact, they meet the other two conditions laid out in the *Gingles* decision. The black vote in North Carolina is cohesive; between 90 and
95 percent of black voters cast ballots for Democratic candidates in
statewide elections. Clearly blacks had been denied an opportunity to
elect "candidates of choice," at least if that distinction is made on the
basis of race alone: it had been more than ninety years since a black
North Carolinian had served in Congress (George H. White, from
1897 to 1901). This legacy made it clear to the redistricting committees
that any plan had to include at least one black majority district.

    One final question had to be considered by the redistricting commit-
tees: the legal status of partisan gerrymanders. The committees wanted
to protect Democratic incumbents, but they were concerned that contorted district lines would not be viewed favorably by the courts. As
noted in chapter 2, the Court has been reluctant to enter this "political
thicket," acknowledging that redistricting is an inherently partisan process. In *Davis v. Bandemer* (1986), however, the Court recognized the
justiciability of partisan gerrymander claims, but failed to overrule the
Indiana redistricting plan. The Court argued that an electoral system
is discriminatory only when "it consistently degrades a voter's or group
of voters' influence on the political process." Furthermore, the ag-
grieved party must prove intent to discriminate and actual discriminatory effects over a period of at least two elections (Research Division,
North Carolina General Assembly 1991, 11). The consequences of this
vaguely worded decision are unclear. Some argue that partisan gerrymanders can be struck down if a stronger case is presented than the
one used in Indiana. Others say that the discrimination suffered by
parties must be comparable to that experienced by minorities in the

South (Butler and Cain 1992, 33–36). The Court seems to be leaning toward the latter interpretation. In *Badham v. Eu* (1988) the Court refused to strike down the 1981 California redistricting plan, claiming that the standard of unconstitutional discriminatory effect had not been met.

Act I—The Drama Unfolds: Plan #6

Early in 1991 the North Carolina General Assembly appointed redistricting committees to take up the task of creating the new state legislative and congressional districts. In addition to the legal constraint to create a new black majority district, the committees were confronted with a political task—to protect as many Democratic incumbents as possible. As the redistricting drama unfolded, one other factor grew increasingly important: unlike many states that have a bipartisan process, North Carolina's redistricting process was completely dominated by the Democrats, who firmly controlled the state legislature and thus the redistricting committees (senate: nineteen Democrats to seven Republicans; house: nineteen Democrats to nine Republicans). Furthermore, the Republican governor, Jim Martin, was the only state executive in the nation without veto power.

Members of the redistricting committees were not solely motivated by broad partisan goals. Some professed altruistic aims of creating fair districts, but others were blunt about their desire to make sure that the redrawing of congressional district lines did not adversely affect their own districts. Still others had their sights on higher office, whether moving from the state house to the state senate or moving from the state level to the national level (personal interviews, August 1991– March 1992). One important feature of both the house and the senate committees was the prominent role of black lawmakers. Six of the ten black house members and three of the five black senators (all Democrats) sat on the redistricting committees. Thus, 60 percent of the black house and senate members were on the redistricting committees, compared to only 20 percent of the whites in the house (22 of 110) and 49 percent of the whites in the senate (23 of 47). Of the nine black lawmakers on the two committees, two (Mickey Michaux and Thomas Hardaway) actually ran for a U.S. House seat in 1992, and three others (Toby Fitch, Howard Hunter, and Frank Ballance) were often mentioned in the newspapers as strong potential candidates. We discuss the influence of these black lawmakers on the creation of black congressional districts later in the chapter.

Two initial questions confronted the redistricting committees as they considered how to create at least one minority district: (1) Which minority groups should be considered in creating the new district? (2) Where would the district or districts be located? Answering the first question was relatively easy. Unlike states such as California or Texas, North Carolina does not have a large Hispanic population. Since the state is only 1 percent Hispanic and 1 percent Native American, it was clear that the focus of minority representation would be on African Americans. Although Republicans and the NAACP made a brief appeal for three minority districts (two black majority and one black and American Indian majority), their argument fell on deaf ears because most members of the black community rejected the notion that Native Americans and African Americans jointly represent a cohesive minority community.[9]

Answering the second question was also relatively straightforward as long as only one black district was created. According to State Representative Thomas Hardaway (D), a black member of the house redistricting committee, the obvious place to put the district was in northeastern North Carolina because that is the "black belt" of the state (see fig. 3.1; personal interview, March 8, 1992). In July and August of 1991 the state house and senate worked out the details of redistricting plan #6, which included a single black majority congressional district in the northeastern part of the state (see fig. 3.2).

The contorted shapes of the resulting congressional districts, however, provoked immediate controversy. Political commentators poked fun at the shape of the new minority-majority district, calling it "modern art," "political pornography," "a bug splattered on a windshield," and the work of an "eight month old baby" or a "chimpanzee playing with a felt-tip pen." Underlying the humor were serious concerns about the new district. In what would be an uneasy alliance, the Republican Party, the NAACP, and the ACLU criticized the new plan for serving the interests of congressional incumbents more than the interests of minorities.

Republican legislators argued that the Democrats did not create a second black majority congressional seat because they wanted to preserve as many safe Democratic seats as possible. Under plan #6 the seven districts that were currently controlled by Democrats were likely

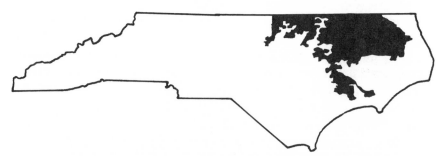

Figure 3.2 Redistricting Plan #6: Proposed by Democrats, June 1991; Approved by General Assembly, September 1991; Rejected by U.S. Justice Department, December 1991
Source: North Carolina General Assembly, Legislative Services Office.

to remain so. The Republicans would also keep their four districts, and the new 12th District would have a majority of Republican voters. Thus, the balance of power would still favor the Democrats, but now the margin would be seven to five instead of seven to four.

As an alternative to the Democratic plan, the Republicans suggested creating a second black majority district in the southern part of the state running from Charlotte to Wilmington. The obvious motivation behind this concern for minority representation is the partisan advantage gained by concentrating traditionally strong Democratic black vote in two districts. Under this Republican alternative, called the Balmer plan for its author, State Representative David Balmer, the GOP would create two strongly Democratic black majority districts and protect all four Republican incumbents (see fig. 3.3). In addition, three other districts would be dominated by conservative white voters who have a history of voting for Republicans, such as Senator Jesse Helms and Governor Jim Martin. Consequently Republicans could have held a seven-to-five majority in the North Carolina congressional delegation under this plan.

While they could not support the Balmer plan, members of the black community were torn between Democratic Party loyalty and the desire to create more than one black majority district. Moderate black state legislators, such as Daniel T. Blue, the first black speaker of the North Carolina House, argued that a single black majority district would be the best way to increase power for minorities. Even progressively ambitious black lawmakers, such as Mickey Michaux and Toby Fitch, who would probably have benefitted from a second minority district, favored the Democratic plan for a single black majority district. But in an interview with the *Durham Herald-Sun* Michaux admitted that the

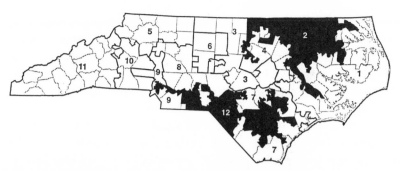

Figure 3.3 The Balmer Plan: Proposed by Republicans, June 1991; Rejected by General Assembly, September 1991
Source: North Carolina General Assembly, Legislative Services Office.

single minority district was not popular in the black community and so most black lawmakers kept a "low profile" in the debate (Lineberry 1992, A1). Fitch was worried that a second black congressional seat could isolate blacks on "political reservations"[10] and "provide major gains for Republicans" (Denton 1991). Leaders in the black community who were not so closely tied to the Democratic Party, such as Mary L. Peeler, executive director for the North Carolina branch of the NAACP, argued that "we wanted to see a maximization of the black voting strength in North Carolina" (Denton 1991a, 8J). The ACLU joined the NAACP in rejecting the single black majority congressional district plan. For these groups the question was one of fairness. In a state that was 22 percent black one of twelve House seats was simply not enough. Despite this resistance, the General Assembly finally approved plan #6 and its single black district in September.

As plan #6 became law, progressively ambitious candidates begin gearing up for the 1992 congressional primaries. Consistent with the expectations of ambition theory and previous work on the candidate-centered nature of congressional campaigns (Rohde 1979; Jacobson and Kernell 1983; Canon 1990) and our supply-side theory, quality challengers emerged in the two new districts that did not appear to have incumbents running. In the newly created 12th Congressional District the absence of an incumbent and the fact that the district had more registered Republicans than Democrats quickly attracted two quality white Republican candidates. North Carolina Representative Coy Privette (R) announced that he would run in the 12th. His motivation for entering the race stemmed from the fact that the new district included his current state house district (Cabarrus County) and the

county in which he was raised (Iredell County). Joining Privette in the
Republican primary was Alan Pugh, an aide to Governor Martin.
Pugh quit his job, rented a headquarters in the 12th District, hired a
campaign manager and a political consultant, and raised more than
$10,000 over the next several months (*Charlotte Observer,* May 14,
1992, 2C).

Activity in the new 1st District was also heavy, but it was mostly on
the Democratic side. The newly created black majority district had
one potential problem for progressively ambitious black candidates: a
white Democratic incumbent. The new 1st was carved out of parts
of four old congressional districts that had produced well-entrenched
incumbents who almost never faced major challengers. In 1991 it
seemed likely that these incumbents would run for reelection in the
following year, with the possible exception of Walter Jones, Sr., the 1st
District incumbent. A challenge to Jones was out of the question, so
prospective candidates were forced to engage in a high-stakes guessing game.

Although Jones, the most senior member of the North Carolina congressional delegation, claimed that he was not retiring, most legislators
and political elites in the state believed that he would. At seventy-eight
years of age the incumbent suffered from poor health and had to be
wheeled through the halls of Congress by an aide. Furthermore, if
Jones retired by 1993, current law allowed him to convert his $300,000
campaign war chest to personal use. Those predicting that Jones *would*
retire also reasoned that the redistricting committees would never have
included so much of his old district in the new 1st if he were *not* retiring. A fellow U.S. Democratic House member told us that Jones initially accepted the redistricting plan, but he thought that the state redistricting committees should have had more contact with him. This
U.S. House member seemed to imply that the state legislature simply
assumed that Jones was retiring without consulting him, thus creating
a "humiliating" situation for Jones (personal interview, August 8,
1991). Jones officially announced his retirement on October 5, 1991,
citing the new black majority district as the primary reason for his
decision (Christensen 1991, 1A).

The clearest signal to state lawmakers that Jones would retire, however, was the fact that he took no interest in the redistricting process.
Danny Lineberry, a political correspondent covering the redistricting
story for the *Durham Herald-Sun,* attended many of the redistricting
meetings and saw quite a few congressional staffers, but never saw a

staff member from Walter Jones's office. Although Jones publicly indicated his displeasure with his new district and never suggested that he planned to retire, one state lawmaker told the *News and Observer* (Raleigh, N.C.), "Other congressmen were heavily involved in trying to protect their districts, but Mr. Jones made no telephone calls and sent no letters objecting to redistricting proposals" (September 25, 1991, 2B).

We asked all potential black candidates who were mentioned by newspaper reporters or political leaders in eastern North Carolina whether Jones was a factor in their decision to run in 1992 (see Canon, Schousen, and Sellers 1994). All of these politicians told us that Jones would have a strong impact on the election if he ran, but none of them believed he would run. For example, Warren County Commissioner Eva Clayton said she thought from the beginning that Jones was going to retire. State Senator Frank Ballance claimed that Jones's wavering about retirement was merely an attempt to help his son, Walter Jones, Jr., by discouraging others from entering the race (personal interviews, March 6, 1991, and others in the spring and summer of 1991).

Although it was too early to file, a number of strong black candidates began organizing their campaigns in the new 1st District. Included in this list of black candidates were Ballance, Clayton, State Representative Toby Fitch, State Representative Thomas Hardaway, State Representative Howard Hunter, the Reverend Staccato Powell, and Willie Riddick, a long-time aide to Walter Jones, Sr.

Act II—Back to the Drawing Board: Plan #10

In compliance with the preclearance provision of Section 5 of the Voting Rights Act of 1965 the General Assembly sent plan #6 to the Justice Department. Democratic lawmakers and party leaders were confident that the plan would be approved. Republicans and members of the black community, however, filed complaints urging rejection of the plan on the grounds that it violated the rights of minorities.

On December 19, 1991, just seventeen days before the beginning of the filing period for congressional elections, the Justice Department rejected the North Carolina redistricting plan. The ruling cited the "unusually convoluted" shape of the black majority district and the fact that the plan created only one such district. Some critics argued that the Justice Department went beyond the intention of the 1982

Amendments and used its Section 5 preclearance power for partisan purposes (Denton 1992b, 10A; 1991, 5A). Particularly the Justice Department ignored the "geographic compactness" condition of *Gingles,* thus going beyond the prevention of minority vote dilution to an actual proportional representation test for minority representation in the U.S. House. The possible partisan motivation is clear when one considers that the creation of black majority districts usually helps the Republican Party by concentrating Democratic voters in a few districts · (Brace, Grofman, and Handley, 1987).

Back in North Carolina the legislature called a special December 30 session to address the Justice Department's decision. Democratic lawmakers knew that a second black majority district in the southern part of the state could deeply hurt their party, so they scrambled to find a less painful alternative. Some wanted to fight for the current plan in court. John Merrit, an aide to U.S. Representative Charles Rose (D–NC), proposed plan #10, which created a second minority district by connecting black voters in Charlotte and Durham by a thin line that traveled northeast along Interstate 85 (fig. 3.4) rather than from Charlotte to Wilmington, as the Republicans proposed in the Balmer plan (fig. 3.3).

Democrats found the Merrit plan appealing because it created a second minority district without diluting Democratic power across the state. In fact, they believed that the new plan might actually increase the number of Democratic seats in the House. In addition to creating another minority district, the plan did not hurt any of the seven Democratic incumbents. Three Republican incumbents would be placed in even safer Republican strongholds, while the fourth Republican, U.S. Representative Charles Taylor, would end up in a marginally Democratic district. Thus, under the Merrit plan Democrats hoped to win nine of the twelve congressional seats in North Carolina. As it turned out, the Democrats won eight seats because Taylor won his reelection bid.

Republicans had been assuming that the second new black majority district would be in the southern part of the state. The new plan left them stunned. They complained bitterly about the new district's odd shape. They had a point. In Guilford County, for example, drivers in the southbound lanes would be in the Republican-controlled 6th District, while drivers in the northbound lanes would be in the new black majority 12th District. As they traveled down the interstate to Randolph County, the congressional districts actually "changed lanes." Southbound drivers were now in the 12th District, and northbound

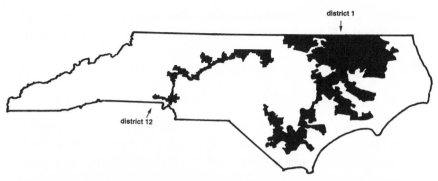

Figure 3.4 Redistricting Plan #10: Proposed by Democrats, January 1992; Approved by General Assembly, January 1992; Approved by U.S. Justice Department, February 1992
Source: North Carolina General Assembly, Legislative Services Office.

drivers were in the 6th District (Denton 1992a, 1C). The strange "u-turn" on the interstate was necessary to keep the 6th District contiguous (without the lane change the 6th would have been cleanly bisected by the 12th District).

The new "I–85" black majority district was literally the width of the interstate in some places. Farther south on I–85, drivers traveling either north or south were in the 12th, but the moment they turned onto any exit ramp (on either side of the road) they were in the 9th (Morrill and Trevor 1992, 4A). This strange configuration led Democratic candidate Mickey Michaux to say that in some counties a driver could travel down I–85 with his doors open and kill everyone in the congressional district. He also joked that it should be an easy district to campaign in because he could meet all the voters by simply visiting at all the rest stops along the interstate.

Plan #10 retained the black majority district in eastern North Carolina. However, the basic outline of the district moved east and south, with tentacles extending into Wilmington and Fayetteville. The most significant change for the eastern black majority district was the exclusion of urban Durham, which accounted for 15.5 percent of the northeastern district under plan #6. The district lines were considerably more contorted than in the earlier plan: the new 1st District has a perimeter that is 2,039 miles long, and it contains nine whole counties and parts of nineteen others.

The primary filing period was due to open on January 5, 1992, but lawmakers postponed it until February 10. Top-ranking Democratic state lawmakers held private meetings with the North Carolina Democratic congressional delegation, state black leaders, and representatives from the NAACP and ACLU. The groups agreed that the Merrit plan was acceptable, and after working out the details, the General Assembly approved plan #10 on January 24, 1992.

Act III—The Final Challenge before the Primaries

Democratic leaders were apologetic, while Republicans were apoplectic about the plan. House Speaker Blue said, "'It is an ugly plan. I will not stand here and tell you these are the most symmetrical, prettiest districts I have ever seen. . . . There are some funny looking districts.'" But Blue argued that Democrats were forced to make the new plan because of the Justice Department's ruling (quoted in Denton 1992b, 10A). Republicans called the plan "idiotic" (*News and Observer* [Raleigh, N.C.], January 29, 1992, 5B). They offered an amendment to add a third black majority district, but it was rejected in a party-line vote. State Republican Party Chairman Jack Hawke said his party would urge the Justice Department to reject plan #10. If it did not, the Republicans would file suit in court. But in spite of this Republican threat, the Justice Department approved the plan on February 7, just three days before the delayed beginning of the filing period. State legislators immediately said that the 1992 primaries would go on as scheduled, with the filing period running from February 10 to March 2.

Hawke made good on his promise to file suit on behalf of the state Republican Party. He argued that a third black majority congressional district should be added. The suit specifically charged that the new plan violated the voters' rights to "freedom of association and to fair and effective representation" (Ruffin 1992, 1A). When the suit was filed, the court left open the filing deadline for congressional candidates until the case could be heard. At a hearing in Charlotte on March 9, a three-member U.S. district court dismissed the case and ruled that the filing period would close immediately. Although the Republicans appealed to the Supreme Court to overturn the lower court decision, Chief Justice William Rehnquist rejected the request on March 11. For the moment the court challenge was over. When the dust settled, the filing period had ended, and the primary campaign was on.

The New 1st and 12th Congressional Districts

In plan #10, the final redistricting plan, the North Carolina General Assembly pieced together the new 1st Congressional District from parts of four old congressional districts. Each of the old districts contained diverse constituencies. The original 1st, 3rd, and 7th Districts included relatively poor farming counties, several sizable military bases, and prosperous coastal counties, which relied heavily on tourism for economic growth. The old 2nd District contained both rural counties and the city of Durham, whose urban constituents made up 22.6 percent of the district's population.

The new 1st District was more homogeneous than the original four districts. The plan removed Durham, the coastal areas that rely on tourism, and the military bases from the 1st District. The remaining counties are covered largely by tobacco fields and drying sheds, and their populations rely largely on farming for income. While some businesses have built plants in the new district, many of the available jobs provide low wages. Political leaders from the area frequently devote attention and resources to increasing economic development. In addition, the district clearly meets the Justice Department's requirements for minority representation. In the new 1st District blacks formed a majority of the total population (57.3 percent) and voting-age population (53.4 percent). Not surprisingly almost 90 percent of voters in the 1st District were registered Democrats.

The new 12th District was, in several ways, similar to the new 1st. The Democrats had a four-to-one advantage over Republicans in the 12th, and over half of total population (56.6 percent) and voting-age population (53.3 percent) was black. Also like the 1st the 12th was pieced together using bits of several counties and other congressional districts. No single North Carolina county was wholly contained within the snake-line district that wound its way through parts of ten counties and seven of the eleven old congressional districts (the 12th contains parts of the 1980s districts 2, 4, 5, 6, 8, 9, and 10).

While they did have some similarities, the two black majority districts also had some fundamental differences. The 1st was primarily a rural district (58 percent of the people were in rural areas), while the 12th was an urban district made up of voters from Charlotte, Winston-Salem, Greensboro, and Durham (93.2 percent urban, according to the 1990 U.S. Census). The two districts also differed on a socioeconomic level. The 1st was the poorest district in the state, while the 12th was about average. For example, in the 1st District only 57.8 percent of those twenty-five years of age or older held high school diplomas. In the 12th the figure was 65.6 percent, which is closer to the 70 percent state average. A similar pattern was evident for median house value and median household income. The 1st was last in the state, with a median house value of $46,100 and a household income median of $18,226. The 12th had a median house value of $58,400 (state median $65,800) and a median household income of $23,068 (state median $26,647).

The two districts also differed in terms of black political organiza-tion. In the 12th the two largest segments of voters were from Charlotte and Durham. Both cities have strong black political organizations, and each city produced a strong black candidate in 1992 (Mel Watt from Charlotte and Mickey Michaux from Durham). In the 1st, as Eva Clayton told us, there are no black political organizations to rally vot-ers or get a candidate's message out. Clayton added that she was sorry to hear that Durham was no longer going to be in the 1st District because at least in Durham voters show up at political events. Clayton said that she was tired of going from small town to small town speak-ing to only a handful of people at a time. When we asked her whether she would like Durham in the 1st if it meant Mickey Michaux would be in the race, she replied, "You're darn right" (personal interview, March 6, 1991). Part of her strategy had been to use Durham as a place to get name recognition, money, and media exposure.

Assessing the Strategic Context of Redistricting

Black state lawmakers played an important role in the redistricting pro-cess. As noted above, three of the five black state senators served on the Senate Redistricting Committee, and six of the ten black state house members served on the House Redistricting Committee. Of these nine black lawmakers five of them either ran for a congressional seat or strongly considered running. All five were considered strong candi-dates. What is most interesting, however, is that until the Justice De-partment required a second black majority district, none of these five potential candidates publicly supported plans that called for the cre-ation of two or three black controlled congressional districts (personal interviews and Lineberry 1992, A1). Black lawmakers generally be-lieved that a second minority district would limit the effectiveness of black politicians and increase Republican clout across the state.

Nevertheless, the redistricting process was subject to manipulation by both blacks and whites. As with many legislative committees, the redistricting committees performed much of their work in informal, "behind-the-scenes" settings, with limited publicity. Consequently it is difficult to uncover the potential candidates' efforts to draw the district lines in ways that furthered their electoral interests (especially because candidates do not readily admit to self-serving strategic behavior).

In one case, however, we were told that a black lawmaker did try to influence the redistricting process. According to two sources, a newspaper reporter and a politically active Democrat, Thomas Hardaway came up with the idea for the "I–85" district and presented it to Merrit. The congressional staffer then refined it and presented it as his own plan. Hardaway denies that he was the source of the plan, but if the story is true, it is an interesting twist to the tale.[11]

Under plan #6 Hardaway would have run against Mickey Michaux in North Carolina's new 1st Congressional District. Our interviews in eastern North Carolina revealed that Michaux did not enjoy extensive support in the rural areas of the 1st District; however, he was considered by many political commentators to be the front-runner.

Michaux ran unsuccessfully for an open seat in the old 2nd District in 1982, narrowly losing a runoff election to Tim Valentine after defeating Valentine and one other white candidate in the primary (Michaux had 44 percent, Valentine had 33 percent, and James Ramsey won 23 percent of the vote in the first round). Therefore, some of the state's black leaders believed that Michaux deserved the seat that he almost won. During the summer of 1991 Michaux expressed active interest in running for the 1st District congressional seat.[12] Under the Merrit plan Michaux's hometown, Durham, was placed in the new 12th District. As a result Michaux did not run in the 1st, and the path was cleared for Hardaway and other ambitious state representatives in the 1st District. However, even without Michaux to contend with, Hardaway still could not win the Democratic primary in eastern North Carolina.

Walter Jones, Jr., was at the center of several other redistricting machinations. Jones, Jr., believed that he had been punished in the drawing of state house lines because of his "independent" record in the state house.[13] His old district was split in half, making it much more difficult for him to win reelection to his state house seat. Jones, Jr.'s plan to run for his father's seat was complicated when his hometown (Farmville) was removed from the 1st Congressional District, after being included in the initial versions of the redistricting plans that were debated in January. Immediately before the final committee vote on the plan Jones introduced an amendment to return Farmville to the 1st District. The amendment passed with the approval of all nine committee Republicans and several blacks on the committee, who, according to Jones, Jr., were later criticized by others in the black community. When the redistricting plan reached the house floor, Jones, Jr., said that a black representative introduced an amendment to take Farmville back out of the 1st District. The amendment was defeated, but the vote had definite racial overtones, according to Jones, Jr. Although he had voted against all the redistricting plans up to this point, he felt compelled to vote for this final one. Jones, Jr., said that the people of Farmville had suffered enough (with their state house district split) and that the General Assembly had treated his people and his father unfairly.

Potential candidates on the redistricting committees in the state legislature were not the only ones trying to influence the district lines for personal electoral gain. The staff of the current congressional incumbents closely monitored the redistricting process and in some cases played an important role. A local reporter saw incumbents' staffers at many redistricting committee hearings, and one member of the North Carolina congressional delegation acknowledged that "we all had people at the redistricting meetings, and we all made suggestions concerning our districts" (personal interview, August 8, 1991). Private memos that were later made public indicate the extent to which North Carolina Democratic members of Congress were kept informed of the redistricting committees' activities. In one memo Congressman Price writes that his new district is "satisfactory" so long as East and West Pittsboro are added and parts of Alamance County are removed. In another memo a staff member from State Senate Redistricting Committee Chairman Dennis Winner's office asks U.S. Representative Martin Lancaster (D–NC) whether moving several precincts in Duplin and Onslow Counties from the 2nd District to the 3rd District would be acceptable. The memo states that the idea is just part of a "draft plan for discussion" and suggests that Lancaster not share the information with others (*News and Observer* [Raleigh, N.C.], August 25, 1991, 6C). Most significantly, as we pointed out earlier, the staff of U.S. Representative Rose played an important role in the formulation of the final redistricting plan that the Justice Department approved.

The Impact of Redistricting on Candidate Decisions to Run and the Campaign

The profound changes in North Carolina's congressional districts created a new strategic context for the black community. David Perlmutt of the *Charlotte Observer* provided evidence for the first causal effect of the supply-side theory, claiming that "[n]ever in North Carolina has a state or federal election drawn so many black candidates—and shaped a debate so central to black voters in a number of the state's major cities" (Perlmutt 1992, 1A). For this reason many in the black community considered the redistricting process a great success.

Samuel Moseley, a political scientist at North Carolina A&T State University, argued that qualified black politicians, such as Mickey Michaux of Durham, simply could not win before the new black majority districts were created. "It was clear here, that we had a man [Michaux] who was black and qualified and who could not win. After all these years of frustration to see the tide turn to a level playing field is gratifying" (Perlmutt 1992, 12A). (Moseley is referring to Michaux's unsuccessful bid for a U.S. House seat in 1982.)

Although the redistricting process provided new opportunities for ambitious black politicians and black voters, it also had some serious short-term costs for other candidates. The two quality white Republicans who decided to run in the Republican-leaning 12th District under plan #6 were forced out of the race when plan #6 was rejected by the Justice Department and the 12th became a second black majority district. Coy Privette ended up in the 8th District, running against the strongly entrenched nine-term Democratic incumbent, Bill Hefner. Alan Pugh, who had quit his job to run, decided to bow out completely and vowed to refund prorated shares of all contributions given to him (*Charlotte Observer,* May 14, 1992, 2C).

Within the black community the late formation of the districts and the uncertainty surrounding their exact location created several problems. In the 12th all four Democratic candidates got off to a late start. It became difficult for the candidates to get their message out because they lacked sufficient time to organize fund-raising for purchasing TV and radio spots. This gave the advantage to Mickey Michaux and Mel Watt. Michaux was advantaged because he had already decided to run under plan #6 when Durham was in the black majority district in the eastern part of the state. Watt was in a relatively strong position because he had previously served one term in the state senate in the area and was campaign manager for Harvey Gantt's successful campaign for mayor of Charlotte and unsuccessful campaign for Jesse Helms's Senate seat. Consequently Watt already had a strong political organization in Charlotte.

Uncertainty about the placement of district lines delayed the initiation of many candidates' campaigns in the 1st District. In our 1st District interviews all candidates said that they did not begin organizing their campaigns until after the General Assembly's approval of the first redistricting plan, and the three white candidates—Brandon, Smith, and Jones, Jr.—started their campaigns after the passage of the second plan. Jones in particular expressed his frustration at how the short period between the plan's final approval and the May primary hurt his ability to raise money and set up a campaign organization. Eva Clayton seemed to be least affected by the uncertainty surrounding redistricting, at least in term of fund-raising. She spent more than all of the other candidates combined and outspent her nearest competitor, Walter Jones, Jr., by more than two to one (see table 3.1). Political action committees (PACs) contributed more than half of her receipts (54 percent), with about half of the PAC money coming from labor. Women's groups, including Emily's List, were the second biggest contributor, giving more than $39,000 to her campaign (about 8 percent of her total receipts). Other candidates complained that it was difficult to get their organization in place when they did not know where the district lines would be drawn.

The late start also influenced the level of voter interest in and awareness of the campaign. The Democratic candidates in the 12th held a series of debates to get their messages out, but the largest meeting in Charlotte drew only thirty-five people. In another debate, in Salisbury, only five people who were not directly connected to one of the campaigns showed up. Although the two strongest candidates, Michaux and Watt, were able to air radio ads right before the primary, all four of the candidates claimed that it was an "uphill" battle to get their message out to the voters (Perlmutt 1992, 12A). Similar problems were created by the shortened campaign season in the 1st District.

The Racial Context

RACE AS A SUBJECTIVE FILTER. Race serves as a filter through which subjective assessments of the electoral context are made. Racial issues and conflict run throughout North Carolina history. Most recently race played a central role in the 1990 and 1996 U.S. Senate contests between incumbent Jesse Helms and challenger Harvey Gantt. The 1st District race is no exception to this pattern of racial tension. Party officials and potential candidates openly described the election as two separate races, one black and one white. A black county party chair expressed concern that the current congressional incumbents (Valentine and Jones, Sr.) had failed to represent black interests. The party chair also expressed doubt about whether any of the current white candidates could adequately represent black interests. Much of the black community holds a strong suspicion of the white candidates and the white-dominated media.[14] In our interviews the black interviewees and potential candidates were much more concerned about our credentials than were their white counterparts. This suspicion explains the secrecy surrounding the meetings and votes of the Black Leadership Caucus; blacks feared that any leaks would be used to divide and exploit the black community. One black candidate described the tension facing the black community between wanting to consider candidates regardless of race and wanting to elect a black member of Congress. Many blacks view the latter as a way of achieving the former.

Most of the white interviewees, in contrast, saw color-blind evaluation of candidates as the proper short-term and long-term goals. Several white politicians mentioned some resentment in the white community over the fact that the new district was created for blacks. One white county party chair criticized the black community's attempts to agree on a consensus black candidate. The party chair did not believe that it was right to deprive voters of a choice in the primary. Another white Democratic Party chair talked glowingly of the strategy that Gantt adopted in eastern North Carolina. He said that Gantt emphasized family issues instead of black issues. Instead of going to black churches, Gantt held rallies at schools, mainly in white areas. The county party chair believed that the ideal candidate in the 1st District must adopt a similar strategy, which would win white votes. The party chair added that while most people are aware of racial issues, it is important to defuse them (personal interview, August 20, 1991).

In our interviews the white candidates in the 1st District claimed a strong commitment to representing black voters. Jones, Jr., believed that race was not a central issue and that he could represent all the people in the district, blacks and whites. The other white candidates also downplayed the tensions that seemed to exist between the two communities. None of the white candidates mentioned the black community's suspicions, which were extremely evident in interviews with black interviewees and candidates. In early March none of the white candidates had contacted the black Democratic Party chair of Edgecombe County, who lives within thirty miles of Jones and Brandon. This county holds 5.8 percent of the 1st District's registered voters, the second-highest percentage of any county in the district (recall there are parts of twenty-eight counties in the district). The lack of contact was perceived by the chair as providing further evidence of the tensions and conflicts between the black and white communities.

RACE AND THE SUPPLY-SIDE EFFECT.   The 12th District is over 80 percent Democratic, and all four of the Democratic candidates were black. These two facts meant that no matter who won the Democratic primary, a black politician would almost certainly be representing the 12th District. It also meant that the black candidate who appealed to the largest percentage of white voters was likely to win given that the black vote would be split, as specified by the second causal effect of the supply-side theory. This is exactly what happened as Mel Watt emerged from the Democratic primary with 47 percent of the vote and strong support in the white precincts.

Descriptive representation was up for grabs, as was substantive representation, in the 1st District, where Walter Jones, Jr., could have taken advantage of a divided black vote and a united white vote to win the new black majority district. This was especially true because the percentage of the vote necessary to win a primary outright had recently been reduced from 50 percent to 40 percent. Ironically this change was intended to help elect more black candidates, but it nearly ended up putting Walter Jones, Jr., in office.

Black leaders in the 1st District recognized their potential collective action problem and acted quickly to try to unify behind a single black candidate. The Black Leadership Caucus (BLC), which is organized by congressional district across North Carolina, met on three occasions. Representatives from each county were to cast weighted votes (one voter per 1,000 black voters) for their preferred candidates. However, the process broke down when one candidate, Willie Riddick, was seen by the other candidates as having unfairly manipulated the meetings to his advantage. Two of the leading candidates did not even attend one of the meetings, and others did not have their supporters there. Thus, the process lacked legitimacy, and several of the candidates refused to bow out when they did not receive the BLC endorsement.

Four black candidates—Frank Ballance, Howard Hunter, Paul Jones, and Toby Fitch—dropped out to enhance the probability of electing an African American. Ballance dropped out before the endorsement vote, and Hunter, Jones, and Fitch were pursuing a mix of altruistic and self-interested strategies. Fitch was most explicit about his motives. As cochair of the state house redistricting committee, Fitch led the effort to create a black majority district. He believed that the entrance of several black candidates into the race would split the black vote and threaten the election of a black member of Congress. Thus, he did not want to have a part in undermining the collective goal that he worked for a year to achieve; in an interview he emphasized that this was his only reason for quitting the race. At the same time, though, he recognized that by dropping out, his political standing in the 1st District black community improved dramatically. If Jones, Jr., defeated the current group of black candidates, Fitch believed that the black community would unite behind him in 1994 and turn out the first-term white incumbent. The fact that Eva Clayton, a black, won the election did not temper his desire to run for Congress. A local reporter told us that Fitch was seriously considering challenging Clayton in the 1994 Democratic primary (personal interview, October 14, 1993), but he ended up not running.

While it may appear that Fitch played a risky game that did not pan out, we believe the strategy may have been less risky than the alternatives. In our interviews in July and August the interviewees referred to Fitch as a potential candidate, but he was rarely described as "the leading candidate." One reporter described his candidacy as "not serious." After his second-place finish in the straw vote Fitch may have decided that his chances in the primary were far from certain and that trying to be the consensus fall-back candidate was his best strategy to win a congressional seat.

With 33.8 percent of the new district comprised of his senate district, Ballance could have been a very strong candidate (see table 3.1). He bowed out of the race to avoid dividing the black vote as well, but his motivations were slightly different. Ballance is clearly not as ambitious as Fitch or the candidates who decided to run. He told us that the only reason he ran for the state house in 1982 was that local political leaders drafted him. His run for the state senate was similarly motivated. Local leaders told him that he would be the best black candidate to run for the senate seat. As the consensus black candidate in his previous elections Ballance did not like the idea of competing against other quality minority candidates in this congressional election. When asked if he would consider running in the future, Ballance said that he would run if a white candidate won this time around and the black community rallied behind him. This potential candidacy illustrates the complex interactions among personal ambition (Schlesinger 1966), race, and constituency.

Relationships between the various candidates also influenced candidacy decisions. For example, another reason Ballance did not run is that he respected Clayton's abilities as a candidate and a potential representative. More uncertain relationships existed among Jones, Sr., his son, and Riddick. Both candidates claimed to be the rightful successor of the elder Jones. Jones, Jr., acknowledged their competing claims to the seat and said that he encouraged Riddick to run (indeed, as we will argue below, it was in his interest to have Riddick split the black vote). Jones, Sr., offered conflicting signals about which of the two he supported. In November, before Jones, Jr., entered the race, he openly endorsed Riddick, but three days later he qualified his support, saying that he had only been saying "nice things" about Riddick. During this same period Jones, Jr., was actively considering running for state auditor or lieutenant governor.[15] He later decided to run in the 1st District congressional race. Jones, Sr., did not endorse either one. One local commentator speculated that the two candidates would simply divide the elder Jones's support and organization, largely along racial lines, though he added that each candidate could expect some support from the opposite race.

An intriguing interpretation of this relationship was that Riddick was running to split the black vote and help Jones, Jr., get elected. At first we discounted this story because the initial source was one of the other black candidates in the race. But later we had independent confirmation from three other reliable sources (one claimed it was "common knowledge"). When asked about Riddick's campaign, one state representative nearly exploded:

> That man! He prostituted himself for a job. He was never a serious candidate. All he wanted to do was help Jones, Jr., win. I don't believe in giving the district to one person and then handing it down to his son. It's wrong. The district was created to help elect a black American and he is trying to help Jones. (personal interview, May 28, 1992)

Another source heard secondhand through Jones, Jr.'s press secretary that Riddick offered to drop out of the race if Jones, Jr., would give him a job. But Jones, Jr., convinced Riddick that he would do him more good if he stayed in the race and hinted that he would get a job if he stayed in the race. This source also claimed that Riddick was just part of the Jones machine and pointed out that Riddick boycotted a last-minute meeting called by Clayton to get the black community behind a single candidate. One week before the primary election Hardaway went public with his charges, saying, "I find it incredible that anyone in the black community would throw their support to Willie Riddick when he is nothing but a part of the plan to keep the Jones machine in control of the first Congressional District." Riddick denied the charges, saying, "It's unfortunate they have to resort to this kind of negative campaigning to try to stop me. There has not been any deal cut" (*News and Observer* [Raleigh, N.C.], April 28, 1992, 2B). Even if this story is false, and honestly we were not sure whom to believe, a substantial proportion of the black leaders we interviewed saw Riddick as a traitor. Perception, in this case, is reality.

Perhaps even more interesting is the chain of events and strategic behavior surrounding the most unlikely of the candidates, Don Smith. Smith entered the race because an article he read in his local paper, *The Daily Reflector,* led him to believe that Jones, Jr., was the only white candidate in the race (Smith thought that Brandon was black). This struck Smith as unfair because the district was created to elect a black and he thought that Jones would win if he were the only white. Smith's candidacy was "an attempt to level the playing field," and so if Jones, Jr., were to win, "he would have to earn it fairly in a one-on-one runoff" rather than by splitting the black vote. At one of the election rallies, Smith met Brandon's campaign manager, Otis Carter, who is black. This reinforced Smith's assumption that Brandon was black. Smith was in for a surprise the first time he met Brandon at a candidate forum, but interestingly Brandon and his campaign manager encouraged Smith to stay in the race to split Jones's vote. As it turned out, Smith did not affect the outcome of the race; he only received 1.5 percent of the vote, while Jones, Jr., missed winning the election by 2.6 percent. Nonetheless he considered it a well-spent $1,250 (the amount of the filing fee) and said that the experience "gave me a good education in politics, and for much cheaper than I could have gotten at Duke!" (personal interview, May 27, 1992).

Summary and Recent Developments in North Carolina

The 1992 congressional elections sent two African Americans to the U.S. Congress from a state that had not sent a black representative to Capitol Hill since 1898. The uncertainty over the future of their careers is being imposed by the courts rather than the North Carolina voters. The legal challenges between 1993 and 1998 provided a roller-coaster ride for Watt and Clayton. *Shaw v. Reno* started things off on a low point in June 1993, but the ride was less turbulent in 1994. On March 9, 1994, a federal court ruled, in a two-to-one decision, that the congressional elections in the two minority-majority districts could go forward even though those districts were being challenged in federal court.

Watt and Clayton were unopposed in the May primary, and they received more good news on August 1, 1994, when a three-member federal court ruled (in *Shaw v. Hunt* 1994) that the new black majority districts passed constitutional muster. Although Watt and Clayton both faced Republican challengers in November, both incumbents won easily (Watt won 66 percent of the district vote against weak Republican challenger Joseph Martin; Clayton faced Republican challenger Ted Tyler again and won 61 percent of the vote). However, in 1996 the Supreme Court overturned that decision. The district lines were allowed to stand for one more election because it was viewed as impractical to redraw the district lines so close to the fall election, and Watt and Clayton were easily reelected once again. The state legislature redrew the district lines for the 1998 elections, but everything was thrown into turmoil again when a federal district court struck down the new 12th District, which was 45.6 percent black, and the Supreme Court refused to postpone the primary elections. The state legislature approved a new plan on May 21, 1998, and reduced the percentage of black voters in the 12th District to 35.6 percent. The Supreme Court will rule on the constitutionality of the 45.6 percent black district in the spring 1999 term.

The other major development concerning redistricting in North Carolina was the shifting partisan implications of the new black districts. As noted above, the Democratic state legislators pulled off a major coup when they were able to protect all the existing Democratic districts, while adding the new black districts in 1992. However, the 1994 Republican landslide reversed those Democratic gains in North Carolina: the state delegation went from eight Democrats and four Republicans to just the reverse. One of the key players of the 1992 1st District race, Walter Jones, Jr., also played a pivotal role in 1994. After his defeat in 1992, Jones, Jr., changed his strategy. He switched parties and congressional districts to run as a Republican in North Carolina's 3rd District. A large portion of the 3rd was made up of the pre-redistricted 1st, which his father held from 1966 to 1992. Although Jones, Jr., did not live in the district, he had strong name recognition and ran a shrewd campaign, linking the four-term Democratic incumbent, Martin Lancaster, to President Bill Clinton. Jones, Jr., flooded the district with television spots showing Clinton and Lancaster jogging together and citing Lancaster's support of Clinton's 1993 budget and tax packages. Jones, Jr., won the general election with 53 percent of the vote. In 1996 Democrats gained back two of the seats they lost in 1994, with David Price winning back a seat that he narrowly lost in 1994 in one of the nation's biggest upsets and Bob Etheridge beating first-term Republican David Funderburk in the 2nd District.

While the long-term partisan and racial implications of redistricting in North Carolina are unresolved, the relevance of the North Carolina case for the supply-side theory could not be more clear. In the introduction to this chapter we posited two causal effects suggested by the supply-side theory: large numbers of candidates should run in the new black majority districts, and the presence or absence of a white candidate should dictate the type of black candidate who wins. Seven candidates ran in the 1st District, and four ran in the 12th, so the new districts stimulated a great deal of candidate activity. The second causal effect is also present in North Carolina. In the 1st District, where one strong white candidate and two weak white candidates ran, Eva Clayton won by appealing primarily to the black voters, while making limited appeals to white voters. She clearly campaigned on the basis of a politics of difference. On the other hand, in the 12th District, where no white Democrat ran, the candidate who had the strongest appeal among white voters, Mel Watt, won the election, as predicted by the theory. Interestingly, this outcome is just the opposite of the conventional constituency-driven, demand-side theories. The conventional view would expect an urban district (the 12th) to produce a traditional black who is more closely linked to black voters and a rural district (the 1st) to produce the new-style, more biracial black.

The case study also provides evidence of a causal mechanism that would not have been evident had we relied exclusively on the multivariate analysis of the following section: racial politics infused the candidate emergence process and political campaign. Two candidates, Riddick and Smith, apparently ran to split the vote of a candidate of their own race and help elect a candidate of the other race. Whites and blacks had extremely different perceptions of the role of race in the politics of the 1st and 12th Districts: blacks were more likely to accentuate racial differences, while whites tended (or perhaps pretended) to ignore them. Finally, many blacks (and whites, as noted below) expressed a sense that it was "their turn" to elect a representative of their race to Congress.

This case study supports our supply-side theory, but more comprehensive analysis is needed to control for alternative explanations. Perhaps the two districts examined here attracted a broad range of candidates because there were no incumbents in either district. Maybe the impact of the presence or absence of white candidates in these districts was atypical. Such concerns can be examined only by analyzing a broader range of districts.

Specifying the Supply-Side Model

This section develops the assertion that perceived electoral opportunities influence the decisions of black candidates to run for Congress.[16] Figure 3.5 outlines the determinants of candidate activity (the number and quality of candidates who run) and the predicted supply-side effects in the Democratic primaries in districts where the population is at least 30 percent black. The factors in the top two boxes capture parts of the "calculus of candidacy" outlined by Gordon Black. He described the decision to run for office as a simple cost-benefit calculation (the utility of running is determined by the probability of winning times the benefits of running minus the costs of running; 1972, 146). New black districts, a high percentage of black voters, and the presence of a runoff primary will all increase the probability that several black candidates will run, while the presence of an incumbent will decrease the probability of winning and thus dampen the amount of candidate activity. The boxes in the bottom two-thirds of the diagram illustrate the impact of various yes-no conditions on the type of representative who will be elected in the district. For purposes of this discussion we categorize three types of candidates: whites, traditional blacks, and new-style blacks. Hypotheses 1–4 capture the expected relationships depicted in the top half of the diagram, while hypotheses 5–7 outline the predicted outcomes at the bottom of the diagram:

1. The number of black candidates will be higher in new black influence and black majority districts than in the existing black districts, due to the pent-up supply of candidates and the higher probability of winning.

2. The higher the district black population, the greater the number of black candidates.

3. More black candidates will run when a runoff provision exists because even if a black field is split, a white candidate cannot win with a plurality of the vote. Therefore, to the extent that the black community is interested in ensuring descriptive representation, the necessity of uniting behind a single candidate is obviated by the runoff provision.

4. The presence of an incumbent will reduce candidate activity. (We test for separate effects for white and black incumbents.)

5. If a single black candidate runs, there is no clear theoretical expectation concerning the nature of the electoral coalition.

6. If a traditional black, a new-style black, and a white run in the same district, the traditional black will win the nomination if there is a runoff election. If there is no runoff and the black vote is deeply split, the white could win; if not, the traditional black will win, as the moderate vote is split.

7. If a traditional black and a new-style black run in a district with a substantial bloc of white voters (at least 30 percent) and no white candidate runs, the new-style black will win the nomination with the support of a biracial coalition.

Hypotheses 5, 6, and 7 constitute the core of the supply-side theory: the racial composition of the candidate pool in the Democratic primary determines the type of representation a district will receive. Hypothesis 5 states that the theory does not produce a clear prediction if a single (or dominant) black candidate runs. In this instance the candidate can count on the support of the black community, and indeed could be elected by ignoring white voters. However, the luxury of running unopposed in the Democratic primary suggests a long-term strategy of laying a base of biracial support that will discourage future challenges from either the black or the white community. If a single black candidate is challenged by a white in a black majority district, the same logic would hold. It is possible that a candidate in this context would campaign on the basis of the politics of difference (because he or she could win without white votes), but it is more likely that the politics of commonality will prevail because of the long-term payoff of building a broader electoral base. The one scenario in which a single black who is running against a white would pursue a politics of difference would occur if a substantial number of black voters were expected

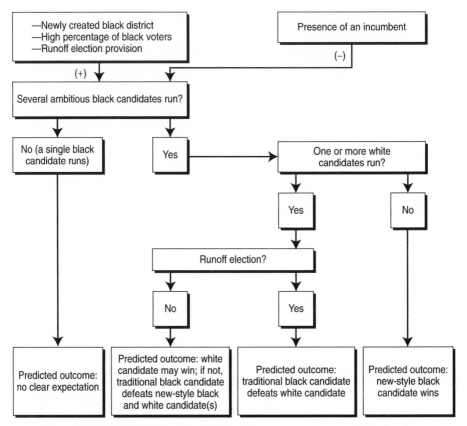

Figure 3.5 Model of the Impact of Supply-Side Effects on the Outcome of Elections in Black Congressional Districts

to rationally abstain from voting if the black candidate moved too far toward the median voter in the district (Downs 1957, 118–120). That is, if the black candidate takes his or her base for granted and tries to capture a sizable portion of the white vote through biracial appeals, black voters may choose to stay home. If rational abstention is a strong enough threat, the single black candidate running against a white could campaign on the basis of the politics of difference.[17]

Hypotheses 6 and 7 state that in districts with both a new-style black candidate who builds biracial coalitions and a traditional black candidate who appeals primarily to African American voters, the presence of a white candidate can influence the outcome of the Democratic primary in one of two ways. In states without runoff elections a divided black vote can translate into a victory for the white candidate. In states with runoffs the new-style black candidate has to compete with the white candidate for moderate voters, thus creating a greater likelihood that the traditional black candidate will win. If no white candidate enters the race, we argue that a biracial coalition of moderate white and black voters elects the new-style black candidate.

These theoretical expectations share a great deal with the spatial theory of electoral politics first articulated by Anthony Downs (1957). Indeed, in the earliest version of this chapter we presented the theory in spatial terms.[18] However, in subsequent versions of the work we moved away from the spatial theory because Downs's core prediction of convergence to the median voter could not explain the election of "difference" candidates in six of the elections in 1992. From a Downsian perspective a difference candidate, who is located with the median black voter, is always vulnerable to a candidate at the district median. This median candidate could win the white vote plus some of the conservative black voters in the district, which should make the politics of commonality a dominant strategy. This logic dictates that difference candidates should *never* win because they will always be defeated by a commonality candidate who appeals to the median voter. However, one-third of the new districts in 1992 (six of eighteen) produced difference candidates who won. The supply-side theory can explain these cases with an equally parsimonious theory: difference candidates win when there is a white candidate who captures most of the white vote and a centrist black who is squeezed in the middle. If there is no white candidate running, then the black candidate who campaigns on the basis of a politics of commonality will win. *Therefore, the location of the median voter is not as good a predictor of the type of black candidate who will win as is the racial composition of the pool of candidates who run in the Democratic primary.*

Stated more formally the median voter theory does not explain patterns of racial representation as well as the supply-side theory does for two reasons: multiple candidacies and a second issue dimension. First, the median voter prediction falls apart when there are more than two candidates running. In the Democratic primaries in the new black districts there were almost always more than two candidates (see table 3.2 below and the related discussion). Second, the median voter theory also does not work if there is more than one issue dimension. When only black candidates are running, the median voter theory holds because the commonality candidate attempts to restrict the debate to the single left-right continuum (and to issues that do not divide blacks and whites, as shown in figure 1.3). These biracial appeals allow the commonality candidate to win by attracting centrist voters. However, when a white candidate runs, race is introduced as a second issue dimension. Keith Poole and Howard Rosenthal find that racial politics produced a second dimension from 1941 to 1971 in an otherwise single-dimensional roll call space (1996, 109–110). This clearly happens in congressional campaigns in the context of racially polarized voting. When a white candidate runs, a median voter strategy no longer makes sense when there are at least two blacks running (or when there is rational abstention, as noted above). The difference candidate who appeals to the median black voter is more likely to prevail, contrary to the expectations of Downsian spatial theory.[19]

Testing the Supply-Side Model

This part of the analysis tests the first four hypotheses outlined above. Our dependent variable is the number of black candidates who received at least 5 percent of the vote in a given district. (The 5 percent cutoff excludes frivolous candidates.) The first three independent variables are expected to increase the level of black candidate activity (see hypotheses 1–3). *New black influence and black majority districts,* most of which were created in 1992, and *runoff elections* are specified as dummy variables. The *percentage of black population in a district* indicates the diversity of the district electorate. As the percentage of blacks increases, candidates representing different factions within the black community are likely to have strong enough electoral bases from which to run. The percentage of blacks in the district will also have a direct effect on the number of candidates through the perception of enhanced electoral opportunity (see hypothesis 2, above). Hypothesis 4 suggests that the presence of an incumbent dampens candidate activity. This variable is captured by two dummy variables, which are coded as one for a white incumbent and one for a black Democratic incumbent. (Open seats are the baseline for this three-level categorical variable.) To test these hypotheses, we collected data on the race of the candidates and other variables in all House districts with at least 30 percent black population in 1972, 1982, and 1992. Collecting the data on race was much more difficult than we had anticipated. But after 239 phone interviews, ranging in length from a minute or two to more than half an hour, we ascertained the race of the candidates in all 144 districts.[20]

Simple descriptive data on the level of candidate activity in black districts reveal whether there is any basis for the hypothesized supply-side effects and a need for more sophisticated tests. If new districts release a pent-up supply of black candidates, as posited in hypothesis 1, the number and quality of black candidates should be higher in new districts than in old districts. As shown in table 3.2, this pattern holds in 1972, 1982, and 1992 (though the differences are not statistically significant in 1982). In each year the average size and quality of the black candidate pool is greater in newly created black influence and black majority districts. In the most recent election forty-eight of the nonfrivolous black candidates in 1992 ran in the fifteen new black influence or black majority districts—more than five times as many candidates per district as in the old districts.

Hypothesis 1 is also supported by a comparison of candidate activity across the three elections. The number of new districts increased

Table 3.2   Challengers in Democratic Primaries in Districts That Are at Least 30 Percent Black

	1972			1982			1992		
	New	Old	Total	New	Old	Total	New	Old	Total
Mean number of black challengers	1.40+	.24+	.36	.67	.32	.34	3.2*	.63*	1.43
Mean quality of black challenger pool**	4.00*	.57*	.92	2.33	.68	.79	10.0*	1.44*	4.17
Mean number of white challengers	.60	1.15	1.10	1.00	1.02	1.00	.73	.47	.55
Mean quality of white challenger pool	1.40	2.47	2.36	3.33	2.32	2.36	2.07*	.94*	1.30
Number of districts	5	45	50	3	44	47	15	32	47

Notes: This table includes only challengers, not incumbents. The differences would be greater for blacks if incumbents were included. Also, the table includes only challengers who receive at least 5 percent of the vote in the primary. New districts are those that are explicitly created in the new apportionment cycle to promote black representation.

+The difference between new and old is significant at the .10 level.

*The difference between new and old is significant at the .05 level.

**The quality of the pool is derived from a four-level measure of quality that is summed across all candidates. Candidates who have held significant elective office receive a 4, minor elective and other public offices receive a 3, ambitious amateurs receive a 2, and regular amateurs receive a 1. See Canon (1990, 87–92, 167) for a more extended discussion of this variable. The figures for each cell are the average for the *pool* of candidates, summed across all candidates. Thus, the pool average of 10 would mean, for example, that there were two state legislators (a 4 each) and two amateurs in the race.

from five in 1972 to fifteen in 1992. Over the same period black candidate activity increased substantially, while there were fewer white
challengers. More than twice as many black candidates ran in black
districts in 1992 (sixty-seven) than in 1972 and 1982 combined (thirty-
two) (the comparable figures are eighty and thirty-seven if all challengers are included rather than only those who received at least 5
percent of the vote). However, change in candidate activity was not entirely confined to the new districts in 1992: there are more black candidates and fewer white candidates in the existing black districts as well.
Overall, the number of nonfrivolous whites running in black districts
fell from fifty-five in 1972, to forty-seven in 1982, to twenty-six in 1992.

The data in table 3.2 do not reflect the changing composition of the
black influence districts (containing between 30 and 50 percent black
voters) and the black majority districts (containing more than 50 percent black voters) between 1972 and 1992. In order to create the new
black majority districts in 1992, the number of black influence districts
was reduced substantially. In 1972 there were thirty-seven black influence districts and thirteen black majority districts. By 1992 only fourteen districts had between 30 and 50 percent black voters, while thirty-
three districts had a majority of black voters. It is important to note,
however, that the levels of candidate activity increased in all black districts in 1992 (although increases were the greatest in the new districts).
So the results presented in table 3.2 are not entirely driven by the increased attractiveness of running in new black majority districts.

An important consequence of the explosion in the number of black
candidates in 1992 is that black voters now have a greater opportunity
to elect a "representative of their choice" (even though it may be a
second choice, as we will discuss more fully below). In 64 percent of
the black districts in 1972 and 55 percent in 1982 supply-side considerations (the absence of black candidates) denied black voters the opportunity to vote for a serious black candidate (defined as one who receives at least 30 percent of the vote). This percentage decreased
dramatically in 1992 to 25.5 percent.

This trend marks an especially significant departure from previous
patterns in southern politics. Malcolm Jewell notes that candidate activity in southern state legislative primaries in the 1960s was the lowest
in the "black belt" (counties with at least 40 percent black population).
These counties were "run by a small clique of politicians hostile to
innovation who have maintained a closed political circle, partly to minimize competition and open controversy that might possibly encourage

Negro registration and voting" (1967, 34). In 1992 these same areas stimulated a much higher rate of candidate activity than is typical in comparable congressional races. In all incumbent primaries between 1972 and 1988 ($n = 3,915$) 63.9 percent of incumbents were unopposed. The average quality of the pool (as defined in table 3.2) was only .64, and in open-seat races it was 6.75 ($n = 722$) (Canon 1989). The comparable figures for black districts in 1992 are 1.93 for incumbent primaries ($n = 30$; only 40 percent were unopposed) and 14.59 in open-seat races ($n = 17$).[21] In 1992 black districts were clearly a hotbed for activity rather than a weak spot in participatory democracy (however, this pattern may have changed in 1994; see Weber 1995b).[22] Of course, there is an important connection between demand-side and supply-side factors in understanding the shift from the South of the 1960s described by Jewell. The increased candidate activity and the success of black candidates in 1992 would not have been possible without the dramatic gains in black voter registration that followed the passage of the Voting Rights Act in 1965 (as described in chapter 2).

The multivariate analysis presented in table 3.3 supports the expectations outlined above. A generalized event count (GEC) model developed by Gary King (1989, 126–131) derives the maximum-likelihood estimates. This technique permits the events that comprise the dependent variable to be correlated (either overdispersed or underdispersed) and estimates a separate dispersion parameter. In our case we expect negative contagion (that is, black candidates are less likely to enter a

Table 3.3   Generalized Event Count Regression Model of Black Candidate Activity in 1972, 1982, and 1992

Variable	Estimate	Standard Error	Estimate/ Standard Error
Constant	−2.41**	0.27	−8.92
New district	1.00**	0.22	4.57
Percentage of black voters	0.041**	0.002	20.25
Black incumbent	−0.99**	0.31	−3.20
White incumbent	−1.14**	0.32	−3.56
Runoff election	0.24	0.23	1.02
Gamma	−.19	0.12	−1.58

Notes: Log-likelihood $= -75.24$.

$n = 144$.

**Significant at the .01 level.

Dependent variable: number of black candidates who receive at least 5 percent of the vote in a given district.

race that is already contested by one black). All of the variables are in the expected direction. We can reject the null hypothesis that each estimate equals zero for all but the runoff variable. (The traditional probability that the estimate equals zero is less than .001 for each of the other four variables.) Approximately .70 additional black candidates run in the new districts, compared to old districts (using the derivative method outlined by King [1989b, 108–110, 130], which multiplies the parameter estimate by the sample mean for the dependent variable). About .69 fewer black candidates run when there is a black incumbent and .80 fewer when there is a white incumbent, compared to open-seat districts. Each 10 percent increase in black population boosts the number of black candidates by about .29. Gamma (which is $exp\sigma^2$), the dispersion parameter) just fails to reach significance at the .05 level; however, the magnitude of the coefficient indicates slight underdispersion (King 1989, 126–131), as expected.

Impact on Descriptive Representation

Given the results from the GEC model and the simple district mean levels of candidate activity, it is certainly possible that a white candidate could have defeated a divided black field in the new districts. An average of 3.86 black candidates ran in these districts in 1992 (3.2 if including only those who received at least 5 percent of the vote), and therefore the conditions described above could easily hold. However, opportunistic whites did not take advantage of the split black vote in most of these districts. Like much of American society congressional campaigns remain largely segregated. Of the 144 races in black districts in 1972, 1982, and 1992, only 40 (27.8 percent) had at least one black candidate and one white candidate. In most of these races one of the candidates did not run a serious campaign and received less than 5 percent of the vote. Only 11 districts (7.6 percent) had a candidate of each race who received at least 30 percent of the vote in the Democratic primary.

As a result, there was only one district where a white candidate won because black candidates split the black vote (the Ohio 1st in 1992). In four other districts the black nominee probably would have lost had it not been for the runoff election (Florida 23rd, Georgia 2nd, North Carolina 1st, and the special election to fill Mike Espy's seat in the Mississippi 2nd). Four of these five districts were new black influence or black majority districts. The exception was the Mississippi 2nd, which was created in 1982. As noted in chapter 2, this impact of the runoff provision is ironic because runoffs have undermined the electoral fortunes of black candidates in the past (though systematic evidence on their impact is mixed; see Bullock and Johnson 1992).

This finding is not terribly surprising given the lack of success by white candidates in black majority House districts. Nonetheless, why did white candidates fail to respond to changing electoral circumstances and exploit the situation for their personal gain? A central reason is a sense of fairness among potential white candidates and a perception that it is "the blacks' turn." Two white Democratic state legislators we interviewed cited the creation of the black majority district as their main reason for not running in the North Carolina 1st.[23] According to one, "The 1st district was created to elect a minority candidate and I think that is a good thing. I would never consider running in the 1st, not now or in the future." The other legislator also cited "not wanting to step on toes" in the new district and was realistic in recognizing she would not be able to win because she is white (personal interviews, May 28, 1992). Indeed, it is difficult to sort out altruistic and self-interested motives. Some potential white candidates may have emphasized more altruistic motives in our interviews, while not expressing the reality that they would not have much of a chance of winning in the new districts anyway. The aggregate data presented in table 3.2 further support this pattern of behavior, whatever the motivations. (Recall that the mean number of nonfrivolous white challengers in black districts fell by almost 50 percent between 1982 and 1992.)

Sometimes the decision of whites not to run in black districts was not entirely voluntary.[24] Pressure from the black community contributed to incumbent Robin Tallon's decision not to run for reelection in the newly created black majority 6th District in South Carolina. Tallon originally announced his intention to run for reelection, despite facing a constituency with 60 percent new voters. Tallon claimed that his campaign would "promote racial harmony" (Duncan 1992, 2536). Since 1982 he had always received strong support from the black voters who made up 40 percent of the old 6th District. However, Phil Duncan reported that the incumbent's "decision to run met with considerable criticism from the black community; some of the black aspirants for the 6th faulted him for trying to block minority political empowerment." Tallon had a change of heart just minutes before the filing period closed on June 25. He decided not to run, saying that his campaign would "further divide the races [and] cause racial disharmony

and unrest" (Duncan 1992, 2536). One ambitious state legislator and
potential candidate we interviewed in the North Carolina 1st District,
Mary McCallister, expressed thinly veiled resentment at having been
pushed from the race; "they" in the following quote refers to the rural,
predominantly black voters in the 1st District:

> Had Fayetteville been in the new district from the get go, I would have
> run. By the time we were added to the district it was an "us versus them"
> [urban versus rural] thing. They did not want us to participate. Fayette-
> ville is a pivotal part of the 1st District as it is drawn up now, but they
> didn't want us in it. . . . It was a rural district and they wanted to keep it
> rural, but the present 1st isn't so rural any more. . . . They didn't want to
> give up the power. (personal interview, May 28, 1992)

Impact on Substantive Representation

Our data indicate that runoff provisions and the segregation of campaigns generally prevent whites from defeating a divided black field.
But a coalition of white voters and moderate blacks often holds the
balance of power in the black districts. Diversity within the black community helps create this situation by encouraging different types of
black candidates to run for Congress. Aggregate-level evidence suggests that the electoral climate facing black candidates has gradually
changed to favor new-style blacks over traditional ones. In districts
that are represented by an African American in Congress, the percentage of black voters has gradually fallen over the past two decades—
from 61.8 percent in 1972, to 59.4 percent in 1982, to 55.9 percent in
1992. At the same time the percentage of white voters in these same
districts climbed from 31.7 percent in 1972, to 32.1 percent in 1982, to
36.9 percent in 1992. These data certainly undermine the notion that
the new districts helped create "political apartheid" and "black reservations." Districts that are represented by blacks are more integrated
today than they were ten and twenty years ago.

Ruth Ann Strickland and Marcia Lynn Whicker argue that blacks
who are political insiders and project a conservative image are more
likely to appeal to white voters: "Only by demonstrating expertise can
black candidates in black-white contests overcome individual racism
where individuals assume that blacks are inferior and less able to govern" (1992, 208–209). New-style black politicians are increasingly taking advantage of the changed electoral environment by appealing to
white voters. From 1972 to 1980, 38.5 percent of the blacks elected
to the U.S. House had no previous elective experience, and only 15.4

percent had more than ten years of previous experience. The pattern changed significantly in 1992. Of the sixteen new black members elected, only one (6.2 percent) had no prior experience, while eleven (68.8 percent) had more than ten years of political experience, which makes them far more experienced than the average new white member of Congress (see table 3.4 for data on black members and Canon 1990, chap. 3, for data on white members). These results are consistent with the expectations of ambition theory (Schlesinger 1966; Jacobson and Kernell 1983): as the probability of winning increases, the quality of the candidates improves.

The dramatic success of new-style black congressional candidates can be attributed in part to the supply-side effects described above. Democratic primaries in newly created black influence and black majority districts often pit one or more traditional black candidates against one or more new-style black candidates. If the black community splits its support between traditional and new-style candidates, whites can play a pivotal role in deciding which candidate will represent the district.

Because data on the policy positions and racial coalitions of black candidates in Democratic primaries are difficult to collect, we tested hypotheses 5, 6, and 7 only for the 1992 election. We examined the seventeen congressional districts in which a newly elected black candidate emerged from the Democratic primaries as well as the new black influence district (the Ohio 1st) in which a black did not win.[25] Thirteen of the sixteen cases support our theory and two districts (FL 17 and TX 30) fall in the category of "no clear prediction" (hypothesis 5—a dominant black candidate ran with no white opposition). In these two cases, the winner made strong appeals to black and white voters alike.[26] Seven cases support hypothesis 6: a white candidate competed with at least one traditional and one new-style black candidate, and either a

Table 3.4 Black Members of the U.S. House of Representatives: Prior Political Experience, 1972–1992

Prior Experience in Public Office	Year Elected to Congress		
	1972–1980	1982–1990	1992
None	38.5%	23.5%	6.2%
More than zero, but less than ten years	46.1%	47.1%	25.0%
Ten or more years	15.4%	29.4%	68.8%
Number of members	13	17	16

traditional black won as the moderate vote was split (CA 37, FL 3, FL 23, GA 11, NC 1, MS 2) or a white won because of the divided black vote (OH 1). The other seven districts support hypothesis 7: no white candidate emerged, and one of the new-style black candidates defeated one or more traditional black candidates (AL 7, IL 1, IL 2, LA 4, NC 12, SC 6).

The three cases that were not were not consistent with our theory were the Georgia 2nd, where Sanford Bishop defeated white incumbent Charles Hatcher; Maryland's 2nd District, where Albert Wynn won a hotly contested primary that attracted thirteen candidates; and the Virginia 3rd, where Robert Scott won a low-turnout (15 percent), issueless primary over two other new-style blacks. In the Georgia case our theory predicted that a traditional black would win, but Bishop clearly ran as a new-style black, touting his legislative experience and attacking Hatcher for his 819 overdrafts. Again, in the Maryland district our theory would have predicted that a traditional black would win because of the presence of seven white candidates (however, only one, Dana Lee Dembrow, was a serious candidate). Nevertheless, both of the leading black candidates, Wynn and Alexander Williams, Jr., realized that overt racial appeals would not work in this heavily middle-class district comprised of federal workers. Similarly, in the Virginia district, ideology and racial politics simply did not emerge in this contest between three similar black candidates. According to our theory the most conservative of the three candidates, Jacqueline G. Epps, should have won (with white support in a divided black field), but Scott used his superior name recognition and fund-raising ability to win this low-key race. Furthermore, Scott made his career in the state legislature by appealing to biracial coalitions and has continued to do so in his congressional career. Thus, this case could easily be coded as verifying our theory.

This test of hypotheses 5, 6, and 7 suggests that the presence of a white candidate can strongly influence the type of candidate who wins the Democratic primary in black influence and black majority districts. It is also interesting to note that in each of the three cases that do not absolutely conform to the theory (though Scott's case is very consistent with the theory), black candidates who emphasized a politics of commonality succeeded by appealing to biracial coalitions.

The conventional wisdom concerning the "apartheid" districts is clearly undermined by the biracial nature of a majority of the 1992 campaigns. Sixteen of the eighteen districts examined here were either new black influence districts (OH 1), older black districts that were substantially altered in 1992 (IL 1, IL 2), or new black majority districts (the rest). The other two were older districts that elected black representatives in 1992 (MS 2, CA 37). Of the sixteen new or substantially altered districts only four produced winning candidates who campaigned on the basis of a politics of difference.

Alternative Explanations

Alternative explanations for variation in the representational styles of members of the CBC are rooted in constituency-based theories of representation (as noted in chapter 1). Rather than looking to the supply-side explanation of the racial composition of the candidate pool and the resultant electoral coalition, two constituency-based arguments point to (1) the conservative influence of rural southern districts and (2) the relatively low proportion of black voters in the new districts, at least when compared to many of the liberal northern urban districts with high concentrations of blacks that elected African Americans to the House in the 1980s. Though the first point clearly has some relevance, the second is not supported by the evidence. Of the seventeen freshman blacks (sixteen were elected in 1992, and Bennie Thompson was elected in a 1993 special election to replace Mike Espy), thirteen are from the South, and many are from largely rural districts.[27] Many of these districts have relatively high concentrations of white voters when compared to some of the northern urban districts of the 1970s and 1980s.

Region and racial composition help explain diversity within the CBC, but these simple explanations cannot account for all the variation in ideology and attitudes toward racial politics found in the new black districts. For example, Cynthia McKinney (D–GA) had a Conservative Coalition (CC) support score of 4 in 1996, while Sanford Bishop, from a neighboring Georgia district, supported the CC 90 percent of the time. The general ideology scores provided by Poole and Rosenthal reveal similar differences: the first-dimension NOMINATE score for Bishop in 1996 was $-.239$ and McKinney's was $-.803$ (by comparison, Bishop was more conservative than the average white Democrat [$-.38$ mean], and McKinney was among the most liberal House members). Before their districts were redrawn, both incumbents had sprawling districts that were a mixture of urban and rural areas with 64 percent and 57 percent black populations, respectively. What accounts for the difference?

Standard explanations of legislative behavior point to the importance of constituency, ideology, and party. In the example noted above, party is the same and attributing the differences to personal ideology only begs the question of why a liberal was elected in one district and a moderate in the other. While the constituencies of the two districts noted above are quite similar, there may be systematic differences in constituencies that could explain the varying representational styles adopted by members of the CBC. One of the most important determinants of varying district interests is the distribution of income within the district. Some black majority districts are uniformly poor, with few differences between the white and black communities. Others are comprised of very poor black inner-city areas and wealthy white suburbs. A few, such as Albert Wynn's district in Maryland, have middle-class black and white constituencies. These varying contexts suggest an answer to my question, "Why do some districts elect proponents of the politics of difference and others practitioners of the politics of commonality?" One demand-side hypothesis is that in districts with a huge economic gulf between the white and black communities, representatives are likely to adopt a politics of difference because the white community does not need their help. In a district with a relatively even distribution of income between the races, on the other hand, interests in the black and white communities are likely to be similar, and the member would be more likely to practice a politics of commonality.[28]

A simple scatterplot of the ratio of per capita nonblack income to black income plotted against the percentage of black residents in the district undermines this hypothesis (not shown here). Districts electing "difference" members run the range from Bennie Thompson's poor Mississippi Delta district, in which nonblacks earn nearly three times as much as blacks, to Walter Tucker's uniformly poor central Los Angeles district, in which nonblacks earn only 1.14 times as much as blacks (this district is 40 percent Hispanic, 34 percent black, and 26 percent white). Districts electing commonality members range from Cleo Field's Louisiana 4th (nonblack-to-black ratio of 2.18) to Albert Wynn's prosperous Maryland district (ratio of 1.39).

A more systematic analysis confirms the supply-side explanation for the style of racial representation in the cases examined here. A logit regression of difference (coded as 1) or commonality (0) on the number of white candidates who received at least 5 percent of the vote in the Democratic primary, the percentage of black constituents in the district, and the ratio of nonblack to black income reveals that the presence of a white candidate is the only significant predictor of whether a difference candidate will be elected. The baseline probability of electing a difference representative when a white is not running is 7.2 percent (holding the percentage black and the income ratio variables constant at their mean levels). When one white candidate runs, that probability increases to 40 percent; with two white candidates a difference representative is almost assured (84.9 percent probability), as black candidates are unlikely to attract many white voters and therefore target their appeals to blacks.

Alternative explanations are not supported by the logit model. The percentage black in the district was even of the wrong sign, and the income ratio variable failed to reach significance (though it had the correct sign). As noted above, the popular press often cited the more rural southern nature of the districts as an explanation for the racially moderate blacks elected in the new districts, but a dummy variable for the South had the wrong sign, and a variable for the percentage of the district in rural areas was insignificant and actually reduced the percentage of cases that were correctly predicted.

Assessing the Impact of Black Districts

Most political solutions to social problems have unintended consequences; the creation of black majority districts is no exception. Black incumbents may become increasingly insulated from their constituents (Swain 1993), and black voters may lose their influence by being grouped in a smaller number of black majority districts (Thernstrom 1987). The most potent concern, we believe, is stated by Lani Guinier, who argues that redistricting forces blacks to "compromise and adjust" their interests to the needs of existing institutions (1991b, 1456). The jury is still out on the charges made by Carol Swain and Abigail Thernstrom. While seeing some merit in Guinier's argument, we reject her call for radical institutional engineering in representative assemblies and adopt a more pragmatic position.

Ultimately the question of how a House member represents constituents depends on how well that member serves the voters' needs. Standards should not be imposed by researchers, but should be set by the voters of each district. *What are the interests of African-American and white voters, and how do different types of representatives serve those interests?* These interests vary within and across districts, and therefore the type of member who is elected should vary. In many established black districts the politics of difference will continue to guide the activities and representation provided by African-American leaders. Representatives such as Cynthia McKinney (D–GA) and Bennie Thompson (D–MS) share these traditional views. In many of the new black majority districts, however, moderate biracial coalitions have elected new-style politicians. These leaders provide valuable, tangible benefits to their districts by working within the political system. The somewhat counterintuitive conclusion of this chapter is that the type of representation a district receives does not depend on demand-side considerations (voters) as much as on supply-side factors (whether a white candidate runs and the supply of black politicians). The precise contours of these differences in representational styles, in addition to the nature of representation of black interests provided by white members of the House, will be tested in the next chapter.

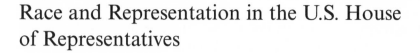

CHAPTER FOUR

Race and Representation in the U.S. House of Representatives

> "We get here in different ways, we stay here by different methods."
>
> Member X (quoted by S27, personal interview)

This pithy summary of the electoral and representative processes captures the essence of my supply-side theory of representation: members of Congress get elected by appealing to different electoral coalitions, and they stay in office by keeping those constituencies happy. The quote also raises a host of questions about *how* this representative process unfolds and how it affects the institutional power of the Congressional Black Caucus (CBC).

We have little understanding of the CBC's relative power in Congress and the representational linkages forged by the creation of new black majority districts in 1992. Do the black moderates who were elected due to the supply-side effects described in the previous chapter change the role and the institutional clout of the CBC? Are these new-style black representatives "authentic," to use Lani Guinier's controversial term? Does the racially charged atmosphere of some campaigns carry over into the governing process, so that some blacks do not represent white voters? Do black members who were elected by biracial coalitions keep their promises to represent both white and black constituents, or do they gravitate toward the preferences of the black majority in their districts? In short, do politicians who are elected with biracial coalitions, while promoting a politics of commonality, attempt to act in a more biracial manner in the House than politicians who were elected in the new black majority districts by primarily appealing to African-American voters? There is much to learn about the nature of representation provided to these new districts, the linkages between campaigning and governing in racial politics, and the usefulness of racial redistricting as a means of empowering minority voters.

An outpouring of research in the past several years on race, redistricting, and representation has illuminated various dimensions of this topic, from the perspectives of both behavior in Congress (Swain 1993; Lublin 1997; Hill 1995; Pinney and Serra 1995; Walton 1995; Menifield 1996; Cameron, Epstein, and O'Halloran 1995; Cobb and Jenkins 1996; Singh 1998; Whitby 1998) and voters' assessment of representation provided in these districts (Gay 1996). However, most studies of racial representation in Congress employ limited measurement of either the constituency or the congressional side of the representational equation and ignore differences in the representational styles of members of the CBC.

My supply-side theory predicts that there will be variation in representational styles and content based on the nature of the campaign and the type of African-American politician elected. The theory produces several specific hypotheses concerning the behavior of members of Congress. Moderate blacks who cultivate biracial themes and issue positions in their campaigns are expected to serve in the leadership, seek committee assignments that will aid both white and black constituents, address issues in the language of commonality, and engage in strong constituency service in both the black and the white communities (the last will be examined in chapter 5).

The balancing approach discussed in chapter 1 should also be evident among commonality members. In most cases this will mean remaining committed to a unified CBC position on racial issues, but trying to serve broader district interests on nonracial issues. However, commonality members will occasionally deviate from the CBC position on racial issues. For example, a staffer for a commonality member indicated that the highly publicized vote to censure Khalid Muhammad, a former minister in the Nation of Islam, for a racist speech was "an important signal to the white voters in the district that Representative M was not beholden to his base constituency. They saw him in a different light after that vote" (S14). But he went on to note that his boss was heavily involved in many issues that were important to minorities in the district as well, such as investigating racial discrimination at the National Institutes of Health, opening up commercial credit markets to minority-owned small businesses, holding two job fairs in the district (which were attended by 8,000 people), and requiring minority involvement in formulating Resolution Trust Corporation rules (S14). This is an excellent example of the balancing perspective.

Black representatives who campaigned primarily in the African-American community and see themselves as representing black interests will be less likely to serve in the leadership (because of the potential conflicts between the party's position and their role as the "conscience of the institution") and more likely to speak in the language of the politics of difference, focus on racial issues in legislation and committee preferences, and focus their constituency service efforts in the black community.

One of my most interesting interviews with a staffer for a difference member addressed some of these issues. This representative had appealed primarily to black voters in her election, and I wanted to know to what extent this had carried over to her behavior in Congress. After telling me that there were some racial tensions on the staff and that white staffers were not trusted, she said:

> Representative J has made a real attempt, at least in her speeches, to appeal to white constituents. She is an inclusionist. She is very cautious and careful not to alienate anyone. But the campaign approach [of appealing to blacks] hasn't gone away. In her relations with the district she has people who will play the race card for her. In Washington everything always has a racial slant—the environmental racism, racial justice . . . this sends a message to the white voters. But it's a subtle message. With black voters it's different. I don't go to Representative J and say, "How do I get the message out to our black voters on this?" It's just understood that is what we should be doing. This is a very different style than someone like Robert Scott (D–VA). He is upwardly mobile and appeals to whites. He will hold state office someday. (S11)

This suggests a different way of representing the district than the balancing approach outlined above. (These comments about Robert Scott also suggest that progressively ambitious members of the CBC are more likely to exhibit the politics of commonality, but this is a topic for future research.)

This chapter will also test the "no racial differences" hypothesis that white representatives with significant black constituencies are just as attentive to black interests as are black members (Swain 1993; Thernstrom 1987). That is, does the race of the member make any difference for the nature of racial representation provided in a district? The extent to which white members pay much attention to their black constituents' interests varies considerably. Included in my analysis are some of the most conservative members of the House, such as Mike Parker, Sonny Callahan, and Sonny Montgomery, who are not very interested in racial issues. However, there are also northern liberals, such as Thomas Barrett, Eliot Engle, and Thomas Foglietta, who are more sensitive to black interests (however, not as much as one might expect).

My interviews with members revealed this variation. One white member hardly mentioned race in his interview. He represented a black influence district for many years and emphasized common issues that are important for the whole district. He did note, however, that there are some issues that divide along racial lines, such as the Martin Luther King holiday. "I voted for it even with an 85 percent white district. I am glad that the vote came in the old district rather than the new one [which now has a much higher black population]," he said with some pride. "I don't want to be accused of being a mere seismograph" (M4). At the other end of the spectrum Mike Parker (a southern Democrat who switched to the Republican Party late in 1995) was described in the following terms by a reporter for a black magazine who urged voters to defeat him: "As one of the most conservative Democrats in the House, Parker consistently voted against the interests of Black constituents, who make up 36 percent of his district's voting-age population. A strong Black vote, plus the support of one in five White voters, can make Parker an example of what can happen to those who treat Black constituents like political stepchildren" (Cooper 1996, 16).

The analysis in this chapter stacks the deck in favor of the "no racial differences" hypothesis and against my argument that race matters by including only the members of the 103rd Congress (1993–1994) who represented districts that were at least 25 percent African American (plus Gary Franks and Alan Wheat, two CBC members who represented districts that were less than 25 percent black). That is, if differences between white members and black members in terms of racial representation are found in this subset of districts in which members should be the most sensitive to racial issues, it is extremely likely that even greater differences will be found if all districts were examined. A few portions of my analysis will consider all 435 districts, but the most detailed analysis is confined to the 53 members described above.[1]

This analysis will proceed on individual and institutional levels. The individual-level analysis, which is the focus of my supply-side theory, attempts to answer the questions posed above and expands the scope of previous studies of race and representation by moving beyond an exclusive focus on roll call voting to consider bill sponsorship and cosponsorship, speeches on the floor of the House, committee assignments, and leadership positions. I also include some data from the 104th Congress to examine the impact that Republican control of the House has on the CBC. However, as Guinier (1994) and others point out, demonstrating responsiveness at the individual level may reveal little about the true nature of racial representation. That is, having a few more black faces in Congress may have little impact on the quality of racial representation in a majority-rule institution. This concern motivates Guinier's call for "proportional interest representation" through controversial institutional reforms, such as minority veto power over issues that are of central concern to African-American constituents and cumulative voting procedures that would permit an expression of intensity of preferences in the electoral process. Failure to adopt such reforms, Guinier claims, will perpetuate the "triumph of tokenism" (Guinier 1991a).

The next section of this chapter will challenge Guinier's argument that the CBC's voice cannot be heard in a majority-rule institution. While it is true that only a relatively small fraction of issues addressed by the House explicitly concern issues of race, the CBC greatly enhanced its institutional power on a broad range of issues as the number of black representatives increased in 1993. It is a mistake to define the CBC's influence in exclusively racial terms. After examining representation at the institutional level, I will examine many of the same variables (roll call votes, committee assignments, leadership, etc.) at the individual level.

Representation at the Institutional Level: The Power of the CBC in the 103rd Congress

The role of African Americans in Congress is changing. With the new size and power of the Congressional Black Caucus, members now have an opportunity to play a significant role in the governing process. This was especially true in the 103rd Congress (1993–1994), when a unified Republican opposition gave the CBC potential veto power over many issues. The CBC's institutional clout was obviously diminished by the Republican takeover of the House in 1995 and by the ascendance of the "Blue Dog" conservative Democrats as the pivotal players within the Democratic Party. In a book that is highly critical of the CBC, Robert Singh argues that the 104th Congress represented "an almost unmitigated political disaster" and the "worst political setback for the caucus in its entire institutional history" (1998, 192). However, the CBC plays an important role within the Democratic Party in Congress, and several moderates within the CBC continue to shape issues like welfare reform, tax policy, and crime policy. Others, such as the CBC's leader in the 105th Congress, Maxine Waters (D–CA), continue the CBC's traditional role of providing a "conscience" for the House.

Cohesion, Diversity, Organization, and Clout

The CBC was viewed as weak and ineffective in its early years, from 1971 to 1983 (see Swain 1993, 37–39, for a review of various studies that make this argument). One of the most favorable studies concluded on this pessimistic note: "[U]nless the Caucus is able to increase its size sufficiently to have a significant impact on roll call divisions and manages to free itself from submersion within the larger Northern Democratic sea, it appears unlikely that the Black Caucus will be able to add substantive success to its already impressive organizational and operational successes" (Levy and Stoudinger 1978, 332). Elsewhere the same authors wondered if the CBC was destined to become "little more than a generalized publicity organ" (Levy and Stoudinger 1976, 44). Burdett Loomis notes that the CBC started to play a more substantive role in the late 1970s, but that "the CBC remains most successful as a symbolic focus for many national black concerns" (1981, 210). Loomis argues that this symbolic focus poses a problem for the CBC because its members' constituents expect substantive results that are difficult to deliver.

   This perceived weakness was both structural and self-inflicted. The CBC's influence was obviously limited by its size (there was an average of fifteen black members in the House through the 1970s and about twenty-one through the 1980s), but often it picked fights that could have been avoided or pushed policies that were sure losers simply to score symbolic points. Most black members of Congress either played the role of agitator and conscience for the institution (Clay 1993) or resorted to nonlegislative means of representation, such as extensive casework (Swain 1993, chap. 2). An older generation of blacks in Congress from urban political machines worked within the system, but as quiet back-benchers who did not exert great influence over the legislative process. The first black elected to Congress in the post-Reconstruction period, Oscar DePreist of Chicago, is a classic example of this type.

In the early 1980s, moderates, such as Julian Dixon (D–CA), William Gray (D–PA), Alan Wheat (D–MO), and later Mike Espy (D–MS), urged the CBC to work within the system rather than hammering away from the outside. The key turning point came in 1983, when Gray and Dixon pushed the CBC to work with the Democratic leadership on the budget rather than focusing on their alternative budget. Gray was the most influential of this group, as he became chair of the Budget Committee in 1985 and worked his way up to number three in the Democratic leadership before retiring from the House in 1991 to become director of the United Negro College Fund. However, there was continued resistance from many influential members of the CBC. John Conyers and others objected to the tactical moderation, arguing that it was critical to take principled positions (Cohadas 1985, 675); thus, throughout the 1980s the CBC's main mark on the legislative process continued to be the alternative budget, which typically received about 70 votes and then was largely ignored.

Both the structural and the self-inflicted sources of weakness were eliminated in the 103rd Congress: the CBC then had the votes to influence legislation, and its members had the experience and leadership to use their power effectively. Halfway through the first session of the 103rd Congress, David Bositis remarked that the CBC has "'gotten more attention in the last five months than it had in the previous 20 years'" (quoted in Cunningham 1993a, 1713). Diversity within the CBC had also reached unprecedented levels. Conservative Coalition (CC) support scores from 1993 to 1996 reveal these differences.[2] CC scores are a good measure of ideological votes that for the most part are not concerned with race. Of the fifty-one CC votes in 1996 none explicitly concerned race, and only five were implicit race issues. The CBC had traditionally been strongly aligned against the Conservative Coalition. Even ten years ago it would have been unthinkable that sixteen members of the CBC would have CC support scores of 30 and above, to say nothing about seven Democratic CBC members who supported the CC more than 50 percent of the time. Sanford Bishop (D–GA) has evolved from a moderate to perhaps the first conservative black Democrat to serve in the House (he supported the Conservative Coalition 90 percent of the time in 1996 and is the CBC's only "Blue Dog" Democrat). Poole and Rosenthal scores, the most general measure of ideology (their scores include all roll calls in which at least 5 percent of the votes were cast on the losing side) show the same general pattern. Of the eighteen most conservative members of the CBC in

1993 and 1994, thirteen were members of the 1992 class (whereas eight would have been expected by chance).

One staffer for a member of the 1992 class explained the increasing diversity in these terms: "Prior to 1992 the CBC's agenda was largely monolithic—urban, inner-city, liberal social activist. Since 1992 there are more conservative members of the CBC from southern, rural areas who bring a totally different perspective. For example, an older member from New York City wouldn't have any qualms about voting for raising the tobacco tax, but that would be a tough vote for us. This has been tough for some of the older members, but we still work together and support each other's bills" (S2). Jim Clyburn, a representative of the 1992 class from rural South Carolina, compared himself to his northern colleagues, saying, "We're different from these guys, no question about it. We have a different style of politics. We are a little more prone to seek consensus" (Katz 1993, 5).

I argued in chapter 3 that these differences within the CBC are attributable not only to the constituency-based factors alluded to by the staffer quoted above, but also to supply-side explanations. Another possibility is that Carrie Meek, Corrine Brown, Eva Clayton, Eddie Bernice Johnson, and Sanford Bishop moderated their positions because they faced a more conservative district after their district lines were redrawn to include more white voters. Nevertheless, both Cynthia McKinney and Bishop had their district lines redrawn in Georgia, but McKinney's CC support scores have not budged from the single digits as Bishop's went from the mid-50s to 90. On average, both difference and commonality members' CC support scores increased by about 20 points from 1993 to 1996, with commonality members remaining more conservative than difference members (45.5 compared to 40.8 in 1996). Thus, difference members who initially campaigned by appealing to black voters are moving closer to the median voter of the district. For example, Bennie Thompson, who ran a very racially oriented campaign in 1993 in a conservative Mississippi Delta district, increased his CC score from 14 in 1993 to 59 in 1996. For the entire 1993–1996 period the members of the 1992 class have CC scores that are about 19 points higher than the older CBC members ($t = 4.71$, sig. at .0001). The new generation of the CBC is clearly moving the caucus in a different direction.

Table 4.1 shows these general patterns for Conservative Coalition and Poole and Rosenthal scores for 1993–1996, broken down by the type of member. According to the Poole and Rosenthal scores, com-

Table 4.1   Roll Call Support Scores for the Congressional Black Caucus, 1993–1996

Type of Member	CC Support 1993	1994	1995	1996	CBC Support	CBC Conflict	Poole & Rosenthal Scores 1993	1994	1995	1996
Commonality	26.5	26.4	27.7	45.5	92.9	70	−.818	−.644	−.660	−.695
Difference	20.5	24	19.8	40.8	93.6	74.8	−.833	−.647	−.732	−.719
Older black	9.6	8.6	9.2	13.5	94.1	78.5	−.819	−.699	−.735	−.783
White Democrat (≥25% black)	60.1	58.6	57.1	52	75.7	26.6	−.420	−.349	−.176	−.179
Hispanic Democrat (≥25% black)	9	8	8	12	95.1	81.0	−.521	−.423	−.353	−.335
White Democrat (<25% black)							−.544	−.432	−.390	−.393
White Republican (≥25% black)	93.3	92	96.3	97.3	33.6	11.4	.406	.351	.690	.797
White Republican (<25% black)							.390	.369	.628	.685
Black Republican	93	86	97	84	43.2	5.0	.298	.149	.449	.527

Notes: CC Support is *Congressional Quarterly*'s Conservative Coalition support. Failing to vote or voting "present" or "abstain" lowers the member's score.

CBC Support is the percentage of times the member supported the majority of members of the Congressional Black Caucus on the 984 roll call votes in the 103rd Congress. Scores are corrected for absences.

CBC Conflict indicates the member's support for the CBC's position when a majority of the CBC voted against a majority of the nonblack Democratic membership. There were 80 of these roll call votes in the 103rd Congress. Scores are corrected for absences.

Poole and Rosenthal Scores are their first-dimension NOMINATE scores (Poole and Rosenthal 1997).

monality members are a bit more conservative than difference or older members. However, the only statistically significant difference is between commonality and difference members in 1995 ($t = 1.38$, sig. at .10). One other interesting pattern evident in this table is that Republicans who represent districts that are at least 25 percent black are somewhat more conservative than other Republicans. However, as noted in chapter 1, one cannot make inferences about racial representation based on general ideology scores because blacks and whites have the same preferences over a broad range of nonracial issues. More refined measures of racial representation will be presented below.

This question remains: How have the new diversity and size influenced the power of the CBC? A staffer who had been on the Hill for many years noted the pros and cons of diversity. He spoke longingly, and with only slight exaggeration, of the "good ol' days" in the 1970s when the "thirteen members were unanimous on every issue." However, he also saw the advantage of "greater numbers, more chairs, and more ideas" (S24). Another said, "We disagree on a lot of issues now, but we try to present a unified front. We have our arguments in private." He also argued that the "quality of the members has greatly improved. Most of the new members are very experienced. The CBC is a much more sophisticated player in the process now. We are picking fights that we can win rather than just lobbing bombs from the outside" (S10).

Other staffers focused more on how the CBC as an organization has increased its clout (rather than looking at the impact of diversity or the characteristics of the members on the success of the CBC). One staffer said, "We have gotten good support from the CBC on our bills. The CBC is adept at understanding the political process and good at working together. We have new ideas and have been able to infuse them into the process. The CBC is a power" (S23). Others were more critical of the CBC as an organization: "The CBC is not as organized as they could be. By the time a bill comes up it is often too late—they don't get the word out as much as they should, and they don't do much lobbying on the floor. They don't have any whip organization" (S5). Another staffer for a freshman who had extensive experience on the Hill was even more critical, saying, "I hope the CBC becomes stronger. At this point issues get lost, everything needs to be fixed yesterday; it's like a perpetual state of emergency. They give you ten minutes to get something done, but that's not the way things work here. You need more lead time. There needs to be a shift in approach—more of a focus on process." He paused and almost apologized for the critical remarks: "Maybe I'm placing too much of a focus on process, but *it is critical.*" Then he shook his head, reaffirming his initial comments: "Relations would be better if they would be more organized. Everything is always on fire!" (S9; see Hammond 1998 and Singh 1998, chapter 3, for an overview of the CBC's organizational problems).

Organizational difficulties certainly have not been improved by the Republican leadership's defunding of the legislative service organizations (LSOs) (of which the CBC is one example). The House rules that were adopted on January 4, 1995, prohibit members from using office accounts to support the LSOs. This move was widely perceived as an effort to weaken opposition to the Republican agenda by eliminating the funding source for powerful liberal organizations, such as the Democratic Study Group, the CBC, the Hispanic Caucus, and the Congressional Caucus for Women's Issues (see Hammond 1998). However, a *Congressional Quarterly Weekly Report* headline midway through 1995 reported, "LSOs Are No Longer Separate, But the Work's Almost Equal: Staff carries on duties of legislative service groups that Congress now forbids members to fund." The article went on to say that "the reconfigured groups have had little trouble changing their ways" (Salant 1995, 1483).

However, organizational prowess has never been the source of the CBC's strength; rather, its members' shared goals and cohesiveness as a group have made it a potent voting bloc in the House. One staffer commented on the importance of the CBC as a source of cues: "The chief of staff and AA take their cues from the CBC. They place a premium on the CBC, even over the state delegation and party" (S11; also see Menifield 1996). Table 4.1 reveals that the increasing diversity in the CBC has not undermined its basic cohesion. Overall, Sanford Bishop was the only Democratic member of the CBC who did not support the CBC's position (defined as the side of the vote on which a majority of the CBC voted) on at least 90 percent of the roll calls in the 103rd Congress, and there are virtually no differences across the three types of black members (commonality, difference, and older). Most members were in the low to mid-90s. However, the significance of these numbers can be overstated. After all, the entire Republican Party in 1995–1996 had party unity scores of 91 and 87, so the CBC is not much more cohesive than the House Republicans (though this clearly is a historically high level of party unity). Second, unlike party unity scores that are based on roll calls on which a majority of Republicans are opposed by a majority of Democrats, the CBC support scores include all roll calls, including many consensual votes (27.7 percent of all roll calls in the 103rd Congress had at least 80 percent of the members voting on the same side). Thus, even conservatives, such as Sonny Montgomery and Mike Parker, had CBC support scores of 73 and 65, respectively. In fact, only one white Democrat in the study had a CBC support score lower than 65 (Norman Sisisky's 46).

Another measure of unity within the CBC is the behavior of members when they are confronted by conflict between two strong voting cues: when a majority of the CBC members are opposed to a majority of the non-CBC Democrats. The CBC opposed the party on important domestic and foreign policies a total of 80 times on the 984 roll calls taken in the 103rd Congress. For example, a slim majority of the CBC voted in favor of HR 3759, which would have cut aid to Bosnia, Somalia, Haiti, and the Iraqi no-fly zone, against the wishes of President Bill Clinton and a majority of Democrats. They also voted 28–5 in favor of a proposal to increase education funding to Puerto Rico, while the rest of the Democratic Party voted against the measure by a 168–44 margin.[3] Only rarely has a majority of the CBC made good on a threat to join with Republicans to defeat a Democratic measure. However, table 4.1 reveals that the Republicans in the sample sided with the CBC on 11.4 percent of the roll calls examined here. Thus, coalitions of the CBC and Republicans against the rest of the Democratic Party were not entirely unheard of. The most important instance was the surprise move by the CBC to block action on a bill that would have enhanced the president's line-item veto powers (Hager 1993, 1008).

Most of these bills that pitted the CBC against a majority of the Democratic Party did not have explicit racial content (other examples were nine votes on various aspects of the crime bill and votes on gay rights, cuts in defense spending, disclosure of lobbying activity, and registration requirements for the Selective Service). However, when forced to choose between these two powerful cues, most members of the CBC voted against the Democratic Party at least three-fourths of the time (see the column in table 4.1 labeled "CBC Conflict"). Only five members of the CBC supported the party on 40 percent of these conflict votes, but there was substantial variation within the CBC. In general, commonality members were somewhat less likely to support the CBC on these votes than were difference or older members (difference members were 4.8 percent more likely than commonality members to support the CBC over the party, and older members were 8.5 percent more likely than commonality members to support the CBC over the party).

This show of independence is probably important for strategic reasons—to make sure that the Democratic leadership does not take the CBC's support for granted. One staffer expressed some frustration on this very point: "It is expected that blacks will submerge their interests in the pursuit of partisanship. Where is the compromise and give and take? If the Democratic Party relies on the black vote, you cannot disrespect the base that is your margin of victory" (S29). The next section examines legislation on which the CBC *did* provide the needed margin of victory for the Democrats.

Influencing Legislation

Typical headlines in *Congressional Quarterly Weekly Report* and newspapers throughout the first session of the 103rd Congress read "Black

Caucus Flexes Muscle on Budget," "Black Caucus Forces Delay," and "Black Caucus Using Its Clout." One observer called it "quite possibly the single most influential block in the Democratic Caucus" (Lawrence 1993, 3A)—a far cry from the "generalized publicity organ" or "conscience of the institution" of the 1970s and 1980s. The CBC played a central role in shaping and then passing (in the House) legislation on the budget, the space station, crime, and campaign finance reform. The CBC played hardball with the budget, threatening to kill it unless more funding was provided for the inner cities, the earned-income tax credit, food stamps, and mandatory immunization for poor children. They did not receive everything they bargained for, but they viewed the final package as a substantial improvement over recent budgets (Cunningham and Katz 1993, 2126). The caucus provided the decisive votes to save the space station (which survived by a single vote in 1993) and used its leverage to protect PAC contributions in the version of campaign finance reform that was approved by the House in November 1993.[4]

The CBC also had a major impact on the crime bill, joining Republicans and conservative Democrats to defeat the rule, but then ultimately working to ensure its ultimate passage. The CBC also helped shape legislation on banking issues, welfare reform, and environmental justice (opposition to dumping toxic waste in poor, black areas). They even played an expanded role in foreign policy, an area in which the CBC typically has limited its involvement to African issues. The CBC expressed its displeasure when Clinton reversed himself on Haitian immigration and eventually played a pivotal role in pushing Clinton to reinstate Aristide, provided the critical votes in support of Clinton's Somalia policy, and balked at aid to the former Soviet Union (though twenty-one of the thirty-seven CBC Democrats still supported Clinton's position on Soviet aid).

Overall, the CBC provided the margin of victory on nine of the sixteen "key votes" identified by *Congressional Quarterly* in the first session of the 103rd Congress. On five of those votes the Democrats faced nearly unified Republican opposition (the three budget-related votes had no Republican defections, the Somalia vote had two, and campaign finance reform had three), which placed the CBC in a more critical position. When the chips were down, they delivered a unanimous bloc of votes on seven of the nine votes. In general, there are three measures that can be used to define the CBC's role as a "pivotal" voting bloc in the U.S. House. The most simple measure, and the one that is typically used by the media when they claim that the CBC "defeated

President Clinton's crime bill," is whether the CBC members would
have altered the outcome by switching their votes. The logic is as fol-
lows: the rule on the crime bill was defeated by a 15-vote margin (210–
225); 10 members of the CBC voted against it; therefore, if 8 of those
members would have voted for the rule, it would have passed (218–
217). The logic may seem airtight at first glance, but there are two
problems. First, any eight of the *other* forty-eight Democrats who
voted against the rule could also be seen as pivotal. Second, on most
votes in which CBC members play a potential pivotal role, they would
have to side with the Republicans to defeat a measure that is preferable
to any legislation that they could pass with the Republicans (in this
respect the crime bill is not a particularly good example because most
members of the CBC who voted against the Democratic Party on the
crime bill could have easily supported it—indeed, they fought hard
in conference for the additional spending on prevention programs).
Nonetheless, on 216 of the 984 roll calls in the 103rd Congress the
CBC could have altered the outcome of the bill by switching some or
all of their votes.

A second definition of a pivotal position is when the outcome of the
vote would have changed if the members of the CBC who voted in
favor of the winning side had abstained rather than voting in favor.
Under this more restrictive definition (and more realistic because they
would not have to actually side with the Republicans), the CBC still
played a pivotal role on 63 of the 984 votes. Finally, the most restrictive
definition would label the CBC's collective vote as pivotal only if the
outcome would have been reversed if their votes in favor of the winning
side were subtracted and replaced with the average position of the nonblack Democrats who voted on the winning side of the bill (this formulation is used because the CBC never voted with a majority of Republicans on these pivotal votes). Table 4.2 shows the twenty-one votes on
which the CBC was pivotal with this definition. For example, HR 2264,
the Omnibus Budget Reconciliation of 1993, passed by a vote of 219–
213. Democrats supported the measure by a 219–38 margin, with the
CBC unanimously in favor (37–0). Therefore, non-CBC Democrats
supported the bill by a 182–38 margin. If that rate of support were
applied to the CBC, its members would have voted for the bill by a
31–6 margin, which would have sent the bill down to a 213–219 defeat.
Similar calculations could be made for the other twenty bills.[5]

The answer to the first of the central questions posed above is clear:
the CBC has become an institutional player rather than an outside

Table 4.2   Votes on Which the Congressional Block Caucus Was Pivotal (103rd Congress)*

Year-Cong. Roll Call Number	Description of the Bill	Tally	Democratic Vote	CBC Vote**
93-167	Rejected Duncan amendment to HR 820, which sought a 10% across-the-board cut in all authorizations.	208–21	36–212	0–36
93-191	Rejected McInnis amendment to HR 2244, which sought to cut $14 million for Sec. 24 of the Small Business Act.	209–215	45–208	0–35
93-199	Passed HR 2264, Omnibus Budget Reconciliation Act.	219–213	219–38	37–0
93-238	Rejected the Kasich Amendment to HR 2295, which sought to strike $55 million for World Bank contribution.	210–216	62–193	1–36
93-278	Rejected amendment to HR 2491 to continue funding for Selective Service by cutting $20 million from HUD.	202–207	71–169	3–30
93-317	Passed HR 2492, District of Columbia Appropriation for FY94.	213–211	201–50	37–0
93-406	Agreed to the conference report on HR 2264, Omnibus Budget Reconciliation for FY1994.	218–216	218–41	37–0
93-434	Passed HR 1340, providing funding for the resolution of failed savings associations.	214–208	190–60	31–4
93-453	Rejected the Hefley amendment to HR 2705, which sought to strike funding for the Interstate Commerce Commission.	207–222	53–203	2–35
93-476	Agreed to the conference report on HR 2403, making appropriation for Treasury, Postal Service, and EOP.	207–206	196–48	36–0
93-502	Rejected a motion to recommit HR 2351 and require the Education and Labor Committee to cut funds to illegal immigrants.	210–214	47–204	0–35
93-609	Rejected the Penny amendment to HR 3400, which sought to cut federal spending by $90.4 billion over five years.	213–219	57–201	0–37
94-43	Rejected the Boehner amendment to HR 6, which sought to eliminate funding for	203–213	37–208	0–33

(continues)

Table 4.2 *continued*

Year-Cong. Roll Call Number	Description of the Bill	Tally	Democratic Vote	CBC Vote**
	the Native Hawaiian Education Program.			
94-125	Rejected the Schiff amendment to HR 4092, concerning management of correctional programs.	205–216	43–207	1–35
94-126	Agreed to the Hughes amendment to HR 4092, which authorizes $10 billion in FY95–FY99 to build prisons.	216–206	214–36	35–0
94-156	Passed HR 4296, making the transfer or possession of assault weapons unlawful.	216–214	178–77	36–1
94-216	Passed HR 4454, making appropriations for the Legislative Branch for the FY95.	210–205	208–35	35–0
94-322	Fiscal 1995 District of Columbia Appropriation.	213–210	200–50	36–0
94-389	Defeated the Fingerhut amendment, which would have barred congressional aides from serving as the Executive Director of the Office on Congressional Compliance (concerning workplace laws).	216–220	83–173	2–34
94-418	Agreed to funding for 266 HUD "Special Purpose" projects.	189–180	153–59	31–0
94-484	Removed requirement to receive written permission from landowners before their property could be designated as an American Heritage Management Area.	217–202	174–72	31–2

Notes: Votes in the Committee of the Whole by Delegates to the House are not included.

*Pivotal votes are defined as those in which the outcome would have changed if the CBC's votes were replaced with the average nonblack Democrat's vote on that specific vote.

**Excludes Gary Franks (R–CT).

critic or "conscience for the institution." But for what end is this new power being used? To further black interests or a broader liberal agenda? Of the twenty-one pivotal bills listed in table 4.2, only six can be viewed as even partially related to race (93–278, 93–317, 94–125, 94–156, 94–322, and 94–418). Of these, the bills cutting funding for

HUD, adding HUD special projects, and banning assault weapons were probably the most important for black urban districts, while funding for the District of Columbia and for correctional institutions had taken on symbolic importance for the CBC, even if most of their constituents were not directly affected by these votes. Most of the other bills were spending measures that would not have passed without the support of the CBC. These bills had the strong support of large majorities of the Democratic Party, but were nearly defeated by the Conservative Coalition. Thus, the most central role for the CBC, at least on these pivotal votes, was to serve the broader interests of the party, biracial coalitions, and a politics of commonality rather than the more narrow black interests implied by a politics of difference.

After the Republicans took control of Congress in 1995, the power of the CBC declined. However, the CBC was still pivotal on 69, 29, and 11 of the 1,165 roll call votes in the 104th Congress, using the three definitions of "pivotal" outlined above, including two "key votes" (a vote to restore provisions of a bill that would have weakened the Clean Water and Clean Air Acts and the Delany Clause, concerning the regulation of pesticides on food, and a vote defeating an amendment that would have restricted lobbying by federal agencies). While this may not sound like a large number, Republican unity was so strong in 1995–1996 that the Democrats were virtually shut out of the legislative process. A stunning 38.3 percent of all roll calls in the 104th Congress had no more than two Republican defections (a cohesion rate of 99 percent). At least 90 percent of Republicans voted together on 71.6 percent of the roll calls, and on 54.7 percent of the votes the Republicans actually had 218 votes on the winning side, meaning that the Democrats *were* shut out on these votes. Therefore, white Democrats were not in the position to influence the outcome of legislation much more often than were black Democrats. Using the second definition of a pivotal vote (being able to alter the outcome of the vote by simply abstaining), white Democrats could have shifted only forty-five votes in the 104th Congress (compared to twenty-nine for the CBC.) Thus, while it is true that the CBC lost substantial power in 1995, its members were not much worse off than white Democrats.

Committee Assignments

One of the initial goals of the CBC when it was formed in 1971 was to gain influence over important legislation by securing key committee assignments (Rules, Appropriations, and Ways and Means) (Smith 1981, 216). Louis Stokes, a founding member of the CBC, noted, "'In the history of the Congress no black has even sat as a member of these committees. We were not in the system. Essentially, we had no power in Congress'" (quoted in Cohadas 1985, 676). The CBC won assignments on each of the three prestige committees in 1973, and by 1979 they had doubled their representation on those committees (Stokes, Dixon, and Stewart served on Appropriations; Rangel and Ford were on Ways and Means; and Chisholm served on the Rules Committee in the 96th Congress). The CBC had a goal of placing at least one member on each of the important standing committees, but until the 103rd Congress they simply did not have the bodies to fill the necessary slots.

Despite the limited coverage that was possible with only fifteen to seventeen members, it is interesting to note the types of committees on which blacks elected to serve.[6] In the 96th Congress the only black representative on *any* of the seven constituency committees was Ronald Dellums (D–CA) on Armed Services (no blacks served on Agriculture, Public Works, Merchant Marine, Interior, Science and Technology, or Veterans).[7] This underrepresentation is in strong contrast to their ample representation on the prestige committees, as noted above; the policy committees (ten slots on six committees); and even the undesired committees (seven positions on four committees). By the 102nd Congress eight additional members had been added to the CBC (which grew from seventeen to twenty-five members), allowing increased coverage on a broader range of committees, but the same pattern persisted (see table 4.3). Six of the eight committees with the lowest percentage of blacks were constituency committees (the other two committees, which were fifth and seventh from the bottom, respectively, were Budget and Appropriations). The only two constituency committees to rank above the expected proportion of blacks in the 102nd Congress were Small Business and Public Works.

This pattern changed dramatically in the 103rd Congress. First, black members increased their representation on nearly every committee (Armed Services; Natural Resources, which is currently the only standing committee without any black members; Budget; and Education and Labor were the only exceptions).[8] Craig Washington (D–TX) noted the significance of this broader presence of the CBC on subcommittees: "'Very little [legislation] can move around here without a black person seeing it. Our ability to legislate has been enhanced a great deal.

Table 4.3   Comparison of Black Representation on House Committees (102nd Congress [1991–1992] through 104th Congress [1995–1996])

Rank 1991	Rank 1993	Rank 1995	Committee Name	% Black on Committee* 1991	% Black on Committee* 1993	% Black on Committee* 1995	Committee Type**
1	1	—	District of Columbia	25	40.0	—	Unrequested
2	2	—	Post Office	17.4	28.6	—	Unrequested
4	3	3	Government Operations	12.5	23.8	12.5	Policy
5	4	1	Small Business	11.4	20.0	19.5	Constituency
9	5	2	Banking	5.9	13.7	13.7	Policy
10	6	9	Ways and Means	5.6	13.2	8.3	Prestige
18	7	4	Veterans	2.9	11.4	12.1	Constituency
11	8	6	Judiciary	5.6	11.4	11.1	Policy
20	9	7	Agriculture	2.2	10.4	10.2	Constituency
3	10	5	Education and Labor	15.0	10.3	11.9	Policy
8	11	11	Public Works	7.0	9.7	8.1	Constituency
14	12	8	Foreign Affairs	4.4	9.1	9.8	Policy
13	13	13	Energy and Commerce	4.6	9.1	6.7	Policy
			Expected Proportion	5.8	8.7	9.0	
6	14	18	Rules	7.7	7.7	0	Prestige
7	15	18	Official Conduct	7.1	7.1	0	Unrequested
23	16	12	Science	0	5.5	7.7	Constituency
12	17	14	Select Intelligence	5.3	5.3	5.9	Unrequested
15	18	10	House Administration	4.2	5.3	8.3	Unrequested
17	19	16	Appropriations	3.4	5.2	3.6	Prestige
22	20	—	Merchant Marine	2.1	4.2	—	Constituency
19	21	17	Budget	2.7	2.3	2.3	Prestige
16	22	15	Armed Service	3.6	1.8	5.7	Constituency
21	23	18	Natural Resources	2.1	0	0	Constituency

Notes:
  *% Black on Committee indicates the percentage of the total committee membership that is black.
  **Committee Types is from Smith and Deering (1990, 87).

Heretofore, our strongest hand was played on the floor'" by offering amendments (quoted in Cooper 1993a, 24). Dellums, the former chair of the Armed Services Committee, noted, "We can win now—we've gone beyond just being the 'conscience' of the House" (*New Pittsburgh Courier,* October 20, 1993, A-5). Second, the distribution of committee assignments shifted. Newer members showed their pragmatism and their desire to reach out to all voters, black and white alike, by choosing constituency committees over some of the more traditional black committees. Four constituency committees now rank above the expected proportion of blacks (although four of the bottom five are still constituency committees). Blacks dramatically increased their pres-

ence on the Veterans and Agriculture Committees from 2.9 percent
and 2.2 percent in the 102nd Congress, respectively, to 11.4 percent
and 10.4 percent in the 103rd Congress. The proportions stayed very
stable in the 104th Congress.

Despite the Republican takeover and the loss of slots on committees
for the Democrats, the CBC fared well in the reshuffling because they
comprised a larger proportion of the Democratic Party in the 104th
Congress (17.7 percent) than in the 103rd (14.3 percent). More telling,
while the Democrats lost fifty-four seats in 1995, only one of them was
held by a black member. The Republican majority dealt a major blow
to the CBC by eliminating the two committees on which its members
held the largest proportion of seats (the District of Columbia and Post
Office Committees). The only other substantial change in black membership on committees in the 104th Congress was the exodus from the
Government Operations Committee (black membership dropped from
23.8 percent to 12.5 percent on that committee), which probably became a less attractive assignment when William Clinger replaced John
Conyers as chair.

Subcommittee assignments in the 103rd Congress also reveal some
interesting changes. First, the CBC nearly cut in half the number of
subcommittees on which it had no members (from fifty-eight in the
102nd to only thirty in the 103rd; however, some of this change is accounted for by the elimination of seventeen standing subcommittees
in the 103rd Congress). Second, there were thirty-seven subcommittees
on which at least 15 percent of the members were black in the 103rd
Congress, though this number dropped to twelve in 1995. Another indication of the power of the CBC in the committee system was the
fifteen subcommittees chairs within the CBC (not counting the two
chaired by Eleanor Holmes Norton, the delegate from the District of
Columbia), in addition to the three standing committee chairs (Dellums on Armed Services, Clay on Post Office, and Conyers on Government Operations). Twelve of the twenty nonfreshman Democratic
members of the CBC chaired a committee or subcommittee in the
103rd Congress. Table 4.4 shows another recent development: in addition to the traditional "black politics" subcommittees (Africa subcommittee on Foreign Relations, Civil and Constitutional Rights
subcommittee on Judiciary, District of Columbia Appropriations subcommittee, etc.) blacks were overrepresented on the oversight committees. Part of this can be explained by the popularity among African-
American members of the Government Operations Committee, which

Table 4.4   Black Membership on Subcommittees, by Subcommittee Type (103rd Congress)

Subcommittee Type*	0	.10–10%	10.1–20	>20%	Total
Prestige	9	4	5	1	19
Constituency	9	8	3	3	23
Undesired	6	0	2	0	8
Economic development/human resources	2	2	5	1	10
Black politics/civil rights	0	0	2	7	9
Energy, environment, natural resources	12	3	3	0	18
Technology	4	4	0	0	8
International trade, foreign policy, intelligence	16	3	2	1	22
Oversight	4	1	4	9	18
Other domestic	0	2	5	0	7

Note:

*Subcommittees are classified on the basis of subcommittee jurisdiction and perceived motivations for membership selection of a specific subcommittee rather than the motivations for serving on the parent committee. For example, the District of Columbia subcommittee of Appropriations and the various subcommittees of the D.C. Committee are all classified as "black politics" subcommittees rather than "prestige" or "undesired," respectively.

increased its stature under the chairmanship of Conyers. But most oversight subcommittees on the other standing committees have at least one black member.

The combination of constituency and oversight committees is perfect for these lean fiscal times: protect as many benefits as possible, but use the formidable oversight powers of Congress to bring attention to areas where valuable resources are being wasted or where black interests are not being served. Conyers's interest in holding hearings on the "environmental justice" question is a good example (Cunningham 1993a, 1712–1713). Interestingly one of the only areas in which blacks are seriously underrepresented is on subcommittees concerned with environmental and natural resource issues. Much of this can be explained by the dearth of black members from western states, which are traditionally strong in these areas.

The distribution of committee assignments clearly shows that the CBC had moved into a new era in terms of its role in policy-making. The CBC had evolved from strategic placement on a few policy committees and prestige committees to a broad presence on all committees, with a special focus on oversight and black politics. This distribution of assignments should serve the CBC well in coming years as it takes on greater policy responsibilities. Minority districting in 1992 has been the catalyst in this change in the CBC institutional role. Half of the assignments received by the seventeen first-term members of the CBC (nineteen of thirty-eight) were on constituency committees, such as Small Business, Agriculture, Veterans, and Public Works, compared to 24 percent of the assignments for the twenty nonfreshman CBC members (eleven of forty-six slots). While serving in the minority party has limited the CBC's influence on legislation, it continues to help shape the Democratic Party's policy alternatives.

Leadership Positions

With their early institutional role defined in terms of confrontation and consciousness-raising, there was little incentive for black members of Congress to become team players and join the leadership. Early moves in this direction were viewed with skepticism by some observers. "These new powers and responsibilities have enabled black Representatives to exert policy influence but not as a Black Caucus per se. These individual successes have therefore detracted from a common Caucus identity and strategy, and weakened its impact" (Levy and Stoudinger 1978, 332).

This perception started to change in the 1980s, when the first African American broke into the top Democratic Party leadership in the House. William Gray served as cochair of the Democratic Leadership Council, chair of the Budget Committee, Democratic Caucus chair, and then majority whip, the number three leadership position, in his thirteen-year tenure in the House. While his retirement in 1991 left a hole in the black leadership, Gray set the stage for the continuing evolution of the role of the CBC within the House. As blacks move into leadership positions, the CBC will continue to grow into its role as an institutional player. While few today would assert that having blacks in high leadership positions weakens the impact of the CBC, there are tensions that come from having institutional loyalties to both the CBC and the Democratic Party. Kitty Cunningham notes that John Lewis is a "leader of the party, not a leader of the caucus. . . . Lewis conceded that there is some conflict between his leadership duties and his responsibilities to the caucus. He was one of several members pushing for moderation in the group's reaction to the Guinier nomination" (1993a, 1715). Carol Swain points out that Gray voted "present" on several of the CBC budgets in the 1980s (along with Mike Espy), much to the chagrin of many of his colleagues. According to Swain, "[A]s more and more blacks climb the leadership ladder, it seems likely that [the CBC] will cease being an organization geared primarily toward advancing a black-focused agenda" (1993, 40–41). While my evidence shows that most members of the CBC currently balance their legislative efforts between racial and nonracial issues, to the extent that blacks in Congress become more fully integrated into the leadership, black members' legislative influence will continue to grow.

Race and the Legislative Process

The pivotal role played by the CBC on roll call votes and its increasing presence on a broader array of committees and subcommittees and in the House Democratic leadership provide strong evidence of the increased clout of the CBC in the 103rd Congress. However, Guinier, or any skeptic who questions whether a minority can ever have power within a majority-rule institution as it is currently constituted, would be unsatisfied with this range of evidence. So what if there are more blacks on the Agriculture and Small Business Committees? So what if the CBC provided the pivotal votes to save funding for the Native Hawaiian Education Program or to fund the Post Office (see table 4.2)? The bottom line is what happens when issues of race are discussed. Does legislation that concerns race have a tougher time making it through the legislative labyrinth than nonracial legislation?

To examine systematically these questions, I coded the racial content of all roll call votes in the 103rd Congress and all bills that were co-sponsored by at least one of the fifty-three members in my primary sample (members of the CBC and all members who represent districts that are at least 25 percent black in the 103rd Congress). The roll call votes provide a good first cut at the analysis, but as I argue below, selection bias produces an unrepresentative sample: bills that make it that far in the legislative process will be more moderate than the universe of proposals. The subset of 2,751 proposed bills provides a good approximation of the universe of the racial agenda in Congress. While it is conceivable that an issue that is of central importance to African Americans would have been completely ignored by all fifty-three members who represent more than half of the nation's blacks (50.9 percent), it is unlikely that this process would have missed more than a handful of proposed bills. To test whether racial issues are disadvantaged in the legislative process, I calculated the average roll call vote margins on racial, part-racial, and nonracial issues and tracked the progress of each of the 2,751 proposed bills through the legislative process. If Guinier's assertions are correct, roll call votes on racial and part-racial issues should have closer margins than nonracial issues. However, due to selection bias this is a relatively weak test of her claims. The fate of introduced bills, based on their racial content, is a much stronger test. If Guinier is correct, racial and part-racial bills should die in committee more frequently than nonracial bills, and fewer should be passed by the House or signed into law.

Before describing the results, I will briefly explain the coding procedure. The racial and nonracial categories are relatively easy to code. Bills dealing with civil rights, discrimination, minority businesses, and historically black colleges; the Racial Justice Act; the Anti-redlining in Insurance Disclosure Act; and dozens of pieces of commemorative legislation (e.g., bills regarding Louis Armstrong, Thurgood Marshall, Dizzy Gillespie, and National African American Health Awareness Week) are coded as racial. Nonracial bills are also straightforward—anything that has no obvious racial impact is coded as nonracial. This category includes the vast majority of Congress's business. However, in making these decisions, one cannot always rely on the title of the bill. In many cases bills appear to be nonracial, such as Charles Rangel's National Son-in-Law Day bill, but upon reading the legislation it is clear that there was a racial motivation (in this case the resolution calls attention to the special contribution of African-American sons-in-law to their families and to society). In such cases the bills were coded as part racial. Other part-racial bills are those that not only *affect* African-American constituents, but also *have a disproportionate impact* on them; examples would include legislation concerning public housing, food stamps, welfare, inner-city revitalization, and gun control. These issues include, but are not restricted to, the "implicit racial" issues shown in figure 1.2 (and discussed by Kinder and Sanders 1996, 30).

Finally, I also make a distinction between symbolic and substantive legislation. The former mostly includes commemorative legislation and comprises a small proportion (11.9 percent) of the 2,751 bills. This distinction is important to provide an accurate test of Guinier's claims because many white members may be willing to vote for renaming a post office to honor a civil rights leader, but unwilling to strengthen programs to promote diversity in higher education. In making the distinction between substantive and symbolic legislation, I do not attempt to discern the motivation of a member of Congress. A large proportion of proposed legislation could be seen as symbolic if one had perfect information on members' motivations. For example, members of Congress often propose legislation that they know has little chance of success, such as John Conyers's repeated submission of a slavery reparations bill, simply to please a constituency or an interest group or to preempt a challenger's policy agenda. Others may propose legislation knowing that it will be struck down by the U.S. Supreme Court if it does pass (such as a proposal to allow prayer in the schools) or will die in the Senate (such as a constitutional amendment requiring a balanced budget or term limits). Such behavior could be considered symbolic. However, given that it is virtually impossible to discern members' motivations for proposing a bill, instead I rely on the more practical coding rule: *would the bill have a substantive impact on public policy if it became law?*

Most joint resolutions are coded as symbolic legislation (the primary exceptions are proposed constitutional amendments), and simple House resolutions are the source of most other symbolic proposals. While an argument could be made for coding all House resolutions as symbolic, given that they do not require action by the Senate or the signature of the president and do not have the force of law, resolutions often have important policy consequences. The House uses simple resolutions to express the "sense of the House" on important foreign policy issues or to provide funding for investigative committees (as for the recent campaign finance hearings in the House). Simple resolutions are also the vehicle for reporting a rule from the Rules Committee and, therefore, are an integral part of the legislative process.[9]

A few additional examples should help clarify the categories. In the 104th Congress Robert Scott, a commonality member from Virginia, cosponsored the following legislation: several substantive nonracial measures that were of special interest to Virginians, such as H.R. 2189, price supports for peanuts, and H.R. 1091, to improve the quality of the national park system in Virginia. He also cosponsored many substantive nonracial bills with more general orientations, such as H.R. 447, to establish a toll-free telephone number in the Department of Commerce to assist consumers in identifying domestically produced merchandise, and H.R. 2963, which concerned the treatment of government contracts during a government shutdown. Others, such as H.R. 616, to design a $1 coin to commemorate Martin Luther King, Jr., and H.R. 1129, to designate the route of the voting rights march from Selma, Alabama, to Montgomery, Alabama, as a National Historical Trail, were coded as symbolic racial issues. A proposal to authorize appropriations for programs relative to the health of individuals from disadvantaged backgrounds (H.R. 1314) was coded as substantive and part racial.

That the overwhelming proportion of bills and roll call votes has nothing to do with race provides some support for the view that minority voices are not being heard in Congress. Only 86 of the 984 roll calls in the 103rd Congress had anything to do with race, and 23 of these took positions that were opposed to the CBC's position. Only eleven roll calls explicitly concerned race; six were in favor of the CBC's position. Only 80 of the 2,751 bills had a substantive pro-CBC racial focus, while 301 (10.9 percent) had a part-racial focus. However, it is not clear that Guinier's proposals would increase the *volume* of racially oriented legislation; rather, she is interested in improving the responsiveness of the institution and thus the rate of success.[10]

The vote margins on roll calls (defined here as the percentage of members voting "yes") from the 103rd Congress do not support the notion that the deck is stacked against minority interests in the House. The 898 nonracial votes had an average vote margin of 62.6 percent, while part-racial issues had the highest average margin of any category (65.6 percent, $n = 57$), and racial issues' average margin was 51.9 percent ($n = 6$). Roll calls that were opposed to part-racial issues had the lowest margin (46.5 percent, $n = 18$), while the five roll calls that opposed explicitly racial issues had an average of 58.4 percent. None of the differences between pairs of these averages was statistically significant. Thus, by this simple measure racial interests are not disadvantaged in the House.

The more complete analysis of the racial agenda in the House reveals the same thing: black interests are not disadvantaged. If anything, they are slightly favored (see table 4.5). To track the progress of a measure through the legislative process, I coded nine possible outcomes for the bill, from dying in committee, to passing one house and failing in the other, to dying in conference, to being signed into law. I collapsed these nine outcomes into three: "stayed alive" (did not die in committee), passed the House, and was signed into law. I also coded the number of hearings that were held on the legislation. Substantive bills with some racial content had more hearings than nonracial bills (while racial bills were about the same as nonracial); substantive racial

bills were also more likely than nonracial bills to make it out of committee ($t = 1.85$, sig. at .03), twice as likely to pass the House as nonracial bills ($t = 2.43$, sig. at .008), and nearly twice as likely to become
law ($t = 1.17$, sig. at .12). Substantive part-racial bills were slightly less
likely than nonracial bills to survive the various stages of the legislative
process, but the differences were not statistically significant. However,
these bills do attract about a third more cosponsors than do nonracial
bills ($t = 1.69$, sig. at .05).

There are two noteworthy points about symbolic legislation: First,
symbolic bills, both racial and nonracial, attract more than three times
as many cosponsors on average as substantive bills, and they enjoy
much higher levels of success. It clearly is more attractive to vote on
or cosponsor legislation concerning the naming of a post office, regardless of the honoree's skin color, than it is to vote on substantive legislation. Symbolic legislation is a low-cost means of advertising; few voters
would be upset about the name on a post office, while any substantive
legislation is bound to alienate some segment of a member's constituency (Mayhew 1974, 61–69). Second, symbolic bills rarely receive hearings; it is somewhat reassuring that members waste limited amounts of
valuable time on these symbolic exercises.

Another way to test Guinier's assertion is to examine the relative
success a bill has based on the race of the sponsor rather than the
racial content of the bill. Bills that have a black sponsor are 60 percent
more likely to become law than those that do not have a black sponsor.
Of the 472 bills introduced by black members, 7.4 percent became law,
compared to only 4.5 percent of the 2,297 bills introduced by nonblack
members ($t = 2.67$, sig. at .004). This finding undermines both Guinier's claims that black interests cannot be served in a majority-rule
institution and the "no racial differences" hypothesis that the race of
the member does not influence representation.

A multivariate logit analysis provides a more systematic test of some
of these patterns.[11] Table 4.6 reveals that racial bills are more likely
than nonracial bills to make it out of committee and pass the House
(though the coefficients fail to reach statistical significance because of
the small numbers of racial bills), part-racial bills are less likely than
nonracial bills to make it through the various stages, and, perhaps the
most surprising result, the bivariate relationship between black sponsorship and a bill becoming law remains significant in the multivariate
analysis. Using the derivative method for interpreting logit coefficients

Table 4.5   Racial Content of Bills and Their Legislative Outcome (103rd Congress)

	Racial Content	Number of Hearings per Bill	Number of Sponsors per Bill	Stayed Alive	Passed One Chamber	Became Law
Substantive bills	Nonracial	.20	30.0	9.9%	7.6%	3.7%
		(2,024)	(2,024)	(2,024)	(2,024)	(2,024)
	Part-racial	.32	34.4	8.0%	5.3%	2.3%
		(301)	(301)	(301)	(301)	(301)
	Racial	.21	23.4	16.3%	15%	6.3%
		(80)	(80)	(80)	(80)	(80)
	Against racial	.32	46.2	5.3%	5.3%	0
		(19)	(19)	(19)	(19)	(19)
Symbolic bills	Nonracial	.03	109.8	23.0%	21.9%	15.3%
		(274)	(274)	(274)	(274)	(274)
	Part-racial	0	100.9	25%	25%	16.7%
		(12)	(12)	(12)	(12)	(12)
	Racial	.03	39.7	23.7%	23.7%	18.4%
		(38)	(38)	(38)	(38)	(38)
	Against racial	0	0	0	0	0
		(3)	(3)	(3)	(3)	(3)
Totals		.20	38.7	11.4%	9.2%	5.0%
		(2,751)	(2,751)	(2,751)	(2,751)	(2,751)

Note: The table includes all bills that had at least one cosponsor from a member in my sample in the 103rd Congress (districts that are at least 25 percent black or are represented by a black member of the House).

outlined by Gary King, starting from the underlying probability of passing a bill (5 percent), having a black sponsor increases the probability of passage to 8.9 percent (the marginal effect is .05 * .95 * .82 = .039; added to the underlying probability of .05, this equals .089) (King 1989, 108–110). The relative difficulty that part-racial bills have in making it through the process is the only bit of evidence that would support Guinier's position.

Several of the control variables also have substantial effects: having symbolic content, two hearings, or 125 Democratic cosponsors (which is about 100 more than the mean number of cosponsors) increases the underlying probability of a bill becoming a law from 5 percent to more than 10 percent. The impact of Democratic cosponsorship is larger than that found in previous research (Wilson and Young 1997). The last column in table 4.6 reveals a slightly different set of relationships when cosponsorship is considered a dependent variable rather than an

Table 4.6 Logit Analysis of the Racial Content of Bills and Their Legislative Outcome (103rd Congress)

Independent Variable	Stayed Alive	Passed One Chamber	Became Law	Number of Cosponsors
Black sponsor	.20	.37*	.82**	−28.3**
	(.18)	(.20)	(.25)	(2.74)
Number of Democratic cosponsors	.014**	.013**	.011**	—
	(.0018)	(.0019)	(.0023)	
Number of Republican cosponsors	−.0080**	−.0079**	−.0041	—
	(.003)	(.0034)	(.0041)	
Racial bill	.26	.30	−.019	−7.0[+]
	(.28)	(.30)	(.38)	(5.04)
Part-racial bill	−.51*	−.78**	−.90**	11.05**
	(.23)	(.28)	(.30)	(3.10)
Symbolic bill	.32*	.90**	1.20**	72.65**
	(.19)	(.20)	(.24)	(2.95)
Number of hearings	—	.77**	.58**	3.05**
		(.076)	(.086)	(1.04)
Constant	−2.41**	−3.01**	−3.82**	33.37**
	(.088)	(.11)	(.15)	(1.15)
Percentage predicted correctly	88.8%	90.8%	95.0%	Adj. R^2 = .21
Naive prediction	88.6%	90.8%	95.0%	F = 119.7**
Number of bills	2,751	2,751	2,751	2,751

Notes: Standard errors are in parentheses.

The number of cosponsors is calculated with OLS regression; the other three models are logistic regressions.

Dependent variable: for the first three models, coded as 1 if the bill stayed alive, passed one chamber, or became law; 0 otherwise; for the fourth model, the dependent variable is the number of cosponsors for each bill.

[+]Significant at the .10 level.
*Significant at the .05 level.
**Significant at the .01 level.

independent variable. Part-racial bills attract about eleven more co-sponsors than nonracial bills, but racial bills and bills sponsored by a black member do not fare as well.

The finding that racial legislation and bills that are sponsored by black members of Congress have a slight advantage in the legislative process surprised me as much as anything in this book. I expected that the evidence would support Guinier's argument that minorities have a tough time in majority-rule institutions. The majoritarian nature of the legislative process in the House is well established (Krehbiel 1991), and nothing in the black politics or congressional literature prepared me for this finding. I do not want to exaggerate the point. The CBC clearly does not run the House—and did not even when the House was controlled by the Democrats. A relatively small fraction of the work of the House touches on racial issues. However, when racial legislation does come up, it has as good a chance as any (and slightly better) of making its way through the legislative process.

Racial Representation at the Individual Level

Overview of the Analysis

In this part of my analysis I will examine Leadership Conference on Civil Rights (LCCR) scores, broader measures of roll call voting, committee and leadership positions, sponsorship and cosponsorship of legislation, and speeches on the floor of the House of the members in the 103rd Congress to determine the nature of racial representation in each district in the sample (members of the CBC and those who served in districts that were at least 25 percent black). Speeches, bills, and roll calls were coded as racial, nonracial, or part racial and as substantive or symbolic according to the procedures outlined above. This analysis differs from the previous section by shifting the focus of analysis from the institutional to the individual level.

This multifaceted approach has several advantages over the typical focus on roll call voting used to study race and representation in Congress. First, using a variety of data sources to tackle the same substantive question increases confidence in one's findings. Second, roll call analysis that relies on aggregate measures of behavior is a blunt instrument that masks huge differences in racial representation. For example, Tom Barrett, a white representative from Milwaukee, and John Conyers, a black representative from Detroit, both had LCCR scores of 100 for the 103rd Congress. One might conclude that there is no difference in the extent of representation provided to black constituents in those two districts. However, that conclusion is wrong. John Conyers has been one of the strongest advocates for civil rights and black interests in his thirty-two-year tenure in the House. Representative Barrett has supported most black concerns that arise on a roll call vote, but he has not focused most of his legislative activity on black interests. Conyers tirelessly pushes legislation even when he knows it cannot succeed (such as the slavery reparations bill), constantly seeking out black constituents and attending to their needs. His speeches on the floor of the House are studded with references to black interests and racial politics. In short, John Conyers views legislative politics through the lens of black politics; Tom Barrett (or any other white representative who is sympathetic to black interests) does not. Blunt measures based on aggregated roll call scores are part of the story, but only a relatively small part. Furthermore, as I will explain below, an exclusive focus on roll call voting produces biased estimates of racial representation because of the censored sample problem.

Finally, a content analysis of speeches and bills permits a more nuanced analysis of how a member presents issues to his or her constituency. On an issue such as the North American Free Trade Agreement (NAFTA), some members of the CBC, such as John Lewis (D–GA), addressed the issue in a completely nonracial manner, focusing on how the policy would affect his entire district. Others, such as Barbara Rose Collins (D–MI), focused almost exclusively on how NAFTA would affect the African Americans in her district. A roll call analysis would note that both of these members voted against NAFTA, but the *racial motivation* of that vote could not be inferred. Furthermore, as the deliberative democrats reviewed in chapter 1 argue, the nuances of legislative positions and the nature of debates can have a critical impact on the issue agenda and can raise a new perspective that can alter the terms of debate (Gutmann and Thompson 1996; Bessette 1994).

William Riker addresses this same point from a formal theory perspective, arguing that members can create new equilibria by manipulation of the issue dimension through political debate. He gives the example of Senator Warren Magnuson's brilliant "heresthetic maneuver" that prevented a shipment of nerve gas from Japan from being brought through his home state of Washington. Rather than employing the standard parochial NIMBY ("not in my backyard") arguments, Magnuson was able to carry the day by turning the issue into a "Senate versus the president" battle over an important matter of foreign policy (having to do with Senate consultation according to the terms of the Okinawa treaty) (Riker 1986, 109–110). Race can similarly alter the issue dimension when interjected into the debate; for example, when our policy toward South Africa became widely perceived as a domestic civil rights issue in the 1980s, many white southern Democrats pressured President Ronald Reagan to toughen his stand against apartheid. More recently the CBC has shaped our policy toward Haiti, Somalia, and Rwanda by devoting extensive attention to those nations.

This analysis will examine differences between white and black representatives and explain variation within the CBC. The central explanatory variable for the latter point is whether the House member was

elected with an electoral coalition rooted in the politics of difference
or the politics of commonality. The central theoretical expectation is
that practitioners of the politics of difference will have a larger proportion of their legislative agenda and speeches dedicated to racial issues
and their roll call votes will more closely match African-American interests relative to practitioners of the politics of commonality, who will
be more likely to pursue biracial politics.

Constituency characteristics comprise the other explanatory variables. As I argued in chapter 1, constituency interests can be thought
of as wants (which imply a delegate model of representation) and needs
(which imply a trustee model). Alternatively these facets of constituency interests could be thought of as subjective interests (wants) and
objective interests (needs) (see Swain 1993, 7–11). I will rely on objective district characteristics (median income, percentage urban, percentage African American, and whether the district is in the South) to
control for district needs.[12]

Aggregate Roll Call Analysis

The standard approach used to assess the nature of black representation regresses district-level characteristics on various interest group
ratings, such as ADA (Americans for Democratic Action), COPE
(Committee on Political Education), or LCCR (Leadership Conference on Civil Rights) scores (see Swain 1993; Lublin 1997; Whitby
1998). While the practice is widely used in the literature, this tendency
can largely be explained by the "law of available data." Roll call data,
especially interest group ratings, are readily available and easily analyzed, but are not accurate measures of a member's overall behavior
in Congress because of the "censored sample problem" (King 1989,
208–213). Assume a range of activities in support of black interests on
a continuum from 0 to 100, with one extreme of the scale anchored by
Senator Jesse Helms (R–NC) and his opposition to most racial issues
that would be of interest to the black community and the other by
Representative John Conyers (D–MI) and his slavery reparations bill,
which he introduces every session. On this 0–100 scale, only activities
in the middle range of concerns ever make it to a roll call vote. The
more extreme positions on either end are weeded out in the legislative
process or are reflected in different aspects of the process, such as
speeches on the floor of the House or constituency service. A statistical

analysis based on this censored sample (in effect, the two tails of the distribution are chopped off) yields biased parameter estimates. In other words, one can say very little about the extent of black representation based on roll call votes or on the interest group support scores that are derived from roll call votes.

Furthermore, LCCR scores are not an especially good measure of black interests. Many of the issues included in the LCCR measure are not of central importance to the African-American community. Diane Pinderhughes notes, "'The LCCR, founded by two blacks and one white, is no longer seen by black organizations as a black coalition, since black groups constitute only about a third of its membership'" (quoted in Cobb and Jenkins 1996, 7). An analysis of the roll call votes included to derive the LCCR support scores for the 103rd Congress reveals that only two of the fourteen votes—D.C. statehood and the amendment to delete the Racial Justice Act—are clearly related to black interests (see table 4.7). On three other votes the LCCR's position was opposed by a majority of blacks. The LCCR opposed the amendment to the Elementary and Secondary Education Reauthorization Act that would have allowed Title 1 funds to be used for public school choice programs and would have prohibited the use of public money for family planning or reproductive services. However, blacks generally favor public school choice and are more opposed to abortion than whites (though blacks are about evenly split on the issue). A recent poll by the Joint Center for Political Studies in Washington, D.C., showed that 88.2 percent of blacks who have heard of school choice or voiced an opinion on choice favor the policy (Bositis 1993, table 4). The abortion issue is more complex. A 1994 National Election Survey (NES) showed that 22 percent of blacks, but only 11 percent of whites were willing to ban abortions in all circumstances. Katherine Tate shows that blacks are between 1 and 13 percent more supportive of the pro-life position than whites depending on the year and question wording (Tate 1993, 39). The average support by blacks for abortion over the past 40 years has been almost exactly 50 percent (NES, University of Michigan, 1956–1996).

Therefore, given that the ban on abortion funding was tacked onto a bill concerning elementary and secondary education (which was supported by a large majority of blacks), it is reasonable to assume that a majority of blacks would have supported this pairing of issues, whereas the LCCR opposed the bill. The LCCR also supported lifting the ban

Table 4.7   LCCR Key Roll Call Votes (103rd Congress)

Subject of the Roll Call Vote	Black Interests in the Bill?			LCCR Position	Position of the LCCR Consistent with the Position of Black Voters?
	Yes	Part	No		
Elementary and Secondary Education Reauthorization Act*			X	Oppose	No
Education Act without Choice and Abortion Amendments		X		Favor	Yes
Optional Family and Medical Leave			X	Oppose	Yes
Mandated Family and Medical Leave			X	Favor	Yes
Motor Voter Law with Proof of Citizenship Amendment		X		Oppose	Yes
Motor Voter Registration		X		Favor	Yes
Amendment to Delete the Racial Justice Act	X			Oppose	Yes
Grants to States to Reduce Violent Crime against Women			X	Favor	Yes
Statehood for the District of Columbia	X			Favor	Yes
Balanced Budget Constitutional Amendment			X	Oppose	No
Prohibition against Hiring Permanent Striker Replacements			X	Favor	—**
Congressional Compliance with Federal Labor Laws			X	Favor	—
Brady Bill—Five-Day Waiting Period for Handgun Purchase		X		Favor	Yes
Lifting the Ban on Gays in the Military			X	Favor	No

Notes:

*Included a public school choice provision and a prohibition against using money in the bill for family planning or reproductive services.

**I did not have polling data on these two issues that were broken down by race.

on gays in the military, a position that is opposed by large majorities of blacks. Tate reports that blacks are generally less tolerant of gay rights than whites (who are also not very tolerant), ranging from 5 to 17 percent less supportive of gay rights (Tate 1993, 39). Finally, various national polls have shown that blacks favor a balanced budget amendment along with a majority of all Americans.

Thus, on two issues the LCCR votes are consistent with black interests, but on three others they are clearly opposed. Four votes—the two "motor voter" votes, the Brady bill vote, and the education bill vote—were partly related to black interests (blacks are more likely to be registered under the provisions of the bill than whites, blacks are more affected by handgun violence than whites, and blacks support higher levels of spending on education than whites), but the eight other bills, such as those concerning violence against women and Congress's compliance with labor laws, are not issues that are specifically relevant to the black community. In fact, the fourteen votes are indistinguishable from a liberal Democratic agenda that is mostly unrelated to race.

However, LCCR scores can provide a baseline test of whether descriptive representation translates into substantive representation. Because the censored samples yield conservative tests of hypotheses, failing to reject the null hypothesis of no difference between blacks and whites, or different styles of black representation, would be inconclusive, but finding more positive evidence of differences would be encouraging. However, these tests will not indicate anything about racial representation. The simple difference of means test reveals a twenty-five-point difference in LCCR scores between black and white members of Congress in districts that are at least 25 percent black and a seventeen-point difference between whites and blacks overall (table 4.8).

The multivariate analysis shown in table 4.9 supports the hypothesis that members of the 1992 class who were elected on the basis of the politics of difference support an agenda that appeals more to African Americans than do practitioners of the politics of commonality (to the

Table 4.8   LCCR Scores by Race and Party (103rd Congress)

Party and Race of the Representative		>25% Black Districts	All Districts
Democrat	African American	97.9	97.9
		(36)	(37)
	Other minority	100	91.2
		(1)	(17)
	White	72.6	80.7
		(11)	(204)
Republican	African American	—	21
			(1)
	Other minority	—	37.3
			(4)
	White	14.3	24.4
		(3)	(171)
Differences in mean LCCR score for black and white Democrats		25.3*	17.2*
t-statistics for differences in means		6.31	5.67

Notes: Table entries are LCCR support scores, adjusted for absences; House Speaker Tom Foley did not have an LCCR score and is omitted from the analysis. Numbers of cases are in parentheses.

*Significant at the .0001 level (one-tailed test).

Table 4.9   Regression Analysis of LCCR Support Scores (103rd Congress)

Independent Variable	Model 1
African-American member of Congress—commonality	21.35**
	(9.57)
African-American member of Congress—difference	26.94**
	(10.65)
African-American member of Congress—older	11.62+
	(8.25)
Median family income	.00011
	(.00017)
Percentage of black constituents (×100)	.0056
	(.14)
Percentage of district in urban area (×100)	.13**
	(.044)
Southern district	−13.85**
	(5.29)
Party (1 = Republican; 0 = Democrat)	−56.44**
	(2.33)
Other minority member of Congress	9.33**
	(5.11)
Constant	73.16*
	(5.38)
F-statistic	97.85**
Adjusted R-square	.67
Number of districts	434

Notes: Dependent variable: member's LCCR support score, adjusted for absences.
   Standard errors are in parentheses.
   House Speaker Tom Foley did not have an LCCR score and is omitted from the
analysis.
   +Significant at the .10 level (one-tailed test).
   *Significant at the .05 level.
   **Significant at the .01 level.

extent that LCCR scores reveal much about racial politics). "Difference" members have adjusted LCCR scores that are 5.6 points higher than those of "commonality" members, who, in turn, have scores that are nearly ten points higher than the "older" members of the CBC and twenty-one points higher than those of whites. Other minorities in the House (Latinos and Asian Americans) have LCCR scores that are about nine points higher than those of whites, and southerners' scores are fourteen points lower than those of nonsoutherners. Thus, a southern "commonality" member would have a slightly lower score than would an older member from the non-South. A member from an entirely urban district would have an LCCR score that is nearly thirteen points higher than that of a member from an entirely rural district.

The most striking variable is the huge fifty-six-point difference between Democrats and Republicans, which supports the assertion above that the LCCR's agenda is quite similar to a liberal Democratic agenda.

In table 4.1, I displayed the CBC support scores and "conflict" scores, which showed the percentage of times that members supported the CBC's position when a majority of CBC members and nonblack Democrats were on opposite sides of an issue. The latter measure is an especially good indicator of the "balancing" hypothesis for commonality members. That is, commonality members should have significantly lower scores on the conflict measure (they should support the party position when it is in conflict with the CBC position) than do difference members.

Table 4.10   Cohesion and Opposition within the Congressional Black Caucus on Roll Call Votes (103rd Congress)

Independent Variable	CBC Support	CBC Support2
African-American member of Congress—commonality	16.2**	20.1**
	(3.48)	(8.10)
African-American member of Congress—difference	13.9**	34.9**
	(3.35)	(8.42)
African-American member of Congress—older	13.1**	24.6**
	(2.93)	(7.07)
Other minority member	15.1*	36.7*
	(6.67)	(16.1)
Percentage of black constituents (×100)	.13*	.76**
	(.08)	(.19)
Percentage of district in urban area (×100)	.02	.19*
	(.045)	(.11)
Southern district	−4.21*	−6.67
	(2.41)	(5.83)
Party (1 = Republican; 0 = Democrat)	−40.26**	−7.54
	(4.11)	(9.91)
Constant	113.1**	−3.01**
	(8.41)	(.11)
F-statistic	44.0**	19.2**
Adjusted R-square	.87	.74
Number of bills	53	53

Notes: Dependent variables: CBC Support is the percentage of times the member supported the majority of members of the Congressional Black Caucus on the 984 roll call votes in the 103rd Congress. Scores are corrected for absences, times 100.

CBC Support2 indicates the member's support for the CBC's position when a majority of the CBC voted against a majority of the nonblack Democratic membership. There were 80 of these roll call votes in the 103rd Congress. Scores are corrected for absences, times 100.

*Significant at the .05 level.

**Significant at the .01 level.

Table 4.10 shows the results of a multivariate regression that explains variation in support for the CBC's position. In the first model there are few differences within the CBC (which is consistent with the descriptive data shown in table 4.1), but a huge forty-point difference between Democrats and Republicans. The second model shows strong support for the supply-side theory. Difference members show the strongest level of support for the CBC position when it is in conflict with the Democratic Party's position, and commonality members show the lowest level of support (of the three groups of black members). The percentage of black constituents in the district also exerts a strong influence: for a 20 percent increase in the percentage of black constituents, support for the CBC's position increases by more than 15 percent. This finding is unusual in the race and representation literature because most other works exclude either the percentage of black voters (Whitby 1998) or the race of the member (Lublin 1997) or they report each of them in separate regressions (Swain 1993, table 1.3 [p. 16] reports the impact of percentage black, but not race; table 10.2 [p. 215] reports the impact of the race of the member, but not percentage black).[13] To truly understand the nature of racial representation, both of these key explanations must be included. But more important, analysis must move beyond the focus on roll call voting. The next sections will take up that challenge.

Committee Assignments

Students of Congress from Woodrow Wilson (1885) to Richard Fenno (1973) have pointed to the central role that congressional committees play in the policy-making process. Recent theories of congressional institutions focus on the informational (Krehbiel 1991) or distributional advantages (Weingast and Marshall 1988) that committees provide to members. Both of these approaches provide some leverage in explaining the distribution of committee assignments within the CBC. From an informational perspective members of the CBC provide useful signals to the floor on a broad range of racial and part-racial issues. Thus, the floor should have an incentive to distribute assignments to black members across a broad range of committees that address these issues. Like the attorney who has lower costs of specialization to serve on the Judiciary Committee or the farmer who gravitates to the Agriculture Committee, African Americans who have a background in the civil rights movement or on broader issues that are relevant to black politics will have lower costs of specialization and lower barriers to entry for subcommittees such as the Judiciary subcommittee on Constitution and Civil Rights or the Small Business subcommittee on Minority Enterprise and Development. The distributive perspective would explain the same patterns of behavior by focusing on the constituent demands for policy benefits in those areas. My supply-side theory adds the representational perspective of the politics of commonality and difference. Difference members are more likely to seek committee assignments that focus more narrowly on black politics, while commonality members are more likely to seek a broader range of assignments, especially those that focus on constituency interests.

My interviews provide some anecdotal evidence to support these hypotheses. A staffer for a commonality member said, "We were very pleased with our assignments. Public Works will be an important committee. With Clinton's emphasis on building up the infrastructure, this will provide an opportunity to get some jobs for the district. Also, Representative B should be able to become a player on this committee more quickly than some of the others" (S2). A commonality member noted a similar constituency-based motivation: "My committee assignments were selected with a view to serving the district. Banking and Finance was the big one. We have more banking in our district than just about anybody else" (M7). On the other hand, a difference member said that he pursued a seat on Small Business to address issues like redlining in the insurance industry and access to capital and credit for minority businesses (M8). Sometimes the motivation to join a committee may be more idiosyncratic; a staffer for a difference member mentioned that his boss took a "seat on Post Office as a favor to Bill Clay. At first he looked at it as a temporary assignment, but now he likes it and may stay" (S4).

The decision to join a committee may also be based on a more complex interaction of constituency and race. A staffer for a difference member said, "He got on the Agriculture Committee to appeal to the white farmers in the district. Also, Rep. X [a senior white Democrat with interests in the area] pushed him to get on it. He also saw it as a vehicle for some of his pet projects, and he didn't realized how commodity-oriented the committee was. He speaks the rhetoric now, but he will never get involved in agricultural policy. He will never immerse himself in the issues—it's not where his heart is" (S11). Thus, contrary to expectations, a difference member sought a constituency committee to serve the interests of white voters rather than blacks. This evidence is consistent with the roll call data discussed above that showed difference members moderating their positions to appeal to whites and broaden their political base (see pp. 150–151).

The first of these hypotheses, that difference members are more likely to sit on subcommittees that concern minority politics, is relatively easy to test. There were nine subcommittees in the 103rd Congress that were identified with minority politics to varying degrees. The second hypothesis concerning constituency committees is more difficult to test. Given the complexity and fluidity of committee jurisdictions (King 1997), members can use a broad range of committees for narrowly or broadly focused policies. Furthermore, a member could use a constituency committee, such as Agriculture, to serve district-wide interests or to focus more narrowly on the needs of rural black constituents (or white farmers). There is simply no way to sort out these complex relationships with the blunt instrument of assignment data. However, an individual-level analysis of committee assignments can provide an indirect test of the argument that CBC members' presence on a broad range of committees indicates a diversified base of power. If this argument is true, one might expect black members to hold a greater number of committee assignments than nonblack members.

Table 4.11 shows the mean numbers of committee assignments for black and white members of the House. The most noteworthy figure is that blacks hold nearly one more committee assignment on average than do their colleagues (6.55 versus 5.71; a separate analysis showed that there were no significant differences within the CBC on the number of assignments). The regression model in table 4.12 shows that even after controlling for seniority, freshman status, prestige committee assignments, and party, blacks are still more likely to sit on a greater number of committees (about one-half an assignment on average).[14] The overrepresentation of blacks on committees had important implications for reform efforts in the 103rd Congress. One recommendation from the Joint Committee on the Organization of Congress was to rationalize committee jurisdictions and cut the number of committee assignments that each member held. Members of the CBC forced the removal of this provision because they feared a loss of legislative power if committee assignments were limited. However, as noted above, when Republicans gained control of the House in the 104th Congress, they were able to impose their changes in the committee system over the objections of the CBC. A regression of committee as-

Table 4.11   Average Number of Committee and Subcommittee Assignments by Party and Race (103rd Congress)

Race	Democrats Committee	Subcommittee	Republicans Committee	Subcommittee	Total Committees + Subcommittees
White	2.04	3.89	1.98	3.50	5.71
	(208)	(208)	(172)	(172)	(380)
Black	2.27	4.38	1.0	2.0	6.55
	(37)	(37)	(1)	(1)	(38)
Hispanic	1.86	3.71	1.67	2.67	5.35
	(14)	(14)	(3)	(3)	(17)

Notes: The number of cases in each cell is in parentheses.

Bernie Sanders is included with the Democrats.

This table includes only the standing committees and the permanent Select Committee on Intelligence.

signment in the 104th Congress (not shown here) reveals that blacks no longer have an advantage in committee assignments after the Post Office and District of Columbia Committees were abolished (the regression coefficient for the black dummy variable was insignificant).

All of the other variables in the model are significant and in the expected direction: Republicans hold about one-half of an assignment less than their Democratic colleagues, and freshmen hold two-thirds of an assignment less than nonfreshmen, but the most senior members also hold fewer assignments (an average of one fewer assignment per twelve years of seniority). Members who serve on prestige committees are not allowed to hold other major assignments; thus, a control variable for prestige committees shows that members on these committees hold, on average, about two and a half fewer assignments than those who do not serve on prestige committees.

I also tested the hypothesis that blacks are less likely to receive prestige committee assignments, which could account for their greater number of other assignments. The second set of coefficients in table 4.12 shows that this is not the case. In fact, the coefficient for African-American representatives was positive, though it did not approach statistical significance. As expected, seniority had a significant positive impact on receiving a prestige assignment, and freshman status had a negative impact (holding other variables constant at their mean level, a ten-term member was 9.4 percent more likely to be serving on a prestige committee than was a three-term member, while a freshman was 29.9 percent less likely than a nonfreshman to be on a prestige

Table 4.12   Determinants of the Number of Committee Assignments (103rd Congress)

Variable	All Standing Committees			Prestige Committees		
	Regression Coefficient	T-Ratio	Significance Level*	Maximum Likelihood Coefficient (B)	Wald Statistic	Significance Level*
New member	−.66	−2.95	.0016	−2.09	20.24	<.0001
Republican	−.49	−2.91	.0020	.46	3.78	.026
Black	.49	1.70	.0450	.35	.64	.21
Prestige	−2.58	−14.02	<.0001	—	—	—
Seniority	−.08	−7.38	<.0001	.028	4.10	.021
Constant	7.62	40.46	<.0001	−1.06	18.78	<.0001

*One-tailed test. $n = 435$
$n = 435$ Correct classification = 71.0%
$R^2 = .43$ Naive Prediction = 71.6%
$F = 65.53$ Significance of $F < .00001$ −2 Log Likelihood = 469.58 430 df; $p = .0913$
                                                   Model Chi-Square = 57.57 4 df; $p < .0001$

New member: coded as 1 if the member was a freshman, 0 otherwise.

Republican: coded as 1 if the member was a Republican, 0 otherwise.

Black: coded as 1 if the member is an African American, 0 otherwise.

Prestige: coded as 1 if the member served on Appropriations, Budget, Rules, or Ways and Means (Energy and Commerce is also a prestige assignment for Republicans). This is the dependent variable in the second model.

Seniority: number of consecutive years the member had served in the House (as of 1994).

committee). Unlike the standing committee model, Republicans were 9.5 percent more likely to be on prestige committees than were Democrats. However, this is because Republicans consider Energy and Commerce a prestige assignment, while Democrats do not.

The limited test of the supply-side theory was inconclusive. As expected, difference members held a slightly higher proportion of minority politics subcommittee assignments than did commonality members (33 percent, compared to 27 percent in the 103rd Congress, and 20 percent, compared to 10 percent in the 104th Congress), but these differences were not significant. More noteworthy is the relatively low level of interest in these committee assignments from *both* difference and commonality members. There was much greater interest in constituency-based subcommittee assignments. The six difference members held a total of thirteen constituency subcommittee assignments in the 103rd Congress, compared to fifteen for the eleven commonality members (these numbers shrank to seven and ten, respectively, for the 104th

Congress). Thus, the evidence supports the notion that the CBC has broadened its political base since 1993 and has become more involved in a broader array of nonracial, constituency-based issue areas.

Leadership Positions

In the section on the institutional level of analysis I argued that the integration of the CBC into the Democratic leadership provides strong evidence of the rapidly evolving role of the CBC. In the 103rd Congress ten blacks held positions in the Democratic leadership, up from only four in the previous Congress. John Lewis was highest ranking as one of the three chief deputy whips. Other members of the leadership in the 103rd Congress included deputy whips Charles Rangel (D–NY) and Alan Wheat (D–MO); at-large whips Barbara Rose Collins (D–MI), William Jefferson (D–LA), Bernice Johnson (D–TX), Bobby Rush (D–IL), and Maxine Waters (D–CA); and assistant whips Donald Payne (D–NJ) and James Clyburn (D–SC). Blacks also doubled their representation on the Steering and Policy Committee (from two to four) in the 103rd Congress. Despite this large delegation, blacks are slightly underrepresented in the leadership. With the explosion in the size of the "inclusive" Democratic leadership of the 1980s (Sinclair 1995; Rohde 1991, 82–93), 39.6 percent of nonblack Democrats serve in the extended leadership (88 of 222), while only 27 percent of blacks (10 of 37) are in the leadership. Blacks are also underrepresented on the Steering and Policy Committee (10.8 percent of blacks and 13.5 percent of nonblacks) and the Democratic Congressional Campaign Committee (5.4 percent of blacks and 14 percent of nonblacks).

A multivariate logit analysis reveals that African Americans were still underrepresented in the Democratic leadership in the 103rd Congress, despite recent gains (see table 4.13). The variable of central concern shows that blacks were still 24.5 percent less likely to serve in the leadership than were nonblacks (holding all other variables constant at their mean levels). A member serving in his or her fifth term is 7.1 percent more likely to be in the leadership than is a member with two years of seniority. Those who are more loyal to the party, not surprisingly, are also more likely to be in the leadership. A ten-point increase in party loyalty over the party mean increases the likelihood of being in the leadership by 13 percent.[15] I also included controls for openings in the member's region (the fourteen regions defined by the Democratic

Table 4.13   Determinants of Democratic Party Leadership (103rd Congress)

Variable	Maximum Likelihood Coefficient (B)	Wald Statistic	Significance Level*
Regional opportunity	−.21	2.27	.066
At-large opportunity	−.25	.81	.184
Black	−1.00	5.49	.001
Party support	.059	11.76	.0003
Seniority	.036	6.14	.0067
Constant	−5.46	13.55	.0001

Notes:
  *One-tailed test
  $n = 256$
  Correct classification = 65.8%
  Naive prediction = 37.9%
  −2 Log Likelihood = 317.42 251 df; $p = .0028$
  Model Chi-Square = 23.26 5 df; $p = .0003$
  Dependent variable: coded as 1 if the member was in the Democratic leadership (from the majority leader all the way down to at-large whips and regional whips—the speaker is not included because he did not vote often enough to have a party support score); 0 otherwise. This model includes only Democratic members of the House and is estimated with a maximum-likelihood logistic regression.
  Regional opportunity: coded as 1 if there was an opening in the member's whip region; 0 otherwise.
  At-large opportunity: coded as 1 if there was an opening in the member's whip region for an at-large whip; 0 otherwise.
  Black: coded as a 1 if the member is an African American, 0 otherwise.
  Party support: the members' party support score from the second session of the 102nd Congress for nonfreshman members or from the first session of the 103rd Congress for freshmen.
  Seniority: number of consecutive years the member had served in the House (as of 1994).

leadership) for both regional and at-large whips. The logic for including this control is that the leadership attempts to achieve regional balance, so an opening in one's region would increase the probability of being elected or appointed to a whip position. However, neither of these variables was significant, and their signs were unexpectedly in the negative direction.

The overall picture of the role of African Americans in the Democratic leadership is mixed. Blacks are starting to play a more prominent role in the leadership, but there is still some resistance within the CBC to fully accepting the "team player" model at the expense of fighting for black interests (or perhaps the continued underrepresentation of the CBC may reflect inertia within the Democratic leadership to recognize the evolving role of the CBC). However, the impact of minority districting on the influence of the CBC within the House is quite evident. Three of the new black members of the leadership in the 103rd Congress were elected in the newly created black majority districts.

The impact of the 1992 class was even more evident in the leadership for the 104th Congress. Bernice Johnson (D–TX) and Bobby Rush (D–IL) were both promoted to deputy whips, which produced a net gain of one for the CBC in that leadership position with the departure of Alan Wheat. Sanford Bishop (D–GA) and Chaka Fattah (D–PA) replaced Johnson and Rush in the at-large positions, and Donald Payne (D–NJ) moved from being an assistant whip to an at-large whip, for a net gain of one in that position. Cardiss Collins (D–IL), Cynthia McKinney (D–GA), Bennie Thompson (D–MS), and Albert Wynn (D–MD) all became assistant whips, for a net gain of three for the CBC in that position. Of the nine promotions or new additions six were from the 1992 class. With fifteen of their thirty-six members now in the leadership (41.7 percent), Democratic members of the CBC are nearly equal to nonblack members in their representation in the leadership (46.1 percent of nonblack members of the House [77 of 167] are in the leadership).

The supply-side theory predicted that commonality members would be more likely to serve in the leadership than would difference members. This clearly was the case in the 103rd Congress, when three of the eleven commonality members and none of the difference members were in the leadership. In the 104th Congress there was no difference in the proportion of commonality and difference members in the leadership (four of ten and two of five, respectively). Thus, overall one-third of commonality members have served in the leadership in their first two terms, compared to only 18.2 percent of the difference members.[16]

Speeches on the Floor of the House

The casual viewer of C-SPAN knows what was previously observed only by tourists in the House and Senate galleries and the handful of Washington insiders who spent time in the Capitol: speeches on the floor are typically made in front of a nearly empty chamber. As noted in the American Enterprise Institute/Brookings Institution report *Renewing Congress,* "[T]he quality of debate in Congress has been diminished as members spend less time on the floor and come to votes pre-programmed on issues by information gleaned from staff and lobbyists.

There is little real interaction and discussion among members. What passes for debate are often lonely declamations by members or senators at times when legislative business has been concluded" (Mann and Ornstein 1993, 57). However, deliberation *does* occur in the House, much of it out of the public eye (Bessette 1994, chap. 6; Smith 1989, 236–246).

Speeches made on the floor of the House, while not the hallmark of reasoned discourse and deliberation, do provide insight into how members view race and representation. However, one member cautioned me, "Speeches on the floor are not always the best indicator of what the member is really thinking. They often are playing to the D.C. audience. Also, their schedule might prevent them from talking even when they really did have something to say. Special orders speeches are better. Those speeches are geared for the broader audience" (M4). For my purposes, however, the content of speeches is more important than the number of speeches (thus, the scheduling issue raised by the member is not a concern), and the specific audience the member has in mind when making the speech is not relevant either. What matters is that the member cared enough about the issue to make a speech and that the speech reveals something about the member's preferences on an issue before the chamber. My assumption that activities such as speaking on the floor and sponsoring or cosponsoring legislation reveal something important about member preferences is consistent with Richard Hall's theory of participation with its focus on "revealed intensities" (1996, 3).

My research assistants analyzed the content of all 3,722 speeches made on the floor of the House (and those that were not actually delivered, but inserted into the *Congressional Record*) by members of the CBC and representatives from districts that are at least 25 percent black in the 103rd Congress. I expect nuances of position-taking to vary among representatives, even when their substantive positions are the same. For example, two members may cast votes in favor of the crime bill, but one would explain his or her position in terms of saving the inner city, while the other would characterize his or her position in biracial terms. Members' speaking on the floor was broken down into speeches (which include actual floor debates and remarks that are made at the beginning of legislative sessions) and symbolic addresses (which include tributes and many extensions of remarks). Examples of the former would be the extended debates on the crime bill, health care, and NAFTA. An example of the latter would be speeches noting the designation of African American Music Month (H.J. Res. 364, *Congressional Record,* May 5, 1994, H3155). Speeches were then coded for racial content using three categories—centrally concerned with race, partly or implicitly concerned with race, and not concerned with race—according to the procedures outlined above. These nuances obviously are not evident in an analysis that relies strictly on roll call votes.

The total number of speeches given by black and white members was nearly identical (means of 71.7 and 66.4 speeches, respectively). However, the racial focus of those speeches was dramatically different. On average, only 6.1 percent of the speeches given by white members explicitly concerned race, compared to 32.6 percent of the speeches given by black members of Congress. An additional 18.3 percent of the speeches given by blacks partly concerned race, but only 5.7 percent of the white members' speeches were in this category. Thus, 88.2 percent of the speeches given by white members did not concern race at all, compared to 49.1 percent of the speeches given by blacks. While a somewhat crude comparison when one considers that the average percentage of black constituents is 33.4 percent in the white members' districts and 56 percent in the black members' districts (in districts that are at least 25 percent black), it appears that blacks are closely representing the interests of their black and white constituents (if anything, blacks spend a disproportionate time on general political issues rather than racial issues), while white representatives are largely ignoring the interests of their black constituents.[17]

Breaking down these simple descriptive statistics by the commonality-difference distinction reveals the expected pattern: 58.5 percent of the speeches and tributes given by difference members involved race, 50.6 percent of the speeches by commonality members, and 48.9 percent of the speeches by older members involved a direct or indirect reference to race. These differences are not an artifact of my coding procedure because one of the precautions that I took to make sure that the supply-side theory would receive rigorous testing was to conceal the coding of the member's representational style from the graduate research assistants who were doing the coding (when the assistant did the content analysis of a speech, he or she did not know whether the speech was given by a commonality or a difference member).

The multivariate analysis shows that the differences in representational style are statistically significant after controlling for district income, racial composition, percentage urban, and region (see table

Table 4.14   Regression Analysis of Speeches on the House Floor (103rd Congress)

Independent Variable	Tributes/ Racial	Speeches/ Racial	Speeches/ Part-Racial	Total Racial Speeches/Tributes
African-American member of Congress— commonality	29.9** (9.5)	14.2** (7.0)	15.1** (5.6)	26.5** (7.5)
African-American member of Congress— difference	37.4** (9.5)	19.8* (7.0)	12.8** (5.5)	37.5** (7.5)
African-American member of Congress— older	30.3** (8.2)	12.5* (6.0)	6.6[+] (4.8)	26.9** (6.5)
Median family income	−.00046 (.00057)	−.00068[+] (.00042)	.000050 (.00033)	−.00061[+] (.00045)
Percentage of black constituents ($\times 100$)	.055 (.24)	.32* (.18)	.14 (.14)	.39* (.19)
Percentage of district in urban area ($\times 100$)	−.021 .12	.09 (.09)	−.044 (.072)	.036 (.097)
Southern district	2.2 (6.9)	−.93 (5.1)	−8.2* (4.1)	−3.9 (5.5)
Party (1 = Republican, 0 = Democrat)	−10.6 (11.1)	4.6 (8.2)	−4.4 (6.5)	−2.1 (8.8)
Constant	15.4 (21.6)	6.9 (15.9)	11.8 (12.6)	13.8 (17.1)
F-statistic	5.56**	5.49**	3.56**	11.9**
Adjusted R-square	.44	.44	.31	.65
Number of districts	53	53	53	53

Notes: Dependent variables: the percentage of speeches given by the member of Congress in each category ($\times 100$).

Standard errors are in parentheses.

[+]Significant at the .10 level (one-tailed tests).

*Significant at the .05 level.

**Significant at the .01 level.

4.14). For each of the types of speeches (tributes and extensions, speeches and remark, racial and part racial) a greater percentage of those given by difference members have racial content than do those given by commonality or older members (ranging from about 3 percent to 11 percent). The differences between each of these three groups within the CBC and white members are mostly statistically significant. The largest differences are for the symbolic tributes and extensions of remarks and the category that includes all speeches. In both instances about 37 percent more of the speeches given by difference members have racial content than do those given by whites, controlling for relevant district-level variables. Speeches given by commonality members also have a significantly higher racial content than do those given by white members (26.5 percent more in the "total" category), but as predicted by the supply-side theory, this figure is 11 percent lower than the comparable coefficient for the difference members. The most significant of the control variables was the percentage of blacks in the district, which was significant in two of the four models, including the model that included all speeches.

Sponsoring and Cosponsoring Legislation

Examining the introduction and cosponsorship of legislation is one of the best ways to address the "censored sample" problem that occurs when relying on roll call data. Thousands of bills are introduced every year that do not become law. Such activity could be dismissed as merely symbolic, but bill introduction and cosponsorship are useful measure of legislative behavior for several reasons. First, they provide a good measure of the intensity of a member's opinion, or "revealed intensities" (Hall 1996), as I argued above concerning floor speeches. A member who not only votes for a bill, but actually sponsors or cosponsors the legislation cares more intensely about the bill than does a member who only supports it through his or her vote. Second, members engage in position-taking and credit-claiming through the use of sponsorship and cosponsorship of legislation (Mayhew 1974). In campaigning for reelection members often tout their legislative activity by referring to the bills that they have been actively involved with. In the member newsletters that I analyze in chapter 5 many members listed the bills that they had sponsored and cosponsored. The CBC publishes a document for every Congress that lists many of the bills that its members have sponsored, and other groups monitor who is sponsoring legislation to determine who supports their political agendas. Third, cosponsorship can be used as a tool to signal preferences to colleagues within the House (Kessler and Krehbiel 1996; Wilson and Young 1997), and sponsoring legislation, even bills that do not pass, shapes the legislative agenda (Schiller 1995).

As with speeches the significance of sponsorship and cosponsorship can be overstated. One study concluded that the number of cosponsors had very little effect on the likelihood that a bill would become law (Wilson and Young, 1997).[18] Cosponsorship may be of limited value as a measure of legislative behavior aimed at the district (as Kessler and Krehbiel [1996] argue). One staffer concurred with this conclusion, noting that cosponsoring legislation had more strategic than substantive value: "It is more important for the politics up here than it is for the district. It's all about building coalitions, helping friends, and getting their help on stuff you want" (S8). Another staffer supported the notion of helping friends through cosponsorship, saying, "The CBC sticks together. They cosponsor each other's bills even if it has nothing to do with their own constituents. Some members will cosponsor without even looking at the bill. For example, one bill to expand lending authority under the Farm Credit program was sponsored by [Carrie] Meek [D–FL] and [Edolphus] Towns [D–NY] and it got fifty-seven cosponsors— many from the CBC. The bill would not have benefitted low-income farmers, but that is how they sold it—as rural development. If it sounds right, they go for it" (S12). However, my interviews also showed that in many cases district interests weighed heavily in the decision to cosponsor.

My interviews also revealed some variation in the personal role that the member plays in cosponsorship decisions. One member noted that he "signs off [has to give his personal approval] on everything" and will only "cosponsor bills that interest me." "I get a lot of 'Dear Colleague' letters, and I turn quite a few of them down—some that I disagree with and some that I don't know enough about. Other times I will cosponsor a bill because of a constituent's request" (M4). Other members were involved in some decisions, but other decisions would be made by staff. However, even when decisions are made by staff, they are acting on behalf of the member and should reflect the member's preferences.

In the 103rd Congress, members of the CBC sponsored 511 pieces of legislation and amendments and cosponsored 11,540 bills (means per member of 13.4 and 303.7, respectively). White members sponsored 248 pieces of legislation and amendments and cosponsored 4,010 (means per member of 17.8 and 286.4, respectively) (see tables 4.15 and 4.16).[19] Each of the bills (720) and amendments (55) was coded for racial content using the same methods that were outlined above. In addition, bills were divided into substantive and symbolic categories. As a validity check on my categories I had several of the chief legislative assistants I interviewed go through a list of thirty to forty bills that the member had sponsored and cosponsored and asked him or her to categorize the bills as racial, part racial, or nonracial. This allowed me to check their coding against the coding that my research assistants had already done, but perhaps more important, the exercise also re-

Table 4.15   Sponsorship of Legislation (103rd Congress)

	Topic of Bills	White Members	Black Members	Latino Members
Substantive legislation	Nonracial	95.1% (212)	57.6% (197)	75.0% (6)
	Racial	1.3% (3)	13.2% (58)	12.5% (1)
	Part-racial	3.6% (8)	29.3% (129)	12.5% (1)
	Totals	100% (223)	100% (441)	100% (8)
Symbolic legislation	Nonracial	88.0% (22)	45.7% (32)	100% (1)
	Racial	8.0% (2)	47.1% (33)	0
	Part-racial	4.0% (1)	7.1% (5)	0
	Totals	100% (25)	99.9% (70)	100% (3)

vealed that the coding scheme had strong face validity. That is, none of the staffers laughed at the thought of making such distinctions or ridiculed the task as one of those silly games that academics play. They all tackled the task with seriousness and thoughtfulness, implying that similar calculations are made by staffers and their members on a routine basis. How can the member best serve the diverse racial interests of the district? As I have indicated elsewhere in this book, some staffers were not very willing to talk openly about race, but even those who had sworn ten minutes earlier that it was "class and not race" that mattered in their district were quite willing and able to code forty bills according to the racial constituency that the member had in mind when he or she sponsored or cosponsored the bill.

The most important finding of this part of the analysis is that 95 percent of the substantive legislation that is sponsored by white members of Congress does not have any racial content, while about 58 percent of black members' bills are in that category. About 84 percent of the substantive bills cosponsored by white members had no racial content, compared to 63 percent of blacks' cosponsored legislation. Once again, it is evident that black members of Congress are more balanced in their division of legislative activity between racial and nonracial concerns than are white members. I should emphasize that this is not an artifact of the coding procedure because the unit of analysis of the coding was the bill ($n = 2,751$) rather than the individual cospon-

Table 4.16   Cosponsorship of Legislation (103rd Congress)

	Topic of Bills	White Members	Black Members	Latino Members
Substantive legislation	Nonracial	83.7% (2,247)	62.7% (5,008)	69.4% (200)
	Racial	3.1% (84)	10.9% (870)	4.2% (12)
	Part-racial	13.2% (353)	26.4% (2,110)	26.5% (76)
	Totals	100% (2,684)	100% (7,988)	100.1% (288)
Symbolic legislation	Nonracial	89.4% (1,186)	83.2% (2,957)	90.6% (115)
	Racial	5.7% (75)	12.8% (453)	5.5% (7)
	Part-racial	4.9% (65)	4.0% (142)	3.9% (5)
	Totals	100% (1,326)	100% (3,552)	100% (127)

sorship ($n = 14,560$) or member. That is, if a specific bill is coded as a racial bill, all members who cosponsor that bill are automatically recorded as having cosponsored a racial bill. Two other interesting patterns are evident in the table: While most of the bills sponsored by white members are nonracial, a larger proportion of their cosponsored bills (about 14 percent) have some racial content. For blacks the only deviation from a relatively even split between racial and nonracial bills is that about 83 percent of the symbolic legislation blacks cosponsored was nonracial. Perhaps this is a relatively easy way for many blacks who are attempting to build biracial coalitions to reach out to white voters in the district.

Differences between types of representational style within the CBC are examined in the multivariate analysis presented in tables 4.17 and 4.18. One note of caution however: because the number of bills sponsored is relatively low for many members and the variation across members is high, the results are very unstable (I attempted to correct for this by using the proportion of bills sponsored that have varying types of racial content, but this did not entirely correct the problem). For example, Andrew Jacobs sponsored seventy-nine bills and amendments, while Mel Watt sponsored only two (and Harold Ford sponsored no bills and is excluded from this part of the analysis). In general, the commonality and difference members sponsored far fewer bills than did their more senior colleagues (7.3 and 5.2 bills, respectively,

Table 4.17 Regression Analysis of Sponsored Legislation (103rd Congress)

Independent Variable	Part Racial/ Substantive and Symbolic	Racial bills/ Substantive and Symbolic	Total Racial/ Substantive and Symbolic
African-American member of Congress—commonality	22.7 (19.5)	2.0 (8.4)	19.6[+] (12.0)
African-American member of Congress—difference	11.5 (21.4)	3.8 (8.7)	8.8 (12.4)
African-American member of Congress—older	5.6 (16.5)	13.4* (7.3)	22.7* (10.4)
Hispanic member	−15.4 (36.2)	10.9 (16.6)	8.0 (23.6)
Income ratio (per capita white income/per capita black income in district)	.13 (12.6)	2.1 (5.7)	2.4 (8.1)
Percentage of black constituents (×100)	−.59[+] (.45)	.34* (2.0)	.76** (.29)
Percentage of district in urban area (×100)	−.23 (.27)	.12 (.11)	.039 (.16)
Party (1 = Republican, 0 = Democrat)	−25.1 (29.1)	.33 (10.1)	−1.53 (14.3)
South	−36.7** (14.8)	19.5** (6.5)	3.2 (9.3)
Constant	112.9** (40.6)	−28.1* (16.7)	−15.3 (32.4)
F-statistic	1.07	2.80*	4.43**
Adjusted R-square	.01	.24	.38
Number of districts	44	52	52

Notes: Dependent variables: the percentage of bills sponsored by the member of Congress in each category (×100). The part-racial category is part-racial bills/racial bills; the second model is the number of racial bills sponsored divided by the total number of bills sponsored; the third model is the number of racial and part-racial bills divided by the total number of bills.

Standard errors are in parentheses.

[+]Significant at the .10 level (one-tailed test).

*Significant at the .05 level.

**Significant at the .01 level.

compared to 17.8 for white members and 20 for nonfreshman blacks). The first model, which examines the proportion of part-racial bills sponsored by the member, is the least reliable of the three.

With these caveats in mind some interesting patterns are evident. Commonality members sponsored a higher proportion of part-racial bills and a lower proportion of racial bills than did difference members (when compared to the baseline white member). Commonality members were expected to introduce a higher proportion of part-racial bills

Table 4.18   Regression Analysis of Cosponsored Legislation (103rd Congress)

Independent Variable	Part Racial/ Substantive and Symbolic	Racial bills/ Substantive and Symbolic	Total Racial/ Substantive and Symbolic
African-American member of Congress— commonality	11.3 (9.9)	16.3** (3.6)	27.6* (12.5)
African-American member of Congress—difference	12.8 (10.3)	20.8** (3.8)	33.6** (13.0)
African-American member of Congress—older	7.5 (8.5)	15.3** (3.2)	22.8* (10.8)
Hispanic member	30.3+ (19.6)	−2.1 (7.2)	28.2 (24.8)
Income ratio (per capita white income/per capita black income in district)	−4.1 (6.7)	−4.8* (2.5)	−8.9 (8.5)
Percentage of black constituents (×100)	.57** (.24)	.20* (.088)	.77** (.30)
Percentage of district in urban area (×100)	.18+ (.13)	.013 (.049)	.19 (.17)
Party (1 = Republican, 0 = Democrat)	−5.8 (11.9)	−7.1+ (4.3)	−12.9 (15.0)
South	−5.4 (7.4)	−2.5 (2.7)	−7.9 (9.3)
Constant	13.0 (19.2)	16.3** (7.8)	29.3 (24.3)
F-statistic	5.39**	17.4**	8.76
Adjusted R-square	.43	.74	.57
Number of districts	53	53	53

Notes: Dependent variables: the number of bills cosponsored by the member of Congress in each category.

Standard errors are in parentheses.

+Significant at the .10 level (one-tailed test).

*Significant at the .05 level.

**Significant at the .01 level.

because these are pieces of legislation that affect the entire district, but disproportionately benefit the African-American constituents in the district (for example, the assault weapon ban). These are the types of issues that got them elected in the first place. At the same time, the balancing perspective holds that commonality members should pay *some* attention to explicitly racial issues, but not as much as difference members, which is exactly what the models show. However, these differences are relatively small and are not statistically significant. In the overall model, which includes all part-racial and racial bills, commonality members sponsor about 19 percent more racial bills than do white members, holding everything else in the model constant; older black members sponsor about 23 percent more racial legislation than do whites. The percentage of black constituents is also significant in the overall model, with members sponsoring about 7.6 percent more racial legislation for each 10 percent increase in the black constituency.

In general, the models of cosponsored bills perform better than the models of sponsored bills, with a much higher proportion of explained variance, higher F-statistics, and more variables reaching significance at the .05 level. The dependent variable in this model is simply the number of bills cosponsored in each category. It is not necessary to use the proportion of bills because all members cosponsored a large number of bills (the range is from 122 to 551), and there is surprisingly little variation across the categories of members (difference members cosponsored an average of 297 bills; the average for commonality members and the overall average were 299 and 301, respectively). Evidently the apprenticeship norm (or, alternatively, simply the time that it takes to "learn the ropes") that appears to be operating with bill sponsorship is not evident with cosponsorship of legislation. In general, the results shown in table 4.18 are consistent with the supply-side theory, but the differences among types of black members are relatively small. The significant differences are between black members and whites in the number of racial bills sponsored and the overall model. In the overall model difference members cosponsor thirty-three more bills than do white members, while commonality and older members sponsor twenty-eight and twenty-three more, respectively. The percentage of black constituents is also significant: every 10 percent increase in the percentage of black constituents produces about eight more cosponsored bills that are related to race.

The final model takes a slightly different approach. Here I look at the patterns of cosponsorship across type of member and examine their impact on the likelihood that any given bill will make it out of committee, pass the chamber, or become law. Here the unit of analysis shifts from the member ($n = 53$) to the bill ($n = 2,751$). The key independent variables of interest here are the proportions of commonality, difference, and older members that cosponsored a specific piece of legislation. This analysis replicates the model presented in table 4.6 and simply adds the three variables for the type of black member. The results are very robust: most of the original coefficients and their standard errors are largely unchanged from table 4.6. The results show that

Table 4.19   Logit Analysis of the Success of Bills, by Racial Content and Proportion of Various Types of Cosponsors (103rd Congress)

Independent Variable	Stayed Alive	Passed One Chamber	Became Law
Black sponsor	.21	.29+	.74**
	(.18)	(.20)	(.25)
Number of Democratic cosponsors	.015**	.016**	.013**
	(.0036)	(.0039)	(.0048)
Number of Republican cosponsors	−.0088**	−.010**	−.0059+
	(.0032)	(.0037)	(.0045)
Racial bill	.26	.36	−.0023
	(.31)	(.33)	(.41)
Part-racial bill	−.54**	−.72**	−.86*
	(.23)	(.27)	(.38)
Symbolic bill	.31*	.52**	.87**
	(.19)	(.20)	(.24)
Percentage of commonality	1.01*	1.68**	1.74*
members who cosponsored the bill	(.57)	(.61)	(.78)
Percenatage of difference members	−.18	−.35	−.79
who cosponsored the bill	(.46)	(.50)	(.65)
Percentage of older CBC member	−.95+	−1.58*	−1.05
who cosponsored the bill	(.67)	(.74)	(.92)
Constant	−2.39**	−2.69**	−3.55**
	(.088)	(.10)	(.14)
Percentage predicted correctly	88.7%	90.8%	95.0%
Naive prediction	88.6%	90.8%	95.0%
Number of bills	2,751	2,751	2,751

Notes: Dependent variable: coded as 1 if the bill stayed alive, passed one chamber, or became law; 0 otherwise.

Standard errors are in parentheses.

+Significant at the .10 level (one-tailed test).

*Significant at the .05 level.

**Significant at the .01 level.

when the proportion of commonality members who cosponsor the bill is high, the chances of passage increase dramatically, while difference and older members actually reduce the chances of success (though their coefficients are not significant).

Using the derivative method outlined above (King 1989, 108–110), if a bill had an underlying 10 percent probability of passing, having all eleven commonality members as cosponsors (as opposed to none of them) would increase that probability to more than 25 percent. I would not argue that the cosponsorship from commonality members *causes* the bill to succeed (or to make it farther through the legislative process). Instead, the causal arrow probably runs the other way. However, this is highly suggestive of an important difference in the representational and legislative styles of commonality and difference members. *Commonality members are more likely to attach themselves to legislative winners, while difference members are more likely to stake out positions without considering the chances for success.* Commonality members are working within the CBC tradition established by William Gray and Mike Espy, while difference members are gravitating toward the style of William Clay, John Conyers, and Maxine Waters. This is one of the strongest pieces of evidence for the supply-side theory in this chapter.

Conclusion

Race matters in the U.S. House of Representatives, at both the institutional and the individual levels. At the institutional level the CBC is highly cohesive, but increasingly diverse. It is a strong supporter of black interests, but instrumental in helping mainstream Democratic Party positions succeed. CBC members provided the pivotal votes on crucial legislation in the 103rd Congress, served on a broader array of committees, and played an increasing role in the leadership. The common wisdom (among both academics and House members) holds that there is a trade-off between cohesion and dispersion. As a group becomes more diverse and its interests more dispersed, its cohesion and ability to speak with one voice decline (Singh 1998, 135–138, 166). In one sense this is obviously true. More diverse groups will not be as cohesive by definition. However, it does not necessary follow that diversity and cohesion cannot peacefully coexist *across a range of issues.* For many members of the CBC it makes sense to break with the CBC and work with the Democratic leadership on one piece of legislation, while simultaneously speaking out for minority interests on another. Furthermore, it does not make sense to measure the success of the CBC by examining only racial issues or general ideological ratings, such as LCCR, ADA, or COPE scores.

As the analysis of NES data showed in chapter 1, black constituents have preferences identical to those of whites over a broad array of nonracial interests; evidence in this chapter shows that black members also distribute their efforts and time over a broad range of concerns. Most important for the policy debates surrounding black majority districts, the first section of this chapter showed that the CBC *can* have its voice heard in a majority-rule institution. My analysis of 2,751 bills in the 103rd Congress showed that bills that had a black sponsor had a significantly higher chance of making it through the legislative process than did those that did not and that the margin of victory on roll call votes did not vary substantially across racial, part-racial, and nonracial issues.

The individual-level analysis provided strong confirmation of the supply-side theory by demonstrating significant differences across the types of representational styles. Commonality members were more likely than difference members to serve in the leadership, slightly more moderate in their roll call behavior, less likely to emphasize race in their speeches on the floor and in their sponsorship and cosponsorship of legislation, and more likely to cosponsor bills that were successful in the legislative process. This broad range of evidence emphasizes the value of moving beyond an exclusive focus on roll call voting as the primary tool for examining racial representation.

While I found systematic differences among black members, even larger differences between white and black members were found. Blacks were disproportionately represented on committees that addressed black interests, their speeches touched on racial issues more frequently than did those of whites, and a far greater proportion of the bills they sponsored and cosponsored had racial content. This is strong evidence against the "no racial differences" hypothesis. While white members certainly *can* represent black interests, as Swain (1993) has shown, on average, the white members in the 103rd Congress who represented districts that were at least 25 percent black did not show much interest in racial issues. This chapter provides the most systematic evidence to support the argument made by Bernard Grofman, Lisa Handley, and Richard Niemi in their book on minority representation: "[A]lthough we recognize that white liberal legislators may vote similarly to their black counterparts on roll call votes, this does not mean that they have the same commitment to a leadership role on civil rights or on economic issues of concern to the black community" (1992, 135). The next chapter will explore whether these varying levels of commitment to racial issues are evident in the linkages that are forged with constituents.

CHAPTER FIVE

Links to the Constituency

"[W]e cannot know all we need to know about House members in Washington unless we do move beyond the capital city into the country and into its congressional districts," Richard Fenno reminded us over twenty years ago (1978, 214). However, previous studies of racial representation in Congress have largely ignored the district half of the representational relationship. Nearly all of our scholarly efforts in this area are directed at measuring the strength of the relationship between indicators of congressional behavior and district characteristics rather than district behavior or information that is received by constituents.[1] While the basis for representational linkages is clearly rooted in making speeches on the floor, sponsoring legislation and amendments, casting roll call votes, and carrying out other Washington activities, a research design that uses the district's urban and racial composition to explain LCCR (Legislative Conference on Civil Rights) scores ignores *how* members attempt to transmit that information to their constituents. Most constituents, to the extent that they are aware of a member's activities at all, will receive information through the member's staff, constituency newsletters, and the news media's reports of the member's activities. These measures of member-constituency linkages are the focus of this chapter.

The transmission of information to constituents may reveal as much about the emphasis a member places on racial issues as does behavior in Washington. For example, consider the behavior of two white members, both of whom represent a 35 percent black district. Both members are relatively moderate on the standard ADA (Americans for Democratic Action)- and LCCR-type measures and occasionally sponsor legislation and make speeches that would be of interest to black constituents. The first member has an all-white staff, locates her district offices in the mostly white suburbs, and does not mention any legislative activities that would be of primary interest to black constit-

uents in her newsletters. The second member has a racially diverse staff
in both Washington and the district, locates one district office in the
inner city and another in the suburbs, and proudly trumpets in his
most recent newsletter his legislative activity on "redlining" in the insurance and financial sectors. The standard roll call analysis of Washington behavior (or even my more detailed analysis presented in the
previous chapter) would not uncover any difference between these two
members. However, the second member is clearly making more of an
effort to maintain a biracial coalition than the first member. These two
styles of representation perfectly describe a difference member and a
commonality member.

Thus, this chapter will provide additional evidence to test the supply-side theory. I will test four specific hypotheses. When compared to
difference members, commonality members are expected to (1) have a
more racially diverse staff, (2) attempt to achieve a balance between
white and black neighborhoods in the location of district offices, (3)
have a better balance of racial and nonracial issues in their newsletters,
and (4) have less of a focus on racial politics in their news coverage.
As in the previous chapter, I also expect that on average black members will have a higher baseline of representing black interests than
white members.

These empirical tests represent a significant advance over previous
work. Indeed, *none of the four measures employed here has ever been
systematically applied to racial representation in the House of Representatives.* However, this approach has limitations. First, these measures
of "presentation of self" and "allocation of resources" (to use Fenno's
terms) are relatively indirect. More direct measures would include content analysis of district speeches and town hall meetings over the
course of a term and analysis of each member's travel schedule (I attempted to gather district travel data, along with the aides' assessments
of the racial composition of each audience over a one-month period,
but most offices were not willing to divulge this potentially sensitive
information). It also would be useful to have access to the constituency
service conducted by the members in my sample, coded for racial content and the race of the constituent and his or her satisfaction with the
casework. These measures would provide a better test of how a member balances his or her time between black and white constituents.

The second limitation of these data is the absence of a direct measure of constituent evaluations of member behavior. The raw material

for such tests should be available in the standard fare of the congressional electoral behavior literature, such as reported contacts with the member, likes and dislikes of the incumbent, and candidate feeling thermometers (Jacobson 1997), broken down by the race of the respondent, the race of the member, and the supply-side-driven representational styles. However, the sampling for the 1992 and 1994 National Election Studies (NES) produced only nine respondents in districts represented by a "difference" member, and only seventy-two were represented by commonality members. Therefore, systematic analysis of the supply-side theory from the constituents' perspective is left for future research.[2]

Members' Perceptions of the Constituency

House members and their staff have varying perceptions of their constituencies depending on their representational styles. Difference members have simplified their representational task by focusing their attention on the racial majority in their districts. Thus, white members who ignore black voters and black members who ignore white constituents do not have to worry about the balancing act that their commonality colleagues struggle with. One staffer for a commonality member was very explicit about his boss's desire to represent all his constituents, but noted the difficulty in pursuing this approach, "We split our district time 50/50 between the white and black communities. Despite this balancing, there is a constant tension between the two groups—each side is concerned that he will be seduced or won over by the other side. The African-American political community is especially restless, young, and ambitious" (S14). Robin Tallon, a former white representative from South Carolina, was committed to biracial representation, as reflected in his political campaigns and the racial diversity of his staff. When asked whether the racial diversity of his staff made it difficult to convince white voters that he would represent their interests, he replied, "'Well, I can tell you, that it was difficult, real difficult. It was so difficult that I just backed away from it for a while, because people really resented [that I had defeated] this clean-cut incumbent [who had the support of white people]'" (quoted in Swain 1993, 153).

Staffers also noted the difficulty of establishing links to the various groups within the district. One staffer said that her boss conducted weekly call-in radio shows, community meetings, and other meetings with groups, both in the district and in Washington, because "you just can't count on the mainstream media. You have to take the message directly to the people" (S6). Another staffer echoed the importance of being proactive in reaching out to constituents: "You can't wait for the folks to call. They won't pick up the phone because there is a general distrust of D.C. We have to get out and drive to their homes. This is a reflection of Representative G's background. He knows poverty and the problems of the poor. He gets out there and works with the poor" (S8). Many members mentioned that they would attend black churches every Sunday that they were back in the district.

While members clearly target different racial constituencies, much of the content of the interaction between member and constituent does not appear to involve explicitly racial issues. This observation is consistent with the data presented in the previous chapter on the relatively small number of explicitly racial topics that are taken up in the House. While I do not have systematic evidence to support this claim, many of the interviews indicated that most of the issues that constituents raised during "listening" sessions were mostly nonracial.

To experience some of these interactions first hand, I spent an afternoon with a member and one of his staff at a local mall in a predominantly black area as he met with his constituents. The member met with twenty-six constituents (twenty-four black and two white) during the three-hour session. Of those, only three had concerns that were racial in nature (one harassment case, one discrimination case, and one that was more generally about racial politics). The rest all had to do with more typical constituency issues: several people wanted jobs; one wanted an endorsement for a state's attorney race; most needed help with the federal bureaucracy. One white constituent was representing a group of residents who wanted to get a noise barrier built on the interstate highway that cut through their neighborhood. After she left, the representative quipped, "That certainly is an issue that isn't black or white. We all have the same color eardrums" (M3). However, the crucial point from the perspective of this research is whether a member makes an effort to reach out to whites and blacks in a district to hear all of their concerns. Indeed, we all have the same color eardrums, but the member who holds listening sessions only in all-white suburbs or all-black inner-city neighborhoods will not hear the range of complaints from all of his or her constituents. The next sections will examine how members attempt to achieve a balance in their constituent contacts by examining the racial composition of their staffs, the location of their district offices, the content of their newsletters, and the coverage they receive in the press.

Congressional Staff

Congressional staff may not be one of the first things that spring to mind when thinking about how to measure the representation of racial interests in Congress. However, the racial composition of a member's staff, both in Washington and in the district, is critical for three reasons. First, the racial composition of a member's staff provides some insight into how he or she thinks about race and representation. A member who practices a politics of commonality is likely to reach across racial lines in filling staff positions. Having a staff that resembles the racial composition of the district is a good indication that the member is sensitive to the importance of descriptive representation. Carrie Meek (D–FL), whose staff was comprised of seven African Americans, four whites, three Latinos, and one Native American, is one of the best examples of this approach to staffing.[3] Personal interviews revealed that balancing the racial composition of the staff was a conscious strategy. One staffer noted, "We have a black campaign manager and a white office manager. The staff is split in the district office as well, which reflects the diverse racial composition of our district" (S3). One member who represents a very racially diverse district also has one of the most racially diverse staffs. He said, "We need a staff that reflects the diversity in the district. We want some people in each office who will have the pulse of that specific community" (M8). Another staffer, who worked for a commonality member and was very proud of their integrated staff (eleven blacks and seven whites), said, "Nobody else in the state comes close [to that level of integration]. Representative Z [a white Democrat] has two blacks on his staff and all of the Republicans are lily white" (S9).

Other representational styles will be reflected in a less integrated staff. Norman Sisisky (D–VA), whose sixteen staffers were all white in the 103rd Congress, and Bennie Thompson (D–MS), who had eighteen blacks among his twenty staffers, are good examples of members who practice a politics of difference. A white staffer for an black inner-city member said, "Representative N feels a personal responsibility to hire blacks. On the personal staff there is more of an emphasis on skin color than quality. For committee staff, it's not so much that way. The policy even affected the interns. When he was first elected, we had lots of white interns. Free labor, right? Well, some people from the district came here and saw all these white interns running around and assumed they were permanent staff. They went back to the district and made a big stink, so we pulled back a bit" (S26).

Second, the racial composition of a member's staff is not important only for its symbolic value or the insight it provides concerning the member's views on race and representation. To the extent that people have different life experiences based on their racial background, a racially diverse staff is more likely to push the member in different directions than is a racially homogeneous staff. The scholarly literature has documented the growing importance of staff on Capitol Hill (Malbin, 1980; Hammond, 1985, 1996; Whiteman 1995; DeGregorio 1994, 1995). Norman Dicks (D–WA) lamented the loss of power he suffered when he was elected to the U.S. House after serving eight years as aide to Senator Warren Magnuson. "'I never thought I would give up *that much power* voluntarily'" (quoted in Smith 1988, 281). To truly understand the nature of racial representation in Congress, it may be nearly as important to examine the race of the staffers as it is the race of the member.

Finally, the racial composition of the staff is also important for constituents. Many constituents' primary contact with a member of Congress is more likely to be with his or her staff than directly with the member. Given the unfortunate racial divide that still exists in our nation, constituents are likely to feel more comfortable if they can confide in a staffer who shares their background and perhaps their experiences. Representative Donald Payne (D–NJ) noted in an interview with Carol Swain, "'Black constituents feel comfortable with me, and see that I feel comfortable with them. I always have, because I have always been a minority in this majority. They don't take me as a threat. They know that I'm very concerned about issues that affect them. If you don't care about your number one, there's something wrong with you'" (quoted in Swain 1993, 219). Constituency relations based on racial identification are probably more important in the district offices than in the Washington offices, but even in the nation's capitol tourists probably notice the racial composition of the member's office when they walk in the door. In many members' offices it is difficult not to notice. In my experience members who have few black constituents have very few black staffers in their Washington offices.

Members varied in their perceptions of the racial backgrounds of constituents that contact them in their Washington and district offices.

Many black members noted that a large majority of the visitors in Washington were white. One staffer noted, "Most of the businesses in our district are white-owned, and those are the folks we see the most" (S2). However, there were exceptions to this general pattern. One staffer (S3) noted that the visitors to Washington were split about 50/ 50 between blacks and whites, while another estimated that the Washington contacts were 70 percent white and the district contacts were 70 percent black (S8). Given the inconsistency of the responses, I did not separately analyze the racial composition of the district and Washington offices (in addition, there is the problem of having a smaller number of cases for each member if the data are split between district and Washington offices, which makes it more difficult to discern patterns).

One of the staffers I interviewed summarized many of these points and is worth quoting at length:

> If you look at the members' offices that are not represented by blacks, Hispanics, and women, they are basically lily white. The few staffers who are there don't have any influence. These members ignore an important base in their own districts. The absence of minority staffers has implications throughout the legislative process: witness lists for hearings are all white, there are few minority committee staffers . . . they are all white males for the most part. You lose a lot by not having a more diverse set of witnesses or staffers. Diversity creates more sensible policy. When you ask white members why they don't have more minority staffers, they say, "But there aren't any blacks in my district." I respond, "Hell, you are making policy for the whole country." I get people in here all the time from white members' districts who will say things like "I have this school project on Black History Month. Can you help me out?" Well DUH! The white members can't deal with requests like this because they don't have people who care about their black constituents. (S29)

The overall averages of the racial composition of the staff for the members in my sample are revealing. Black members of Congress hire an average of 10.6 minority staffers, compared to 4.4 minority staffers for white members. On the other hand, black members hire only 3.7 whites on average, while whites hire 11.1 white staffers. Thus, 71.6 percent of white members' staffs are white, and 74.2 percent of black members' staffs are minority (68.4 percent of the staffers are black). When controls are introduced for the racial composition of the constituency, differences between white and black members persist. If one applies simple descriptive representation, or the "politics of presence" (Phillips 1995), to a member's staff, the racial composition of the staff should be the same as the racial composition of the district. To test whether representatives met this ideal, I subtracted the percentages of each member's staff who were white, black, and "other" from the percentages of the member's constituents who were white, black, and "other." The staffs of white representatives were 13.7 percent "more white" and blacks' staffs were 10 percent "less white" than their districts (difference of means significant at .0001, $t = 6.01$), while whites' staffs were 11.1 percent "less black" and blacks' staffs were 11.4 percent "more black" than their districts (sig. at .0001, $t = 4.1$). Thus, yet another measure of the nature of racial representation indicates a significant difference between white and black representatives.

The data on the racial composition of members' staffs also provide support for my supply-side theory. The theory predicts that commonality members should make an effort to provide a multiracial staff that "looks like the district," while difference members will have staff that are disproportionately black (with the control group of older black members in between). The data in table 5.1 show this is exactly the case. The commonality members have the smallest absolute differences between the racial compositions of their staff and their districts (about 4.5 percent and 6.9 percent for black and white staff, respectively) and are the only type of member for whom the null hypothesis of no difference for black staff cannot be rejected (however, white staffers are slightly underrepresented among commonality members). Difference

Table 5.1   Racial Composition of Members' Staff

Type of Member	(% staff that is black) − (% black constituents)	(% staff that is white) − (% white constituents)
Commonality	4.51%	−6.91%*
($n = 8$)	$t = 1.11$	$t = -2.43$
Difference	19.07%*	−16.26%**
($n = 6$)	$t = 2.53$	$t = -5.31$
Older	14.0%**	−9.47%**
($n = 17$)	$t = 4.42$	$t = -3.2$
White	−11.09%**	13.73%**
($n = 9$)	$t = -3.42$	$t = 4.01$

Notes: *t*-tests are for the difference computed by the percentage of the staff that is black or white minus the percentage of the constituents that are black or white.

 *Significant at the .05 level (one-tailed test).

 **Significant at the .01 level (one-tailed test).

 Source: Data on the staff collected by the author; constituency data from the 1990 U.S. Census.

members have the largest gap between the percentage of blacks on the staff and the percentage of blacks in the district (19.1 percent) and also underrepresent whites to the greatest extent (16.3 percent), as predicted by the theory.[4] Older members are between difference and commonality members, and their staffs also tend to overrepresent blacks and underrepresent whites.

I also coded the race of each member's top staffers (those listed in the staff directory). I noted the race of the chief of staff, the administrative assistant, and the legislative director. The correspondence between the race of the member and the race of the top staffers is striking. Only one of the fifteen top staffers for white members (6.7 percent) was black, while thirty-four of the forty-seven top staffers (72.3 percent) were black in the black members' offices. Given that 35.7 percent of the constituents in the white members' districts for which there are data are black, compared to 55.3 percent of the black members' constituents, black members' staff are somewhat more representative than white members' staff. The supply-side theory's predictions also hold for the top staff positions: commonality members have the highest proportion of whites among their top staffers (25 percent), while difference members have the lowest (11 percent), and older members are in between (23 percent).

Location of District Offices

A massive literature, primarily from the 1970s and 1980s, explored the various linkages between members and constituencies through district contacts. Scholars examined such topics as the members' general representational styles, allocation of resources, and "explanation of self" (Fenno 1978); casework and the electoral connection (Fiorina 1989; Johannes 1983, 1984); and travel to the district (Parker 1986) (see Clapp 1963, chap. 2, for an earlier contribution).[5] While there is some disagreement about the specific impact of constituency service on electoral success, there is no doubt that constituency contact is an important part of the representational relationship. Furthermore, an increasing proportion of constituency service is now being done through district offices. In 1972, 22.5 percent of all House members' personal staffs were based in the district; by 1997 that figure had nearly doubled to 44.1 percent (Ornstein, Mann, and Malbin 1998, 137).

Constituency service in the district provides another opportunity to examine racial representation and to test the supply-side theory. The location of a member's district offices indicates the priority he or she places on serving that group of voters; if a member places all of his or her offices in the white suburbs, that sends a very different signal than if the member balances the offices between the inner city and suburbs or places all the offices in black neighborhoods. While the symbolic importance of the decision on where to locate offices is clear, office placement may also have substantive implications. It is much more difficult for poor inner-city residents to seek out the member if his or her office is not in their neighborhood. Ronald Dellums (D–CA) was criticized by local blacks when he closed his district office in the poor black area of Oakland: "'Dellums closed the [ghetto] office because he did not want the brothers and sisters coming in off the streets'" (quoted in Swain 1993, 138). Swain notes that closing the inner-city office inconvenienced many black constituents: "From the black ghetto, trips to the Oakland office require a long bus ride to the downtown post office" (1993, 138). Without this personal contact black residents are likely to become even more alienated from the political system.

The racial composition of the neighborhoods in which members place their offices has its limitations as an indicator of racial representation. The main problem with the indicator is that urban areas are disproportionately black and many members want to have their offices downtown. That is, many members may decide to locate their district offices in urban centers not because they are heavily black, but because they are close to the main business districts. Thus, the primary motivation may be to reach the business people who work in the city, but live in the suburbs. For example, Norman Sisisky, a white representative from Virginia who does not spend a great deal of time on racial issues, located all three of his offices in heavily black, urban areas. However, if a member places his or her offices in a white neighborhood, this is more likely to reflect a conscious decision to reach out to white voters (because the member would be making a decision to *not* locate the office in the more obvious urban area). Therefore, this measure of racial representation may tend to overestimate the extent of black representation (though it is impossible to tell for sure), but is a fairly good measure of efforts to reach out to white voters.

In this analysis I calculated the racial composition of the areas in which 108 district offices of fifty-two members in my sample are situated (Gary Franks was excluded because he is such an outlier; he was the only black Republican in the 103rd Congress and was elected from a district that is only 5 percent black). My initial effort to make this

calculation used the Land View CD–ROM, published by the Environmental Protection Agency and the Department of Commerce. This
database allows one to enter a street address and calculate the racial
composition for a radius of 1 mile, $\frac{1}{2}$ mile, or 1/5 mile from that point.
The only problem was that sometimes the map could not locate the
address or, if the area was too sparsely populated, the program could
not calculate a population for the smaller radii. Therefore, I relied on
Census data broken down by zip code. This had the virtue of selecting
areas that were somewhat more uniform in size and had almost no
missing data.[6]

Styles of racial representation were very evident in many instances.
Some members made a real effort to reach black and white voters. For
example, the zip code containing Mike Andrews's (D–TX) Southmore
Street office in Pasadena had only 36 blacks out of 31,426 residents,
but his other office was in downtown Houston, with a 50.8 percent
black population. Albert Wynn (D–MD) placed one office in Land-
over, in an 86.4 percent black area, and another in Silver Spring, in a
neighborhood that was only 29.8 percent black. At the other extreme,
Bennie Thompson (D–MS) illustrates the politics of difference in placing all five of his district offices in areas that were at least 56 percent
black (including one in a Mound Bayou zip code that had only 76
whites among its 3,200 residents and another in Bolton, which is 83
percent black).

The histograms shown in figure 5.1(a)–(d) indicate the differences
between the percentage of black voters in the zip code that contains
the district office and the percentage of black voters in the district as
a whole. Thus, the positive side of the histograms indicates "overrepresentation" of black constituents, while the negative side represents overrepresentation of whites. Commonality members would be expected to
be as close to the percentage of blacks in the district as possible if they
only had one office, or they would split their offices between black and
white voters if they had more than one office. Difference members
would be expected to be heavily tilted in the direction of representing
black constituents, while white representatives would be slightly biased
toward whites and older members slightly toward blacks. Given that
balancing between constituencies could not occur if the member had
only one office, the histograms are presented only for members who
had at least two offices.

The contrast in figure 5.1 among (b), (c), and (d) should help put to
rest the idea that the Congressional Black Caucus (CBC) is a mono-

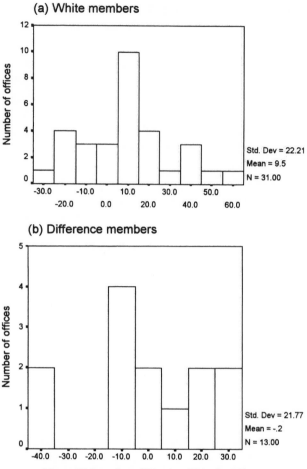

Figure 5.1 Location of Members' District Offices

lithic group that has little internal variation. While the means for all three groups of black representatives are nearly identical, the distributions are dramatically different. Older blacks have an almost perfect normal distribution around the mean of zero (no difference between the racial composition of the zip code in which the district office is located and the overall racial composition of the district). Commonality members, on the other hand, clearly are attempting to serve both racial groups, which is consistent with the biracial, balancing approach outlined in chapter 1 [there are no district offices in the −5 to 5 percent category for commonality members; see fig. 5.1(c)]. Difference members, on the other hand, are tilted toward the positive side of the figure,

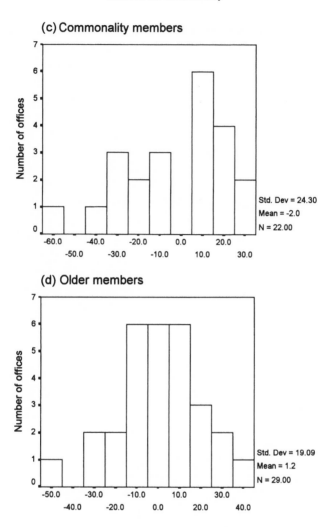

(c) Commonality members

(d) Older members

and only two of their thirteen offices are located in heavily white areas. The only surprise is that white members significantly overrepresented blacks. As noted above, this could be explained by the tendency to place offices in urban areas for reasons other than race.

This figure uses the district office as the unit of analysis. However, this is potentially misleading: for example, the gulf in the middle of the commonality histogram could be explained by some members placing all their offices in white areas and others placing them in black areas rather than *each member* balancing racial representation within his or her own district.[7] Therefore, it is also important to examine the data with the member as the unit of analysis rather than the office. To check this possibility, I summed the differences displayed in the above figure to produce a single measure that would reflect the racial balance of the district office placements. By this measure, zero would represent a perfect balancing of racial representation for a given member. Members who have only one office are included in this analysis because, as noted above, a commonality member with a single office would simply shoot for the district percentage of black constituents. This aggregate measure produced a mean of -5.5 percent for commonality members and 8.8 percent for difference members. This means that on average commonality members placed their district offices in areas that have slightly fewer black residents than the district average, while difference members placed their offices in more heavily black neighborhoods. Corrine Brown (D–FL) is an extreme outlier for the difference members; she was the only one who overrepresented whites (her score was -91.3; she had three district offices that were all in predominantly white neighborhoods). If her case is excluded, the mean for difference members goes to 28.8 percent. The 34.3 percent gap between difference and commonality members is significant at the .01 level ($t = 2.36$). Older black members were very close to the district mean (1.7 percent overrepresenting blacks), and whites' offices were more commonly placed in black areas (18 percent more black residents than the district mean).

Caution must be used in interpreting these results because district offices are placed in a specific area for reasons other than access to various racial groups within the constituency (convenience, rent levels, access to the business district, proximity to public transportation, or good parking). District office location is an incomplete measure of members' efforts to reach out to parts of the constituency because many members have "mobile units" that travel around the district to reach constituents that are not served by a district office. Most members also hold listening sessions and town hall meetings throughout the district. As noted above, a complete travel schedule, broken down by the racial composition of the constituency, would be needed to provide a complete test of this dimension of racial representation. However, the data on district office location demonstrate that commonality members make more of an effort to reach both black and white voters than do difference members, which is consistent with the expectations of the supply-side theory.

Member Newsletters

The "franking privilege"—the ability to send mail by simply using a representative's signature rather than stamps—is one of the many tools that members use to keep in touch with their constituents. The tool is freely used. From 1981 to 1992, congressional mailings averaged 1.21 *billion* pieces of mail per two-year electoral cycle (ranging from a high of 1.48 billion pieces in 1983–1984 to a low of 717.8 million in 1991–1992) at a cost of nearly $100 million a year (in inflation-adjusted dollars) (Ornstein, Mann, and Malbin 1998, 172, 149).[8] Despite the importance of the frank, there is very little research on the content of material that members mail to their constituents or its significance. Albert Cover and Bruce Brumberg (1982) conclude that mailing a pamphlet on infant care helped create more positive evaluations of the incumbent (however, these effects erode over time). Another study found that most newsletters and press releases focused on position-taking, but there was also a healthy dose of advertising and credit-claiming; furthermore, the content of the mailings was shown to be systematically related to district and member characteristics, such as seniority, marginality, urban/rural, and income (Yiannakis 1982).

However, there are no systematic studies of the racial content of member communications. This omission is especially surprising given that newsletters and press releases are the best possible sources for understanding the message that members want to convey to their constituents. All other spoken or written messages from the member are either mediated (such as television or newspaper stories) or partially targeted at an audience other than the constituents (for example, speeches on the floor of the House are partly intended for other members of Congress or for interest groups, and campaign ads or speeches are aimed at voters and the incumbent's opponent). Diane Evans Yiannakis supports this view, noting that "member-initiated communications provide perhaps the best available assurance that members will reach all of their constituents with the images of themselves that they wish to portray. . . . Moreover, such communications are probably the only way in which members reach the majority of their constituents in the interelection period. Thus, examination of the styles which they adopt therein can tell us a great deal about what representatives think are the appropriate linkages between themselves and their constituents" (Yiannakis 1982, 1050). One staffer I interviewed argued that newsletters are especially important for keeping in touch with black constituents: "The blacks in our district want us to keep in touch. They don't want you to become a stranger. Most whites figure they can just catch it on the evening news" (S14).

To determine the racial content of the messages that members convey to their constituents, I collected copies of 123 newsletters from forty-five of the fifty-three members in my sample when I was in Washington conducting interviews in the summer of 1994. Two members in my sample did not send newsletters, and one staffer was adamant in stating that his boss thought that newsletters were a "waste of money. They are abused by many members and are basically just propaganda" (S17). However, most members are willing to use the frank, and staffers were happy to show me the tools of their trade; in addition to the newsletters I received favorable newspaper articles, press releases ($n = 81$), issue-specific flyers ($n = 82$), and in one case, a glossy $8^{1}/_{2}'' \times 11''$ photo of the member. I did not code the newspaper articles or targeted mail that was not sent to the entire district. The selection of newspaper articles would clearly be a biased sample; my systematic analysis of newspaper coverage of members appears in the next section. Targeted mail would be a potentially useful indicator of the balancing perspective of representation (sending one message to white constituents and another to primarily black voters). For example, Carrie Meek (D–FL) sent a separate newsletter to community organizations announcing a range of federal grant programs and another letter that was targeted for environmentalists touting her achievement in this area. However, I did not collect enough targeted mail to have an adequate sample for analysis.

My research assistant coded the racial content of the newsletters, press releases, and issue-specific flyers according to the same procedures used in the previous chapter to code speeches and legislation (racial, implicit racial, and nonracial for substantive and symbolic issues). Press releases and flyers typically addressed only one issue, and therefore only one observation was coded for each member communication. However, newsletters contain many different messages with varied racial content. Therefore, the content analysis was broken down into what Ole Holsti calls the "context unit" (see Yiannakis 1982, 1058). In most cases these units were an article or legislative update within the letter. Most newsletters are organized like newspapers with pictures and short stories with headlines such as "Relief for Farmers" or "Tax Enterprise Zones." My research assistant and I coded 637 articles and 522 legislative updates (typically a brief note about a bill that the member was working on). Other separate items that were coded from the newsletters included letters or columns from the member ($n = 78$), pictures ($n = 302$), surveys ($n = 14$), and letters from constituents ($n = 50$), for a total of 1,766 observations (or "context units").[9] The only item that was not coded with the three-level racial content variable was the pictures, where we counted the numbers of whites, blacks, and other minorities and recorded the percentage for each observation.

Why include letters from constituents and member surveys? The former would seem to reveal voters' views, not the member's, and the latter are so poorly constructed that they could be seen as providing little useful information. First, constituent letters were included as one of the indicators of the member's message because letters are carefully selected by the staff to help demonstrate a claim of credit or to explain a member's vote. For example, several members printed excerpts from letters supporting the member's vote on tough bills, such as the 1993 Reconciliation Act. Often there were letters from popular politicians in the state or from well-known groups or organizations that could help inoculate the member from criticism.

Second, member surveys are certainly useless as a serious survey instrument. The question wording for many items would make a serious pollster blush. For example, Craig Washington's (D–TX) Winter 1992–1993 newsletter contained the following question: "Do you consider health care to be a right or simply a commodity? A) a right, B) a commodity." Clearly the survey is attempting to elicit responses that will support the member's position on this issue that health care is a right. Therefore, while Gallup or Harris polls would not recognize these surveys as legitimate, they do provide some additional insight into the member's position-taking and some explanation of future votes. After receiving the self-selected and probably unrepresentative responses to the biased survey, the member may use this "evidence" to support a potentially controversial position. One can imagine a campaign speech that would rely on the survey to make the following comment: "I support an overhaul of our health care system because 85 percent of my constituents see health care as a fundamental right that must be provided for all Americans."

The content of the newsletters is very similar to the letters that Yiannakis examined from 1975 to 1977. While I did not code the categories of position-taking, credit-claiming, and advertising, as she did, the newsletters in my sample were mostly a judicious mixture of these three ingredients, with strong emphasis placed on Washington activity. However, I have two minor amendments. First, I sensed that advertising constitutes a larger proportion of the newsletters of the mid-1990s than of those of the mid-1970s. Yiannakis found that about 20 percent of newsletters and 11 percent of press releases contained advertising (1982, 1062). In my sample it was not unusual to find a letter that was *exclusively* devoted to publicizing the member's services and asking for casework. For example, Carrie Meek (D–FL) had a four-page letter in the second session of the 103rd Congress entitled "At Your Service," outlining the services her offices could provide across a number of areas. Topics included Need to Cut Red Tape?, Educational Grants, Courtesy Greetings, Passports, Military Academy Appointments, and Want a U.S. Flag Flown Over the Capitol? (I was surprised to learn that these flags only cost between $6.50 and $17.38). The second amendment to the earlier study is that explanations of members' votes (Fenno 1978) were also quite common in newsletters. Both of these observations might be explained by the disproportionate number of first-term members in my sample, who are in the expansionist stage of their careers (Fenno 1978) and more eager to advertise their services and stay in the voters' good graces.

The analysis of the racial content of the newsletters and press releases reveals patterns that are very similar to the data on speeches and legislation presented in chapter 4. Very few articles are explicitly concerned with race: only 6.1 percent of members' communications had racial content. In general, members emphasized issues that were of interest to the entire district. For example, the headline of James Clyburn's Winter 1994 newsletter was "There Are Many Things to Unite Us." Clyburn, who is classified as a commonality member, goes on to write: "Over the past year, I have sought to make the office of the 6th Congressional District more accessible to its people. . . . Much has been written about the broad spans and great diversity of our District. . . . There are common threads running throughout. We all want better conditions for our families, our state and our country. We all want a secure and safe environment for our children." While there are relatively few explicit references to race, 22.4 percent of the content of the communications was "implicit racial" issues that are of central concern to the minority community, such as welfare reform, crime, and the earned income tax credit.

Another similarity to the data in chapter 4 is the additional evidence to reject the "no racial differences" hypothesis. While overall levels of racial content were low, newsletters and press releases from members of the CBC ($n = 37$) were more focused on race than the newsletters from white House members ($n = 8$) (6.6 percent of the content of black members' communications was racial, compared to 2.6 percent of the white members'; $t = 2.18$, sig. at .024). Black members' communications had twice the proportion of implicit racial issues, compared to white members (24.6 percent, compared to 12.6 percent; $t = 2.97$, sig. at .006).

Evidence in support of the supply-side theory is relatively weak for the overall data on member communications. Difference members emphasized more substantive racial issues than commonality members, which is consistent with the theory, but differences were both substantively and statistically insignificant. Commonality members had a slightly higher level of implicit racial emphasis than difference members (25.7 percent, compared to 19.2 percent; 25.1 percent of older members' communications were implicit racial), but these differences were not significant.

However, interesting patterns are evident when the overall analysis is broken down by the source of the representational message. I will briefly discuss two of these: the press releases and the pictures included in newsletters. CBC members' press releases have a much higher racial content than do the articles in their newsletters. For example, James Clyburn (D–SC) issued a press release on May 26, 1994, that touted his efforts to authorize posthumous commissions for two African-American cadets who had been unjustly driven from the Military Academy at West Point in 1870 and 1878. In both cases the cadets had been subjected to extreme racial harassment. In one instance the Army claimed that the cadet had inflicted wounds upon himself, not suffered a racially motivated beating. In the press release Clyburn said, "It is time to right the wrong of a different era, and time for the trailblazing spirit and uncelebrated valor of Whittaker and Smith [the two cadets] to reach the annals of history, where their courage and intellect can be recounted for future generations." This issue was not raised in the newsletter that went to the entire district. In fact, the only mention of race in Representative Clyburn's newsletters was to announce scholarships sponsored by the CBC.

Overall, there are dramatic differences in the racial content of the press releases when compared to articles in the newsletters. There is a relatively small sample of members who provided press releases, so conclusions must be made with some caution (there were fifteen members, twelve black and three white, who gave me seventy-seven press releases). Seventy-five percent of the press releases from the twelve black members, averaged across members, had some racial content (22.7 percent racial and 52.5 percent implicit racial). This compares to the overall average for the thirty-seven black members' newsletters of 6.6 percent racial and 24.6 percent implicit racial content. A paired-samples t-test for the twelve members who had both press releases and newsletters reveals that the former had more than twice the level of racial content ($t = 5.81$, differences significant at .0001).[10]

Targeted messages are common for any savvy House press operation, but how could the member be sure that the press release reaches the intended audience? If anything, it would seem that the press release is *more* public and less targeted than a newsletter. Any media outlet could pick up the press release and publish a story on it. *However, as I will show in the next section, African-American members of the House have learned that the major papers ignore most of their press releases, but the black newspapers often print them verbatim.* Thus, the message aimed at the black constituents is most efficiently distributed through press releases.

The racial content of the pictures that appear in members' newsletters provides strong evidence in support of the supply-side theory. As noted above, 302 pictures were coded for the number of whites, blacks, and other minorities who appeared in the pictures.[11] Table 5.2 shows

Table 5.2   Racial Composition of Pictures in Members' Newsletters

Type of Member	Blacks	Whites	Other
Older member	43.0%	53.8%	3.2%
	(18)	(18)	(18)
Difference member	64.8	32.3	2.9
	(6)	(6)	(6)
Commonality member	37.6	62.4	0
	(9)	(9)	(9)
White member	28.2	71.0	.8
	(7)	(7)	(7)
Hispanic member	40.1	27.5	32.5
	(1)	(1)	(1)
Total	42.1	55.2	2.7
	(41)	(41)	(41)

Notes: Table entries are the percentages of each racial category that appeared in pictures in members' newsletters that were mailed to the district.

Numbers of cases are in parentheses.

the simple means broken down by race and representational style. Overall, 28.2 percent of the people pictured in white members' newsletters were black, compared to 45 percent for nonwhite members ($t = 2.21$, sig. at .025); this is yet more evidence to reject the "no racial differences" hypothesis. Even more compelling is the evidence in support of the supply-side theory. Difference members are much more likely to have blacks in their pictures than are commonality members (64.8 percent, compared to 37.6 percent; $t = 2.84$, sig. at .01). A regression that controls for the percentage of black constituents in the district, the percentage of the district that is urban, and the race and representational style of the member reveals that commonality members are the *least* likely to have African Americans in their newsletter pictures (30 percent less likely than difference members, who serve as the baseline in this regression, compared to whites, who were 26.1 percent less likely to have pictures of blacks than were difference members). The percentage of black constituents in the district is also significant: a 10 percent increase in the percentage black corresponds to a 6 percent increase in the percentage of blacks in the pictures.

Symbolic images clearly matter. Social psychologists have demonstrated the impact of racially diverse or homogeneous images on the

Table 5.3   Regression Analysis of Racial Composition of Pictures in Members' Newsletters, 1993–1994

Variable	B	t	Significance*
Constant	39.6	2.27	.015
	(17.4)		
Percentage urban (×100)	−.092	−.79	.214
	(.15)		
Percentage black in district	.57	2.13	.02
(×100)	(.26)		
White member	−26.1	−2.37	.012
	(11.0)		
Hispanic member	−27.1	−1.35	.093
	(10.0)		
Commonality member	−30.0	−3.05	.002
	(9.8)		
Older member	18.8	−1.95	.03
	(9.6)		

Notes:
   $n = 41$ $R^2 = .376$ Adjusted $R^2 = .266$
   *One-tailed test.
   Dependent variable: the percentage of blacks in pictures (×100)

perceptions and attitudes of children. Similarly constituents who see their black representative in pictures with whites and blacks will probably infer that the member takes a biracial approach to politics. Whether or not this interpretation of the symbolic images could be empirically demonstrated, it is irrefutable that members send different signals concerning their representational styles to the district. Patterns this clear are extremely unlikely to have occurred by chance. Furthermore, these data are among the most objective in this entire book: counting the number of faces in pictures did not require any interpretation or special coding rules. As the saying goes, "Pictures don't lie."

Newspaper Coverage of Members of Congress

Examining the newspaper coverage of members of Congress helps establish a crucial link in the underlying patterns of racial representation. Speaking on the floor, cosponsoring legislation, and offering amendments would matter very little for representation if voters did not have the opportunity to discover what was going on in Washington. Legislation and committee work obviously have an impact on people's lives whether or not constituents can trace out the causal chain of the legislative process. However, the representative process is a two-way linkage. As noted in chapter 1, the strongest theories of representation require that constituents be aware of what the member is doing and eventually take that knowledge with them to the voting booth.

Very few people are attentive to the legislative process in Congress. Even fewer, mostly lobbyists and interest groups, carefully scrutinize a member's record. C–SPAN junkies have some understanding of how things work, but even they could not provide many generalizations about what happens in Congress. The Internet is a new source of useful information about Congress, but this resource is also utilized by an elite few. Most people do not directly receive their information about Congress; instead, it is mediated through television, radio, or newspapers. Thus, the extent to which a voter *perceives* that his or her interests are being served by a member of Congress will depend very heavily on the images he or she receives from the news media. Furthermore, even though most constituents do not closely follow politics, the interested public and potential challengers do, which may serve as a basis for arousing the sleeping public if its interests are not being met (Arnold 1990). In the context of this study, if a member who was elected with biracial support suddenly started ignoring one group of voters, it would be important to know whether this shift was reflected in the news coverage of that member. Without accurate coverage, one important ingredient of electoral accountability and representation would be missing.

Ideally this study would assess the coverage members receive in both the print and the broadcast media. My interviews revealed that while most members thought that newspapers were more important than television, several took advantage of the Democratic Congressional Campaign Committee's Wednesday media feeds from the Capitol. Also, one staffer noted that local television news stations were "eager to cover [her boss] on trips back to the district. We will get pretty good coverage on a fifty-stop tour that is coming up from July 1–12. Richard Petty would have been proud of me" (S7). Coverage from local television stations varied by the urban or rural status of the districts. Members from large urban areas said it was "simply impossible to get on local TV" (according to S10). However, they often mentioned that there were greater opportunities on local access cable TV and C–SPAN. Several staffers also mentioned the importance of black radio. One said, "They are very community oriented, at the forefront of black issues" (S14).

However, documenting the broadcast media's coverage (television and radio) of even a single incumbent, to say nothing about the fifty-three members in my sample, was prohibitively expensive. Therefore, I relied on an extensive content analysis of more than 11,000 stories that appeared in 128 newspapers. I will examine two aspects of newspaper coverage of the members of Congress in my sample. First, I will discuss the members' perceptions (most typically as expressed through their staff) of press coverage.[12] Is the coverage racially biased? How difficult or easy is it to get the member's legislative activities covered? Second, what is the racial content of the mediated message? Do the stories focus on issues of race? How does the focus correspond to the message that the member is attempting to deliver? Are black members of Congress more likely to emphasize issues that concern black constituents than are white members from districts with substantial black constituencies? Will this point of view come across in the news stories? Are there differences between the types of newspapers (African-American and the large-circulation, or "white," papers)?[13] Finally, are there differences within the representational styles of African-American members of the House in the press coverage they receive?

Previous research does not provide many clues for answering these specific questions concerning the racial content of coverage of House incumbents. However, there is an extensive literature over a broad range of topics that uses newspaper coverage to measure the behavior of political figures and links this coverage to individual-level preferences and behavior within the electorate or to the behavior of the politicians. For example, one study used newspaper editorials prior to the confirmation of Supreme Court justices to provide a measure of ideology that would be independent of votes on cases (Segal and Cover 1989). Another study used newspaper coverage of senators' initial campaigns for office to create an ideology scale that is independent of their behavior in office (Hill, Hanna, and Shafqat 1997, 1395).

Others have linked newspaper editorials to voting in presidential elections (Erikson 1976) and the content of weekly issue-oriented newspapers to the information received by readers about their representatives and their evaluations of the politicians (Larson 1990). Russell Dalton, Paul Beck, and Robert Huckfeldt provide the most comprehensive evidence for the argument that the content of newspaper coverage of a campaign has a significant effect on voters' preferences for candidates. Their study, which examined 6,537 items from forty-six newspapers during the 1992 presidential election, demonstrates that "the press performs a persuasive role and an information function" (1998, 124). Examining the 1989 mayoral races in New York City and Seattle, Keith Reeves has found that 22 percent of the newspaper stories about the election in New York were primarily about race, compared to 9 percent in Seattle (1997, 52). This work supports my argument that newspaper coverage can help establish the nature of the representation linkages between members and constituents.

Members' Perceptions

My interviews of staffers and members revealed an almost universal perception among blacks that they were not being fairly treated by at least part of the white press. Though some made distinctions among papers in their district, others made blanket statements about the bias. This bias was manifested in two ways: the content of the stories and the difficulty of getting coverage at all. White members and their staff had many fewer complaints about the white press. White and black offices both agreed that the black newspapers were much more accessible. I will develop each of these points.

Complaints about the content of the coverage that black members received occasionally noted that the white press often made race a polarizing issue or drew attention to race when it was not necessary for the story. More commonly they complained about what one staffer called the "gotcha press," which always focused on negative stories. While many politicians, regardless of race, make this same observation, some staffers believed that African-American members were singled out for harsher treatment. "The white press is very biased in our district. We are always the first one to be criticized and the last one to be praised," one staffer exploded. "The big local paper ran a story about a 'foreign junket' that Representative A took. But it was only for a few days—one trip! The same paper didn't say anything about two white members from our state who were globetrotting all around the world. Another story claimed that he was missing business in Washington while he has a 96 percent voting record. That paper is the worst. It's run by a bunch of autocratic old white guys who shape the news and dictate policy. Only one of their twenty-seven reporters is black" (S1). Another press secretary said, "They try to find any way they can to put on a negative spin; if they can't find a way, they just won't mention [the black member]" (S7). "It's their ink," one staffer acknowledged, "but you wish there was more fairness. The good things we do get stuck on a back page; the allegations of any wrongdoing end up on page one. It's the culture of reporting today. Many of the older guys cut their teeth on the Watergate story, and they have been scandalmongers ever since. I just *know* they are looking for the bad stuff" (S23).

Several staffers noted that there are substantial differences between papers in the degree of racial bias. One said that any bias in the large white papers was mostly partisan rather than racial. "I don't think it would be any different if he was white." He noted that some of the smaller white papers were more racially biased, but they were not as worried about them simply because fewer voters read the low-circulation papers (S8). One southern black member echoed some of these observations, noting the differences between both the sizes of the papers and their ideological leanings. "Most of my difficulties come with the small, conservative papers in the district. I don't think it's primarily a racial issue for them—it's more ideological. However, the way this plays out ends up having a racial slant. I get good coverage from [the major city paper], but the [small city paper] is always after me. We tried hard to work with them, but they always want to report every story as black versus white. Every story about me starts with the line 'black member of Congress. . . .' They have a hard time getting past race" (M7).

A few other comments combined the various observations of racial bias and difficulty of getting stories covered. One press secretary identified two biased papers in his district. "The editors at [paper Z] are a bunch of rednecks. They never help us out, never will print favorable stories. One time Representative C worked his butt off getting a grant for an airport. They ran a story on the front page, but didn't even mention him. They knew he played an important role, but they didn't want to give him the credit. They never have liked him. In the editorial about the election they pretty much cut his dick off" (S3). Another staffer had a similar story about naming a courthouse. This was the first bill sponsored by the new member, but the local paper did not even mention the representative's name. "They mentioned the mayor and the mayor's assistant, and they had nothing to do with it. We did everything we were supposed to do [to get some coverage]. We busted our butts, but nothing happens. They just ignore our press releases" (S7). It was amazing how similar the stories are from office to office— even using the identical language.

Staffers for the older members of the CBC concurred. If anything, from their perspective coverage was even more biased. A press secretary for an inner-city member said, "Representative F is the darling of the black press, but we have to fight the white press constantly. We beg and beg to get any news. For a while I thought there was a complete boycott. Even on biracial issues they won't print our stuff. Once we gave a reporter complete access, but they ended up printing a story that was very negative. We work one hundred times harder to get the few crumbs from the white press. I do everything I am supposed to do—op eds, press releases, access—still we get next to nothing. I understand that Representative F isn't [a white, senior Democratic member], but still, there needs to be more balance. . . . At one point the white press was actually trying to push for a Republican challenger to try to get him to run" (S6). Another inner-city staffer said, "[A major city paper] ran a story on minority members taking PAC contributions from tobacco companies. An editorial dubbed Representative Z the 'Marlboro Man.' Was he captured by the industry? Well, he got more money from the health industry than tobacco, so by that logic he should be called the 'Health Czar' instead" (S27).

However, the view of a biased white press was not universally held by the African-American members and their staffs. "Fortunately, we have gotten very good press coverage," a staffer noted. "Maybe there are have been one or two articles that were not favorable, but I can't complain." He cited an example where the freshman member had a dispute with the senior U.S. senator in the state over the naming of a new federal court building and the editorial page of the major newspaper sided with the freshman (S2). Another staffer attributed his member's good relations with the white press to his previous experience in the state senate and the relationships he developed in the state capital (S8).

The assessment of the black media was dramatically different. One staffer put the contrast in these terms: "The black radio stations are key, and thank god for the black papers. They will run whatever we send them. Press releases, whatever. The white papers never run a damn thing we send them. Anything they can find fault with and you can bet it will be on the front page" (S1). Another staffer noted the importance of the black weekly newspapers; his boss had a bimonthly editorial that they run (S2). Two staffers referred to the black papers as a "godsend" (S7, S12), and nearly all of them had something good to say about the black press.

One staffer was also appreciative of the favorable coverage the member gets from the black papers, but at the same time indicated that he did not have much respect for the journalistic quality of the papers. "The black papers are lazier," she said. "They just run news stories verbatim from our press releases" (S3). Another staffer had a more charitable, and in my view more accurate, explanation for the content of the black papers; he noted that the black papers "don't have the resources and press people to edit; they will generally print what we send them. You have to be careful to say what's right when you have that kind of power" (S12). The same point was made by a staffer who said, "The black press doesn't have the resources to do much of their own reporting. The more you give them, the more they print. The white press is more of a sifter" (S16).

White members' comments about the black press were more favorable than black members' comments about the white press. One staffer for a white member made the same observation that "it is easier to get stuff in the black papers. They will actually publish our press releases. We also held a 'Youth Summit' on issues that were important to inner-city youth, and the only reporters that showed up were from the black papers. They gave us good coverage on that one" (S18). Another said, "The major black daily is very fair. They give us good coverage for the things we have done well. They are especially interested in our activity on the Education and Labor Committee. They regularly report on this" (S31). One staffer said that his boss was ignored by the black press; the difference was that they did not perceive the sort of hostility in the black press that so many of the black members' staffers described when talking about the white press (S15).

If members' perceptions are correct, I expect to find that the black papers provide more coverage of racial issues than do the white papers and that white members will figure more prominently than black members in the stories in which they do appear in the white papers (but no differences would be expected in the black papers). Also, the supply-side theory predicts that difference members should have a higher percentage of their press coverage on racial issues than do commonality members.

Racial Content of the Coverage

To see whether these predicted patterns hold, my research assistants coded 11,319 stories and editorials from 128 newspapers for the fifty-three members in my sample between 1992 and 1994. There were three sources for these stories: Ethnic News Watch, a CD–ROM database that provides full-text searching of stories gathered from forty-eight African-American and Latino newspapers; CD Newsbank, another database of major newspapers; and Nexis, the nation's largest full-text media database, which was used to fill in the gaps for districts that were not covered by the other two sources. I included all stories in the Ethnic News Watch and CD Newsbank data sets on the fifty-three members in my sample. Nexis searches were limited to the *New York Times, Washington Post, Los Angeles Times,* and any papers that were in the member's district. (A complete listing of the newspapers used appears in the References.) The unit of analysis is a member/story. That is, if a newspaper story mentioned five members in my sample, it would appear in the data set five times.

Each story was coded for its racial content along three dimensions: the focus, the member's point of view, and the generic topic. First, did the story have a racial focus? If so, did the article emphasize a biracial or an implicit approach to racial politics, did it emphasize a more explicit approach to racial politics, or was the story balanced between the two? Second, did the member express a point of view along the racial lines used in the focus coding? An article was coded as expressing the member's point of view only if there was a quotation from the member from which his or her position could be inferred. The third dimension of the coding scheme, the racial content of the generic topic of the story, serves as a check on the coding procedure. Each article was coded as "racial," "implicit racial," or "race not involved." This coding was done independently, after the focus and member point of view were coded, based on a four- to five-word summary of the article that was coded in the first stage. This second stage of coding was conducted without knowledge of the type of newspaper (white or black) in which the article appeared or of which member was the focus of the article. This provides a measure of the racial content of the article that is independent of any potential biases that may creep into the coding process based on contextual knowledge. The coding may also approximate the impressions of a reader who skims headlines and topic paragraphs. See Appendix B for a more detailed discussion of the coding procedure and the differences between the focus and the generic topic.

Tables 5.4, 5.5, and 5.6 all have the same basic format: they break down the coverage of members in my sample by the type of paper (major or African-American) and the racial content of the stories (no race, biracial, or racial); tables 5.5 and 5.6 also have the "balanced" category. For example, the upper-left cell in table 5.4 shows that 61.7 percent of the stories in the major papers that included a reference to African-American members of the House had no racial content (2,681 of 4,348 stories). The data on the generic topic of the stories reveals several fascinating patterns (table 5.4). First, while the white papers do not give much attention to explicitly racial issues (only 7.1 percent of the stories obviously concern race), when they do cover race they almost always turn to a black member of Congress as a source for the story (452 of 459 articles, or 98.5 percent of the time). Blacks are also heavily represented on implicit racial stories (with nearly 90 percent of the 1,358 stories). Even if one corrects for the different baseline (about two-thirds of the stories coded from white papers are on black members), this is a large difference. That is, if major papers mentioned members of Congress randomly in their articles across different categories of racial content, black members should have appeared in 67.7 percent of the racial politics stories (4,348/6,426). However, they appeared in 98.5 percent of those stories.

There are several competing explanations for this pattern that cannot be sorted out with these data (the analysis required to figure this out would require inside access to daily editorial decisions: Which sto-

Table 5.4   Racial Content of the Generic Topics of Articles

		Topic of the Article			
	Race of Member	No Race Involved	Biracial Politics	Racial Politics	Total
Major newspapers (Nexis, CD Newsbank)	African American	61.7% (2,681)	27.9% (1,215)	10.4% (452)	100% (4,348)
	White	93.0% (1,862)	6.7% (135)	1.3% (6)	100% (2,003)
	Latino	88.0% (66)	10.7% (8)	1.3% (1)	100% (75)
	All members	71.7% (4,609)	21.1% (1,358)	7.1% (459)	99.9% (6,426)
African-American newspapers (Ethnic News Watch)	African American	41.2% (1,923)	31.5% (1,469)	27.3% (1,274)	100% (4,666)
	White	84.8% (151)	7.9% (14)	7.3% (13)	100% (178)
	Latino	67.3% (33)	24.5% (12)	8.2% (4)	100% (49)
	All members	43.1% (2,107)	30.6% (1,495)	26.4% (1,291)	100% (4,893)
All newspapers	All members	77.2% (8,732)	9.9% (1,116)	10.0% (1,137)	2.9% (332)

Notes: Cell entries are the percentage of newspaper stories in each racial category for each type of member. See text for descriptions of the various categories.

  Numbers of cases are in parentheses.

  Includes all fifty-three members in the sample.

ries get covered and why? Whom do they use for sources on specific stories and why?). The pattern may be explained by the relative efforts of black and white representatives on issues of race, as demonstrated in the previous chapter. Black members are more active on racial issues, so it makes sense that they get disproportionate coverage when issues of race arise. However, the size of the gap cannot be explained by relative effort. It is possible that white members have to make the extra effort if they want to have their views stated on a racial issue, and most of them apparently do not. On the other hand, maybe they *do* try, but are ignored by the mainstream press on issues of race. Finally, there is a more simple explanation that could be called "Rolodex journalism." When an issue of race comes up and the journalist needs a quote, he or she probably has a list of CBC members on the Rolodex who are likely to get the first call. The overall pattern is probably explained by a combination of relative effort, conscious exclusion, and a more passive selection mechanism.

On the other hand, white members are somewhat overrepresented in the white press on topics that do not concern race (40.4 percent of the total, compared to their baseline of 31.2 percent of all stories in the white papers). According to the member interviews and the evidence presented in chapter 4, the lack of exposure on nonracial issues for black members is not from lack of trying. This is the first bit of evidence of the racial bias against black members in the white press that was so strongly perceived by the members of their staffs.

The same patterns were evident in the black papers, and if anything, the bias toward covering black members on racial and implicit racial issues and whites on nonracial issues is even more pronounced. Because the number of stories on white members is relative small in the black paper data set (mostly due to the small number of black papers in the white members' districts, and perhaps because of the same processes of conscious and passive exclusion that were noted above for the white press), the more meaningful comparisons can be made across types of members rather than across types of topics. White members have about 85 percent of their stories on nonracial topics, compared to only 41.2 percent of the stories on blacks that do not concern race in the black papers (see table 5.4).

Table 5.5, which shows the results of the analysis of the member's point of view as it is represented in the news story, reveals similar patterns. The central finding is that a vast majority of stories about members of Congress who represent substantial numbers of blacks do not reveal any racial perspective presented by the member of Congress. An amazingly low 1 percent of the stories in the major papers that covered white members contained any racial angle (racial, implicit, or balanced), as stated by the member of Congress; this compares to 16.2 percent of the stories in the white papers involving black members of Congress having some racial content. Even for the black members a very small percentage of the articles contained the member's racial or balanced views (3 percent). Not surprisingly the African-American papers were more likely to present the member's point of view from a black politics perspective. But even in the black papers only 39 percent of the 4,666 stories about black members portrayed the member as emphasizing any one of the three racial categories (compared to 11 percent for the white members). However, a large proportion of the stories on African-American members had a primary focus on race (22.9 percent of the total), as opposed to the biracial (10.4 percent) or balanced (5.3 percent) category.[14]

Table 5.5   Newspaper Coverage of Race: Member's Point of View

		Racial Content of Member Point of View				
	Race of Member	No Race Involved	Biracial Racial Politics	Racial Politics	Balanced View	Total
Major newspapers (Nexis, CD Newsbank)	African American	83.8% (3,645)	13.2% (573)	1.2% (51)	1.8% (79)	100% (4,348)
	White	99.0% (1,981)	1% (20)	0% (1)	0	100% (2002)
	Latino	73.3% (55)	26.7% (20)	0	0	100% (75)
	All members	88.4% (5,681)	9.5% (613)	.8% (52)	1.2% (79)	99.9% 6,425
African-American newspapers (Ethnic News Watch)	African American	61.4% (2,865)	10.4% (485)	22.9% (1,070)	5.3% (246)	100% (4,666)
	White	88.8% (158)	5.1% (9)	3.4% (6)	2.8% (5)	100.1% (178)
	Latino	59.2% (29)	18.4% (9)	18.4% (9)	4.1% (2)	100% (49)
	All members	62.4% (3,052)	10.3% (503)	22.2% (1,085)	5.2% (253)	100% (4,893)
All newspapers	All members	77.2% (8,732)	9.9% (1,116)	10.0% (1,137)	2.9% (332)	100% (11,318)

Notes: Cell entries are the percentage of newspaper stories in each category. See text for descriptions of the various categories.

Numbers of cases are in parentheses.

Includes all fifty-three members in the sample.

Table 5.6 shows the same data for the racial focus of the article. The most striking difference between the two tables is the huge increase in the proportion of stories that focus on race in the African-American papers—only 12.6 percent of the stories on black members do not focus on race, and more than half are from a racial politics perspective. In contrast, more than half of the stories on white members of Congress in the African-American papers do not focus on race, and only 18 percent are from a racial politics perspective. The white papers focus much less on race (55.2 percent do not focus on race for blacks, and 90.7 percent do not for whites). Thus, once again, it is clear that the race of the House member has a significant impact on the nature of racial representation provided for the district. *Regardless of motivations or biases of the papers, white or black, constituents living in districts that are represented by a black House member are substantially more likely to receive news that touches on or focuses on issues of race.*

Table 5.6   Newspaper Coverage of Race: Focus of the Article

	Race of Member	No Race Involved	Biracial Racial Politics	Racial Politics	Balanced View	Total
			Racial Focus of the Article			
Major newspapers (Nexis, CD Newsbank)	African American	55.2% (2,400)	36.3% (1,579)	1.0% (44)	7.5% (325)	100% (4,348)
	White	90.7% (1,816)	7.1% (142)	2.0% (41)	.2% (4)	100% (2,003)
	Latino	56.0% (42)	44.0% (33)	0	0	100% (75)
	All members	66.3% (4,258)	27.3% (1,754)	1.3% (85)	5.1% (329)	100% (6,426)
African-American newspapers (Ethnic News Watch)	African American	12.6% (590)	14.8% (689)	54.7% (2,552)	17.9% (835)	100% (4,666)
	White	57.9% (103)	10.7% (19)	18.0% (32)	13.5% (24)	100.1% (178)
	Latino	32.7% (16)	20.4% (10)	24.5% (12)	22.4% (11)	100% (49)
	All members	14.5% (709)	14.7% (718)	53.1% (2,596)	17.8% (870)	100% (4,893)
All newspapers	All members	43.9% (4,967)	21.8% (2,472)	23.7% (2,681)	10.6% (1,199)	99.9% (11,319)

Notes: Cell entries are the percentage of newspaper stories in each category. See text for descriptions of the various categories.

Numbers of cases are in parentheses.

Includes all fifty-three members in the sample.

Some interesting patterns appear within the "racial" and "biracial" categories in the white papers. For black members of Congress thirty-six times as many stories are presented from the perspective of biracial politics (36.3 percent) as from a racial politics point of view (1 percent). Thus, to the extent that constituents receive information about Congress from white newspapers, they are not being inundated with messages of racial divisiveness. For the most part the mainstream papers either ignore questions of race or present them in a balanced or implicit manner.

Table 5.7 allows a more detailed analysis of this point by examining the interaction between the generic topic and the focus of the article. There are some large differences between black and white papers in the focus they choose for racial and nonracial issues. Of the issues that are explicitly racial in the generic content, such as voting rights, racial bias, or affirmative action, black papers present the story with a focus

Table 5.7 Interaction between the Topic and Focus of the Article

	Racial Content of the Generic Topic of the Story	Focus of the Story				
		Race Not Involved	Biracial	Racial	Balanced	Total
Major newspapers (Nexis, CD Newsbank)	Race not involved	85.6% (3.947)	12.3% (569)	.7% (32)	1.3% (61)	99.9% (4,609)
	Biracial	22.0% (299)	66.7% (906)	1.3% (17)	10.0% (136)	100% (1,358)
	Racial	2.6% (12)	60.8% (279)	7.8% (36)	28.8% (132)	100% (459)
	All topics	66.3% (4,258)	27.3% (1,754)	1.3% (85)	5.1% (329)	100% (6,426)
African-American newspapers (Ethnic News Watch)	Race not involved	30.6% (645)	17.0% (358)	34.4% (724)	18.0% (380)	100% (2,107)
	Biracial	3.8% (57)	17.9% (267)	53.9% (806)	24.4% (365)	100% (1,495)
	Racial	.5% (7)	7.2% (93)	82.6% (1,066)	9.7% (125)	100% (1,291)
	All topics	14.5% (709)	14.7% (718)	53.1% (2,596)	17.8% (870)	101.1% (4,893)
All newspapers	All topics	43.9% (4.967)	21.8% (2,472)	23.7% (2,681)	10.6% (1,199)	100% (11,319)

Notes: Cell entries are the percentage of newspaper stories in each category. See text for descriptions of the various categories.

Numbers of cases are in parentheses.

Includes all fifty-three members in the sample.

on race 82.6 percent of the time, compared to only 7.8 percent of the racial topics with a racial focus in the white press. The white papers are much more likely to present the issue in a biracial fashion (60.8 percent of the time) or in a balanced fashion (28.8 percent). At the same time 85.6 percent of the 3,947 stories on nonracial topics in the white press were treated in a nonracial fashion, compared to only 30.6 percent in this same category in the black papers ($n = 645$). Recall that these differences cannot be explained by bias in the coding because the coding of the topic was done with no knowledge of whether the story appeared in a white or black paper and applies equally across both types of papers (that is, a story on Lani Guinier is always coded as a racial issue, and one of food stamps is always biracial, regardless of the type of paper).

A more systematic test of the "no racial differences" hypothesis and of the supply-side theory is shown in the multivariate analysis in table

Table 5.8   Regression Analysis of Racial Coverage of Members in Newspapers, 1992–1994

Independent Variable	Model 1: Article Focus	Model 2: Member's Point of View	Model 3: Generic Topic	Model 4: Article Focus (White Newspapers)
African-American member of Congress—difference	43.84** (7.78)	11.31** (4.61)	28.06** (7.71)	8.30** (2.91)
African-American member of Congress—commonality	34.30** (7.38)	11.95** (4.37)	28.59** (7.32)	3.23 (2.84)
African-American member of Congress—older	35.04** (6.07)	14.38** (3.60)	29.62** (6.02)	6.64** (2.52)
Hispanic member of Congress	20.97+ (14.79)	20.06** (8.77)	2.57 (14.67)	−2.15 (5.49)
Ratio of white to black income in the district	−5.76 (4.96)	−3.17 (2.94)	−1.86 (4.92)	−3.29* (1.76)
Percentage of black constituents (×100)	.49** (.18)	.32** (.11)	.32* (.18)	.192** (.068)
Percentage of district in an urban area (×100)	—	—	—	−.10** (.034)
Party (1 = Democrat; 0 = Republican)	4.47 (8.50)	3.59 (5.03)	3.84 (8.43)	.13 (3.29)
South	−10.40* (5.08)	−5.16* (3.01)	−3.68 (5.03)	—
Constant	13.11 (15.09)	−1.36 (8.94)	2.27 (14.97)	7.58 (7.23)
F-statistic	18.63**	11.24**	10.07**	6.55**
Adjusted R-square	.73	.61	.58	.46
Number of cases	53	53	53	53

Notes: The dependent variable for models 1 and 2 is the percentage of newspaper stories on the member of Congress that was concerned with a racial, biracial, or balanced issue for white and black newspapers. The dependent variable in model 3 is the percentage of newspaper stories on the member of Congress that were concerned with a racial or biracial issue for white and black newspapers. Model 4 examines only white papers and racial and balanced issues.

Standard errors are in parentheses.

+Significant at the .10 level (one-tailed test).

*Significant at the .05 level (one-tailed test).

**Significant at the .01 level (one-tailed test).

5.8. The regressions in models 1–3 combine all the newspaper stories into one data set,[15] while model 4 is based only on the white newspapers (many white members did not have enough stories in the black papers, so there were too many missing cases to do a regression for the black papers). Model 1 shows that nearly 10 percent more stories focusing on difference members have a racial focus, compared to commonality members (who, in turn, have about 34 percent more of their stories from a racial perspective than do white members). The racial content of stories from the member's point of view is nearly identical for commonality and difference members, who both had between 11 and 12 percent more of their stories from a racial angle than white members (model 2). However, the similarity between commonality and difference members in this instance may be a function of the data: it was often very difficult to determine the member's point of view in an article. The generic topic model (model 3) shows no differences among types of black members, but this is not surprising given that it is a blunt measure that does not pick up the nuances of various stories. However, even in this model about 29 percent more of the newspaper articles about black members concern race than those on white members.

The controls for the percentage of black voters in the district and the dummy for southern districts were both in the expected direction. A 10 percent increase in the proportion of black constituents produced a 3.2 percent increase (member point of view and topic) or a 4.9 percent increase (focus) in the proportion of racial stories. Racial coverage of southern House members in districts that are at least 25 percent black is about 10.4 percent less than in nonsouthern districts (5.2 percent less from the member's point of view; not significant for the topic). This is consistent with the members' perceptions that some of the smaller (and in a few cases even the larger) southern papers are more biased in their coverage.

The party of the member failed to reach significance, probably because there are only four Republicans among the fifty-three members in the study. The income ratio variable (simply per capita white income in the district divided by per capita black income) did not have the expected sign and was not significant. I had expected a positive sign for the variable—as the income gap between whites and blacks grew, I thought that members would be more inclined to address racial and implicitly racial issues (such as welfare and food stamps) to try to redress the imbalance.

Model 4 presents a separate analysis of the white newspapers, where the dependent variable is the proportion of stories on the member that are racial and/or balanced between racial and implicitly racial issues. This is a more direct test of the supply-side theory, as the focus is on more explicitly racial issues (rather than explicit or implicit racial issues). The theoretical expectation is that difference members would have a higher proportion of their news coverage on racial issues than commonality members, and the evidence supports this proposition. Difference members have a higher proportion of racial stories than any other category of member (8.3 percent more than whites). The proportion of commonality members' stories devoted to racial issues was not statistically significantly different from the proportion of racial stories concerning white members. Both the percentage of the district that is urban and the income ratio had unexpected signs, and both were statistically significant. The size of the urban variable is quite small, but its negative sign may indicate the impact of the increasing diversity of the CBC (with more blacks being elected from rural areas in 1992). The income ratio is still negative in this model and is significant at the .03 level. Its substantive significance is relatively small— as white income doubles, relative to black income, the percentage of stories about race in the white newspapers would fall by about 3 percent—but the negative relationship is still puzzling. One possibility is that districts with higher income inequality between whites and blacks are disproportionately represented by whites who have less of a racial focus. However, I control for the race of the member, and in any case the means of the income ratio are nearly identical for white members' districts (1.94) and those of blacks (1.90).

The last cut at the newspaper coverage data examines access to the papers. Is there evidence to support the black members' perception of bias among the white papers and the general view that black papers were more accessible? There are a few limitations of my newspaper data set that prevent me from conclusively answering this question. First, it was not possible to record the "nonevents" of the failure to get a press release published in a paper. Ideally I would have had access to all the members' press releases and been able to determine the proportion that the white and black papers published. Second, I will employ an indirect measure of access: the average number of mentions of the member in the articles and whether the member was a major focus of the story. The more simple option of counting the number of stories for each member in the black and white papers would not be valid because my newspaper database does not contain all the stories on the members in the three years of the study (mostly because the black newspapers were not available in a format that included all stories; Ethnic News Watch provides only a selection of stories).

The data in table 5.9 provide strong evidence for differential treat-

Table 5.9   Mentions of and Focus on Members in Articles

	Race of Members	Number of Mentions	% of Major Focus
White newspapers	White members	2.50[a]	40%[b]
		(2,003)	(2,003)
	Black members	2.02[c]	31%[d]
		(4,348)	(4,348)
	Difference of means t-test	t = 7.00**	t = 7.33**
African-American newspapers	White members	2.17[a]	35%[b]
		(178)	(178)
	Black members	2.63[c]	36%[d]
		(4,666)	(4,666)
	Difference of means t-test	t = 2.26*	t = .25

Notes:

*Difference of means test significant at the .05 level.

**Difference of means test significant at the .01 level.

Numbers of cases are in parentheses.

t-ratios in the table are for the pair of numbers directly above the t score. The pairs of superscripts indicate the t-ratio for that given pair (listed below). For example, the [a] pair compares the mean number of mentions for whites in the white newspapers (2.5) and black newspapers (2.17), and the t-ratio listed below ($t = 1.42$) shows that this difference is significant at the .08 level.

[a]$t = 1.42$, significant at .08.

[b]$t = 1.32$, significant at .09.

[c]$t = 5.20$, significant at .0001.

[d]$t = 9.53$, significant at .0001.

ment based on the member's race. Both black and white papers are inclined to focus more on their respective race; the differences are nearly identical, with white papers giving about one additional mention per two stories for white members, while black papers do the same for black members. In percentage terms this is nearly a 25 percent advantage in coverage based simply on the race of the member. The racial bias in whether the member was a major focus of the story holds for the white papers, with nearly a 10 percent difference, but not for black papers, where both white and black members were a major focus of about one-third of the stories. Turning the focus of the difference of means test to the member rather than the type of paper (see the listing under table 5.9), white members do not receive differential treatment in the white and black papers (differences are not significant at the standard .05 level, but they are significant at the less stringent .10 level), while black members receive significantly less coverage in the white papers than in the black papers (or viewed more positively, they receive more coverage in the black papers).

These differences persist in a separate analysis (not shown here) that controls for seniority. That is, the differences in newspaper coverage may simply be a function of the number of years a member has been in the House. Given that a disproportionate number of the blacks in my sample were freshmen, this could account for some of the observed differences. However, this hypothesis was firmly rejected. A regression of seniority on mentions and major focus yielded coefficients that were insignificant, and in three of the four models I ran, the seniority variable even had the wrong sign.

Overall, the analysis of newspapers provides stark evidence of differences across types of papers and the race of members, and fairly strong evidence of differences among black members based on their representational styles. The most benign explanation for these differences is the different missions and audiences of the two types of papers. Black papers serve a largely black audience and see one of their central purposes as serving as a voice for the minority community. The lines between editorial and reporting practices are much more blurred in the black press (though the same criticism is often leveled at the white press). Black papers are much more likely to include a triumphant endorsement of the increase in black representation in reporting on the 1992 House election returns than are white papers.[16] White papers served a more racially mixed constituency and are therefore less likely to present racial issues from the perspective of the racial minority, at least not without considering the arguments on the other side of the issue. My own view is that nothing is wrong with this arrangement: different styles of journalism serve different constituencies.

The only disturbing part of this analysis was the evidence of racial bias in the amount of coverage that papers provide to members of the race of their primary audience. This bias may have been expected in the black newspapers, where their purpose has a strong racial motivation, as noted above. However, the bias was even stronger in the white press, which may reflect lingering discrimination. Shying away from divisive racial issues and trying to report on them in a biracial fashion can serve a useful purpose; giving less coverage to black members than white members on the stories that *are* covered cannot be justified.

On a more positive note, this analysis also shows that newspaper coverage may serve the interests of members who try to promote a politics of commonality and build biracial coalitions. In a sense the newspapers are doing the members' work for them. The African-American papers emphasize issues of race, whereas the mainstream papers do not, which allows members to appeal to both constituencies. Obviously the member must act in a manner that promotes such reporting by serving the interests of all his or her constituents. As I point out in the previous chapter, this is largely the case. Given the recent spate of media-bashing, it is refreshing to see that the reality of biracial politics in Congress is being reflected in the newspapers (the broadcast media may be a different story, but they are not examined in this study).

Conclusion

This chapter provides strong evidence to support the three central conclusions of this book: (1) race matters, (2) white voters are not disenfranchised by having black representatives, and (3) there are important differences among black members in the racial representation provided to their districts. These conclusions are based, in part, on the most "objective" evidence I have produced to demonstrate differences between white and black members and among black members in how they represent their districts. The racial composition of the staff, the location of the district office, the number of mentions of a member in newspaper articles, and one component of the analysis of the district newsletters (the racial composition of the pictures) do not depend on subjective coding.

The race of the member matters in two ways. First, the data in this chapter undermine the assertion by advocates of the "no racial differences" perspective that white representatives address black interests as thoroughly as black representatives. The newspaper accounts of the issues stressed by white members of Congress and the content of their newsletters do not support this conclusion. A vast majority of these links to the constituency were devoid of racial content. White members do not focus much of their attention on issues of race. However, by two symbolic measures, the racial composition of the staff and the location of the district offices, white members were somewhat more attentive to the needs of their blacks constituents. Second, the race of the member matters because the coverage of racial issues is substantially higher in black and white papers alike and in the members' newsletters when the House member is black. This clearly has an impact on the type of information that constituents receive. Constituents are more likely to be aware of racial issues and more likely to be exposed to a variety of positions on issues. This has to improve the quality of deliberative democracy.

However, white constituents are not "disenfranchised" by this relatively more intense focus on race when the member is black. More than two-thirds of the topics of all newspaper stories in black members' districts have nothing to do with race, and 60 percent of the foci of the stories are not related to race. Black members of Congress stress issues that are not only of interest to the black community. Based on this analysis of more than 11,000 newspaper stories; nearly 300 newsletters, press releases, and issue flyers; district office location; composition of the staff; and interviews with members and their staff, it is difficult to understand the claim that white constituents are being ignored. The newsletter data may be the most convincing on this issue because they are the most direct measure of the image that the member is trying to portray to the district. Only 6.6 percent of the content of the newsletters of the thirty-seven CBC members in this part of the data set had an explicitly racial focus.[17] Furthermore, it is important to recall the conclusive evidence presented in chapter 1 that black and white preferences are the same on nonracial issues. Therefore, black members of Congress are representing the entire district when they balance their time and efforts between racial and nonracial issues.

The supply-side theory also receives strong support by examining the linkages to the constituency. Commonality members' staffs were the only ones that did not over- or underrepresent the black composition of the district, and they had the smallest disproportionate representation of whites on their staffs of any type of member. Difference members were the most likely to overrepresent blacks, just as predicted by the theory. In other words, commonality members' staff "looked like" the district, while difference members made more of an explicit effort to represent blacks. Commonality members also pursued a much more obvious balancing strategy in the placement of their district offices, in an effort to reach both black and white voters, while difference members were more concerned about placing their offices in black neighborhoods. Finally, there were dramatic differences in the racial composition of the pictures in the member newsletters and significant differences in some dimensions of the newspaper coverage between commonality and difference members. Clearly the standard view of homogeneity within the Congressional Black Caucus is in need of revision.

The final chapter will develop some of these general conclusions, explore the broader significance of the findings, and demonstrate their relevance for the broader literatures on congressional politics, the legal aspects of redistricting, normative theory, black politics, and the policy process concerning racial politics.

CHAPTER SIX

Black Majority Districts: Failed Experiment or Catalyst for a Politics of Commonality?

Racial issues, such as multiculturalism, diversity, affirmative action, quotas, identity politics, reverse discrimination and "the new racism," urban unrest and poverty, and welfare reform, figure prominently on the current social and political agenda in the United States, but until recently the participation of black politicians on these issues was primarily examined at the local level. African Americans first achieved significant political power in urban politics. Thus, it made sense that political scientists focused most of their attention at that level. Similarly blacks in Congress had relatively little power, so scholars largely ignored them in that context. Of the 350 citations in Paula McClain and John Garcia's extensive review of the minority politics literature that was written before the size of the Congressional Black Caucus (CBC) exploded (1993), only seven concerned African Americans in Congress. Racial redistricting in 1992 and the nearly 50 percent increase in the size of the CBC permanently changed the relative lack of interest in race and representation in Congress. Research on the CBC since 1993 has contributed greatly to our understanding of racial representation in Congress (Swain 1993; Canon 1995; Cobb and Jenkins 1996; Singh 1998; Whitby 1998; Lublin 1997; Walton 1995; Pinney and Serra 1995; Menifield 1996; Johnson and Secret 1996; Clay 1993; Overby and Cosgrove 1996; Cameron, Epstein, and O'Halloran 1996; Di Lorenzo 1997; Canon, Schousen, and Sellers 1996). I hope to have contributed to this literature in several ways.

First, I provide a theory that links the electoral and institutional arenas through the racial coalitions that elect the member. My supply-side theory simply states that if there are at least two black candidates and no white candidate running in a Democratic primary in a black majority district, the candidate who campaigns on the basis of biracial politics—the politics of commonality—will beat the candidate who campaigns by using the politics of difference. If a white candidate runs

in a field with at least two black candidates, the candidate who campaigns on the basis of the politics of difference will win. The necessary
conditions for the theory were tested with data from the 1972, 1982,
and 1992 elections and then applied to the 1992 elections involving
African Americans who were elected to the House. My coauthors and
I found that of the seventeen black members elected in 1992, eleven
were elected on the basis of the politics of commonality and six on the
basis of the politics of difference. Of these seventeen districts, thirteen
had been explicitly drawn to provide an opportunity for black voters
to elect "candidates of their choice."[1]

Second, I tested this theory in a variety of institutional settings and
found that the increased size of the CBC did not produce an exclusive
focus on racial issues, contrary to the expectations articulated by Justice Sandra Day O'Connor in *Shaw v. Reno* (1993). Indeed, black
members focus a majority of their attention on issues that do not concern race. However, African-American members of the House *are*
more attentive to the distinctive needs of the black constituents than
are their white counterparts who represent substantial numbers of
blacks. The "no racial effects" argument has been thoroughly undermined with a broad array of data, including roll call voting, sponsorship and cosponsorship of legislation, committee assignments, leadership positions, speeches made on the floor, constituency newsletters,
placement of district offices, the racial composition of the staff, and
the coverage that members receive in newspapers. Many of these indicators of the representational relationship between members and constituents have never been used to examine racial representation. I employed a variety of research methods to examine these data, including
simple descriptive and multivariate statistical techniques, in-depth case
studies, and extensive personal interviews of politicians and their staff.
The quantitative analysis provides a more comprehensive test of the
causal effects, while the qualitative case studies provide an understanding of the causal mechanisms.

This triangulation (or, more accurately, dec-angulation) of methods
and measures (Tarrow 1995) should provide greater confidence in the
central conclusions of this book: (1) *The race of the representative has
important implications for the type of representation that is provided to
a district with a significant number of black constituents.* Black members
do a better job of walking the racial tightrope and balancing the distinctive needs of black voters and the general interests of all voters,
black and white alike. White members tend to have a more exclusive

focus on nonracial issues. This central conclusion has been largely overlooked by studies that focus on roll call voting.[2] (2) *The supply-side theory can explain differences in the representational styles of members of the CBC.* This conclusion runs strongly against the grain of the common wisdom concerning the CBC, which has focused on its cohesiveness and unity. One reviewer of a proposal for this project was quite skeptical that I would find any differences. While the differences within the CBC are not as great as the differences between white and black members, distinctive representational styles are evident, and they matter. Sanford Bishop, Robert Scott, and Jim Clyburn are different politicians than Cynthia McKinney and Bennie Thompson. The supply-side theory provides a basis for predicting which elections will produce which types of candidates, based entirely on the racial composition of the candidate pool. Given the simplicity of the theory, its ability to successfully predict differences within the CBC over such a broad range is quite striking.

The policy consequences of this research are bound to be controversial. Proponents of "authentic" black representation will not be pleased with what will be perceived as the "triumph of tokenism," to use Lani Guinier's phrase. Guinier says, "For those at the bottom, it is not enough that a representation system give everyone an equal chance of having policy preferences physically represented. A fair system of political representation should include mechanisms to ensure that a disadvantaged and stigmatized minority group also has a fair chance of having its needs and desires satisfied" (1992, 288–289). Building biracial coalitions will also be seen by these critics as sublimating the interests of blacks to the institutional pressures of majority coalition-building. However, blacks *are* a potent force in the House. As my analysis in chapter 4 shows, they often provide pivotal votes for passing important legislation, they are forceful advocates for black interests in their speeches and sponsorship of legislation, and the bills they sponsor are more likely to succeed than those with nonblack sponsors.

Critics from the other side of the ideological spectrum who favor a color-blind approach to redistricting may also be unconvinced. This research shows that commonality members engage in a *balancing biracialism* rather than a *color-blind biracialism.* My personal view is that the former is preferred over the latter because there are distinctive black interests and wants, as demonstrated in chapter 1, and these interests are not adequately addressed by the color-blind approach, which is favored by most white members. Furthermore, these critics may see the representational effects of black districts as irrelevant: they argue that voters should not be placed into districts on the basis of race, period. But for political scientists who have a theoretical interest in understanding racial representation and citizens who want to fully explore the various options for enhancing racial representation and improving race relations in this country, representation must be at the center of the discussion. My hope is that both sets of critics may reevaluate their positions in light of these findings and conclude that the minority districting that is rooted in a balancing politics of commonality represents a reasonable middle-ground position.

This chapter will place these findings and arguments within the broader policy and theoretical context. I will organize these comments around the goal established in the first two chapters of increasing the dialogue among the normative, legal, black politics, and legislative literatures. I conclude by briefly exploring the implications of my research for policy debates in this area.

Before I turn to these issues, I want to briefly address the question of political context and relevance. The Republican takeover of Congress in 1995, the series of court cases challenging the constitutionality of minority districting, and the general movement in the political system toward color-blind policies may all point in the direction of diminished interest in the topic. However, race still infuses the politics of Congress. A recent article in *Congressional Quarterly Weekly Report,* with the headline "Surface Racial Harmony on Hill Hides Simmering Tensions," provides ample evidence that the politics of difference and commonality are alive and well in the House (Doherty 1998). Members frequently work together across racial lines to build a local airport or solve common problems, but the debates become intense over issues such as affirmative action. Black incumbents who must campaign in redrawn districts face the same challenges of building new racial coalitions that they confronted in their initial election in 1992, and the same supply-side forces outlined in chapter 3 will be present. The legal challenges to the 1990s round of redistricting that continue as of this writing may be overtaken by the next Census and the next round of redistricting.

Furthermore, my supply-side theory of representation is general and broadly applicable to a variety of institutional settings; it does not require Democratic or Republican control of the House and could be applied to state legislatures or other political institutions. Arguments about the relative power of the CBC are important for the policy debates that I examined in the first part of chapter 4 and will return to below, but they do not affect the broader theoretical argument that I make about race and representation in Congress or the main conclusions outlined above.

Theoretical Implications

Implications for Normative and Democratic Theory

The central normative question of the study is "What happens when equality of rights, a basic tenet of liberalism, comes into conflict with the politics of difference?" (Taylor 1992, 51–61). Should African Americans have congressional districts explicitly drawn to provide them with additional representation? The answer of this study is a resounding yes. Minority districting provides valuable symbolic representation and a growing substantive voice for African Americans in the political system. While the traditional argument over minority districting would balance these values against the harm done to liberal principles, I argue that the apparent trade-off was not present in most districts. Whites did not have their Fourteenth Amendment protections violated, and the politics of difference did not prevail in most of the new minority districts. Even in districts that are represented by difference members, white voters still receive extensive attention from their member of Congress.

This normative conclusion and the empirical evidence on which it is based fit most comfortably within the work of normative theorists such as Anne Phillips and Will Kymlicka, who attempt to bridge the gap between political liberals and difference theorists. While both Phillips and Kymlicka have expressed reservations about minority districting, they endorse the importance of incorporating racially based differences into a liberal political system or, in Phillips's terms, recognizing the centrality of the "politics of presence." The politics of presence suggests that there is value in both descriptive and substantive representation that flows from diversity. While descriptive representation is often viewed as less important than substantive representation (Pitkin 1967), the following counterfactual exercise suggests that it matters: Consider a Congress populated by 535 white, middle- to upper-class men. Most Americans would not be comfortable with such a representative body. Why? Because, in part, Congress should "look like us," at least to some extent. But also because many people assume some relationship between descriptive and substantive representation. The evidence in this book suggests that this assumed connection exists: the race of the member matters for racial representation.

Another group of normative theorists, the deliberative democrats (Gutmann and Thompson 1996; Bessette 1994), suggests a mechanism through which descriptive and substantive representation may be linked. Politicians of different races, genders, and ethnic backgrounds have different life experiences that help shape their outlook on politics. Having a broader range of experiences in a representative assembly means that the quality of deliberation is improved through the expression of diverse political views. Amy Gutmann and Dennis Thompson's dramatic example of Senator Carol Moseley Braun changing the outcome of an amendment concerning the use of the Confederate flag illustrates this point. My data presented in chapter 4 provide strong support for the view that racial diversity *does* provide a broader range of viewpoints. It is important to have issues such as health care reform, crime, and free trade agreements debated from the perspective of black politics. Without a substantial number of African Americans in Congress, the evidence indicates that this would be far less likely to happen. The supply-side theory also shows that there are diverse viewpoints within the CBC, which also is a healthy development for representation in Congress.

Others have written extensively about the relationship between democratic theory and minority districting (Cain 1992; Guinier 1992, 1994; Graber 1996; Natapoff 1996). The focus of this debate shifts from commonality and difference to majority rule and minority rights. How can a racial minority with distinct interests have its voice heard in a majority-rule system? This question looms even larger in nations such as South Africa, the former Yugoslavia, India, and Sri Lanka, which are currently attempting to maintain or create democracies amid racial or ethnic divisions that run far deeper than those in the United States. Comparative scholars emphasize that creating stable political systems that address the needs of various constituencies may be facilitated by picking the right type of electoral institutions. One study on South Africa noted, "Electoral-system design is increasingly being recognized as a key lever that can be used to promote political accommodation and stability in ethnically divided societies" (Reynolds 1995, 86). Placing the U.S. experience with racial redistricting in this broader comparative context draws attention to the general importance of these issues for democratic theory.

The debate over majority rule and minority rights in the American context typically is drawn back to James Madison's famous arguments in *Federalist #10*. Scholars on both sides of the debate have appropriated Madison to support their views. In *The Tyranny of the Majority*, Guinier, for example, approvingly quotes Madison's assertion that "'[i]f a majority be united by a common interest, the rights of the minority will be insecure'" (1994, 3). Applying this idea to a broad range of racial issues, Alexandra Natapoff observes that "the Voting Rights Act, race-based economic preferences, school desegregation measures, and antidiscrimination laws that aim to equalize the participatory power of racial minorities should be seen as Madisonian salve on this nation's factional wounds" (Natapoff 1996, 755–756). On the other hand, Mark Graber points out that Guinier's institutional and electoral remedies to promote interest representation (such as minority veto power over certain legislation or cumulative voting) run directly counter to Madison's institutional solutions of separation of powers and checks and balances that were aimed at *reducing* the evil effects of self-interested factions (1996, 292–293). To paraphrase Richard Nixon's comment about John Maynard Keynes, in the area of voting rights and redistricting, apparently "we are all Madisonians now."

Madison recognized that it was impossible to get rid of factions because they are rooted in self-interested human behavior. He believed that the large and diverse republic and the elaborate system of divided power would ensure that no majority could permanently dominate the political system. While sectional and class interests were Madison's concern rather than racial minorities, his insights can be applied to the current debates over minority districting. I believe that Madison would have been pleased with the actual results of the black majority districts that I outline in this book, but not for the reasons promoted by difference theorists. The new black majority districts provide a voice for minority interests that may not otherwise be heard in the system of majority rule, thus limiting the possibility of majority tyranny. But this has been accomplished without polarizing interests or inflaming factional politics. Rather, the emergent biracial politics that balances racial interests and general concerns strives to achieve the public good sought by Madison.

This balancing version of the politics of commonality shares ground with good old-fashioned pluralism. First, both place an emphasis on the intensity of preferences. As Robert Dahl argues in his classic pluralist tract, *Preface to Democratic Theory*, those who care more deeply about a given issue should have a greater say in the formulation of policy in that area (1956, chap. 4). Balancing commonality provides more attention to black constituents on issues such as affirmative action and racial discrimination, to white business interests on issues of central concern to them, and to districtwide interests on issues such as health care and tax policy that are of concern to all constituents. Both approaches strive to ensure that every active and legitimate interest can have its voice heard, to paraphrase Dahl's characterization of the pluralist process (1956, 137–145). Second, both approaches maintain that majority tyranny will be controlled in the long run, over a range of issues. If the members of a segment of the population lose on one round, they must reorganize to win on the next round. The open and divided system ensures that there are no permanent majorities. Evidence I present in chapter 4 demonstrates that the CBC has been a successful participant in this pluralistic system: it has placed racial issues on the agenda and enacted them into law with greater success than is accorded to nonracial issues.

However, the balancing commonality approach differs from pluralism in several important ways. First, while Dahl argues that institutional solutions to fundamental problems of democratic representation are insufficient, the balancing commonality approach produced by the supply-side effects in the new black majority districts shows that institutional solutions can work. Dahl argues that social customs and mores are necessary supplements to the Madisonian system of checks and balances in order to hold majority tyranny at bay. However, the experience in the black majority districts turns this argument on its head: the institutional engineering actually helped alter political attitudes and firmly entrenched patterns of racial voting. Black politicians who have practiced the politics of commonality in the new districts have helped break down racial barriers. However, *they would not have had this opportunity without the institutional change of the new black majority districts that were created in 1992.*

Second, while pluralism has a group-based focus, the supply-side theory is rooted in individual-level politics. The type of politician elected shapes the nature of racial representation that a district will receive. Third, the balancing commonality approach is not as normatively neutral as pluralism. Under pluralism the Ku Klux Klan would have the same access to a member as the National Association for the Advancement of Colored People (NAACP). On the other hand, racial issues have a special place on the agendas of all members of the CBC, including those who practice the politics of a balancing commonality.

Finally, because of historical patterns of underrepresentation, racial issues are less likely to be compromised in a "split the difference" approach that may be more characteristic of the distributive politics of pluralism. Rather, positions on racial issues that are consistent with the interests of black constituents are balanced with positions on non-racial issues.

Implications for the Legal Literature

Given the murkiness of the central legal concepts in the *Shaw*-type cases, especially the notion of "race as a predominant factor," minority districting is likely to be litigated well into the next century. After a three-judge district court panel struck down the newly redrawn and much more compact "I–85" district, which was 45.6 percent black, because race was still the predominant factor in drawing the district lines, State Attorney General Mike Easley expressed frustration at the high-stakes guessing game: "'We never get real clear direction from the court. We just keep getting told what the proper boundaries are not. The General Assembly is beginning to narrow it down'" (quoted in Rawlins 1998, A3).

My research may help inform the legal debate in two areas: the responsiveness of elected officials and the standing of white plaintiffs in districting cases. Neither of these issues has been accepted by a majority of the Court as relevant for the *Shaw*-type cases. The Court has shied away from an analysis of representational harms suffered by white plaintiffs. Instead, the Court has accepted the white plaintiffs' claims that they were denied equal protection of the laws under the Fourteenth Amendment by being classified by race and placed in a black majority district. Thus, while my research is not relevant for white plaintiffs, it could aid defendants in *Shaw*-type cases whose districts come under strict scrutiny. My evidence that white representatives are not as responsive to black constituents as black representatives are could help establish a Section 2 justification for the creation of a black majority district under a "totality of circumstances" analysis that demonstrates blacks did not have an equal opportunity to participate. As I noted in chapter 2, the responsiveness of politicians is not one of the central factors mentioned in the 1982 Senate report that is often used to define the "totality of circumstances" in vote dilution cases. However, it is one of the two additional factors mentioned in the report and has been used in some pre-*Shaw* cases (*Rogers v. Lodge* 1982).

The issue of standing, which has drawn some of the most intense debate among the Supreme Court justices in the *Shaw*-type decisions, is centrally related to this research. The liberal justices—Justices John Paul Stevens, Byron White, Harry Blackmun, Stephen Breyer, David Souter, and Ruth Bader Ginsburg—have continually raised the issue of standing, but they have never had more than four votes on this issue. The dissenters' argument is that white voters have not been prevented from voting, they have not been denied representation, and there is no constitutional right that guarantees a color-blind election; therefore, white plaintiffs have not suffered any concrete harm and as a result have no standing to sue.[3] Instead, the majority of the Court has endorsed a thin conception of "stigmatic harm," and a new category of Fourteenth Amendment protections and a new basis for standing in these types of cases (see Justice Stevens's dissent in *Shaw v. Hunt* 1996). The evidence presented in chapters 4 and 5 on the extensive attention that black members of the House give to nonracial issues would lend support to the liberal justices' views that white plaintiffs have not been harmed by racial redistricting. It seems unlikely that a majority of the Court will suddenly endorse this position, but maybe Justice O'Connor, the pivotal vote in all of these cases, will listen to Justice Souter's plea for judicial restraint in *Bush v. Vera* (1996, 1074–1075) and leave the political process of drawing district lines up to the state legislatures.

Implications for the Black Politics Literature

In a recent review article Paula McClain asks if black politics is "at the Crossroads, or in the Cross-Hairs?" (1996). The mid-1990s were certainly a difficult time for black politics. While evidence of distinctive black interests and needs continued to mount (see chapter 1 for a summary of these data), the political system was backing away from policies aimed at providing opportunities for blacks. Even in the area of higher education, long perceived as the best way to reduce the gap between blacks and whites, several states abandoned affirmative action programs. These developments have produced a range of responses in the black politics literature from a scathing critique from the left of the failure of black politics to address the needs of poor blacks (Smith 1996) to an edited book on the "bold new voice of black conservatives in America," which endorses the move away from affirmative action policies (Faryna, Stetson, and Conti 1997).

This book attempts to address some of the central issues raised by

McClain in her essay. She says that the *Shaw v. Hunt* and *Bush v. Vera* decisions "raise a broader question for black and American politics and theories of representative democracy: What does representation mean, and what does it mean to be represented? These two questions, I predict, will dominate research in black politics over the next several years" (1996, 872). The view of representation I endorse is the commonality perspective described in chapter 1. How does this view of representation, and the evidence of its expression in the U.S. House, relate to the recent black politics literature?

In another review essay McClain and Garcia chart the evolution of the black politics subfield through several different generations: early studies on Negro leadership, the protest/accommodation paradigm, the ethnic politics/pluralism approach, and the power relations approach (1993, 248–253). The current generation of work, they argue, is characterized by a "diversity of scope and heterogeneity of approaches" (1993, 253). However, one common thread that runs through much of this literature is the tension between integration and incorporation versus separation and self-reliance. Robert Smith makes one of the strongest arguments for the latter approach, arguing that Black Nationalism is the only path for serving the interests of poor blacks (1996). Ronald Walters has also been very critical of the "deracialization" perspective that is rooted in the biracial politics of the integrationist side of the debate (1992).

Proponents of the integrationist side of the debate range from those on the right, such as Shelby Steele (1990), Thomas Sowell, Clarence Thomas, and Stephan Thernstrom and Abigail Thernstrom (1997), who argue for a color-blind society, to those who argue for building biracial coalitions in black influence districts (between 30 and 50 percent black) as a way of maximizing black political power (Perry 1991a, 1991b; Swain 1993). Those in this latter category recognize the distinctive interests of blacks, but argue that whites can adequately represent black interests and that black majority districts are a self-limiting and ultimately ineffective tool to serve black interests. Others are less optimistic that blacks can be elected in white majority districts due to racially polarized voting and support minority districting when there is evidence of racial vote dilution, while endorsing biracial politics as the ultimate goal (Grofman, Handley, and Niemi 1992, 135; Cain 1992). Finally, this side of the debate includes a vast majority of black politicians at the national level, including most members of the CBC and the leadership of the NAACP. This view sees integration and incorporation as the ultimate long-range goal for black politics, but in the interim it also sees a strong need for addressing the concerns of black Americans.

I see my research as fitting squarely in these last two groups. In chapter 1 I presented evidence that only thirty-five elections between 1966 and 1996 in the U.S. House of Representatives in white majority districts produced black winners. Until racially polarized voting is less pronounced, black majority districts will be needed to produce significant numbers of blacks in the House. The balancing commonality view recognizes the importance of building biracial coalitions, but within the context of serving black interests as well. Too many debates on racial representation assume a polarized stance. Either one is an "authentic" black or not. If a black candidate receives white votes, he will not adequately represent blacks. On the other hand, one is color-blind or not. If a politician endorses a program to help disadvantaged black youths, then she is part of the problem, not the solution. These are overly simplistic views of the messy world of congressional politics. It is possible to champion peanut subsidies or catfish sales to support the white farmers in one's district (as Sanford Bishop and Mike Espy have done), while at the same time pushing for money for a historically black college or minority enterprise program. It is absurd to claim that a black politician is not "authentic" if he or she pays attention to the needs of white voters in the district and is elected with their support. Most black members of Congress view their representational role from a perspective of balancing various interests; thus, it makes sense for political scientists to build theories of racial representation that accommodate this complexity.

Ronald Walters, while skeptical of the deracialization perspective, endorses this pluralistic view. "In any society, if you have a minority group that's down, they need every strategy in their arsenal—they need the Mike Espys, the Maxine Waterses, the Jesse Jacksons, all of them. It's a question of complementary roles. It's not a question of one group superseding the other" (Donohoe 1993, E1). William Jefferson, a black member of Congress from Louisiana, summarized his notion of the balancing commonality perspective in the following way:

"When the civil rights battles were at their height in the late '50s through the '60s, most of us were outside the institutions of government. Part of the civil rights struggle was to empower us to get here. And our work after we've got here is to improve on civil rights laws. But that is not our main charge in this place. Our job is not strictly as civil-rights advocates.

There are other areas now: lack of income, dependency on a government that refuses to empower us to carry our own load, welfare reform issues that take people out of the cycle of dependency, and training for education. My job is just to be the best legislator I can be." (quoted in Donohoe 1993, E1)

Implications for Legislative Politics Research

The two dominant approaches to understanding congressional institutions and behavior—the rational choice variant of new institutionalism, in its distributive, informational, and partisan incarnations (Weingast and Marshall 1988; Krehbiel 1991; Shepsle and Weingast 1995; Cox and McCubbins 1993; Aldrich 1995, chap. 7), and behavioralism (Kingdon 1989; Hall 1996)—do not emphasize race. Indeed, the only one of these leading works that mentions race is Richard Hall's analysis of the Job Training Partnership Act, in which the race of the member is one of the explanations of participation in legislative activity on the bill (1996, 206–209). Rather than focusing on race, these theories emphasize the time and resource constraints members face (Hall 1996, 21–24), bargaining and gains from exchange (Weingast and Marshall 1988), or informational benefits from specialization and expertise (Krehbiel 1991). To this list I add the supply-side theory and the different styles of racial representation members bring to the institution. These ideas about representation influence member behavior— their patterns of roll call voting, how they frame debate on an issue, which bills they cosponsor, and how they present themselves to their constituents. Informational and distributive theories may explain the central tendencies of member behavior, but for members of the CBC the politics of commonality and the politics of difference shape racial and implicitly racial issues.

In the introduction to this chapter I cited the importance of moving beyond the analysis of roll call data and advocated the use of multiple methods and data to test theories. This approach provides the basis for both explaining and understanding member behavior. On a sensitive and complex topic such as race it is important to confirm the validity of theoretical constructs by talking to the politicians and their staff who are involved in the daily battles. My theory is essentially deductive; it was in place a year before I started collecting any of the institutional data and was based on abstract principles that had strong roots in rational choice theory and spatial analysis in its earliest incarnation. But the Washington interviews and mucking around in the data provided one important nuance of the theory—the balancing perspective. In my initial thinking on this topic I only had two categories—commonality and difference. After talking to politicians I realized that there were color-blind and balancing versions of the commonality approach. This also raised an important normative implication, addressed above: racial representation did not need to be an "either/or" proposition. I would have missed this without the interviews. The case study of North Carolina was also useful for uncovering the causal mechanisms that produced the supply-side causal effects.

The other implication that my work has for the legislative politics field is that it adds my voice to Richard Fenno's admonition for the past twenty years that legislative scholars need to pay more attention to linking electoral and governing activities (1978, 1996). In Fenno's recent work on the Senate he sees the "representational relationship as a continuous negotiation between politician and constituents" (1996, 332) and focuses on the political career and the political campaign as important variables in the representational relationship between politicians and voters. He ends his book on a note that is consistent with my supply-side theory, stating, "A focus on the campaigning candidate may encourage us to think of campaigns in the context of the candidate's career and constituency connections. And it may lead us to broaden our focus beyond the study of election outcomes toward the study of representation" (1996, 336). My argument has been precisely that the behavior of the campaigning candidate will have an important impact on the nature of representation that is provided to the constituent. However, the supply-side theory also points out that part of the campaigning strategy may be determined for the candidate by the racial composition of the candidate pool. If a black candidate is running against a white challenger in a district that is highly polarized and 55 percent black, it probably will not make much sense to make a biracial appeal. If, on the other hand, there are two blacks running with no white candidate, this biracial approach will be the winning ticket.

Future research will have to extend Fenno's challenge to examine what happens to the politics of difference and commonality over the course of a career. There is some indication in the roll call data examined in chapter 4 that difference members may be moderating their views to solidify their political base. Does a primary challenge dictate a change in representational philosophy, in either direction? That is, a commonality member who has campaigned and governed from a biracial perspective may be challenged by a difference candidate if the incumbent has moved too far from representing the racial interests of the district. The opposite may happen to a difference member who is challenged by a commonality black candidate or a white opponent.

One of the central conclusions of this book, which is consistent with the focus suggested by Fenno, is that campaigns matter—not in the typical way debated in the presidential election literature that goes back two generations (as in "campaign effects" versus partisan identification and long-term commitments), but rather by determining the type of electoral coalition that produces a winner and the impact this has on representation.

Policy Implications

Partisan Considerations

The Introduction and chapter 2 of this book examined the impact of minority districting on Republican success in House elections. After reviewing the research on this topic, I concluded that the Democrats lost somewhere around ten seats in the 1992 and 1994 elections due to minority redistricting, which was fewer than Democratic partisans feared and not as many as Republicans hoped. While this was not enough of a swing to give control of the institution to the Republicans, there is no doubt that the Republican control of Congress has undermined the power of the CBC and harmed black interests (Singh 1998, 192–199). To the extent that black majority districts contributed to Republican control, this should be a concern to Democratic partisans. Another concern of advocates of black representation was that the "bleaching" of the white Democratic districts would make them less responsive to black interests; however, this does not appear to have happened (Whitby 1998, 130–131; Bullock 1995).

This leaves open the question of how many black voters should be placed in a district if the goal is to maximize black representation. The only attempt to simultaneously consider the electoral side (electing a black) and the representational side (in terms of congressional behavior) concludes that the optimal size for black influence districts in the South is 42 percent (Cameron, Epstein, and O'Halloran 1996). However, that study is based exclusively on roll call votes, so it does not consider the rather dramatic differences between black and white members demonstrated in chapters 4 and 5. Also, as noted above, the prospects for electing blacks in white majority districts remain quite slim, despite the recent success of J. C. Watts in Oklahoma and Julia Carson in Indianapolis.

An additional partisan consideration faced by the CBC is its new role as a minority within the minority party. The CBC's options are limited because, for the most part, the Democratic Party appears to be the only game in town. Republicans have elected two blacks to the House in the past decade, J. C. Watts (OK) and Gary Franks (CT), who lost his seat in 1996. Nationally, however, Republicans have been able to win only 10–20 percent of the black vote. The Republican Party has started nominating blacks in black majority districts and black influence districts in an effort to broaden its political base. In fact, in three congressional districts in 1998 (GA 4, GA 2, and FL 3), black Democratic incumbents defeated black Republican challengers. However, one white member I interviewed thought the Republicans were hypocritical and engaging in empty symbolism. "The white establishment thinks it's cute to nominate blacks in races they can't win. It's just tokenism. If they thought they had a chance to win, they would nominate a white so fast it would make your head spin" (M4). It seems clear that the long-range fortunes of the CBC will be best served within the Democratic Party.

Alternative Electoral Institutions

Some critics of racial redistricting argue that alternative electoral institutions, such as proportional representation and cumulative voting, may provide a more efficient voice for minority interests in a majority-rule political system than minority-majority districts (or single-member geographic representation more generally). Richard Morrill says, "With single-member districts, it is manifestly impossible to satisfy any but one dimension of these interests—that of the majority" (1996, 4). Guinier's advocacy of these positions, in addition to her even more controversial views on minority veto powers, supermajorities, and cumulative voting on legislation of interest to the minority community in Congress (1991a; 1991b; 1994, 4–7, 94, 107, 260 n. 118) led to the demise of her nomination to serve as assistant attorney general for civil rights in the spring of 1993. These views constitute a subtle, but important shift from voting rules that favor black candidates to rules that would favor black interests. Guinier's position is based on the belief

that the "right to fair representation" under the Voting Rights Act
should be measured by "the extent protected minority groups are provided meaningful voice in government" (1994, 93). This is the view
that got Guinier in trouble. One critic responds, "With all due respect,
it is simply impossible to reconcile this idea with any theory of gover-
nance that is called 'democratic' in ordinary, common speech" (Polsby
and Popper 1996, 19). While Guinier's proposals for procedural
changes in the legislative process are extreme (and in my view unworkable),[4] her cumulative voting plan (which she calls "semi-proportional
representation") is more plausible.

Cumulative voting works in the following fashion: Members of the
legislature would be elected from multimember districts in which voters
would have one vote per legislative seat. Voters could allocate their
votes among the candidates in any proportion, including "plumping"
their votes by casting them all for one candidate. Thus, minorities who
comprised at least $1/n$th of the district (where n is the number of legislative seats) should be able to elect at least one of their preferred candidates. This electoral arrangement has received some attention in the
popular press and among empirical scholars and formal theorists.

Formal theorists have long been interested in the process of aggre-
gating individual preferences into collective outcomes. When more
than two options are presented, there is no voting system that ensures
consistently fair and just results (see Riker 1982, chap. 4, for a summary of the various voting methods). While cumulative voting cannot
satisfy all the conditions of a fair voting system, formal work suggests
that it can serve as a mechanism for increasing minority representation. Most formal work has focused on the optimal voter strategies to
elect candidates of their choice under various voting systems. Gary
Cox (1984) finds that in two-member districts under straight voting, it
is optimal to "plump" votes for a single candidate. Cox also concludes
that in multimember districts cumulative voting promotes a dispersion
of ideological positions among the candidates (1990, 927). Elizabeth
Gerber, Rebecca Morton, and Thomas Reitz (1998) find that under
straight voting, the majority candidates in a three-candidate two-seat
election (with two majority candidates and one minority candidate)
constitute one equilibrium. However, they also find that there are equilibria that predict either a close three-way race or even the minority
candidate winning. Under cumulative voting in the same context the
minority candidate wins when minority voters have no preference be-

tween the majority candidates and cumulate their votes for their first choice. However, if the minority voters split their votes, one of the majority candidates can win (1998, 141–142).

The empirical literature is relatively thin on the topic of cumulative voting in the United States because there are only a few offices for which the practice is used. The most commonly cited examples in the literature are Chilton County, Alabama; Peoria, Illinois (which held only one election under cumulative voting); Alamogordo, New Mexico (which ended its experiment in 1994); and the Illinois General Assembly from 1870 to 1982 (Adams 1996; Sawyer and MacRae 1962; Van Biema 1994; Issacharoff and Pildes 1996).[5] Greg Adams (1996) provides strong empirical evidence that the cumulative voting system in Illinois produced more ideologically extreme members of the state assembly than did the single-member district system that was employed in 1982, contradicting Cox's formal results (1990).[6] Chilton County, Alabama, which is 12 percent black, used cumulative voting to elect its first black commissioner since Reconstruction, Bobby Agee. Agee received votes from only 1.5 percent of the white voters (Issacharoff and Pildes 1996, 10), yet managed to win the most votes overall because nearly every black voter in the county cast all seven of his or her votes for the only black candidate (Van Biema 1994, 43). Furthermore, in the second election under cumulative voting in Chilton County, Issacharoff and Pildes report that white candidates were courting black voters and Agee was able to attract a few more white votes. In addition to providing descriptive representation, cumulative voting may help break down racial barriers (1996, 10).

However, there are several potential problems with cumulative voting: (1) it is relatively complex and will produce voter confusion, at least in the short term; (2) it will shift power to groups of voters with higher turnout rates (the elderly, wealthy, highly educated, and whites) because they will be able to influence elections in a broader geographic area; (3) it will most likely benefit minorities of the right; (4) multimember districts in which the cumulative voting occurs will be so large as to virtually do away with the concept of geographic representation, which is so central to American politics (Morrill 1996, 4–5); and (5) it could produce a less stable, more fractured political system (Forest 1996, 10). One other unintended effect often not mentioned by proponents of the system is that Republicans are likely to benefit from cumulative voting even more than they did from the creation of black majority districts. If Republicans "plump" their votes, they should be able to elect candidates roughly in proportion to their population, just like minorities would. For example, in Chilton County, a area where Republicans rarely won local office, three of the seven commission seats went to Republicans.

Furthermore, minorities will need to construct powerful slating organizations to limit the supply of candidates or risk splitting their limited voting power. In Centre, Alabama, another community that tried cumulative voting, a black city councilman was elected when the plan was implemented in 1988. But in 1992 another black candidate ran, splitting the black vote, and the city council reverted to all-white (Van Biema 1994, 43). The practice of cumulative voting is clearly not a panacea for minority representation.

Implications for Minority Districting and Its Place in the Policy Process

The broader significance of this research lies in the theoretical issues raised above concerning the implications of embracing a politics of difference or a politics of commonality. The central question is "How can a pluralist system that places an emphasis on process over outcomes provide a voice for minorities who have not received equal treatment in the political marketplace?" My research reaches the surprising conclusion that the *outcome* of embracing a politics of difference by creating black majority districts is, in fact, consistent with a *procedural* focus of the liberal pluralist tradition. In other words, what appeared to be another example of mandating outcomes based on racial classifications actually turned out to promote a broader biracial politics in most of the new districts.

The unanticipated impact of the new minority districts is all the more surprising given that our system generally has difficulty dealing with issues that lie at the intersection of race and mandated outcomes (for example, affirmative action and busing). Our political system is more comfortable producing policies in the liberal, pluralist tradition of focusing on process rather than outcomes. The conventional wisdom implies that politics should help provide a level playing field, protect individual autonomy and dignity, and promote equal access to the economic and political systems.[7] The civil rights laws passed in the 1960s were clearly in this tradition. They attempted to provide African Americans with the protections they had been denied since the nation's inception, but did not guarantee equality of outcome. Similarly issues

Table 6.1   Racial Policy and the Political Process

Politics of the Policy	Involvement of Race in the Policy		
	Explicit	Implicit	No Race
Concern with outcomes	Minority districting Affirmative action Busing MLK day	Death penalty Immigration quotas Sentencing guidelines	Veterans' benefits Pell Grants Progressive income tax
Focus on process/equal access and opportunity	1960s civil rights laws	Bilingual education Welfare reform	Social Security Medicare

such as bilingual education, though increasingly controversial in some areas, are often defended as providing all children with an equal opportunity to receive a good education, regardless of ethnic or cultural background. Welfare reform has enjoyed broad bipartisan support because most Americans are willing to provide a "hand up" (equal opportunity), but not a "handout" (equal outcomes), to use the old cliche. Major social programs, such as Social Security and Medicare, have broad support because of equal access provisions.

The difficulty of sustaining a political coalition in support of an issue increases as one moves from the right to the left (from "no race" to "explicit" involvement of race) and from the lower half to the upper half of the diagram. The political system is not as comfortable when shifting to a focus on outcomes rather than process or opportunity. Policies that target specific groups in society for special treatment or regulation will enjoy support if they serve some greater social good. Veterans' benefits and Pell Grants are good examples of policies that are targeted to specific individuals to promote specific outcomes, but are widely accepted because they are viewed as serving useful ends. The progressive income tax, though under increasing attack from the "flat tax" reformers, also is widely accepted, demonstrating that such targeted policies can transcend class boundaries.

When the issue of race is interjected into policies that focus on outcomes, politics becomes more volatile. Policies in the middle category, those that have racial undertones, will be accepted despite their focus on outcomes if the members of the majority see them as serving their interests, as with many issues of criminal justice. Targeted policies involving explicit racial classification, such as busing and affirmative action, are initially controversial and then difficult to sustain if the majority perceives that it is bearing some significant cost due to "preferential treatment" for minorities. Symbolic policies, such as the Martin Luther King Day, are somewhat controversial, but will not be difficult to sustain because they do not impose large costs on the majority.

Minority districting appears to be a policy with a very specific, targeted outcome in mind: promote black empowerment and representation by electing more African Americans to Congress. The *appearance* of an outcome-based policy does not comport with reality. First, nothing in the Voting Rights Act or its amendments guarantees an outcome. It guarantees an *opportunity* to elect "candidates of choice." Second, even if the proponents and critics of black majority districts both expected that race would be the primary focus of these districts, *those expectations were overturned by the supply-side effects documented in chapter 3—the process of candidate emergence and the resultant biracial coalitions—and the institutional and behavioral effects demonstrated in chapters 4 and 5.* Rather than representing a politics of difference, the new minority districts actually represent a politics of commonality. A dominant focus on black politics is not evident in these new districts. Indeed, a great majority of the activity of the entire CBC is focused on issues that are of general concern to most Americans. Finally, as I argue in the section on the legal literature, minority districting does not impose direct costs on the majority, unlike affirmative action and busing.

Unintended consequences have a fascinatingly different impact on redistricting than the other issues in the upper-left cell of the table. With affirmative action and busing the unintended consequences worked to undermine support for the policies. Busing helped produce "white flight," which eroded urban tax bases and increased underlying segregation, exacerbating the initial problem (though Hochschild [1984, 32–33] notes that the relationship between white flight and busing is not entirely clear). Affirmative action produced a backlash against "reverse discrimination" and contributed to the "new racism," which caused a growing divide between the races in support for the policy (Edsall and Edsall 1991, 186). Ironically in the case of minority districting the unanticipated results of the policy help strengthen its appeal with the moderate majority (white and black) and solidify its position as a permanent fixture in the political landscape—if the courts do not entirely abolish the districts.[8] Black incumbents who make biracial appeals expand their base of white support rather dramatically within a few elections. If the polarization and politics of difference hypothesis were correct, racial bloc voting would have increased over time (rather than diminishing) as whites grew increasingly dissatisfied with the black representative. Thus, unlike "white flight" due to busing or the backlash against affirmative action, the new black majority districts appear to break down racial barriers rather than erecting them.[9] Minority districting in the 1990s is not "the experiment that failed," but rather "the experiment that must be given a chance to succeed."

APPENDIX A

Data Sources

Chapter	Topic/Data Used	Unit/Subject of Analysis	Number of Cases	Source	Time Period
1	Black interests/ national survey	National random sample	1,490	1992–94 NES	1992–1994
2	Legal issues/ various court cases	Federal court cases	44	Standard legal references, relevant legislation, and congressional hearings	Focus on 1960–1990
2	Electing blacks to Congress	House elections since 1870	26,670	ICPSR elections data set; recent data collected by the author (CbA) from *Congressional Quarterly*	
3	Supply-side theory: the decision to run for office from the individual-level case study of two elections in North Carolina	Actual candidates and potential candidates in the 1st District and actual candidates in the 12th District House race	2	CbA (with Schousen and Sellers), 239 interviews, newspaper articles, and other publicly available sources	1991–1992
3	Supply-side theory: data on the racial composition of House candidate pools, district characteristics, and racial coalitions that elected members in 1992 and 1993	House candidates in districts that were at least 30% black	144	CbA (with Schousen and Sellers), 239 interviews, public electoral records, and newspapers	1972, 1982, and 1992
		Newly elected blacks	17	30 interviews, public records, newspapers	1992–1993

Chapter	Topic/Data Used	Unit/Subject of Analysis	Number of Cases	Source	Time Period
4	Racial content of member	Members of the House	435	CbA from LCCR scores	1993–1994
	behavior,	Roll call votes	984	CbA from Nexis	1993–1994
	cohesion within the CBC/roll call voting	Roll call votes	1,165	CbA from Nexis	1995–1996
4	Racial content of member behavior/ committee assignments	Member committee assignments	7,320	CbA from *Congressional Quarterly*	1991–1996
4	Impact of race on bill success/ analysis of outcome of legislation	Bills cosponsored by members in standard sample (SS)	2,751	CbA from Thomas web site (thomas.loc.gov)	1993–1994
		Roll call votes	984	CbA from Nexis	1993–1994
		Hearings	537	CbA from Congressional Information Service	1993–1994
4	Racial content of member behavior/ leadership positions	Democratic members	257	CbA from *Congressional Quarterly*	1993–1994
			204		1995–1996
4	Racial content of member behavior/ speeches on the floor of the House	Members from SS	3,722	CbA from *Congressional Record*	1993–1994
4	Racial content of member behavior/ sponsored and cosponsored legislation	Bills sponsored by SS	720	CbA from *Congressional Record*	1993–1994
		Amendments offered by SS	55		
		Cosponsorship of bill by SS	14,560		
5	Links to the constituency/ racial composition of personal staff	Members from SS	40	CbA from personal meetings with staff in Washington, D.C.	1994
5	Links to the constituency/ location of district offices	Members from SS	52	CbA from the Census Bureau's web site (zip code data)	1993–1994
		Offices	108		

Chapter	Topic/Data Used	Unit/Subject of Analysis	Number of Cases	Source	Time Period
5	Links to the constituency/ member newsletters, flyers, and press releases	Members from SS Newsletters Press releases Flyers Context units	45 123 81 82 1,766	CbA, content analysis	1993–1994
5	Links to the constituency/ newspaper coverage	Newspaper stories	11,318	CbA, content analysis	1992–1994

Notes: Standard sample refers to the fifty-three-member sample from the 103rd Congress that includes all members of the CBC, plus other members who represent districts with a total black population of at least 25 percent.

Also used my interviews with thirty-two staffers and eight members, conducted in the summer of 1994 in Washington, D.C.

APPENDIX B

Procedures for Coding the Newspaper Stories

As discussed in chapter 5, each story was coded for its racial content along three dimensions: the focus, the member's point of view, and the generic topic. The categories of racial, implicit racial, nonracial, and balanced were assigned for the focus and the member's point of view, and the first three were coded for the generic topic.

For example, one of the primary issues stressed by Robert Scott (D–VA) in the 103rd Congress was the crime bill. Stories were coded as having a racial focus if race was prominently featured (as it often was with the Racial Justice Act, an amendment to the crime bill that was primarily concerned with racial bias in the application of the death penalty), while other stories on the same topic were coded as having a biracial focus if crime was discussed in a manner that appealed to both black and white voters. Implicit racial stories have a slightly different quality than biracial stories, but distinguishing between the two on a reliable basis is too difficult. Therefore, I combined the two into an intermediate category between "racial" and "nonracial." For purposes of my theory, the difference between implicit and biracial stories is not important, but the distinction between this intermediate category and the racial and nonracial stories is crucial. Difference members would be expected to have a greater proportion of racial stories than commonality members, and commonality members should balance their racial stories with a greater focus on nonracial and biracial or implicit racial stories than difference members.

News stories on crime often had an implicit racial focus. For example, Representative Scott was quoted in a wire service story as saying, "We have to decide whether we want to reduce crime or play politics." The story went on to say that Scott prefers prevention programs over locking more people up. He also expressed his opposition to the "three strikes provision" (*Cleveland Plain Dealer*, February 1, 1994, 8A). These are "liberal" positions on crime, but they are not positions that are different from those of dozens of white Democrats who fought for similar provisions in the crime bill. Such a story was coded as an implicit racial story because the story's primary focus is an issue that has a disproportionate impact on the black community and often has racial overtones. This is consistent with the discussion of implicit racial issues in chapter 1 (and with the method used by Kinder and Sanders 1996, 30). Stories that were coded as having a balanced focus talk about racial concerns, but attempt to present the issue in a manner that combines racial and implicit racial politics (this was more typical in the African-American newspapers than in the white newspapers).

Stories with a racial focus typically advocate stronger black representation, endorse or report approvingly on affirmative action, or point out the prevalence of racism. Biracial articles take these racial issues and focus on opportunity rather than outcomes, current progress on fighting discrimination rather than continuing problems in that area, or elements of an issue that bring the races together rather than divide them. For example, an article on the Million Man March could focus either on the show of black solidarity and strength (racial focus) or on the effort by some participants to embrace support from all races (biracial).

The foci of many other stories, a large majority, have no racial content at all. They simply report the results of an election, note that the representative appeared at the local Lions' Club meeting, or announce funding for a local highway project. Another story on Robert Scott that received extensive coverage in the local press is his connection to Energy Secretary Hazel O'Leary. At O'Leary's confirmation hearing the *Washington Times* reported, "It matters that a newly minted Virginia congressman, Rep. Bobby Scott, 46, could bring himself to tell the committee that when he was a youngster in Newport News, he had a baby sitter who grew up to be the woman seated before them" (February 4, 1993, E1). Not exactly earth-shattering news, but typical of the racially neutral or nonracial coverage that dominates newspaper stories on members of Congress from black districts.

In coding the focus of the story, my coding rules erred on the side of inclusiveness; that is, if race (implicit or explicit) is a factor in the part of the article that includes the reference to the member, it was included in one of the three racial categories. If the article mentions the member in a context different than the main focus of the article, the article was coded according to the part of the article that refers to the member. For example, consider a fifteen-paragraph article summarizing recent legislative activity in the House in which the first thirteen paragraphs talk about the crime bill and the Racial Justice Act. In the last two paragraphs the article turns to an item of local interest—the representative's bill to name a local federal office building. In this case the article would be coded as nonracial because the part of the article that refers to the member has nothing to do with race. On the other hand, if the member is mentioned in the second paragraph talking about the Racial Justice Act and in a later paragraph talking about the office building, the article would be coded as a racial article.

A more detailed coding scheme could have broken the article down by paragraph, but this simpler procedure has two attractive features. First, it approximates the way the most constituents read the paper. They scan headlines, find an article in which they are interested, scan the article, and maybe remember a salient point or two. They are very unlikely to make a detailed assessment of the article. Instead, they are probably more likely to zero in on a racial issue (such as the Racial Justice Act) rather than the naming of an office building. Second, because the scheme is relatively simple, it allowed me to analyze many more articles than I would have been able to do with a more labor-intensive process, thus providing greater assurance that I am measuring the actual racial content of newspaper coverage of the member.

There are always trade-offs in any research strategy; in this instance I maximized the scope of the coverage (to make sure that I had a broad sample of papers and topics) rather than the depth of the analysis of any given article. However, I did include two other items in the coding scheme that allow a more detailed analysis: the number of times that the member is mentioned in the article (this allowed me to address the perception of the black members that they do not receive as much attention as the white members) and whether the member is the major or minor focus of the article. In any event this coding scheme provides a conservative test of the claim that the white newspapers are biased in their coverage of members of the Congressional Black Caucus (CBC) (that is, the level of reporting of racial issues should be somewhat overstated in this data set). The member's point of view was coded with the same rules outlined above for the focus. The distinguishing feature here is that a racial, biracial or implicit, or balanced coding was made only in instances in which the member of Congress made his or her position known (typically through a direct quotation in the article).

As noted in chapter 5, the third dimension of the coding scheme, the racial content of the generic topic of the story, serves as a check on the coding procedure. Each article was coded as racial, implicit racial, or race not involved, using a four- to five-word summary of the article that was coded in the first stage. This second stage of coding provides a measure of the racial content of the article that is independent of any potential biases that may creep into the coding process based on contextual knowledge. It also provides the basis for testing some of the claims of racial bias made by members of the CBC.

The generic racial issues are fairly clear cut and include (1) general categories such as racial bias, discrimination, civil rights, voting rights, set-asides, affirmative action, and minority businesses; (2) specific issues such as the Racial Justice Act and proposed legislation on environmental racism and slavery reparations: and (3) people who triggered racial debates in this period such as Kahlid Muhammad, Louis Farrakahn, Lani Guinier, and Rodney King. If a story was coded as racial on the generic topic dimension, it may or may not have been coded as such on the focus dimension. Some generic racial topics may have a biracial focus—for example, a story on Rodney King could focus on his question "Can we all get along?" rather than on the brutality and racism of the Los Angeles Police Department. In fact, more than half of the racial topics had a biracial or balanced focus in the white newspapers (56 percent), compared to roughly a quarter in the black newspapers (27.5 percent). The biracial topics include domestic issues such as crime, gun control, welfare reform, food stamps, the earned income tax credit, and redistricting (which was coded as a racial issue if it clearly dealt with minority districting and as a biracial issue if it was unclear from the summary). They also include foreign policy issues such as Somalia, Haiti, South Africa, and Rwanda. Nonracial topics include articles on commencement addresses, town hall meetings, highway bills, health care reform, Dan Rostenkowski's ethics problems, military spending, and general reports on election returns. Some of these (such as a commencement address or a report on an election) again could have a racial or a biracial focus, just as the biracial topic of crime could have a focus that is nonracial or racial, as noted above with the example of Robert Scott.

Notes

Preface

1. Guinier defines authenticity in these terms: "Authenticity refers to community-based and culturally rooted leadership. The concept also distinguishes between minority-sponsored and white-sponsored black candidates—Black representatives are authentic because they are elected by blacks *and* because they are descriptively similar to their constituents. In other words, they are politically, psychologically, and culturally black." In a footnote she acknowledges that white candidates elected from majority black districts could be considered authentic, but that the typical usage refers to black politicians (1991a, 1103; for an extended discussion of the term see 1991a, 1102–1109).

Introduction

1. Of course, pluralist theorists have been guilty of equating parts of Madisonian theory with their own. Most important is the divergent starting point: Madison was concerned with controlling the effects of "evil factions," while pluralists embraced factions as the essential embodiment of political action and expression of political interests.

2. The exception was Republicans who supported the creation of black majority districts because they anticipated gaining seats from white Democratic incumbents in adjacent districts who would be weakened by the loss of some of their most loyal constituents.

3. The central legal question in the *Shaw* case and its progeny is whether the state may classify people based on race. Thus, a narrow reading of *Shaw* could lead to the conclusion that "political apartheid" is present in black majority districts regardless of the representation provided in those districts (commonality or difference) because people are placed in voting districts on the basis of race. I see that as an overly narrow reading (as do Justice David Souter in his *Shaw* dissent and Justice John Paul Stevens in his *Miller v. Johnson* dissent). The broader significance of the concern over racial classification is rooted in a debate over the nature of representation provided in the black majority districts, as the quotation from Justice O'Connor in this paragraph makes clear.

4. The "supply-side" perspective of politics has provided new explanations for divided government (Jacobson 1990; Ehrenhalt 1991), partisan realignments (Hurley 1991; Canon and Sousa 1992), and the impact of the economy on election outcomes (Jacobson and Kernell 1983). However, there is no systematic analysis

of the relationship between redistricting and candidate behavior. The only study of the supply side of redistricting and minority representation I am aware of is an analysis of black mayoral elections that concludes black incumbents deter future black challengers (Watson 1984).

5. Robert Cushman notes, "The city [Tuskegee], which had been square in shape, was transformed 'into a strangely irregular twenty-eight sided figure,' with the intention and result of removing from the city 'all save four or five of its 400 Negro voters while not removing a single white voter or resident.' The Negroes thus excluded could not, of course, vote in municipal elections" (Cushman 1966, 222). Justice Stevens also makes this point in his dissent in *Shaw v. Hunt.* In comparing *Gomillion* to *Shaw v. Hunt,* Justice Stevens says, "There, the plaintiffs had been prohibited from voting in municipal elections; here, all voters remain free to select representatives to Congress. Thus, while the plaintiffs purport to be challenging an unconstitutional racial gerrymander, they do not claim that they have been shut out of the electoral process on account of race, or that their voting power has been diluted as a consequence of race-based districting" (1996, 921).

6. This observation is consistent with our interviews in which several white North Carolina state legislators said that they did not plan on running in the new districts because it was time to provide equal representation to black constituents (personal interviews, May 1992).

7. Charles Hamilton argues that this is a more realistic possibility for local office (1992, 178).

8. Two additional districts, the 1st in Missouri in the 1980s (William Clay) and the 7th in Illinois in the 1970s (George and Cardiss Collins), were barely majority white if voting-age population rather than total population was used.

9. Additional evidence of the difficulty of electing blacks in majority white districts in the South is provided by state legislative races, where only 1 percent of all white majority districts elected black state legislators in the 1980s. On the other hand, 77 percent of black majority districts elected blacks to the lower house and 62 percent of black majority districts sent black representatives to the upper house in the 1980s (Handley and Grofman 1994, 345).

10. Where I part company with Guinier is in her assertion that black representatives cannot adequately represent black voters' interests under current legislative institutions and rules (Guinier calls for supermajority votes on racial issues in Congress and other procedural protections for the minority within a majority-rule institution). I show that members of the Congressional Black Caucus have done an excellent job of representing the interests of all their constituents.

11. Hochschild says, "[A] white partakes of race as much as does a black, and is no more or less privileged an interpreter of the meaning of race in America" (1995, 10). I had an interesting experience that suggests some participants in the racial redistricting debate believe that African Americans also face obstacles to understanding. In my deposition as an expert witness in the U.S. district court case *Moon v. Meadows* (1997), the attorneys for the plaintiffs grilled me for fifteen minutes on the backgrounds of my graduate research assistants. They asked questions about the assistants' race and involvement in partisan politics or civil rights issues. At the time I naively thought they were interested in whether my assistants' background would produce the empathy and understanding discussed above. I reluc-

tantly admitted that no, they were all middle-class whites. Later I realized that they were fishing for evidence that would allow them to claim my research was biased because the researchers were *too close* to the issue. They assumed that African-American research assistants would have been more likely to stack the deck in favor of theory because of their normative commitments. I do not share this view and wish that I would have had a racially diverse research team; however, it is interesting that at least in this instance the "outsider" was seen as more objective.

12. While I obviously cannot know for sure whether difference members were as forthcoming as commonality members, any potential biases would have minimized observed differences between these two types of members. Therefore, this potential bias makes any evidence used from interviews a conservative test of my theory. That is, my theory maintains that difference members should be more likely to ignore white voters than are commonality members. But if difference members are hiding these true attitudes from me because I am white, they will appear to look more like commonality members. Because I found differences between these two styles of racial representation despite this potential bias, it should provide even greater confidence that the differences are real.

13. I do not want to turn this into an extended discussion of the philosophy of social science, but briefly it is possible to have explanation without understanding. While this violates common usage of these terms, an example from political science is the realist and neorealist theorists in international relations who argue that state behavior can be *explained* by knowing the relevant state interests and the international balance of power without *understanding* anything about the specific beliefs, motivations, or intentions of a specific actor. Furthermore, those who emphasize understanding, such as interpretivists like Winch and Geertz, resist the generalizations that are made by social scientists who seek explanations (and even predictions) (see Hollis and Smith 1990). My personal view is that theoretically grounded social science can provide both explanation and understanding.

Chapter One

1. While these questions will be examined in the context of the U.S. House of Representatives, the problem of how to represent minority interests and the tensions between racial and ethnic groups figure prominently in Bosnia, Rwanda, India, and dozens of other nations. Students of comparative politics have examined these issues in great detail, but I would have been working on this book for another five years if I had attempted to engage this research in any serious way. I will provide an occasional reference to comparative research, but I plead guilty to the "division of labor" rationalization that I critique above in limiting the scope of this study to the American case. I develop the links to the comparative literature in a review essay in *Legislative Studies Quarterly* (Canon, forthcoming [1999]).

2. Myrdal is one of those "classic" authors that everyone cites and nobody reads. When I finally looked up the book, I discovered why—at two volumes and nearly 1,500 pages it easily qualifies as the *Wealth of Nations* of the racial politics literature.

3. Stephan Thernstrom and Abigail Thernstrom (1997) tend to use relative gains when it supports their argument that the condition of blacks is improving, but

they use absolute gains when that serves their purposes. Compare, for example, their data on education and class on pages 190, 191, 192, and 200 to the tables on poverty on page 233.

4. http://www.census.gov/hhes/www/wealth/wlth93f.html.

5. Data are from the Bureau of Labor Statistics web site at http://146.142.4.24/cgi-bin/surveymost.

6. However, these intraracial divisions are dwarfed by black-white differences. Michael Dawson concludes, "As long as racial divisions remain prominent, racial tensions will take precedence over class divisions" (1994, 197). Throughout his book Dawson demonstrates that "linked fate" and group interests cut across class lines. Indeed, in many parts of his analysis class status and group perceptions are positively related, counter to the common wisdom on this issue (1994, chap. 4).

7. The only differences are that I used a broader range of questions (twenty instead of six) and that I employed the panel data from 1992–1994 in addition to the 1993 pilot and 1994 pre-election surveys. I calculated an average score across questions for each respondent, with a minimum of five responses required for the case to be included (white: n = 1,486; black: n = 197). The only advantage of including the panel data is that it provides a slightly more reliable measure of the respondent's position given the broader range of questions. Following Kinder and Sanders (1996), all questions were rescaled on 0–1 intervals, with 1 coded as the pro–civil rights position. The racial index was then aggregated into deciles for purposes of presenting the data. The twenty questions used in this index are variables 1001, 1002, 1004, 1005, 1048–1051, 5929, 5930, 5932, 5935, 5936, 5938, 5947, 5948, and 6126–6129 from the 1994 National Election Studies survey.

8. Variables 309, 820, 822, 946–949, 1041, 1042, 3725, 3726, 3746, 5318, 5933, and 5934 were used to make the implicit racial index. These are the same issues cited by Kinder and Sanders in their "implicit racial issues" category in table 2.2 (1996, 30). Each respondent had to answer at least five questions to be included (white: n = 1,490; black: n = 198).

9. The skeptic could argue that whites cannot be "extremely conservative" across this range of issues because they comprise 85 percent of the population. One reviewer made this point, noting that "conservative" and "liberal" should be used only as relative terms. However, the mean for white respondents on implicit racial issues is three standard deviations below the mean for white respondents on non-racial issues, which far exceeds the normal standard for evidence of relative differences. While comparing arbitrary scales across issues is always problematic, the similarity of wording on options across the two scales makes the inferences tenable (most of the questions use five- or seven-point scales). Comparing blacks to whites on the same set of questions poses no comparable problems of inference, and on implicit racial issues the mean for whites is twelve standard deviations below the mean for blacks (in the conservative direction).

10. The weighted index takes into account the different number of roll calls used by the ADA on various topics. For example, there are seven questions on defense issues, but only one on many of the issues. I calculated a mean score for each respondent on each topic, multiplied it times the weight, and then divided the score by the number of weighted questions the respondent answered. The twenty-eight questions used to make this index were variables 317, 318, 817, 818, 823, 826,

827, 925, 926, 929, 940, 950, 1014, 1016, 1042, 3603, 3717, 3732, 3736, 3738, 3802, 3815, 3818, 5934, 7280, 7309, 7327, and 7331. To create the index on nonracial issues, I dropped the two topics that were implicitly related to race (the death penalty and the CBC budget vote). Even if these votes are included, the difference between whites and blacks is only .03. Each respondent had to answer in at least five of the ten categories to be included in the index (white: $n = 1,499$; black: $n = 199$).

11. There were eleven issues on which I could not find an NES question that was reasonably close to the topic, but most of them were not issues that would create more of a gap between whites and blacks; if anything, they seem even *less* likely to produce a gap than the questions that were included in the index (motor voter, striker replacement, the national science program, the Brady bill, the constitutional amendment requiring a balanced budget, lobbying reform, black lung disease, rules changes in the House, and the super collider). Only two of the ADA votes would probably have had a racial gap: U.S. policy toward Haiti and statehood for the District of Columbia. One other issue, the Racial Justice Act, did not have a directly related NES question, but there were two questions on the death penalty. None of these implicitly racial issues would have been included in the nonracial index anyway. I only mention them here to show how few of the issues included by the ADA directly or implicitly deal with race.

12. I interviewed thirty-two staffers and eight members of Congress in the summer of 1994. I refer to each interview by number (S for staff and M for member), but anonymity was guaranteed to encourage members and their staff to be candid with me. I also randomly changed references to the gender of the member of Congress to provide further protection of anonymity for the members.

13. One implication of this trend is that the central racial tensions in the future may be not between blacks and whites, but between "blacks and browns" (Miles 1992).

14. I use the term "deracialization" in a slightly different fashion than is standard in the literature. The term was first used by Charles Hamilton (1977) to refer to the strategy of raising issues that appeal across racial lines. This strategy allows black candidates to win office in white majority districts. My use of the term as meaning "color-blind" politics is a logical extension of this usage.

15. Greg Streich's dissertation (1997), cited below, spends more than three hundred pages analyzing and critiquing this literature. Even his thorough presentation is not exhaustive.

16. However, Amy Gutmann and Dennis Thompson have reservations about the long-term implications of black majority districts. "Representatives from racially gerrymandered districts have greater need to speak exclusively for the groups that predominate in their districts where different groups predominate. Some exclusiveness in representation may be desirable if it is the only way that the long-standing grievances of black citizens can be effectively addressed. But as a permanent mode of representation, it is likely to further divide citizens and discourage deliberation" (Gutmann and Thompson 1996, 153). I disagree. In chapters 4 and 5 I will demonstrate that the impact of the districts has been just the opposite.

17. However, see Bianco 1994, 162, for a contrary view. William Bianco argues that constituents view such efforts at improving the quality of deliberation as "cheap talk" and that informational advantages (Krehbiel 1991) are already provided by the institutional structures within Congress.

18. Twenty members of the CBC voted to condemn Muhammad's speech, eleven voted no, four voted "present," and three did not vote; thus, while the rejection of the speech was not unanimous, those who voted against the condemnation justified their vote on the basis of freedom of speech or the fact that they felt Muhammad was unfairly singled out for his racist speech. Several members pointed out that two months earlier Senator Ernest Hollings (D–SC) made a comment that African leaders were cannibals, but that no articles of censure were proposed for a "member of the other body." Kweisi Mfume (D–MD) attempted to draw attention to this double standard, but was ruled out of order by the speaker pro tempore (members are not allowed under House rules to refer to comments made by "members of the other body"). Representative Mfume amended his comments to refer to "someone from South Carolina" and was allowed to proceed (*Congressional Record,* February 23, 1994, H572).

19. Alan Lichtman made a very similar argument earlier in the testimony (House 1994a, 26–27).

20. One systematic test that could provide some evidence of black representatives' ability to win over white voters is the electoral performance of the 1992 class in the 1994–1998 elections. However, there are three problems with this analysis. First, black members of the 1992 class were elected from safe districts, so there is relatively little room for improvement (the seventeen blacks elected in 1992 won an average of 72.2 percent of the vote, compared to 54.8 percent for the eighty-five white members in the 1992 class). Second, national forces in 1994 confound any effort to uncover the typical "sophomore surge" that members receive in their first reelection bid. Finally, many of the black members' districts were substantially redrawn in 1994–1998, so their vote margins declined.

With these caveats in mind, blacks in the 1992 class increased their vote totals by nearly two points (to 74.1 percent) in 1994, while white Democratic freshmen lost exactly two points (Republican freshmen increased their margins by six points). However, in 1996, the fourteen remaining blacks of the 1992 class dropped to 70 percent, while the twenty-five surviving white Democrats increased their margins by ten points. In 1998, the gains for the remaining black and white members were more similar (a 5.5 percent average gain for the blacks and an 8 percent gain for the whites). It is interesting to note that the survival rate for black Democrats has been much higher than that for whites (fourteen of the seventeen blacks elected in 1992 were serving in 1999, compared to twenty-one of the forty-one white Democrats; thirty-seven of the forty-seven Republicans elected in 1992 were still in office in 1999). Thus, some blacks have been able to expand their political base, and most remain electorally secure with the advantages that come from incumbency, despite losing significant portions of their constituents.

21. However, Senator Roman Hruska of Nebraska challenged Griffith's argument. In defending President Nixon's appointee to the Supreme Court, G. Harrold Carswell, Hruska said, "'Even if he were mediocre, there are a lot of mediocre judges and people and lawyers. They are entitled to a little representation, aren't

they, and a little chance? We can't have all Brandeises and Frankfurters and Cardozos and stuff like that'" (quoted in Barone, Ujifusa, and Matthews 1975, 494).

22. Later he explained that the district had the most people claiming the earned income tax credit and the second most people earning over $100,000.

23. See Kousser 1995, 18–21, for a discussion of the unsupported empirical assumptions made in *Shaw v. Reno.*

Chapter Two

1. This list is very limited. A Lexis search on the term "racial gerrymandering" produced 270 law review articles between 1983 and 1997; about 200 of these were directly related to racial redistricting and the Voting Rights Act. Other useful sources are the symposia in several leading law journals on the future of the Voting Rights Act and racial redistricting: *American University Law Review* (Fall 1994), *Michigan Law Review* (December 1993, February 1997), *Rutgers School of Law–Camden Rutgers Law Journal* (Spring 1995), *Stanford Law Review* (May 1995), and *Texas Law Review* (June 1993).

2. For example, the Louisiana grandfather clause read, "[N]o male person who was on January 1, 1867, or at any date prior thereto, entitled to vote under the Constitution of the United States, wherein he then resided, and no son or grandson of any such person not less than twenty-one years of age at the date of the adoption of this Constitution, shall be denied the right to register and vote in this State by reason of his failure to possess the educational or property qualifications." Grandfather clauses, as they applied to voting, were ruled unconstitutional in 1915 (Key 1949, 538, 556).

3. The original "covered" jurisdictions were the six states of the Deep South, twenty-six counties in North Carolina, Alaska, and one county in Arizona. States in which less than 50 percent of the voting-age population either registered or voted in the 1964 presidential election and that had various discriminatory prerequisites for voting as of November 1, 1964, were subject to Section 5 preclearance. States and jurisdictions could "bail out" from coverage if they could prove the absence of discriminatory practices. The list of covered states has evolved with various bailouts and the addition of other jurisdictions in the 1970, 1975, and 1982 amendments. There are currently twenty-two states that have at least some covered jurisdictions.

4. There were only twenty-two DOJ objections to electoral changes submitted by covered states under Section 5 between 1965 and 1969, compared to 251 from 1970 to 1974 and 534 from 1975 to 1980. The number of submissions also exploded after the *Allen* decision (583 from 1965 to 1970, compared to 34,215 from 1971 to 1980. However, much of this increase cannot be attributed to the *Allen* decision. For example, Texas submitted 15,959 changes between 1976 and 1980 after submitting only 249 from 1971 to 1975 (and none before 1970) (Senate 1982a, 430, 433) because the 1975 Voting Rights Act Amendments added language discrimination as a covered activity (Days 1992, 57).

5. Single-shot voting refers to the practice of voting for a single candidate in a multimember at-large district. For example, if five whites and one black are running for five at-large city council seats in a city that is 30 percent black, African-

American voters enhance their chances of electing the black candidate if they vote *only* for the black candidate (thus choosing not to cast their other four votes).

6. See Guinier 1991, 1091–1101, for a discussion of the evolution of Court decisions on vote dilution; Schockley (1991, 1039–1045) and Ballard (1991, 1150–1156) explain the necessary conditions to establish a claim of vote dilution.

7. The House version passed 385–324, the Senate version passed 85–8, and the House passed the Senate version by unanimous consent; the bill was signed into law by President Ronald Reagan on June 29, 1982.

8. After reviewing the case law and noting that the *White* and *Zimmer* standards were used in nearly fifty vote dilution cases in the 1970s, the committee report concludes, "[T]he prevailing standard in voting dilution was the 'results' test and intent was not a prerequisite" (Senate 1982b, 23). Despite this overwhelming evidence, Hatch strenuously argued that *Bolden* did not create a new intent standard (Senate 1982a, 33–35).

9. The *Gingles* case concerned multimember districting, but the three conditions were applied to single-member districts in *Growe v. Emison* (1993). See Grofman, Handley, and Niemi 1992, chap. 5, for a discussion of the lower court decisions that applied *Gingles* to single-member districts.

10. See Grofman, Handley, and Niemi 1992, chaps. 3–4, for a discussion of the lower court decisions that discuss these issues.

11. However, the 4th Circuit Court of Appeals was reluctant to reach this conclusion because there were other black candidates who received a higher percentage of the black vote in a multimember at-large district than the white candidate (who received a majority of the black vote), but were not elected (*Collins v. City of Norfolk* 1989, cited in Grofman, Handley, and Niemi 1992, 77).

12. The DOJ did not preclear the initial plan that created only one black majority district, perhaps thinking that the second district would help Republicans; but when the Democrats came up with the I–85 surprise, the DOJ precleared it even if it appeared to help the Democrats more than Republicans. Thus, the North Carolina case provides evidence for both sides of the argument concerning the DOJ's partisan motivations.

13. Strict scrutiny is the most rigorous standard applied by the courts to determine whether group-based classifications are permissible. Typically racial classifications must be justified by the state under the standard of strict scrutiny. Very few policies survive strict scrutiny (the internment of Japanese Americans during World War II is one of the few exceptions). Weaker standards apply to gender (intermediate scrutiny) and age. Thus, for example, it is permissible to deny twenty-year-olds the "right" to drink alcohol, but it would not be permissible to distinguish between twenty-year-old women and men, or whites and blacks, when establishing drinking laws. Similarly, some classifications based on gender would be allowed (separating men and women in military barracks), but not race.

14. Morgan Kousser goes on to note that "the fears of liberals and the hopes of opponents of the voting rights revolution have been exaggerated" (1995, 1). However, it is clear that he sees serious flaws in the *Shaw* decision.

15. Many critics have argued that judicial activism is one of the greatest failings of the *Shaw* decisions. Christopher Eisgruber argues, "[T]his judgement [*Shaw v.*

Reno] is empirically contingent in a way that makes it appropriate for legislative, rather than judicial, resolution. That is why I think *Shaw* is a monster: not because I agree with the policy it declared unconstitutional (I don't), but because the *Shaw* Court wrongly interfered with legislative discretion to treat America's most severe and most intractable problem, the problem of racial inequality" (Eisgruber 1996, 525).

16. *Vera* also is inconsistent with *Wright v. Rockefeller* (1964), in which the Court held that even though racial motivation was evident in the drawing of district lines, the districts did not violate the Fourteenth Amendment because other motivations were evident in the process (Grubert 1997, 1841).

17. There are two relevant lines of pre-*Shaw* cases for the issue of standing: those that established the "judicially cognizable injury" in redistricting and vote dilution cases and those that addressed standing more generally. *Davis v. Bandemer* (1986), a partisan gerrymandering case, established that plaintiffs suffer no injury if they receive "adequate representation" or "virtual representation." The Court held that supporters of the losing candidate are represented adequately "by the winning candidate and have as much opportunity to influence that candidate as other voters in the district" (*Davis v. Bandemer* 1986, 132). Virtual representation is provided by representatives elected from other districts. Racial vote dilution cases, such as *White v. Regester* (1973), *Rogers v. Lodge* (1982), and *UJO* (1977), established a heavy burden of proof that had to be met, showing that plaintiffs did not have an equal opportunity to participate in the political process and that they were not being represented (Karlan and Levinson 1996, 1209–1211).

18. Justice Stevens goes on to make a clever argument about logical incompatibility between the reliance on stigmatized harm and the *Hays* decision, which established that plaintiffs must live in the district to have standing. Justice Stevens points out that while representational harms would be suffered only by those living in the district, general stigmatic harms would be suffered by all citizens in the state (because all voters would victimized by the "balkanization" of the races).

19. See Justice Souter's dissent in *Vera* 1995, 1054–1056, for an eloquent discussion of the contextual differences between the subjugation of blacks and the placement of whites in black majority districts. Erving Goffman's classic book *Stigma: Notes on the Management of Spoiled Identity* (1963) presents an interesting contrast to *Shaw*'s use of the term. Goffman examines the lives of truly stigmatized people—drug addicts, prostitutes, people with physical deformities, and ex–mental patients—who do not conform to the "normal" expectations of society. It is difficult to see how the concept can be stretched to fit white plaintiffs.

20. The Court did not entirely adopt the color-blind view, noting that "race conscious" districting may be constitutional. However, the Court did recognize the individual-level basis for the constitutional challenge to the districts in *Shaw v. Hunt* (1996, 904).

21. *Bush v. Vera* 1996, 1030–1035 (Souter, J., dissenting). Also see Issacharoff 1995.

22. Of course, in some of these instances a majority of whites would have voted against the black Democratic nominee (when white Republicans are included). Thus, if all whites are considered, the black representative may not be the whites'

candidate of choice. However, this does not contradict the reality that white voters were pivotal in the nomination and thus the election of more than half of the newly elected blacks in 1992. This point will receive more attention in the next chapter.

Chapter Three

1. Cynthia McKinney makes an interesting argument that could be dubbed the "trickle down" version of our supply-side theory. "My opportunity to run for office and win in the state of Georgia has inspired dozens of African-American candidates at the local level to seek public office for the first time. Most of them had never dreamed that would be possible" (McKinney 1996, 64).

2. Blacks in the South have often played that role when they comprise a sizable minority. Although white voters are less often in the position of the cohesive minority, there are several instances of large-city mayoral races (Detroit, Chicago, Atlanta, Cleveland, and New Orleans) where whites tried to elect black moderates (see Perry 1990, 141–159; Eisinger 1980, 69).

3. A more complete study of the politics of difference, the politics of commonality, and the linkages between electoral coalitions and behavior in Congress would chart how these representational linkages evolve over the course of a career. That is, a politician may begin his or her career having been elected from a biracial coalition and practicing a politics of commonality. However, through time the district may become electorally secure, the demographics of the district may change, and the member may evolve toward a politics of difference—focusing primarily on issues that are of interest to his or her African-American constituents. Alternatively a member might begin a career having been elected on the basis of the black vote, but shift toward biracial representation, as the example of Bennie Thompson seems to indicate. Thus, some of the more senior members of the CBC (Alan Wheat, John Lewis, William Jefferson) will be practitioners of a politics of commonality, and others (John Conyers, Barbara Rose Collins) will practice a politics of difference. Although we are sure that both types of evolution have happened, a study incorporating such movement would span several decades and is beyond the scope of this analysis. While we do not attempt to measure the key explanatory variable for the older members, this control group will serve as a useful baseline for comparison to the white members, showing whether basic descriptive representation translates into substantive representation.

The supply-side theory could also be applied to white candidates. As noted in the previous footnote, a black minority may also play the role of electing white candidates who practice a politics of commonality. However, there were only two whites newly elected in 1992 in districts with at least 25 percent black voters; thus, there are not enough cases for analysis.

4. Gary King, Robert Keohane, and Sidney Verba define the causal effect as "the difference between the systematic component of a dependent variable when the causal variable takes on two different values" (1994, 85). They are careful to note that one can "never hope to know a causal effect for certain" because one cannot observe the two different values of the causal variable simultaneously (1994, 79). In our instance a district is either a new black majority district or not—it cannot be both in the same election (or for our second causal effect either a white candidate is running or not). Therefore, the best social science can offer is

a strong theoretical basis for the causal effect and statistical controls for alternative explanations.

5. They go on to note: "However, we should not confuse a definition of causality with the nondefinitional, albeit often useful, operational procedure of identifying causal mechanisms" (1994, 87). I agree; I see the identification of causal mechanisms in the case studies as complementary to the causal theory rather than as a substitute.

6. Joseph Schlesinger coined the terms "progressive ambition" (desiring higher office) and "static ambition" (making a career in a single office) (1966, 10).

7. We conducted thirty-seven interviews with thirty-four people, including newspaper reporters, Democratic Party chairs of the most populous counties in the district, members of the General Assembly, a member of the U.S. Congress, and all of the identified potential and actual candidates. Most of the interviews were conducted between October 1991 and May 1992. The interviews ranged in length from twenty minutes to more than two hours, with an average length of about one hour. All but five of the interviews were face to face. These interviews were conducted only in the 1st District. The 12th District was added later, after the election; therefore, we had to rely on newspaper accounts for this race.

8. For an excellent discussion of different measures of compactness and how different values are traded off in the redistricting process, see Butler and Cain 1992, 60–90; Niemi, Grofman, Carlucci, and Hofeller 1990; and Young 1988.

9. While the North Carolina legislature did have one Native American member (State Representative Adolph Dial), the members of this minority community did not have much interest in congressional redistricting. They were active in trying to create more Native American majority districts at the state level (personal interview, October 14, 1993).

10. This debate also rages in the black community nationally. Carol Swain echoes Blue's and Fitch's sentiment: "The evidence suggests that the present pattern of drawing district lines to force blacks into overwhelmingly black districts wastes their votes and influence [and] place[s] them in districts where their policy preferences can become separated from the majority in their states" (1993, 235).

11. Another version of the source of the Merrit plan came from Glenn Newkirk, a staffer from the North Carolina state house redistricting committee, who claims that a Republican intern concocted the plan at a public access terminal. This story was not confirmed by an independent source; furthermore, it does not make sense that a Republican invented the plan because it was the perfect solution to the Democrats' dilemma of having to create a second black district while protecting their incumbents (or if a Republican did think of it, he or she certainly should have not discussed it with anyone).

12. We did not find any evidence that Michaux actively resisted the move of his home from the 1st to the 12th District. Michaux may have been aware of his limited rural support and believed that his chances for election would be better in a more urban district, such as the 12th.

13. In 1988 Jones, Jr., joined a group of Republicans and independent-leaning Democrats in an overthrow of the established house leadership. Since that time he has sponsored numerous bills to reform state government and has voted against the house leadership on important legislation.

14. One black interviewee called the main newspaper in Raleigh "The News and Disturber."

15. Jones, Jr.'s indecision about which race to enter led the *News and Observer* (Raleigh, N.C.) to label him "the Mario Cuomo of North Carolina politics," in reference to the former New York governor's inability to decide whether he would run for president in 1988 and 1992. A critic of Jones, Jr., charged that the state representative expressed interest in the state auditor position only in an attempt to hide his true ambition for the House seat and confuse the black community. But several sources expressed disbelief at this allegation. In their opinion Jones, Jr.'s interest in the state auditor position was consistent with his record as a proponent of government ethics and campaign finance reform.

16. This analysis assumes that blacks tend to vote for black candidates and whites for white candidates. Although we do not provide new evidence of racially polarized voting, there are voluminous studies that demonstrate the point (Reeves 1997; Loewen 1990; Vanderleeuw 1991; Bullock and Johnson 1992; Parker 1990; Guinier 1991a, 1113, notes 165–169). Furthermore, our study examines candidate activity in Democratic primaries. Racial bloc voting is likely to be more prevalent in these races than in general elections, where party considerations can dominate racial voting (Strickland and Whicker 1992).

17. This is a refined version of our original theory (Canon, Schousen, and Sellers 1996), in which we posited that a single black candidate would reflect a politics of difference. Subsequent research on the two districts in question and reflection on the long-term implications of appealing only to black voters led to this modification of the theory. The only other change from earlier versions of this research was to correct a coding error of Albert Wynn's campaign. Also, figure 3.5 does not show the expectation for a contest between a single black candidate and one or more white candidates. This matchup occurred only once in a new black majority or influence district in 1972, 1982, and 1992 (in the second district in Mississippi in 1982).

18. We also presented the supply-side theory in the context of a collective action problem faced by ambitious black candidates. Ambitious black candidates want to get elected, but by acting in their own self-interest, they can destroy the collective goal of electing a black (if the black vote is split too many ways, a white candidate may be able to win, as noted in hypothesis 6). However, we ended up dropping the collective action language because it did not contribute anything to the predictive or explanatory power of the theory and only complicated some of the conceptual issues.

19. I thank Mark Hansen for helping clarify the arguments in this paragraph.

20. We were surprised to discover that no institution systematically records the race of House candidates. We called the Joint Center for Political Studies, the Congressional Black Caucus, the Urban League, the NAACP, Vote America, the Democratic National Committee, the Democratic Congressional Campaign Committee, *Congressional Quarterly,* and individual state election boards. The public record contained two problems. First, minor candidates (those receiving less than 10 percent of the vote) often were mentioned only in passing. Second, the race of leading candidates was not provided in some cases. To continue our search, we called party officials (starting with the state party headquarters in each relevant state), newspaper reporters, campaign workers, offices of current incumbents (this

approach was especially useful for 1992), and the candidates themselves to fill in the substantial gaps.

21. These data were collected by one of the authors from various issues of *Congressional Quarterly Weekly Report.*

22. More detailed analysis is needed to determine whether these data refute Jewell's findings. The new districts created in 1992 span the rural black belt that Jewell describes (AL, MS, and NC 1) and more urban areas (TX, FL, and NC 12); several of the new districts include both rural and urban voters (SC 6 and GA 11).

23. However, as we noted above, the 1st District already had one very strong white candidate, Walter Jones, Jr., and two weaker white candidates; nonetheless, this calculation is noteworthy and may have helped produce the absence of white candidates in other black majority districts.

24. In many instances the decision to run had nothing to do with the racial politics of the new districts. In our case study of the 1st District we interviewed eight state legislators who were not mentioned by our sources and who had expressed no interest in running to understand the motivations of those who decided not to run. By virtue of their position in the opportunity structure these politicians were similarly situated to many of the candidates who decided to run. The two quoted above cited race as the reason they were not running ("It's their turn"). The other six had a variety of reasons for not running. Two state house members, one white and one black, wanted to establish their careers in state politics before thinking about higher office (both were serving in their first terms). At the other extreme one Republican house member cited his age (62) and health as the main reasons for not running. He also noted that a Republican would not have much chance in the new district anyway. Finally, one state senator said he did not run because he knew he could not win, while another said he had "absolutely no interest in running for Congress" and "wouldn't serve if I was appointed." Thus, seven of our eight "unseen candidates" support David Rohde's assumption that politicians would accept higher office if it were offered to them without cost or risk (1979).

25. We included the special election to fill Mike Espy's seat in this analysis. To ascertain the nature of the racial coalitions and the racial appeals of the various candidates, we conducted thirty personal interviews and consulted newspaper articles, *Congressional Quarterly Weekly Report,* and the 1994 editions of *Almanac of American Politics* and *Politics in America.*

26. Though figure 3.5 specifies that "a single black candidate runs," in these two districts the winner was virtually unopposed. Carrie Meek (FL 17) won 82.5 percent of the primary vote against two weak opponents, and Bernice Johnson (TX 30) won 91 percent of the primary vote against a single opponent.

27. The Census defines a rural area as one that is outside an urbanized areas (SMSA) and not in a town of more than 2,500 people. According to this relatively narrow definition only Eva Clayton, Bennie Thompson, and James Clyburn have districts that are more than 50 percent rural. Overall, the districts created in 1992 are 75.7 percent urban, while the old districts are 98.9 percent urban.

28. In absolute terms black districts are much poorer than white districts. In fact, only three black districts of the thirty-eight have median incomes that are above the national median (Gary Franks [R–CT], Floyd Flake [D–NY], and Al-

bert Wynn [D–MD]). A simple regression of percentage black on median income shows that for every percentage increase in the black population the district median income decreases by $163.65 ($t = 6.93$, sig. at .00001). However, the ratio of black income to white income is more important as a predictor of representational style.

Chapter Four

1. Two related points require noting. First, while my evidence strongly rejects the "no racial differences" hypothesis by showing that white representatives are not as sensitive to black interests as black representatives, whites in this study are almost certainly more responsive to black constituents than white members who are not included in this study. That is, a white member from a district that is 35 percent black will pay more attention to black interests than will a white member who is from a district that is 2 percent black. Second, this case selection criterion amounts to "selecting on the independent variable." This practice does not lead to biased estimates (see King, Keohane, and Verba 1994, 137–138).

2. The Conservative Coalition refers to a voting alliance between southern Democrats and Republicans. It has been a potent force in Congress through much of the twentieth century. Though it has appeared only on roughly 10–12 percent of all roll call votes in the past decade, its success rate has averaged about 90 percent for that period (including a perfect 51–0 record in 1996).

3. In an important stand against President Clinton, thirty of the thirty-seven Democratic members of the CBC voted against NAFTA (though a majority of white Democrats also voted against NAFTA). The final vote margin was such that their votes were not pivotal, but until a few days before the vote it looked like the CBC might contribute to the most important defeat of Clinton's presidency to that point.

4. One staffer I interviewed explained the frustration that some members of the CBC have with PACs: they perceive a racial bias in the levels of contributions, but they still need the contributions. The staffer said, "PACs don't treat African Americans the same [as whites]. They will give us $500–$1,000, and the same PAC will give $5,000 to whites. It blows my mind. However, PACs are key in our fundraising because we don't have a bunch of rich sugar daddies like some districts or like the rich Republicans who can bankroll their own campaigns" (S1).

5. Note that the CBC's role in defeating the initial rule on the crime bill would be defined as pivotal only by the least restrictive of the three definitions. However, even the most subtle of these definitions is still quite crude, failing to take into account the importance of the constituency and other external factors. This discussion is intended only to provide a slightly more rigorous and systematic analysis of the claims made in the media of the CBC's pivotal role in the House. One reviewer was concerned that any other bloc of voters could be seen as "pivotal" using these calculations, but no other group in the House (freshman Democrats, women, the Hispanic Caucus, southern Democrats, or various state delegations) was as cohesive as the CBC and, therefore, would play a pivotal role on far fewer roll call votes.

6. While there is not a perfect correspondence between member preferences and

actual assignments, the Democratic leadership and the Steering Committee make every effort to accommodate member requests. Most members receive at least one of their top choices for a standing committee, and subcommittee service is largely through self-selection (see Smith and Deering 1990).

7. I will identify the committees by the names used in the 103rd Congress rather than by the new names given to most committees by the Republicans in 1995. As one of my formal theory colleagues once said, "I don't update my priors very quickly." More important, these were the names used for most of the period covered in my study.

8. See Friedman 1996 for a longer historical view on the evolution of committee assignments for CBC members.

9. Richard Hall argues that one should not attempt to distinguish between substantive and symbolic legislation (1996, 25). While I obviously disagree with his conclusion, making this distinction was the most difficult of all the coding tasks undertaken in this study (also I do not exclude the symbolic legislation from analysis, which was one of Hall's concerns) (see Preston 1978 and Bullock and MacManus 1981 for other research that examines the importance of symbolic politics for racial representation). To check the validity of the measure, I did an independent coding of 100 bills. There were only four bills on which I differed on the substantive/symbolic coding of the bills. There were no cases where the racial coding differed by two categories (that is, I did not code any cases as "racial" that were coded as "nonracial" by the research assistant, nor did I code any racial bills as nonracial). There were only eight instances where I coded a racial or nonracial bill as part-racial, or a part-racial bill as nonracial or racial. This high intercoder agreement should provide some confidence in the validity of the subjective coding. Obviously it would have been ideal to have double coding for all of the bills, speeches, and so on, but this would have limited the range of material that I could have covered. Similar checks of the coding were performed on other measures. I describe one other check in chapter 5 (of the member newsletters).

10. The volume of racially oriented legislation is likely to be increased by having more black members of Congress. As I will show in the next section, blacks are far more likely than whites to introduced racially oriented legislation.

11. Logistic regression is used when the dependent variable is dichotomous (yes-no; black-white, etc.). Parameter estimates are more difficult to interpret in logit than with ordinary least squares (OLS) regression because the impact of any given explanatory variable on the dependent variable depends on the values of the other variable. Interpretation of the impact of a given independent variable is typically stated in terms of a change in probability (see Aldrich and Nelson 1984).

12. Subjective indicators are more difficult to model at the district level because there are no surveys with adequate district sample size. One approach is to take a sample mean of district opinion from a national survey (Miller and Stokes 1963), but this has been criticized on methodological and theoretical grounds. Christopher Achen (1975) and John Jackson (1989), among others, point out that this sample-based procedure for estimating district opinion is biased because of the error-in-variables problem. Briefly, when there is a nontrivial amount of measurement error, the district sample size must be quite large to get accurate estimates of

mean district opinion. Sample sizes of ten to twenty cases per district, as in Miller and Stokes's seminal study (1963), are too small, yielding large measurement error (40 to 60 percent of the total measured variance) and biased estimates (Jackson 1989, 160–161).

13. Previous researchers have made this decision because of the multicollinearity between the two variables (black members of the House tend to be elected from districts with large numbers of black voters). However, by excluding one variable or the other, scholars are committing specification error. Multicollinearity is a problem only because it makes the variance of the estimates imprecise, which may lead one to fail to reject the null hypothesis when, in fact, the coefficient is significantly different from zero. Even with relatively high levels of multicollinearity, coefficients are still unbiased. In fact, they are BLUE (best linear unbiased estimate) (Kmenta 1971, 380–389). None of the bivariate correlations between percentage black and the dummies for commonality, difference, and older members exceeded .40 (they were .39, .13, and .17, respectively). Furthermore, given that both the variables for the different types of black members and the percentage black in the district were significant in most of the multivariate models, it does not appear that multicollinearity was a serious problem.

14. This model is estimated with OLS rather than a multinominal logit or probit technique despite the ordinal nature of the dependent variable. When there are at least five levels in the dependent variable and the variable has a relatively normal distribution, any bias from using OLS is minimal. In the prestige committee and leadership models, which have a dichotomous dependent variable, logistic regression is used.

15. Party support scores from the second session of the 102nd Congress were used for nonfreshman members, and scores from the first session of the 103rd Congress were used for freshmen. The causal direction hypothesized in this model is that higher support scores make it more likely that the member will be appointed or elected to the leadership. This argument is obviously more difficult for freshmen, who have no established voting record. I assume the leaders make an effort to discern which freshmen will be most likely to support the party and make appointments accordingly. Obviously the causal direction could work the other way to some extent (being in the party leadership increases one's party support score).

16. I attempted to included controls for difference and commonality members in the logit model, but with so few cases the standard errors were quite large.

17. The obvious problem with this crude comparison is that many, if not most, of the nonracial issues addressed by both white and black members are also important to black constituents. Thus, the key point in this comparison is the relative lack of attention to explicit and implicit racial issues by white members.

18. However, recall my data in table 4.6, which finds a significant impact for cosponsorship.

19. I have included the 55 amendments with the 720 bills because there were not enough cases for separate analysis. Members attempt to achieve similar goals by introducing bills and sponsoring amendments; therefore, they can be combined for purposes of analysis. These numbers include seven bills with twenty-one cosponsors that were opposed to the CBC's position. I do not include these seven bills in the tables because there are so few of them.

Chapter Five

1. Swain (1993) mentions some of the topics addressed in this chapter, such as the location of district offices and the racial composition of the staff. However, she does not present her data in a systematic fashion (for example, she mentions the racial composition of the staff for some members, but not others). Thus, one cannot generalize from her limited cases.

2. There is voluminous research on racial attitudes and voting (see Reeves 1997 for a recent contribution), but virtually nothing on race and constituency-member linkages. Claudine Gay (1996) overcomes the limited sample size problem alluded to above by pooling National Election Studies (NES) surveys from 1980 to 1992. She finds that black constituents report higher numbers of contacts and more satisfaction with black incumbents than with whites, and the reverse holds for white constituents. Pooling may provide enough data to test the supply-side theory in a few more electoral cycles, though the solution is not ideal.

3. To ascertain the race of each of the member's staffers, I presented a photocopy of the relevant page from the *Congressional Staff Directory* to the office manager in the Washington, D.C., office to indicate the race of each of the staffers. In two instances the office manager was not able to indicate the race of the staffers in the district offices, and in ten instances I was not able to set up interviews with the office manager. In only one instance did a member's office refuse to cooperate with my inquiry. Thus, I was able to ascertain the information for forty of the fifty-three offices of members who represent districts in this study.

4. A difference of means test shows that the gap between the commonality and difference members is significant at the .05 level (one-tailed test) for both black staff ($t = 1.82$) and white staff ($t = 2.21$).

5. There are literally hundreds of articles on this topic with many conflicting findings on the importance of constituency service. See Fiorina 1989, chaps. 10 and 11, for a discussion of some of the literature from the 1980s.

6. The data may be found at http://venus.census.gov/cdrom/lookup/CMD=LIST/DB=C90STF3B/LEV=ZIP. The size of the zip codes ranged from Mel Reynolds's (D–IL) South Chicago office (94,317 constituents) to Tom Barrett's (D–WI) Milwaukee office, which had only 456 people (one other downtown office, Cardiss Collins's (D–IL) Dearborn Street office had only three people listed as living in the zip code, so that case was deleted). The median number of constituents in the zip codes was 28,841, and the mean was 30,139.

7. As it turns out, this was true of two of the eleven commonality members: Mel Watt (D–NC) placed his three offices in neighborhoods that averaged 71.3 percent black, well above his 57 percent black district, while Jim Clyburn had his three offices in white areas that averaged only 32 percent black, well below his 62 percent black district.

8. The number of mailings fell to 200.7 million in 1993, the lowest level for an odd-numbered year since 1969. Norman Ornstein, Thomas Mann, and Michael Malbin (1998) do not provide the data for 1994, but it appears that the downward shift in the early 1990s may be permanent. This is probably due to the new restrictions imposed in 1990 that set a mail budget for each member and required that expenditures be publicly disclosed.

9. As in the previous chapter, one graduate research assistant was responsible

for coding the material. I did an independent coding of a subset of 100 observations. There was only one instance in which I disagreed on the definition of the "context unit" (a rather lengthy piece on health care that had been coded as a single observation; I decided that it really was five different subtopics. However, in skimming through most of the other newsletters, it looked like this format was unusual). There were no instances of disagreement across two categories (that is, no racial cases were coded as nonracial or vice versa). There were five cases where I coded an implicit racial article as nonracial and three others where I would have coded a nonracial article as implicit racial. This suggests that the categories are well defined and that the constructs have fairly strong face validity.

10. There were only three white members who gave me press releases, so there is not enough information to analyze. One white member had no racial content in his press releases, the second had one racial story out of the eleven I coded, and the third submitted only one press release, which was coded as implicit racial.

11. This count does not include the member himself or herself. Many, if not most, of the pictures include the member posing with constituents, cabinet members, or the president. If the member were included in the count, this would bias this measure toward greater representation for the member's race. I should also note that percentages of each race were calculated for each picture so the final figure for each member would not be skewed by one picture with a large number of people. That is, percentages rather than numbers of people of each race were aggregated by member.

12. This is one topic where the staffer is probably more knowledgeable than the member of Congress. In most instances I attempted to interview the press secretary (if there was one) or the administrative assistant. They are people who deal with the press on a daily basis and have a good sense of the nature of the coverage the member receives.

13. For ease of presentation I will refer to the two types of newspapers as the "black" and "white" papers. While the readership and staff of the papers are not entirely segregated, this is the language used by the press secretaries. Occasionally some would refer to the white papers with more neutral terms, such as "large circulation," but this was the exception rather than the rule.

14. I should note one characteristic of the coding scheme that influences the interpretation of the "nonracial" category: in coding the member's perspective my main interest was in whether or not he or she took a clear position on the topic of the story from a racial perspective. Therefore, the "nonracial" category is really a residual category that includes cases in which the member took a nonracial position and those in which no position could be determined. In retrospect, I wish I would have distinquished these two outcomes in the coding scheme. However, the interpretation of the three racial categories is not affected by this coding rule. This is not an issue for the data in table 5.4.

15. In this regression analysis I created a composite variable for each member of the House who represents a district that is at least 25 percent black. This variable was basically a counter variable for each news story that had a racial perspective (collapsing the racial, implicit racial, and balanced categories of tables 5.6 and 5.7 for models 1 and 2; the racial and implicit racial categories of table 5.5 for model 3; and the racial and balanced categories for model 4). The variable is then

calculated as a percentage of the total number of stories concerning that member of Congress that involve race (both from the member's perspective and for the general topic of the article).

16. From a more theoretical standpoint black papers are probably a better indicator than white papers of the image that the member would like to project to the district. Recall the many references in my interviews to the black papers' willingness to publish press releases without editing, compared to the difficulty in getting these unfiltered messages into the white papers.

17. Furthermore, in a district that is comprised of a significant number of black constituents, the member *should* spend some of his or her time on issues that are of central concern to the black community.

Chapter Six

1. The members from older districts were one difference member (Walter Tucker) and two commonality members (Bobby Rush and Mel Reynolds, both of whom had their districts substantially altered in 1992). Bennie Thompson, another difference member, was elected in 1993 to replace Mike Espy from a district that was created in 1982 to promote black representation. Thus, of the sixteen new districts that were created or substantially redrawn in 1992, only four produced candidates who won on the basis of the politics of difference.

2. A few studies that focus on roll call voting (most important, Whitby 1998) *do* conclude that race matters. However, roll call votes are only one relatively small part of the entire legislative picture.

3. One staffer I interviewed supported this argument: "Nobody questioned the ability of Lindy Boggs [the former white Democrat from Louisiana who represented a black majority district for seventeen years] to represent blacks. She did it wonderfully. Now that a black member represents the district all of a sudden the whites see themselves as disenfranchised. Black voters never assumed they were disenfranchised because they were represented by Lindy Boggs" (S29).

4. An interesting irony is that Guinier's plans for supermajorities and minority veto rights in Congress bear a strong resemblance to John C. Calhoun's concept of "concurrent majorities," which served as the basis for the states' rights perspective in favor of slavery, and ultimately the justification for the secession of the Confederacy from the Union (see Hertzberg 1992 for an analytical treatment of Calhoun's concept of concurrent majorities).

5. Richard Engstrom points to "over 50 local governing units [that] have adopted either limited or cumulative voting systems in response to dilution allegations" (1994, 687).

6. Greg Adams makes one small factual error that has some implications for his argument. He claims that there were typically four candidates in the three-seat elections (1996, 139), when, in fact, 56 percent of the elections between 1902 and 1954 had only three candidates (two from one party and one from the other) (Sawyer and MacRae 1962, 941). More important, in only 3.5 percent of the elections in this period did one party nominate more than two candidates. The logic of nominating ideologically extreme candidates is not as compelling for two candidates as it would be if the party was putting up three candidates. However, Adams's model may still hold even when parties nominate only two candidates.

7. This is not to say that "process-oriented" policies do not have some intended outcome. Clearly all policies attempt to accomplish some end. The difference between the two categories is one of relative rather than absolute focus.

8. The minority districting in 1992 is likely to have a lasting impact for another reason. Because of the power of incumbency, decisions that are made by candidates and voters in watershed years, such as 1992, have repercussions for many years or even decades. This will be especially true in black majority districts, where challenges to entrenched incumbents are relatively rare.

9. This point is recognized by Abigail Thernstrom, who notes: "And where whites—and often blacks—regard skin color as a qualification for office (in part because no experience suggests otherwise), the election of blacks helps to break both white and black patterns of behavior" (1987, 239). However, Thernstrom rejects the practice of using black majority districts to help elect blacks to office.

References

Published Sources

Abrams, Kathryn. 1988. "Raising politics up": Minority political participation and Section 2 of the Voting Rights Act. *New York University Law Review* 63:449–531.

Achen, Christopher H. 1975. Measuring representation. *American Journal of Political Science* 22:475–510.

Adams, Greg D. 1996. Legislative effects of single-member vs. multi-member districts. *American Journal of Political Science* 40:129–144.

Aldrich, John H. 1995. *Why parties? The origin and transformation of party politics in America.* Chicago: University of Chicago Press.

Aldrich, John H., and Forrest D. Nelson. 1984. *Linear probability, logit, and probit models.* Beverly Hills, Calif.: Sage Publications.

Almond, Gabriel. 1988. Separate tables: Schools and sects in political science. *PS: Political Science and Politics* 21:828–842.

Alvarez, R. Michael, and John Brehm. 1997. Are Americans ambivalent toward racial policies? *American Journal of Political Science* 41:345–374.

Arnold, R. Douglas. 1990. *The logic of congressional action.* New Haven, Conn.: Yale University Press.

Ball, Howard. 1986. Racial vote dilution: Impact of the Reagan DOJ and the Burger Court on the Voting Rights Act. *Publius: The Journal of Federalism* 16:29–48.

Ballard, Gregory G. 1991. Application of Section 2 of the Voting Rights Act to runoff primary election laws. *Columbia Law Review* 91:1145–1157.

Barber, Benjamin R. 1984. *Strong democracy: Participatory politics for a new age.* Berkeley: University of California Press.

Barone, Michael, and Grant Ujifusa. 1985. *The almanac of American politics: 1986.* Washington, D.C.: National Journal.

Barone, Michael, Grant Ujifusa, and Douglas Matthews. 1975. *The almanac of American politics: 1976.* New York: E. P. Dutton.

Beitz, Charles R. 1989. *Political equality: An essay in democratic theory.* Princeton, N.J.: Princeton University Press.

Benenson, Bob. 1992. GOP's dreams of a comeback via the new map dissolve. *Congressional Quarterly Weekly Report* 50 (November 7): 3580–3581.

Bessette, Joseph M. 1994. *The mild voice of reason: Deliberative democracy and American national government.* Chicago: University of Chicago Press.

Bianco, William T. 1994. *Trust: Representatives and constituents.* Ann Arbor: University of Michigan Press.

———. 1997. Evaluating descriptive representation: When will constituents do better with "someone like them"? Working paper, Department of Political Science, Pennsylvania State University.

Black, Earl, and Merle Black. 1987. *Politics and society in the South.* Cambridge: Harvard University Press.

Black, Gordon. 1972. A theory of political ambition: Career choices and the role of structural incentives. *American Political Science Review* 66:144–159.

Blissman, Scott E. 1996. Navigating the political thicket: The Supreme Court, the Department of Justice, and the "predominant motive" in district apportionment cases after *Miller v. Johnson. Widener Journal of Public Law* 5:503–548.

Bloom, Allan. 1987. *The closing of the American mind.* New York: Simon and Schuster.

Bositis, David A. 1993. McClosky revisited: Issue conflict and consensus among African-American party leaders and followers. Paper presented at the annual meeting of the American Political Science Association, September 2–5, Washington, D.C.

Brace, Kimball, Bernard Grofman, and Lisa Handley. 1987. Does redistricting aimed to help blacks necessarily help Republicans? *Journal of Politics* 49:169–185.

Brace, Kimball, Lisa Handley, Richard Niemi, and Harold Stanley. 1995. Minority turnout and the creation of majority-minority districts. *American Politics Quarterly* 23:190–203.

Bullock, Charles S., III. 1995. The impact of changing the racial composition of congressional districts on legislators' roll call behavior. *American Politics Quarterly* 23:141–158.

Bullock, Charles S., III, and Loch K. Johnson. 1992. *Runoff elections in the United States.* Chapel Hill: University of North Carolina Press.

Bullock, Charles S., III, and Susan A. MacManus. 1981. Policy responsiveness to the black electorate: Programmatic versus symbolic representation. *American Politics Quarterly* 9 (July): 357–368.

Bullock, Charles S., III, and A. Brock Smith. 1990. Black success in local runoff elections. *Journal of Politics* 52:1205–1220.

Butler, David, and Bruce E. Cain. 1992. *Congressional redistricting: Comparative and theoretical perspectives.* New York: Macmillan.

Cain, Bruce E. 1985. Assessing the partisan effects of redistricting. *American Political Science Review* 79:320–333.

———. 1992. Voting rights and democratic theory: Toward a color- blind society? In *Controversies in minority voting: The Voting Rights Act in perspective,* edited by Bernard Grofman and Chandler Davidson, 261–277. Washington, D.C.: Brookings Institution.

Cameron, Charles, David Epstein, and Sharon O'Halloran. 1996. Do majority-minority districts maximize substantive black representation in Congress? *American Political Science Review* 90:794–812.

Canon, David T. 1989. Contesting primaries in congressional elections, 1972–1988. Paper presented at meeting of the American Political Science Association, August 31–September 4, Atlanta.

————. 1990. *Actors, athletes, and astronauts: Political amateurs in the United States Congress.* Chicago: University of Chicago Press.

————. 1995. Redistricting and the Congressional Black Caucus. *American Politics Quarterly* 23:159–189.

————. 1999. Electoral systems and representation in legislatures. Paper presented at the Shambaugh Comparative Legislative Research Conference, University of Iowa, Iowa City, April 16–19, 1998. *Legislative Politics Quarterly,* forthcoming.

Canon, David T., Matthew M. Schousen, and Patrick J. Sellers. 1994. A formula for uncertainty: Creating a black-majority district in North Carolina. In *Who runs for Congress: Ambition, context, and candidate emergence,* edited by Thomas A. Kazee, 23–44. Washington, D.C.: CQ Press.

————. 1996. The supply-side of congressional redistricting: Race and strategic politicians, 1972–1992. *Journal of Politics* 58:837–853.

————. 1998. Congressional districting in North Carolina. In *Race and redistricting in the 1990s,* edited by Bernard Grofman, 269–289. New York: Agathon Press.

Canon, David T., and David J. Sousa. 1992. Party system change and political career structures in the U.S. Congress. *Legislative Studies Quarterly* 17:347–363.

Carby, Hazel. 1992. The multicultural wars. In *Black popular culture,* edited by Gina Dent, 187–199. Seattle: Bay Press.

Carmines, Edward G., and James A. Stimson. 1989. *Issue evolution: Race and the transformation of American politics.* Princeton, N.J.: Princeton University Press.

Christensen, Rob. 1991. U.S. Rep. Jones decides to retire. *News and Observer* (Raleigh, N.C.), October 5, 1A, 11A.

Clapp, Charles L. 1963. *The congressman: His work as he sees it.* Washington, D.C.: Brookings Institution.

Clausen, Aage R. 1973. *How congressmen decide: A policy focus.* New York: St. Martin's Press.

Clay, William. 1993. *Just permanent interests: Black Americans in Congress, 1870–1992.* New York: Amistad Press.

Cobb, Michael D., and Jeffrey A. Jenkins. 1996. Who represents black interests in Congress?: Sponsoring and voting for legislation beneficial to black constituents. Paper presented at the annual meeting of the Midwest Political Science Association, Chicago, April 18–20.

Cohadas, Nadine. 1985. Black House members striving for influence. *Congressional Quarterly Weekly Report* 43 (April 16): 675–681.

Congressional Quarterly. 1993. *The new Congress: Younger, more diverse House and Senate take aim at political gridlock,* Supplement to *Congressional Quarterly* 51(3) (January 16).

Congressional Research Service. 1989. *CRS report for Congress: Black members of the United States Congress, 1789–1989.* Washington, D.C.: Library of Congress.

Connoly, William. 1991. *Identity/difference: Democratic negotiations of political paradox.* Ithaca, N.Y.: Cornell University Press.

Cooper, Kenneth J. 1990. Helms defeats Gantt: Poll hours disputed. *Washington Post,* November 6, A27.

————. 1993a. Black Caucus flexes muscle, independence. *Emerge,* September, 24.

————. 1993b. Churchgoers courted as crucial in Mississippi house campaign. *Washington Post,* April 11, A12.

————. 1994. Dismantling black political power. *Emerge,* April, 30–37.

————. 1996. Six ways to make a difference in '96. *Emerge,* December/January 1996, 16.

Cover, Albert D., and Bruce S. Brumberg. 1982. Baby books and ballots: The impact of congressional mail on constituent opinion. *American Political Science Review* 76:347–359.

Cox, Gary W. 1984. Electoral equilibrium in double-member districts. *Public Choice* 44:443–451.

————. 1990. Centripetal and centrifugal incentives in electoral systems. *American Journal of Political Science* 34:903–935.

Cox, Gary W., and Mathew McCubbins. 1993. *Legislative leviathan: Party government in the House.* Berkeley: University of California Press.

Cranor, John D., Gary L. Crawley, and Raymond H. Sheele. 1989. The anatomy of a gerrymander. *American Journal of Political Science* 33:222–239.

Cunningham, Kitty. 1993a. Black Caucus flexes muscle on budget—and more. *Congressional Quarterly Weekly Report* 51 (July 3): 1711–1715.

————. 1993b. Contest for Espy's seat drawing large field. *Congressional Quarterly Weekly Report* 51 (March 6): 534–537.

Cunningham, Kitty, and Jeffrey L. Katz. 1993. A test of strength. *Congressional Quarterly Weekly Report* 51 (August 7): 2126.

Cushman, Robert E., with Robert F. Cushman. 1966. *Leading constitutional decisions.* 13th ed. New York: Appleton-Century-Crofts.

Dahl, Robert A. 1956. *A preface to democratic theory.* Chicago: University of Chicago Press.

Dalton, Russell J., Paul A. Beck, and Robert Huckfeldt. 1998. Partisan cues and the media: Information flows in the 1992 presidential election. *American Political Science Review* 92:111–126.

Davidson, Chandler. 1984. *Minority vote dilution.* Washington, D.C.: Howard University Press.

————. 1992. The Voting Rights Act: A brief history. In *Controversies in minority voting: The Voting Rights Act in perspective,* edited by Bernard Grofman and Chandler Davidson, 7–51. Washington, D.C.: Brookings Institution.

Davidson, Chandler, and Bernard Grofman, eds. 1994. *Quiet revolution in the South: The impact of the Voting Rights Act, 1965–1990.* Princeton, N.J.: Princeton University Press.

Dawson, Michael C. 1994. *Behind the mule: Race and class in African-American politics.* Princeton, N.J.: Princeton University Press.

Days, Drew S., III. 1992. Section 5 enforcement and the Justice Department. In *Controversies in minority voting: The Voting Rights Act in perspective,* edited by Bernard Grofman and Chandler Davidson, 52–65. Washington, D.C.: Brookings Institution.

DeGregorio, Christine. 1994. Congressional committee staff as policy making partners in the U.S. Congress. *Congress and the Presidency* 21:49–66.

————. 1995. Patterns of senior staff use in congressional committees. *Polity* 28:261–275.

Denton, Van. 1991a. A new political map: Forces old and new change the face and nature of representation. *News and Observer* (Raleigh, N.C.), August 18, 1J, 8J.

———. 1991b. Party loyalty, black gains clash in redistricting. *News and Observer* (Raleigh, N.C.), December 28, 1991, 1A, 5A.

———. 1992a. District plan would turn candidates into roadrunners. *News and Observer* (Raleigh, N.C.), January 12, 1C, 2C.

———. 1992b. House Democrats offer district plan. *News and Observer* (Raleigh, N.C.), January 19, 1A, 10A.

Di Lorenzo, Vincent. 1997. Legislative heart and phase transitions: An exploratory study of Congress and minority interests. *William and Mary Law Review* 38:1729–1815.

Doherty, Carroll J. 1998. Surface racial harmony on Hill hides simmering tensions. *Congressional Quarterly Weekly Report* 56 (March 21): 715–720.

Donohoe, Cathryn. 1993. Beyond race: It's not just a black agenda anymore, it's an American agenda, say a new crop of leaders. *Washington Times,* April 8, E1.

Downing, Lyle, and Robert Thigpen. 1986. Beyond shared understandings. *Political Theory* 14:451–472.

Downs, Anthony. 1957. *An economic theory of democracy.* New York: Harper and Row.

Drysek, John S. 1990. *Discursive democracy: Politics, policy, and political science.* New York: Cambridge University Press.

Duncan, Phil. 1992. Blacks hope to win House seat after a century of waiting. *Congressional Quarterly Weekly Report,* August 22, 2536–2537.

———. 1993. *Politics in America 1994: The 103rd Congress.* Washington, D.C.: CQ Press.

Dworkin, Ronald. 1989. Liberal community. *California Law Review* 77:479–504.

Dymally, Mervyn M. 1971. *The black politician: His struggle for power.* Belmont, Calif.: Duxbury Press.

Edsall, Thomas B. 1990. Bush takes no stand on ballot plan; program targeted N.C. black voters. *Washington Post,* November 9, A13.

Edsall, Thomas B., and Mary D. Edsall. 1991. *Chain reaction: The impact of race, rights, and taxes on American politics.* New York: W. W. Norton.

Ehrenhalt, Alan. 1991. *The United States of ambition: Politicians, power, and the pursuit of office.* New York: Random House.

Eisenstein, Zillah. 1988. *The female body and the law.* Berkeley: University of California Press.

Eisgruber, Christopher L. 1996. Ethnic segregation by religion and race: Reflections on *Kiryas Joel* and *Shaw v. Reno. Cumberland Law Review* 26:515–526.

Eisinger, Peter. 1980. *The politics of displacement: Racial and ethnic transition in three American cities.* New York: Academic Press.

Engstrom, Richard L. 1994. The Voting Rights Act: Disfranchisement, dilution and alternative election systems. *PS: Political Science and Politics* 27:685–688.

———. 1995a. Voting rights districts: Debunking the myths. *Campaigns and Elections* 16 (April): 24–46.

———. 1995b. *Shaw, Miller* and the districting thicket. *National Civic Review* 84:323–336.

Erikson, Robert. 1976. The influence of newspaper endorsements in presidential elections. *American Journal of Political Science* 20:207–234.

Eversley, Melanie. 1997. Whites positive on race relations, national poll finds. *Wisconsin State Journal,* June 11, 2A.

Faryna, Stan, Brad Stetson, and Joseph G. Conti. 1997. *Black and right: The bold new voice of black conservatives in America.* Westport, Conn.: Praeger.

Fenno, Richard F. 1973. *Congressmen in committees.* Boston: Little, Brown.

———. 1978. *Home style: House members in their districts.* Boston: Little, Brown.

———. 1989. *The making of a Senator: Dan Quayle.* Washington, D.C.: CQ Press.

———. 1996. *Senators on the campaign trail: The politics of representation.* Norman: University of Oklahoma Press.

Fiorina, Morris P. 1989. *Congress: Keystone of the Washington establishment.* 2nd ed. New Haven, Conn.: Yale University Press.

———. 1974. *Representatives, roll calls, and constituencies.* Lexington, Mass.: Lexington Books.

Fletcher, Michael A. 1996. Is the South becoming colorblind? *Washington Post National Weekly Edition,* December 2–8, 13.

Fogg-Davis, Hawley. 1998. Choosing children: Antidiscrimination and the ethics of transracial adoption. Ph.D. diss., Princeton University.

Forest, Benjamin. 1996. Where should Democratic compromise take place? *Social Science Quarterly* 77:6–13.

Friedman, Sally. 1996. House committee assignments of women and minority newcomers, 1965–1994. *Legislative Studies Quarterly* 21:73–81.

Galloway, Jennifer A. 1997. America's future face: Growing number of multiracial identities creates new dynamics in race relations. *Wisconsin State Journal,* June 12, 1A, 3A.

Gates, Henry Louis, Jr. 1992. *Loose canons: Notes on the culture wars.* New York: Oxford University Press.

Gay, Claudine. 1996. The impact of black congressional representation on the political behavior of constituents. Paper presented at the annual meeting of the Midwest Political Science Association, Chicago, April 18–20.

Geertz, Clifford. 1973. *The interpretation of cultures.* New York: Basic Books.

Gelman, Andrew, and Gary King. 1994. Enhancing democracy through legislative redistricting. *American Political Science Review* 88:541–559.

Gerber, Elisabeth R., Rebecca B. Morton, and Thomas A. Rietz. 1998. Minority representation in multimember districts. *American Political Science Review* 92:127–144.

Gilligan, Carol. 1982. *In a different voice: Psychological theory and women's development.* Cambridge: Harvard University Press.

Gitlin, Todd. 1993. Universality to difference: Notes on the fragmentation of the idea of the left. *Contention: Debates in Society, Culture, and Science* 2 (Winter): 15–40.

Glaser, James M. 1996. *Race, campaign politics, and the realignment in the South.* New Haven, Conn.: Yale University Press.

Goffman, Erving. 1963. *Stigma: Notes on the management of spoiled identity.* New York: Simon and Schuster.

Graber, Mark A. 1996. Conflicting representations: Lani Guinier and James Madison on electoral systems. *Constitutional Commentary* 13:291–305.

Grofman, Bernard. 1991. Multivariate methods and the analysis of racially polarized voting—pitfalls in the use of social-science by the courts. *Social Science Quarterly* 72:826–833.

———. 1993. Would Vince Lombardi have been right if he had said: "When it comes to redistricting, race isn't everything, it's the *only* thing"? *Cardozo Law Review* 14:1237–1276.

———. 1995. *Shaw v. Reno* and the future of voting rights. *PS: Political Science and Politics* 28:27–36.

Grofman, Bernard, Robert Griffin, and Amihai Glazer. 1992. The effect of black population on electing Democrats and liberals to the House of Representatives. *Legislative Studies Quarterly* 17:365–379.

Grofman, Bernard, and Lisa Handley. 1989. Minority population proportion and the black and Hispanic congressional success in the 1970s and 1980s. *American Politics Quarterly* 17:436–445.

———. 1991. The impact of the Voting Rights Act on black representation in southern state legislatures. *Legislative Studies Quarterly* 16:111–127.

Grofman, Bernard, Lisa Handley, and Richard Niemi. 1992. *Minority representation and the quest for voting equality.* New York: Cambridge University Press.

Grubert, Jeanmarie K. 1997. The Rehnquist Court's changed reading of the equal protection clause in the context of voting rights. *Fordham Law Review* 65:1819–1854.

Guinier, Lani. 1991a. The triumph of tokenism—the Voting-Rights Act and the theory of black electoral success. *Michigan Law Review* 89:1077–1154.

———. 1991b. No 2 seats—the elusive quest for political equality. *Virginia Law Review* 77:1413–1514.

———. 1992. Voting rights and democratic theory: Where do we go from here? In *Controversies in minority voting: The Voting Rights Act in perspective,* edited by Bernard Grofman and Chandler Davidson, 283–292. Washington, D.C.: Brookings Institution.

———. 1994. *The tyranny of the majority: Fundamental fairness in representative democracy.* New York: Free Press.

———. 1995. Don't scapegoat the gerrymander. *New York Times Magazine,* January 8, 36–37.

Gutmann, Amy, and Dennis Thompson. 1996. *Democracy and disagreement: Why moral conflict cannot be avoided in politics and what to do about it.* Cambridge: Harvard University Press (Belknap).

Hacker, Andrew. 1992. *Two nations: Black and white, separate, hostile, unequal.* New York: Scribner.

Hager, George. 1993. GOP, Black Caucus force delay in line-item veto debate. *Congressional Quarterly Weekly Report* 51 (April 24): 1008–1009.

Hall, Richard L. 1996. *Participation in Congress.* New Haven, Conn.: Yale University Press.

Hamilton, Charles V. 1977. De-racialization: The examination of a political strategy. *First World* 4:1–35.

————. 1992. The politics of deracialization in the 1990s. *National Review of Politics* 3:175–179.

Hammond, Susan Webb. 1985. Legislative staffs. In *Handbook of legislative research,* edited by Gerhard Lowenberg, Samuel C. Patterson, and Malcolm E. Jewell, 273–319. Cambridge: Harvard University Press.

————. 1996. Recent research on legislative staffs. *Legislative Studies Quarterly* 21:543–576.

————. 1998. *Congressional caucuses in national policy making.* Baltimore: Johns Hopkins University Press.

Handley, Lisa. 1991. The quest for minority voting rights. Ph.D. diss., George Washington University.

Handley, Lisa, and Bernard Grofman. 1994. The impact of the Voting Rights Act on minority representation: Black officeholding in southern state legislatures and congressional delegations. In *Quiet revolution in the South: The impact of the Voting Rights Act: 1965–1990,* edited by Chandler Davidson and Bernard Grofman, 336–350. Princeton, N.J.: Princeton University Press.

Hertzberg, Roberta. 1992. An analytic choice approach to concurrent majorities: The relevance of John C. Calhoun's theory for institutional design. *Journal of Politics* 54:54–81.

Hill, Kevin. 1995. Does the creation of majority black districts aid Republicans? An analysis of the 1992 congressional elections in eight southern states. *Journal of Politics* 57:384–401.

Hill, Kim Quaile, Stephen Hanna, and Sahar Shafqat. 1997. The liberal-conservative ideology of U.S. senators: A new measure. *American Journal of Political Science* 41:1395–1413.

Hochschild, Jennifer L. 1984. *The New American dilemma: Liberal democracy and school desegregation.* New Haven, Conn.: Yale University Press.

————. 1995. *Facing up to the American dream: Race, class, and the soul of the nation.* Princeton, N.J.: Princeton University Press.

Holden, Matthew, Jr. 1973. *The politics of the black "nation."* New York: Chandler Publishing.

Hollis, Martin, and Steve Smith. 1990. *Explaining and understanding international relations.* New York: Oxford University Press.

Holmes, Steven A. 1997. Asian American is named to top civil rights position. *New York Times,* June 12, A18.

Horowitz, Donald L. 1985. *Ethnic groups in conflict.* Berkeley: University of California Press.

House of Representatives (U.S.). 1993. Committee on the Judiciary. Subcommittee on Civil and Constitutional Rights. *Hearing on Voting Rights.* 103rd Cong., 1st sess., October 14.

————. 1994a. Committee on the Judiciary. Subcommittee on Civil and Constitutional Rights. *Voting Rights Roundtable.* 103rd Cong., 2nd sess., May 11.

————. 1994b. Committee on the Judiciary. Subcommittee on Civil and Constitutional Rights. *Voting Rights Roundtable.* 103rd Cong., 2nd sess., May 25.

Huckfeldt, Robert, and Carol Weitzel Kohfield. 1989. *Race and the decline of class in American politics.* Urbana: University of Illinois Press.

Hurley, Patricia. 1991. Partisan representation, realignment, and the Senate in the 1980s. *Journal of Politics* 53:3–33.

Hurwitz, Jon, and Mark Peffley. 1997. Public perceptions of race and crime: The role of racial stereotypes. *American Journal of Political Science* 41:375–401.

Issacharoff, Samuel. 1995. Groups and the right to vote. *Emory Law Journal* 46:869–883.

Issacharoff, Samuel, and Richard H. Pildes. 1996. All for one: Can cumulative voting ease racial tensions? *New Republic,* November 18, 10.

Jackson, John E. 1989. An errors-in-variables approach to estimating models with small area data. *Political Analysis* 1:157–180.

Jacobson, Gary C. 1990. *The electoral origins of divided government: Competition for U.S. House elections, 1946–1988.* Boulder, Colo.: Westview Press.

———. 1997. *The politics of congressional elections.* 4th ed. New York: Longman (1st ed., 1983).

Jacobson, Gary C., and Samuel Kernell. 1983. *Strategy and choice in congressional elections.* New Haven, Conn.: Yale University Press.

Jewell, Malcolm E. 1967. *Legislative representation in the contemporary South.* Durham, N.C.: Duke University Press.

———. 1983. Legislator-constituent relations and the representative process. *Legislative Studies Quarterly* 13:303–337.

Joint Center for Political Studies. *Black elected officials: A national roster.* 1987, 1991. Washington, D.C.: Joint Center for Political Studies.

Johannes, John R. 1983. Explaining congressional casework styles. *American Journal of Political Science* 27:530–547.

———. 1984. *To serve the people: Congress and constituency service.* Lincoln: University of Nebraska Press.

Johnson, James B., and Philip E. Secret. 1996. Focus and style of representational roles of Congressional Black and Hispanic Caucus members. *Journal of Black Studies* 26(3) (January): 245–273.

Jones, Charles E. 1985. Three conditions for effective black participation in the legislative process: An inquiry of the Congressional Black Caucus, 1971–1982. Ph.D. diss., Washington State University.

Kairys, David. 1996. Unexplainable on grounds other than race. *American University Law Review* 45:729–749.

Karlan, Pamela S. 1995. Apres *Shaw* le deluge? *PS: Political Science and Politics* 28:50–54.

Karlan, Pamela S., and Daryl J. Levinson. 1996. Why voting is different. *California Law Review* 84:1201–1286.

Karlan, Pamela S., and Peyton McCrary. 1988. Without fear and without research: Abigail Thernstrom on the Voting Rights Act. *Journal of Law and Politics* 4:751–777.

Katz, Jeffrey L. 1993. Growing Black Caucus may have new voice. *Congressional Quarterly Weekly Report* 51 (January 2): 5–11.

Kelly, Michael. 1995. Segregation anxiety. *New Yorker,* November 20, 43–54.

Kessler, Daniel, and Keith Krehbiel. 1996. Dynamics of cosponsorship. *American Political Science Review* 90:555–566.

Key, V. O., Jr. 1949. *Southern politics.* New York: Vintage.

Kilborn, Peter T. 1998. Black Americans trailing whites in health, studies say. *New York Times,* January 26, A16.

Kinder, Donald R., and Lynn M. Sanders. 1996. *Divided by color: Racial politics and democratic ideals.* Chicago: University of Chicago Press.

Kinder, Donald R., and David O. Sears. 1981. Prejudice and politics: Symbolic racism versus racial threats to the good life. *Journal of Personality and Social Psychology* 40:414–431.

King, David C. 1997. *Turf wars: How congressional committees claim jurisdiction.* Chicago: University of Chicago Press.

King, Gary. 1989. *Unifying political methodology: The likelihood theory of statistical inference.* Cambridge: Cambridge University Press.

King, Gary, Robert O. Keohane, and Sidney Verba. 1994. *Designing social inquiry: Scientific inference in qualitative research.* Princeton, N.J.: Princeton University Press.

———. 1995. The importance of research design in political science. *American Political Science Review* 89:475–481.

Kingdon, John W. 1968. *Candidates for office.* New York: Random House.

———. 1989. *Congressmen's voting decisions.* 3rd ed. Ann Arbor: University of Michigan Press.

Kmenta, Jan. 1971. *Elements of econometrics.* New York: Macmillan.

Kousser, J. Morgan. 1992. The Voting Rights Act and the two reconstructions. In *Controversies in minority voting: The Voting Rights Act in perspective,* edited by Bernard Grofman and Chandler Davidson, 135–176. Washington, D.C.: Brookings Institution.

———. 1995. *Shaw v. Reno* and the real world of redistricting and representation. Working paper #915, California Institute of Technology.

Krehbiel, Keith. 1991. *Information and legislative organization.* Ann Arbor: University of Michigan Press.

Kymlicka, Will. 1995. *Multicultural citizenship: A liberal theory of minority rights.* New York: Oxford University Press.

Lamison-White, Leatha. 1997. *Poverty in the United States: 1996.* U.S. Bureau of the Census, Current Population Reports, Series P60–198. Washington, D.C.: U.S. Government Printing Office.

Larson, Stephanie G. 1990. Information and learning in a congressional district: A social experiment. *American Journal of Political Science* 34:1102–1118.

Lawrence, Jill. 1993. Black Caucus using its clout. *Wisconsin State Journal,* July 7, 3A.

Levy, Arthur B., and Susan Stoudinger. 1976. Sources of voting cues for the Congressional Black Caucus. *Journal of Black Studies* 7:29–45.

———. 1978. The Black Caucus in the 92nd Congress: Gauging its success. *Phylon* 38:322–332.

Little, Daniel. 1991. *Varieties of social explanation: An introduction to the philosophy of social science.* Boulder, Colo.: Westview Press.

Lineberry, Danny. 1992. Redistricting fireworks are expected next week. *Herald Sun* (Durham, N.C.), January 8, A1–A2.

Loewen, James W. 1990. Racial bloc voting and political mobilization in South Carolina. *Review of Black Political Economy* 19:23–37.

Loomis, Burdett A. 1981. Congressional caucuses and the politics of representation. In *Congress reconsidered,* edited by Lawrence C. Dodd and Bruce I. Oppenheimer, 204–220. Washington, D.C.: CQ Press.

Lowery, Joseph E. 1997. The place of race in the Census: It's the best way to monitor our fight against discrimination. *Washington Post,* June 16, 21.

Lublin, David Ian. 1995. Race, representation, and redistricting. In *Classifying by race,* edited by Paul E. Peterson, 111–125. Princeton, N.J.: Princeton University Press.

———. 1997. *The paradox of representation: Racial gerrymander and minority interests in Congress.* Princeton, N.J.: Princeton University Press.

MacIntyre, Alasdair. 1971. *Against the self-images of the age: Essays on ideology and philosophy.* London: Duckworth.

MacKinnon, Catherine A. 1987. *Feminism unmodified: Discourses on life and law.* Cambridge: Harvard University Press.

MacManus, Susan A. 1995. The appropriateness of biracial approaches to measuring fairness of representation in a multicultural world. *PS: Political Science and Politics* 28:42–50.

Malbin, Michael J. 1980. *Unelected representatives: Congressional staff and the future of representative government.* New York: Basic Books.

Mann, Thomas E., and Norman J. Ornstein. 1993. *Renewing Congress: A second report.* Washington, D.C.: American Enterprise Institute and Brookings Institution.

Mansbridge, Jane. 1996. In defense of descriptive representation. Paper presented at the annual meeting of the American Political Science Association, San Francisco.

Marable, Manning. 1980. *How capitalism underdeveloped black America: Problems in race, political economy, and society.* Boston: South End Press.

Mayhew, David R. 1974. *Congress: The electoral connection.* New Haven, Conn.: Yale University Press.

McCartney, John T. 1992. *Black power ideologies: An essay in African-American political thought.* Philadelphia: Temple University Press.

McClain, Paula D. 1996. Black politics at the crossroads? Or in the cross-hairs? *American Political Science Review* 90:867–873.

McClain, Paula D., and John A. Garcia. 1993. Expanding disciplinary boundaries: Black, Latino, and racial minority groups in political science. In *Political science: The state of the discipline II,* edited by Ada W. Finifter, 247–279. Washington, D.C.: American Political Science Association.

McCrery, Peyton. 1990. Racially polarized voting in the South: Evidence from the courtroom. *Social Science History* 14:507–531.

McKinney, Cynthia. 1996. The politics of geography. *Emerge,* December/January 1996, 62–66.

Menifield, Charles E. 1996. Caucuses as sources of cues: A look at the Black, Women's, and Hispanic Caucuses. Paper presented at the annual meeting of the Midwest Political Science Association, Chicago, April 18–20.

Merelman, Richard M. 1994. Racial conflict and cultural politics in the United States. *Journal of Politics* 56:1–20.

Miles, Jack. 1992. Blacks vs. browns: The struggle for the bottom rung. *Atlantic Monthly,* October, 41–45.

Miller, Warren E., and Donald E. Stokes. 1963. Constituency influence in Congress. *American Political Science Review* 57:45–56.

Montgomery, Bill. 1992. Bishop touts "progressive" image in push to topple Hatcher. *Atlanta Journal and Constitution,* August 4, E1.

Morrill, Jim, and Greg Trevor. 1992. District's a land of confusion: Contortions show politics at work. *Charlotte Observer,* January 27, 1A, 4A.

Morrill, Richard L. 1996. Territory, community, and collective representation. *Social Science Quarterly* 77:3–5.

Murray, Charles A. 1984. *Losing ground.* New York: Basic Books.

Myrdal, Gunnar. 1944. *An American dilemma.* New York: Harper and Brothers.

NAACP. 1994. Report of the NAACP Legal Defense and Educational Fund: The effect of Section 2 of the Voting Rights Act on the 1994 congressional elections. Mimeographed.

Natapoff, Alexandra. 1996. Madisonian multiculturalism. *American University Law Review* 45:751–773.

Niemi, Richard G., and Alan I. Abramowitz. 1994. Partisan redistricting and the 1992 congressional elections. *Journal of Politics* 56:811–817.

Niemi, Richard G., Kimball W. Brace, and Doug Chapin. 1992. Bright lines, guidelines, and tradeoffs: The conflict between compactness and minority representation in the congressional districts of the 1990s. Paper presented at the annual meeting of the Midwest Political Science Association, Chicago, April 17.

Niemi, Richard G., Bernard Grofman, Carl Carlucci, and Thomas Hofeller. 1990. Measuring compactness and the role of a compactness standard in a test for partisan and racial gerrymandering. *Journal of Politics* 52:1155–1181.

Niemi, Richard G., Jeffrey S. Hill, and Bernard Grofman. 1985. The impact of multimember districts on party representation in U.S. state legislatures. *Legislative Studies Quarterly* 10:441–456.

Ornstein, Norman J., Thomas E. Mann, and Michael J. Malbin. 1998. *Vital statistics on Congress: 1997–1998.* Washington, D.C.: Congressional Quarterly Press.

O'Rourke, Timothy. 1992. The voting rights paradox and the 1982 Voting Rights Act Amendments. In *Controversies in minority voting: The Voting Rights Act in perspective,* edited by Bernard Grofman and Chandler Davidson, 85–113. Washington, D.C.: Brookings Institution.

Overby, L. Marvin, and Kenneth M. Cosgrove. 1996. Unintended consequences? Racial redistricting and the representation of minority interests. *Journal of Politics* 58:540–550.

Parker, Frank R. 1990. *Black votes count.* Chapel Hill: University of North Carolina Press.

———. 1996. Factual errors and chilling consequences: A critique of *Shaw v. Reno* and *Miller v. Johnson. Cumberland Law Review* 26:527–536.

Parker, Glenn R. 1986. *Homeward bound: Explaining changes in congressional behavior.* Pittsburgh: University of Pittsburgh Press.

Patterson, Dennis. 1994. Lawmaker says ugly districts serve a purpose. *News and Observer* (Raleigh, N.C.), April 1, 3A.

Perlmutt, David. 1992. Maligned district has good points: 12th brings together quality black candidates to choose from. *Charlotte Observer,* April 12, 1A, 12A.

Perry, Huey L. 1990. Black electoral success in 1989. *PS: Political Science and Politics* 23:141–162.

————. 1991a. Deracialization as a analytical construct. *Urban Affairs Quarterly* 27:181–191.

————. 1991b. Pluralist theory and national black-politics in the United States. *Polity* 23:549–565.

Peterson, Paul E. 1995. A politically correct solution to racial classification. In *Classifying by race,* edited by Paul E. Peterson, 3–17. Princeton, N.J.: Princeton University Press.

Petrocik, John R., and Scott W. Desposato. 1998. The partisan consequences of majority-minority redistricting in the South, 1992 and 1994. *Journal of Politics* 60:613–633.

Phillips, Anne. 1995. *The politics of presence.* New York: Clarendon Press/Oxford University Press.

Pildes, Richard H., and Richard G. Niemi. 1993. Expressive harms, "bizarre districts," and voting rights: Evaluating election district appearances after *Shaw v. Reno. Michigan Law Review* 92:483–507.

Pinderhughes, Diane M. 1987. *Race and ethnicity in Chicago politics.* Urbana: University of Illinois Press.

Pinney, Neil, and George Serra. 1995. The Congressional Black Caucus: Group agreement and voting influences. Paper presented at the annual meeting of the American Political Science Association, Chicago, August 31–September 2.

Pitkin, Hanna F. 1967. *The concept of representation.* Berkeley: University of California Press.

Polsby, Daniel, and Robert Popper. 1996. Guinier's theory of political market failure. *Social Science Quarterly* 77:14–22.

Poole, Keith, and Howard Rosenthal. 1996. *Congress: A political- economic history of roll call voting.* New York: Oxford University Press.

Preston, Michael B. 1978. Black elected officials and public policy: Symbolic or substantive representation? *Policy Studies* 7 (Winter): 196–201.

Raspberry, William. 1994. Judgement, black and white. *Washington Post,* July 8, A23.

Rawlins, Wade. 1998. Judges rule out May primaries. *News and Observer* (Raleigh, N.C.), April 22, A3.

Rawls, John. 1971. *A theory of justice.* Cambridge: Belknap/Harvard University Press.

Reeves, Keith. 1997. *Voting hopes or fears: White voters, black candidates, and racial politics in America.* New York: Oxford University Press.

Research Division, North Carolina General Assembly. 1991. Redistricting 1991: Legislator's guide to North Carolina legislative and congressional redistricting. Mimeographed.

Reynolds, Andrew. 1995. Constitutional engineering in southern Africa. *Journal of Democracy* 6:86–99.

Riker, William H. 1982. *Liberalism against populism: A confrontation between the theory of democracy and the theory of social choice.* San Francisco: W. H. Freeman.

———. 1986. *The art of political manipulation.* New Haven, Conn.: Yale University Press.

Rohde, David W. 1979. Risk bearing and progressive ambition: The case of members of the United States House of Representatives. *American Journal of Political Science* 23:1–26.

———. 1991. *Parties and leaders in the postreform House.* Chicago: University of Chicago Press.

Ruffin, Jane. 1992. GOP sues over redistricting. *News and Observer* (Raleigh, N.C.), February 29, 1A, 17A.

Rush, Mark E. 1993. *Does redistricting make a difference?: Partisan representation and political behavior.* Baltimore: Johns Hopkins University Press.

Sack, Kevin. 1996. Victory of 5 redistricted blacks recasts gerrymandering dispute. *New York Times,* November 23, A1, A8.

Said, Edward. 1978. *Orientalism.* New York: Random House.

Salant, Jonathan D. 1995. LSOs are no longer separate, but the work's almost equal. *Congressional Quarterly Weekly Report* 53 (May 27): 1483.

Sandel, Michael. 1982. *Liberalism and the limits of justice.* Cambridge: Cambridge University Press.

Sawyer, Jack, and Duncan MacRae, Jr. 1962. Game theory and cumulative voting in Illinois: 1902–1954. *American Political Science Review* 56:936–946.

Schiller, Wendy. 1995. Senators as political entrepreneurs: Using bill sponsorship to shape legislative activities. *American Journal of Political Science* 39:186–203.

Schlesinger, Arthur, Jr. 1992. *The disuniting of America.* New York: Norton Press.

Schlesinger, Joseph A. 1966. *Ambition and politics: Political careers in the United States.* Chicago: Rand McNally.

Schockley, Evelyn Elaine. 1991. Voting Rights Act Section 2: Racially polarized voting and the minority community's representative of choice. *Michigan Law Review* 89:1038–1067.

Schuman, Howard, Charlotte Steeh, and Lawrence Bobo. 1985. *Racial attitudes in America: Trends and interpretations.* Cambridge: Harvard University Press.

Sears, David O. 1988. Symbolic racism. In *Eliminating racism: Profiles in controversy,* edited by Phyllis A. Katz and Dalmas A. Taylor, 53–84. New York: Plenum.

Sears, David O., and Tom Jessor. 1996. Whites' racial policy attitudes: The role of white racism. *Social Science Quarterly* 77(4) (December): 751–759.

Segal, Jeffrey A., and Albert D. Cover. 1989. Ideological values and the votes of U.S. Supreme Court justices. *American Political Science Review* 83:557–565.

Senate (U.S.). 1982a. Committee on the Judiciary. *Voting Rights Act: Hearings before the Subcommittee on the Constitution of the Committee on the Judiciary.* 97th Cong., 2nd sess., January 27–March 1. No. J-97–92.

———. 1982b. Committee on the Judiciary. *Voting Rights Act Extension: Report of the Subcommittee on the Constitution of the Committee on the Judiciary.* 97th Cong., 2nd sess., May 25. S. Rept. 97–417.

Shepsle, Kenneth A., and Barry R. Weingast, eds. 1995. *Positive theories of congressional institutions.* Ann Arbor: University of Michigan Press.

Shipler, David K. 1997. *A country of strangers: Blacks and whites in America.* New York: Knopf.

Sinclair, Barbara. 1995. *Legislators, leaders, and lawmaking: The U.S. House of Representatives in the postreform era.* Baltimore: Johns Hopkins University Press.

Singh, Robert. 1998. *The Congressional Black Caucus: Racial politics in the U.S. Congress.* Thousand Oaks, Calif.: Sage Publications.

Sleeper, Jim. 1997. *Liberal racism.* New York: Viking.

Smith, Hedrick. 1988. *The power game: How Washington works.* New York: Ballentine Books.

Smith, Robert C. 1981. The black congressional delegation. *Western Political Quarterly* 34:203–221.

————. 1990. Recent elections and black politics: The maturation or death of black politics? *PS: Political Science and Politics* 23:160–162.

————. 1996. *We have no leaders: African Americans in the post–civil rights era.* Albany: State University of New York Press.

Smith, Steven S. 1989. *Call to order: Floor politics in the House and Senate.* Washington, D.C.: Brookings Institution.

Smith, Steven S., and Christopher J. Deering. 1990. *Committees in Congress.* 2nd ed. Washington, D.C.: CQ Press.

Sniderman, Paul M., and Thomas Piazza. 1993. *The scar of race.* Cambridge: Harvard University Press (Belknap).

Soni, Sushma. 1990. Defining the minority-preferred candidate under Section 2. *Yale Law Journal* 99:1651–1668.

Steele, Shelby. 1990. *The content of our character.* New York: St. Martin's Press.

Stoker, Laura. 1996. Understanding differences in whites' opinions across racial policies. *Social Science Quarterly* 77(4) (December): 768–777.

Streich, Gregory W. 1997. *After the celebration: Theories of community and practices of interracial dialogue.* Ph.D. diss., University of Wisconsin, Madison.

Strickland, Ruth Ann, and Marcia Lynn Whicker. 1992. Comparing the Wilder and Gantt campaigns: A model for black candidate success in statewide elections. *PS: Political Science and Politics* 25:204–212.

Strong, Donald. 1968. *Negroes, ballots, and judges: National voting rights legislation in the federal courts.* University: University of Alabama Press.

Sunstein, Cass R. 1993. Democracy and shifting preferences. In *The idea of democracy,* edited by David Copp, Jean Hampton, and John E. Roemer, 196–230. New York: Cambridge University Press.

————. 1997. In the court of cautious opinions: Once again, the justices are proceeding only by small steps. *Washington Post Weekly Edition,* July 14, 22–23.

Swain, Carol M. 1993. *Black faces, black interests: The representation of African Americans in Congress.* Cambridge: Harvard University Press.

————. 1995. The future of black representation. *American Prospect* 19 (Fall): 78–83.

Tarrow, Sidney. 1995. Bridging the quantitative-qualitative divide in political science. *American Political Science Review* 89:471–474.

Tate, Katherine. 1991. Black political-participation in the 1984 and 1988 presidential elections. *American Political Science Review* 85:1159–1176.

————. 1993. *From protest to politics: The new black voters in American elections.* Cambridge: Harvard University Press.

Taylor, Charles. 1992. *Multiculturalism and the "politics of recognition."* Princeton, N.J.: Princeton University Press.

Thernstrom, Abigail. 1987. *Whose votes count? Affirmative action and minority voting rights.* Cambridge: Harvard University Press.

———. 1997. The overlooked story. *New York Times,* June 18, A19.

Thernstrom, Stephan, and Abigail Thernstrom. 1997. *America in black and white: One nation, indivisible: Race in modern America.* New York: Simon and Schuster.

Tuch, Steven A., and Michael Hughes. 1996a. Whites' opposition to race-targeted policies: One cause or many? *Social Science Quarterly* 77(4) (December): 778–788.

———. 1996b. Whites' racial policy attitudes. *Social Science Quarterly* 77(4) (December): 723–745.

Tufte, Edward R. 1975. Determinants of the outcomes of midterm congressional elections. *American Political Science Review* 69:812–826.

Valelly, Richard M. 1995. National parties and racial disenfranchisment. In *Classifying by race,* edited by Paul E. Peterson, 188–216. Princeton, N.J.: Princeton University Press.

Van Biema, David. 1994. One person, seven votes. *Time* 143(17) (April 25): 42–43.

Vanderleeuw, James M. 1991. The influence of racial transition on incumbency advantage in local elections. *Urban Affairs Quarterly* 27:36–50.

Walters, Ronald. 1992. Two political traditions: Black politics in the 1990s. *National Political Science Review* 3:198–207.

Walton, F. Carl. 1995. The Congressional Black Caucus and its liberal ideology: A search for explanation. Paper presented at the annual meeting of the American Political Science Association, Chicago, August 31–September 2.

Walton, Hanes, Jr., and Leslie Burl McLemore. 1970. A portrait of black political styles. *Black Politician* 2:9–13.

Watson, S. M. 1984. The second time around: A profile of black mayoral election campaigns. *Phylon* 45:165–175.

Weber, Ronald E. 1995a. Redistricting and the Court's judicial activism in the 1990s. *American Politics Quarterly* 23:204–228.

———. 1995b. The unanticipated consequences of race-based districting: The impact on electoral competition and voter participation. Paper presented at the annual meeting of the Midwest Political Science Association, Chicago, April 6–8.

Weingast, Barry R., and William Marshall. 1988. The industrial organization of Congress. *Journal of Political Economy* 96:132–163.

Whitby, Kenny J. 1998. *The color of representation: Congressional behavior and black interests.* Ann Arbor: University of Michigan Press.

Whiteman, David. 1995. *Communication in Congress: Members, staff, and the search for information.* Lawrence: University of Kansas Press.

Wilentz, Sean. 1996. The last integrationist: John Lewis's American odyssey. *New Republic,* July 1, 19–26.

Wilson, Rick K., and Cheryl D. Young. 1997. Cosponsorship in the U.S. Congress. *Legislative Studies Quarterly* 22:25–43.

Wilson, William Julius. 1987. *The truly disadvantaged: The inner city, the underclass, and public policy.* Chicago: University of Chicago Press.

———. 1996. *When work disappears: The world of the urban poor.* New York: Knopf.

Wilson, Woodrow. 1885. *Congressional government.* Cleveland: World Publishing.

Winch, Peter. 1958. *The idea of a social science and its relation of philosophy.* London: Routledge and Kegan Paul.

Yiannakis, Diane E. 1982. House members' communication styles: Newsletters and press releases. *Journal of Politics* 44:1049–1071.

Young, H. P. 1988. Measuring compactness of legislative districts. *Legislative Studies Quarterly* 13:105–115.

Young, Iris M. 1990. *Justice and the politics of difference.* Princeton, N.J.: Princeton University Press.

———. 1994. Justice and communicative democracy. In *Radical philosophy: Tradition, counter-tradition, politics,* edited by Roger S. Gotlieb, 123–143. Philadelphia: Temple University Press.

Nexis and CD Newsbank Newspapers

AP wire
Arizona Republic (Phoenix)
Atlanta Daily World
Atlanta Journal-Constitution
Austin American Statesman
Baltimore Sun
Boston Globe
Buffalo Globe
Capital Times (Madison, Wis.)
Chapel Hill Herald
Charleston Gazette
Charlotte Observer
Chicago Sun-Times
Chicago Tribune
Christian Science Monitor
Cincinnati Herald
Columbus Dispatch (Ohio)
Commercial Appeal (Memphis)
Commercial Appeal (Nashville)
Dallas Morning News
Dallas Post Tribune
Dayton Daily News
Denver Post
Des Moines Register
Detroit Monthly
Detroit News
Durham Herald-Sun
Durham Morning Herald
Federal News Service
Fort Worth Star Telegram
Fresno Bee

Greensboro News and Record
Hartford Courant
Houston Chronicle
Houston Post
Indianapolis Star
Kansas City Star
Knight-Ridder News Service
Legal Intelligencer (Philadelphia)
Los Angeles Times
Miami Herald
Morning Advocate (Baton Rouge)
News and Observer (Raleigh, N.C.)
Newsday
New York Times
Orange County Register
Orlando Sentinel
Palm Beach Post
Philadelphia Inquirer
Phoenix Gazette
Plain Dealer (Cleveland, Ohio)
Post and Courier (Charleston, S.C.)
Reuters News Service
Richmond Times-Dispatch
Roanoke Times and Worlds News
Rocky Mountain News (Denver)
Roll Call
Sacramento Bee
St. Louis Post-Dispatch
St. Petersburg Times
San Diego Union Tribune
San Francisco Chronicle

San Francisco Examiner
Star and Tribune (Minneapolis)
Star Ledger (Newark)
Sun-Sentinel (Fla.)
Tampa Tribune
The Oregonian
The Record (N.J.)
The Advocate (Baton Rouge)
The Daily Oklahoman
Times Picayune (New Orleans)
US Newswire
USA Today
Virginia Pilot
Wall Street Journal
Washington Post
Washington Times
Wisconsin State Journal (Madison)

Ethnic News Watch Newspapers

Atlanta Inquirer
Baltimore Afro-American
Bay State Banner
Big Red News
Black Enterprise
Black Issues in Higher Education
Black Professional
California Voice
Call and Post (Cincinnati)
Call and Post (Cleveland)
Call and Post (Columbus)
Char-Koosta News
Chicago Citizen
Chicago Weekend
Columbus Times
Community Contact
EEO Bimonthly Career Journal
El Sol de Texas
Emerge
Forward
Hispanic
Hyde Park Citizen
Indianapolis Recorder
Inside

La Prensa de San Antonio
Los Angeles Sentinel
Metro Reporter
Miami Times
Michigan Citizen
National Minority Politics
Network Journal
New Pittsburgh Courier
New York Amsterdam New
New York Beacon
New York Voice
Oakland Post
Philadelphia Tribune
Portland Scanner
Precinct Reporter (Calif.)
Richmond Afro-American
Sacramento Observer
Seattle Scanner
Sun Reporter
Weekly Journal
Washington Afro-American
Washington Informer
YSB (Washington, D.C.)

Court Cases

Abrams v. Johnson, 521 U.S. 74 (1997)

Adarand Constructors, Inc. v. Pena, 515 U.S. 200 (1995)

Allen v. State Board of Elections, 393 U.S. 544 (1969)

Allen v. Wright, 468 U.S. 737 (1984)

Badham v. Eu, 694 F. Supp. 664 (N.D. Cal. 1988)

Baker v. Carr, 369 U.S. 186 (1962)

Beer v. United States, 425 U.S. 130 (1976)

Brown v. Board of Education, 347 U.S. 483 (1954)

Buchanan v. City of Jackson, 683 F. Supp. 1515 (W.D. Tenn. 1988)

Bush v. Vera, 517 U.S. 952 (1996)

Chisom v. Roemer, 501 U.S. 380 (1991)

Citizens for a Better Gretna v. City of Gretna, 834 F.2d 496 (5th Cir. 1986)

City of Mobile v. Bolden, 446 U.S. 55 (1980)

City of Richmond v. J.A. Croson Co., 488 U.S. 469 (1989)

Collins v. Norfolk, 883 F.2d 1232 (4th Cir. 1989)

Davis v. Bandemer, 478 U.S. 109 (1986)

Garza v. County of Los Angeles, 918 F.2d 763 (9th Cir. 1990)

Gayle v. Browder, 352 U.S. 903 (1956)

Gomillion v. Lightfoot, 364 U.S. 339 (1960)

Growe v. Emison, 506 U.S. 25 (1993)

Hays v. Louisiana, 839 F. Supp. 1188 (W.D. La. 1993)

Holmes v. Atlanta, 350 U.S. 879 (1955)

Lujan v. Defenders of the Wildlife, 504 U.S. 555 (1992)

Mayor and City Council of Baltimore v. Dawson, 350 U.S. 877 (1955)

Meadows v. Moon, 952 F. Supp. 1141 (E.D. Va.), *affirmed*, 117 S. Ct. 2501 (1997)

Miller v. Johnson, 515 U.S. 900 (1995)

New Orleans City Park Improvement Assn. v. Detiege, 358 U.S. 54 (1958)

Pope v. Blue, 506 U.S. 801 (1992)

Regents of University of California v. Bakke, 438 U.S. 265 (1978)

Reynolds v. Sims, 377 U.S. 533 (1964)

Rogers v. Lodge, 458 U.S. 613 (1982)

Sanchez v. Bond, 875 F.2d 1488 (10th Cir. 1989)

Shaw v. Hunt, 861 F. Supp. 408 (E.D.N.C. 1994), *reversed*, 517 U.S. 899 (1996)

Shaw v. Reno, 509 U.S. 630 (1993)

Smith v. Allright, 321 U.S. 649 (1944)

Thornburg v. Gingles, 478 U.S. 30 (1986)

United Jewish Organizations of Williamsburgh, Inc. v. Carey, 430 U.S. 144 (1977)

United States v. Hays, 515 U.S. 737 (1995)

Voinovich v. Quilter, 507 U.S. 146 (1993)

Wesberry v. Sanders, 376 U.S. 1 (1964)

Whitcomb v. Chavis, 403 U.S. 124 (1971)

White v. Regester, 412 U.S. 755 (1973)

Wright v. Rockefeller, 376 U.S. 52 (1964)

Wygant v. Jackson Board of Education, 476 U.S. 267 (1986)

Zimmer v. McKeithen, 485 F.2d 1297 (5th Cir. 1973), *affirmed on other grounds*, 424 U.S. 636 (1976)

INDEX

North Carolina (*cont.*)
  12th District, 110, 111, 113–15, 117, 118,
    120, 125
  See also Black majority districts, "I–85"
    district; Clayton, Eva; Durham (N.C.);
    Helms, Jesse; *Shaw v. Hunt; Shaw v.
    Reno;* Watt, Mel
Norton, Eleanor Holmes, 162

O'Connor, Justice Sandra Day, 2, 5, 60, 70,
    77, 78, 81, 86, 89, 90, 244, 252, 273n. 3
One person–one vote, 1, 63, 64, 79
Ornstein, Norman, 289n. 8
Owens, Major, 40

Page, Clarence, 43
Parker, Frank, 83
Parker, Mike, 146, 153
Payne, Donald, 185, 187, 206
Peeler, Mary L., 107
Peterson, Paul, 79
Petri, Tom, 31
Phillips, Anne, 20, 36, 37, 48, 53, 247
Pildes, Richard, 260
Pinderhughes, Diane, 175
Pitkin, Hanna, 20, 55, 56
Pluralism, xiii, 1, 43, 49, 249–51, 253, 261,
    273n. 1
Polarized voting. *See* Racial bloc voting
Political organizations, 6, 95, 114, 117, 118,
    122, 175, 216, 217
Politics of commonality
  balancing approach, 47–51, 58–59, 144–
    45, 179, 196, 199, 203, 211, 245–46,
    250–51, 254, 256
  bill sponsorship and cosponsorship,
    194–99
  black majority districts, 4–6, 19, 42–47,
    94–95, 138, 250, 263, 273n. 3, 291n. 1
  committee assignments, 181, 184–85
  comparison to difference members, 4,
    150–51, 154, 174, 177–80, 184, 189–91,
    195, 197, 199, 200, 202, 208, 209, 214,
    219, 221, 236, 237, 241, 275n. 12,
    289n. 4
  congressional staff, 205, 208–9, 241,
    289n. 4
  critiques of, 46–48
  defined, 3, 4, 38–42
  district offices, 211–14, 289n. 7
  leadership positions, 187
  member newsletters, 218–19, 221, 241

newspaper coverage of members, 228,
    234–37, 239–41, 268
normative theory, 3, 20–21, 34–38, 247–
    51, 261
perceptions of the constituency, 203, 204
roll call voting, 150–51, 153–54, 159,
    177–80
speeches on floor, 189–91
See also Biracial politics; Racial integra-
    tion; Representation; Supply-side the-
    ory, commonality candidates, condi-
    tions for electing; Supply-side theory,
    testing the theory
Politics of difference
  appeal to white voters, 4, 150, 181, 182
  behavior in the House, 145, 173–74, 200,
    202, 203, 245–46, 255, 275n. 12
  bill sponsorship and cosponsorship,
    194–99
  black majority districts, 2, 4, 5, 19, 42–
    47, 94–95, 125, 139, 247, 250, 263,
    273n. 3, 291n. 1
  committee assignments, 180–82, 184
  congressional staff, 205, 208–9, 241,
    289n. 4
  defined, 3, 4, 38–42, 51, 95
  leadership positions, 187
  member newsletters, 219–21, 241
  newspaper coverage of, 228, 234–37,
    239–41, 268
  normative theory, 3, 20, 34–38, 59, 247–
    51, 261
  roll call voting, 150–51, 153–54, 159,
    177–80
  speeches on floor, 189–91
  supply-side theory, impact of, 4, 94, 96,
    243–45
  See also Authentic representation; Poli-
    tics of commonality, comparison to
    difference members; Representation;
    Supply-side theory, difference candi-
    dates, conditions for electing; Supply-
    side theory, testing the theory
Politics of presence. *See* Descriptive repre-
    sentation
Poole, Keith, 30, 130, 149, 150
Pope v. Blue, 75
Poverty, 21, 23–25, 56, 204, 243, 275–76n. 3
Powell, Adam Clayton, 8, 95
Powell, Staccato, 109
Preclearance. *See* Section 5
Price, David, xiii, 53, 100, 116, 124, 167

Steele, Shelby, 94, 253
Stevens, Justice John Paul, 87, 273n. 3,
    274n. 5, 281n. 18
Stimson, James, 51
Stokes, Donald, 287n. 12
Stokes, Louis, 160
Streich, Greg, 35, 48, 277n. 15
Strickland, Ruth Ann, 136
Strict scrutiny, 7, 60, 78, 80–82, 85, 91, 251,
    280n. 13. *See also* Fourteenth
    Amendment
Sunstein, Cass, 83
Supply-side theory, xii, 3, 92–94, 273n. 4
    alternative explanations, 139–41
    causal effect, 96, 97, 117, 120, 125, 244,
        256, 282n. 4, 283n. 5
    commonality candidates, conditions for
        electing, 94, 96, 120, 127–30, 140–41,
        243
    congressional staff, 208
    continuing relevance of, 246–47, 282n. 3
    descriptive representation, impact on, 96,
        120–23, 125–27, 134–36, 282n. 2
    difference candidates, conditions for elect-
        ing, 94, 127–29, 140–41, 243–44,
        284n. 17
    legal debates, implications for, 60–61, 72,
        84–92, 251–52
    location of district offices, 209, 210
    newspaper coverage of members, 234,
        236
    normative and democratic theory, impli-
        cations for, 3–4, 247
    and other theories of legislative politics,
        255–57, 284n. 18
    predictions for behavior in the House,
        144–47, 181, 187, 191, 195–96, 199
    predictions for behavior with respect to
        constituents, 208, 209, 211, 228, 237,
        243, 245
    substantive representation, impact on,
        50, 59, 96, 136–39, 142, 200, 241–42,
        245, 248, 250, 263, 282n. 3
    supply of candidates, impact of new dis-
        tricts on, 93, 96, 126, 131, 132, 282
    testing the theory, 130–39, 177–80, 184–
        85, 187, 189–91, 208–9, 211–14, 219–
        22, 234–37, 241
    unintended consequences, 261–63
    See also Ambition theory; Candidate
        emergence; Congressional Black Cau-
        cus; Politics of commonality; Politics

of difference; Redistricting; Represen-
    tation
Supreme Court. *See* Judicial activism; Judi-
    cial restraint; Standing to sue; *specific
    court cases and justices*
Swain, Carol, 16, 57, 141, 164, 165, 206,
    283n. 10, 289n. 1
Symbolic behavior, 54, 148, 159, 166–70,
    172, 188, 190–92, 210, 216, 221–22,
    240, 262, 287n. 9

Tallon, Robin, 135, 203
Tate, Katherine, 175
Taylor, Charles, 20, 36
Taylor, Stuart, 44–46
Thernstrom, Abigail, 20, 21, 24, 33, 88, 90,
    141, 253, 275–76n. 3, 292n. 9
Thernstrom, Stephan, 20, 21, 24, 33, 253,
    275–76n. 3
Thomas, Justice Clarence, 40, 54, 94, 253
Thompson, Bennie, 41–42, 95–96, 139, 140,
    142, 150, 187, 205, 211, 245, 282n. 3,
    285n. 27, 291n. 1
Thompson, Dennis, 37, 248, 277
Thornburg v. Gingles, 60, 70, 72, 73, 75, 77,
    82, 102, 103, 110, 280n. 9
Thurmond, Strom, 37, 52
Tillman, Benjamin "Pitchfork Ben," 52
Totality of circumstances, 60, 66, 67, 70,
    85, 251. *See also* Responsiveness of
    elected officials to black interests;
    Section 2; Vote dilution
Towns, Edolphus, 192
Traditional blacks. *See* Politics of difference
Tucker, Walter, 291n. 1

Unemployment, 22, 24
*United Jewish Organizations of Williams-
    burgh, Inc. v. Carey,* 78–79, 281n. 17
United States v. Hays, 81, 87–88, 281n. 18
Urban areas
    constituency interests of, 31, 43, 57, 136,
        140, 174
    policies concerning, 29, 39, 159
    political machines, 7, 148
    as predictor of behavior in the House, 178,
        189–90, 201, 210, 213, 221, 223, 237
    and redistricting, 26, 102, 111, 284n. 22
    traditional CBC districts, 26, 44, 57, 125,
        139, 150
    voters, 64, 113
    See also Rural areas